PSYCHOLOGY OF THE DIGITAL AGE

Based on two decades of participant-observation field research in diverse online environments, this engaging book offers insights for improving lifestyles and enhancing well-being in the digital age. John R. Suler, a founder of the field of cyberpsychology, explains its fundamental principles across a wide variety of topics, including online identity management, disinhibition, communication via text and photographs, intimacy and misunderstandings in online relationships, conflicting attitudes toward social media, addiction, deviant behavior, virtual reality, artificial intelligence, and media overload. He provides a new framework, the "eight dimensions of cyberpsychology architecture," which researchers, students, and general readers interested in cyberpsychology can apply as a valuable tool for creating and understanding different digital realms. *Psychology of the Digital Age* focuses on the individual, shedding new light on our conscious as well as subconscious reactions to online experiences and our intrinsic human need to self-actualize.

John R. Suler is Professor of Psychology at Rider University's Science and Technology Center and Honorary Professor at the Royal College of Surgeons in Ireland. He has published widely on cyberpsychology, Eastern philosophy, photographic psychology, psychotherapy, and creativity, including the book *Contemporary Psychoanalysis and Eastern Thought*.

Psychology of the Digital Age

HUMANS BECOME ELECTRIC

John R. Suler

Rider University

CAMBRIDGE
UNIVERSITY PRESS

University Printing House, Cambridge CB2 8BS, United Kingdom

One Liberty Plaza, 20th Floor, New York, NY 10006, USA

477 Williamstown Road, Port Melbourne, VIC 3207, Australia

4843/24, 2nd Floor, Ansari Road, Daryaganj, Delhi - 110002, India

79 Anson Road, #06-04/06, Singapore 079906

Cambridge University Press is part of the University of Cambridge.

It furthers the University's mission by disseminating knowledge in the pursuit of education, learning and research at the highest international levels of excellence.

www.cambridge.org
Information on this title: www.cambridge.org/9781107569942

First published 2016

A catalogue record for this publication is available from the British Library

Library of Congress Cataloging in Publication data
Suler, John R., 1955–
Psychology of the digital age : humans become electric / John R. Suler, Rider University.
  pages   cm
Includes bibliographical references and index.
ISBN 978-1-107-12874-3 (hbk.) – ISBN 978-1-107-56994-2 (pbk.)
1. Internet – Social aspects.   2. Internet – Psychological aspects.   I. Title.
HM851.S8647   2016
302.23'1–dc23   2015022165

ISBN 978-1-107-12874-3 Hardback
ISBN 978-1-107-56994-2 Paperback

Illustration credit: Kira Suler; Cover design by James F. Brisson

To Debra

CONTENTS

FIGURES

FOREWORD

Professor John R. Suler is acknowledged as the world's leading expert in cyberpsychology and the founder of the discipline. As a cyberpsychologist, I am honored to be invited to introduce readers to this text.

Psychology of the Digital Age: Humans Become Electric presents an engaging overview of the field of cyberpsychology as a unique discipline, and will appeal to anyone who is immersed in or fascinated by the experience of online environments. The book you are about to enjoy is a wide-ranging exploration of the profound impact of technology on human beings, and the significance of cyberspace as a new environment humans have created for ourselves.

Cyberpsychology has been considered by some to be a subdiscipline within applied psychology; however, Professor Suler's treatment creates a powerful argument for the consideration of cyberpsychology as a unique and valuable discipline in its own right, and is groundbreaking in this regard. Suler draws on a vast range of theoretical constructs in psychology, including psychodynamic theory, operant theory, group dynamics theory, and theories of human motivation, which not only ground the cyberpsychological arguments in established science, but also showcase his vast knowledge of the psychology of human behavior mediated by technology.

Many current debates and trends concerning the impact of technology on human behavior are explored. I found the section that discusses the psychoanalytic typology of Nancy McWilliams particularly insightful. Professor Suler points out that this typology has explanatory value regarding the full spectrum of human personality, from normal to pathological. This premise is then wonderfully illuminated in an applied context, whereby personality is considered in online environments – for example, psychopathic personality types and the impact of online anonymity, or narcissistic personalities and the forums they select to display themselves.

In an important chapter on the disinhibited self, Professor Suler explores the *online disinhibition effect*. This effect, one of the principal and best-known constructs in the discipline of cyberpsychology, was conceptualized and first proposed by the author over a decade ago. His publications on this phenomenon have been cited thousands of times. As an active researcher in this field, I am perhaps most excited about the new theoretical model that Professor Suler has created. The *eight dimensions of cyberpsychology architecture* provide a unique, comprehensive framework for exploring experiences in cyberspace and have applications in a wide range of fields (consumer psychology, digital marketing, user interface, interactive design, online community development). Suler also explores many important areas such as ethics in cyberspace and Big Data, issues that will only continue to grow in importance and relevance over time.

Suler has a unique style, a philosophical approach grounded in psychology and delivered as cyberpsychology. His transdisciplinary vision is reflective of the discipline itself, and therefore the content will likely resonate with those of us who are immersed in this subject and those who are interested in discovering it. John's elegant writing style, especially the narrative and historical aspects of the book, should delight anyone with an interest in technology and psychology while providing professors and students in all the fields that interface with the digital world a coherent and informed overview of cyberpsychology.

This is cyberpsychology by the ultimate expert, my good friend and colleague Professor John R. Suler. A most enjoyable and engaging read.

Professor Mary Aiken
Director, Royal College of Surgeons in Ireland
CyberPsychology Research Center

PREFACE

My relationship with computers began in the late 1970s as a graduate student in Ed Katkin's psychophysiology lab at the State University of New York (SUNY) Buffalo. Back then, they were called "microprocessors" that we used for real-time control of experimental procedures and data collection. My journey since those days feels like a long one, filled with the many ups and downs that all of us experience in our love/hate relationship with this digital age. I remember angrily smashing my desk chair into the ceiling when I accidentally deleted an almost completed manuscript on my IBM personal computer, learning the hard way the lesson to always back up. I remember my delight the very first time I saw a photograph on my Mac Quadra. In the 1980s, when my students undertook an assignment to analyze the pros and cons of Eliza, the early psychotherapy simulation program, I asked them one day how many of them used this thing called "email." No one raised a hand. Now they all come to class with phones that guarantee their constant connection to social media, while thinking that email is something their parents use.

This book is an account of my journey as a cyberpsychologist through the decades of this digital age – an account of my insights as a researcher, but also as a citizen of what I still like to call "cyberspace." By highlighting the basic cyberpsychological principles of our highs and lows in this new digital land, of our love/hate relationship with technology, I hope that this book can serve as a useful resource for anyone who seeks to maximize well-being and compassion in cyberspace, and for my fellow cyberpsychologists who wish to understand the concepts and methods that guided me in my work.

With the rise of the Internet, we have entered a new era in human evolution, and with it the need for a psychology of this digital age. But as the

xi

subtitle of this book suggests, our voyage into this new era revives many of the basic triumphs and strife depicted in the classic Eugene O'Neill play *Mourning Becomes Electra*, which is itself a retelling of the ancient stories of the *Oresteia* by Aeschylus – archetypal tales of love, aggression, loyalty, betrayal, revenge, and family relationships. Our new electric selves in the digital era transcend the old boundaries of human experience while echoing back to us all the emotional complexities inherent in the ancient depths of our human condition.

ACKNOWLEDGMENTS

The journey that led me to the completion of this book would not have been possible without the many people who guided and supported me along the way. I would like offer my sincere gratitude to Ed Katkin and Steve Goldband, who during my graduate school days taught me about computers, while patiently tolerating my anxieties when the program I had written for my dissertation research kept crashing; to Nancy McWilliams, who raised my understanding and appreciation of psychoanalytic theory to new heights; to Azy Barak, Michael Fenichel, John Grohol, Robert Hsiung, Storm King, Gary Stofle, and Kimberly Young, with whom I joined forces in the earliest days of cyberpsychology; to Lloyd Silverman and Dick Zakia, who encouraged my explorations into understanding images; to Rick Larson, Vince Potenza, the wizards at the Palace, and my friends in Flickr, especially Michael Titus, who so generously shared their ideas and experiences; to my students who appreciated what I had to teach them while teaching me some important things as well; to Mary Aiken, whose dedication to cyberpsychology inspired me; to Dave Repetto and Cambridge University Press, who recognized the potential of this book; to Kira for her wonderful design insights; to Asia for her inspiration; to my loving mother and father; and to my wife Debra, whose unending encouragement, insights, and love sustained my entire career.

Introduction

Newborns in Evolution

We're still in the first minutes of the first day of the Internet revolution.
– Scott Cook

It's 10:30 P.M. and the day seems almost over. The kids finally fell asleep. My wife is reading in the living room. At last, the house is quiet. Doing a bit of reading myself is a possibility, or perhaps a round of channel surfing on TV. But I decide against it. Something more intriguing waits for me beyond the walls of my home, something that uniquely mixes work with play. Having just published my book on contemporary psychoanalysis and Eastern philosophy, which I considered a swan song for that stage of my career, I found something new and exciting to study, another realm to explore as a psychologist who loves to apply his discipline to something seemingly far afield of the mainstream. I settle into the swivel chair at my desk, fire up my brand new and very own computer – for I am the first in my neighborhood to have one – and I head into that wonderfully mysterious new world that I had discovered only a few months before, a world only geeks like me appreciated or even knew existed. Even though we are an oddball collection of people, we all suspect that this new space is leading us onto a path that could empower all people, as long as we avoid the pitfalls along the way.

THE BIRTH OF CYBERSPACE

Just yesterday, comparatively speaking in the many millennia of our evolution, we humans did something quite remarkable. We created an entirely new environment for ourselves, one that intersects but also transcends the physical world as we have known it for all these hundreds of thousands of years. People called this new digital realm "cyberspace."

The coining of that term is attributed to William Gibson, who popularized it in his 1984 debut novel *Neuromancer*, which tells the story of a down-and-out computer hacker hired by a mysterious employer to carry out the ultimate hack. We now associate the term "cyberspace" with any activity or experience that occurs online and via the many devices that connect us to that ubiquitous space. A variety of other expressions have been used to refer to this digital realm, such as the Internet, the net, the web, social networks, social media, or "being online." These terms are often used interchangeably, even though in a strict technical sense they do not mean the same thing. The fact that our terms continually change even when they refer to similar environments reflects our preoccupation with "new and better" as well as our coming to grips with this seemingly ever-changing, elusive world of technology. Whatever terms we do use, and I will use them all throughout this book, the essential idea is that this digital realm is a unique environment for humanity, a special kind of space created by computers – a "cyberspace."

Even though the word "cyber" is usually associated with digital networks and the computers that comprise them, another science fiction writer, Sterling (1992), claimed that we can trace the origin of cyberspace a bit further back in time – maybe the day before yesterday – to the very beginnings of the electronic frontier, when telegraph, radio, television, and especially the telephone enabled humans to communicate with each other in an imaginary space "out there," an ethereal space somewhere between you and me. Although the exact time cyberspace was born might be a matter of debate or definition, its history after the broadcast age of telephones and television, very succinctly outlined, goes something like this:

In the 1960s, wide geographic networks were developed to enable distant computers to communicate with each other. Academics and government researchers used these networks to share information, one of the most successful being the Advanced Research Projects Agency Network (ARPANET). The U.S. Defense Department supported research into these widespread networks, as it was hoping for a flexible communication system that could survive a nuclear attack because it did not rely on a single center of control. Licklider (1960), an American psychologist and computer scientist at the Massachusetts Institute of Technology (MIT), envisioned – some say in a tongue-in-cheek fashion – a "Galactic Network" of globally interconnected computers through which everyone could quickly access information and programs. Other prominent scientists made similar predictions.

By the early 1980s, such visions began to materialize. The invention of the Transmission Control Protocol/Internet Protocol (TCP/IP) communication protocol enabled all the once separate networks to talk with each other. The system of interconnected computers grew larger and larger, culminating in what people called the Internet. Mostly computer experts, engineers, scientists, and librarians used it, but soon nontechnical people joined them in this new realm.

At that time, it was all text communication. There were no pictures or sounds – just lines of letters and numbers.

In the early 1990s, hypertext was invented. It overcame the limiting way cyberspace operated: when people on a personal computer connected to a site somewhere on the Internet, they had to disconnect from that location then return back to their personal computer before going anywhere else. Instead, thanks to hypertext, by clicking on links embedded within text, people could move more freely from one location to another, within an expanding interlaced network of connections, somewhat similar to how the human brain works. Very aptly, it was called the World Wide Web. People used "browsers" such as Lynx to travel through the "pages" of this web. As the term "hypertext" suggests, it was still all text communication.

That would soon change in a way that would dramatically transform the psychological experience of cyberspace. In 1993, with the introduction of the popular graphical browser Mosaic, the web became visual. In addition to reading and writing, people could now see images, including graphics and photographs. Sound files and videos followed. Webpages grew more sophisticated in visual, conceptual, and functional design. Due to the enhanced sensory qualities of this fascinating web, more people began going online, forming many different kinds of relationships, groups, and communities, a movement that boomed when the Internet became commercialized with the relaxing of government restrictions on its use.

The space "out there" first created by radio, telephones, and TVs had blossomed into a complex global environment, far beyond a simple broadcast empire, with levels of participation, interactivity, and media sophistication that surpassed anything previously known in human history. Rooted in the real physical world, cyberspace grew into a complex ethereal world unto itself, with some traditions carried over from the old world and some new ones invented. Eventually every type of communication device linked to cyberspace, including all varieties of institutional and personal computers, as well as phones, TVs, cameras, radios, navigation devices, tablets, glasses, and appliances – to the point where it became hard to define where this cyberspace began and where it ended. Thanks to our creation of these interconnected electronic devices, we humans developed the ability to manifest our ideas, customs, personal identities, and relationships with others in a space filled with buzzing electrons that we controlled.

Humans had become electric.

THE BIRTH OF CYBERPSYCHOLOGY

It was not long after the appearance of the Internet that cyberspace caught the attention of social scientists. They realized that a very unique dimension for human behavior was opening up right in front their eyes, one that enabled versatile communication between individuals as well as the creation of groups of many sizes and configurations. Unlike the mass media of TV and radio, cyberspace offered powerful opportunities for social interactions among many people, among different types of people, from many geographic locations, for all types of purposes. It was a social psychological environment with a magnitude of complexity, subtlety, and adaptability no less sophisticated than the physical world. With the 1985 appearance of such virtual communities as The WELL (Whole Earth 'Lectronic Link), visionary nonfiction writers began recounting tales and offering theories about online human interactions, including Howard Rheingold's groundbreaking 1993 book *The Virtual Community*.

Some of the first psychologists to study online behavior, including myself, proposed a new discipline within our field that we called *cyberpsychology*. Along with colleagues that included Azy Barak, Michael Fenichel, John Grohol, Robert Hsiung, Storm King, Gary Stofle, and Kimberly Young, we advocated the need for psychological investigations into what people were doing on the Internet, including the potential benefits and hazards of cyberspace. Our voices echoed those of other psychologists from around the world, such as Tikhomirov, Babaeva and Voiskounsky (1986) in Russia, who anticipated a "psychology of computerization." When my colleagues and I joined together with clinicians of other mental health disciplines from around the world, we explored the possibilities for conducting psychotherapeutic interventions via email and chat, the use of the Internet for widespread education about mental health, and the psychologically healthy as well as pathological uses of cyberspace.

Many psychologists at the time focused on mental health issues in cyberspace, particularly the prospects for online psychotherapy and controversies about the now widely recognized existence of Internet addiction. Other researchers, including myself, also pointed to the need for expanding our psychological research into other areas of online behavior. After having completed my book that integrated contemporary psychoanalysis with eastern Thought (Suler, 1993) – the same year that the World Wide Web went visual – I saw cyberspace as fertile territory for the kind of qualitative, experiential, and immersive research that I loved. It was also an extension of my interest in computers since my graduate school days, especially the use of "Eliza," an artificial intelligence psychotherapy program that I used in teaching my students about clinical psychology. Relying on such methods as participant observation, case studies, interviews, focus groups, and field research, I began writing about my experiences with computer-mediated communication. In 1996, I launched my online hypertext book *The Psychology of Cyberspace*, the first book about this topic that was widely cited. I continued to revise and expand it over the following decade, with journal articles and book chapters as spinoff publications. In this online book, I explored a broad range of topics that reflected the fundamental questions that have always been important within the diverse discipline that is psychology and that now carried over into this new environment called cyberspace:

- How do individual people react to cyberspace?
- How do people interact with each other online?
- How do people behave in online groups and communities?
- What is normal and abnormal behavior?
- How can cyberspace promote mental health?

The topics I addressed in *The Psychology of Cyberspace* reflected some of the many different types of studies that began to appear in the field of cyberpsychology. As more psychologists and other social scientists joined the research efforts, areas of expertise emerged. New journals devoted specifically to cyberspace appeared, such as *CyberPsychology, Behavior, and Social Networking*; *Cyberpsychology: The Journal of Psychosocial Research*; and the *International Journal of Cyberbehavior*. In 2007 and 2008, the Institute of Art, Design, and Technology in Dun Laoghaire, Ireland, and Nottingham Trent University in the United

Kingdom launched the first graduate programs in cyberpsychology. Research centers devoted specifically to cyberpsychology appeared, such as Cyberpsychology Research at the University of Wolverhampton (CRUW), the University of Bolton Computer and Cyberpsychology Research Unit (UBCCRU), and the Cyberpsychology Research Center in the Institute of Leadership at the Royal College of Surgeons in Ireland. In 2015, CBS introduced its *CSI: Cyber* series about a forensic cyberpsychologist, based on the work of Mary Aiken. Despite some skeptics who perhaps too quickly overlooked cyberpsychology, or who claimed outright that nothing important was happening online, research continued to expand in many directions.

Aspects of cyberpsychology are now incorporated into many areas of study at universities around the world, including law, journalism, sociology, communications, economics, design, information technology, public policy, law enforcement, and international relations. These studies inspired the formation of a variety of centers devoted to online research, such as Pew Research Center's Internet and American Life Project; the HomeNet Group at Carnegie Melon; the Berkman Center for Internet and Society at Harvard University; NetLab in Toronto; the Center for Mobile Communication Studies at Rutgers University; the Multimedia Research Group at University of California, Santa Barbara; the Oxford Internet Institute; the World Internet Project at the University of Southern California (USC); HomeNet Too at Michigan State University; and the MIT Media Labs. While obviously interdisciplinary, cyberpsychology can also lead us back to a renewed understanding of traditional psychology – how it can help us explain human behavior in cyberspace, as well as how it must expand into new avenues of research.

A NEW ARCHITECTURE

Anyone who has taken a course in introductory psychology quickly realizes how vast this territory is – it encompasses everything from brain functioning to existential arguments about the meaning of life. So too since its inception, cyberpsychology has grown increasingly diversified. In his book providing a comprehensive overview, Norman (2008) discussed how an effective computer interface parallels the natural ways humans perceive, think, and behave; individual differences in attitudes about computers; computer-mediated interpersonal relationships; abnormal behavior and psychotherapy in cyberspace; automated interactions with computers; and artificial intelligence. In other edited and single-authored books on cyber-psychology (Aiken, 2015; Amichai-Hamburger, 2005; Attrill, 2015a; Barak, 2008, Joinson, 2003; Joinson et al., 2009; Power & Kirwan, 2014; Yan, 2012), we see a similar explosion of issues concerning cyberpsychology: Internet addiction, cybersex, online flow experiences, mobile phone separation anxiety, identity theft, cyberchondria, deception in online dating, gendered website designs, personality traits that affect social media usage, the use of the Internet in education, and attitudes about computerized psychotherapy. Like its parent discipline of psychology, cyberpsychology has a multifaceted quality that makes it ripe for interdisciplinary efforts with other social sciences. In fact, the interdisciplinary spirit called out to cyberpsychology from its very beginnings, due to its inevitable linkage with communication technology.

In order to establish itself as a new discipline, cyberpsychology needed to embrace its heterogeneous, multidisciplinary nature while also maintaining its unique identity as psychology. And so, holding true to our parent discipline, we cyberpsychologists applied traditional psychological concepts to explaining life online. For example, why do some people act blatantly inappropriately on the Internet? Perhaps it is due to the fact that cyberspace offers a heavy dose of something old school psychology previously identified: the unleashing power of anonymity.

Later we began to wonder whether traditional psychology would be sufficient to understand people in this very new environment. Might we have to modify old theories or propose new ones? As we will see in Chapter 4, "The Disinhibited Self," I discovered a variety of reasons why people behave online in ways they would not in person, rather than just due to anonymity. In what would become one of my most widely cited articles, I proposed the concept of the *online disinhibition effect* (Suler, 2004a), which pinpointed several factors, some of them specific to cyberspace, that account for the unleashing of otherwise suppressed actions. Providing another example of new conceptualizations, Kimberly Young (1998) was one of the first psychologists to suggest that Internet addiction was not just a subtype of other well-known addictions but something quite unique.

Over time, a wide variety of novel terms and theories surfaced in cyber-psychology and related fields. As is always the case in the history of any type of research, newly proposed ideas complement or compete with each other. Some theories endure, others come and some go. Only the test of time reveals which ones offer the most explanatory power. We must always be on the lookout for ideas that are new and good, while remembering that what is new is not necessarily good, and what is good is not necessarily new. Charles Darwin said:

> It is not the strongest or the most intelligent who will survive but those who can best manage change.

The diversity of cyberpsychology is both a blessing and a curse. It lays claim to explaining all varieties of online phenomenon while running the risk of growing so multifarious that it loses a recognizable shape as a unified discipline. For this emerging body of knowledge to succeed as a distinct entity that we call cyberpsychology, it requires grounding in a new type of psychological framework for understanding the unique digital realm we humans created. By identifying the most elemental, technology-driven dimensions of our online world, as I propose in Chapter 1, "Cyberpsychology Architecture," we can decipher the features of cyberspace that determine how we humans perceive, feel, think, and behave within it. This cyberpsychology architecture can follow the tradition in psychology that distinguishes it from other social sciences – the tradition of understanding the individual person, including how the person relates to others, groups, and the online environment itself.

A PSYCHODYNAMIC CYBERPSYCHOLOGY

Given the complexity of cyberpsychology, it would be impossible for any one book to discuss this topic in a fully comprehensive, in-depth manner, covering all research and theories. As such, I would like to clarify the particular approach I take in this book. By examining the table of contents, you can see the topics I have chosen to explore. They come from my many years of research in which I and my students immersed ourselves into different realms of cyberspace, the kinds of topics that would catch the eye of anyone who takes the time to develop an online lifestyle. They also reflect the major categories of psychology that I mentioned earlier: the individual, interpersonal relationships, groups, abnormality, and mental health.

The field of psychology contains several different theoretical positions for studying human behavior, such as the behavioral, cognitive, humanistic, and psychodynamic styles. Although I draw on all of them in this book, I mostly rely on the last two, particularly psychodynamic theory, which includes the traditional ideas introduced by the early psychoanalytic thinkers, along with more contemporary approaches such as object relations, self-psychology, and psychoanalytic phenomenology. No other theory more thoroughly examines the depths of the human *psyche* – which is what the word "psychology" means – including how that psyche determines personality styles, interpersonal relationships, and the social dynamics of groups. Psychodynamic theory also specializes in the investigation of how the unconscious influences us in cyberspace without our realizing it, perhaps even more so than in the real world. As we will see, it is this unconscious mind that leads us to create lifestyles in cyberspace based on things we do not even realize about our "real" lives. With its intense focus on the intrapsychic world, psychoanalytic theory provides many helpful tools to understand cyberspace as an extension of our psyche into the psyche of others, which is why over the years many important insights into the digital realm have been offered by psychoanalytic thinkers (Akhtar, 2013; Balick, 2013; Holland, 1996; Turkle, 1995, 2012; Whitty & Carr, 2006).

WALKING A MILE IN ONLINE SHOES: INDIVIDUAL DIFFERENCES AND SUBJECTIVITY

Ed Katkin, my mentor in graduate school, once told us that there are two types of researchers: lumpers and splitters. Lumpers use statistical methods to study groups of people, ideally in carefully designed experiments that determine cause-and-effect relationships. The aim of this type of research is to discover general principles that apply to everyone, or at least to most people.

Splitters are more interested in *individual differences*, in how people compare to each other. They embrace the fact, which everyone knows, that no two people are exactly alike. They feel inspired by how the lumpers always find at least some exceptions to their research findings. By studying in depth these individual differences, splitters discover the intrinsic diversity in human psychology. They attempt to detect patterns and themes in that diversity, or to classify people into types, while recognizing there will always be exceptions. If you react to a situation in cyberspace in some particular way, you can be sure you are not alone. Others react that way too, although their reactions might be a bit different from yours. Splitters are interested in how people's experiences are similar while realizing that any particular experience is part of a complex, unique individual.

For these reasons, splitters such as myself focus on the subjective experience of the individual person. How do different people feel about their lives in cyberspace? How can we come to see things through their eyes? When addressing such questions, I do not discredit self-report, as some researchers might, even if a person's biases or wishes distort it, because such distortions often reveal unconscious motivations that the researcher must investigate to arrive at a more complete understanding of online behavior.

I often rely on the psychodynamic idea of an *experience-near under-standing*. When I conduct my research, I remain as close as possible to the actual, concrete experience of the person rather than abstract interpretations of it. When I write about what I discover, I rely less on abstruse technical language while concentrating more on descriptions that can be understood in everyday terms. If you are an academic researcher, you will see how I express our theories in a way everyone might comprehend, a challenge that often tests whether we truly understand those concepts, whether they actually make any sense, or whether we are simply hiding behind psychobabble. When I do delve into technical discussions, I hope it gives readers who are not professional psychologists a chance to see how we think. I encourage you to read this book to find those ideas that make sense to you, that feel valuable to you, and then develop from there.

INSIGHTS WITHOUT NUMBERS: QUALITATIVE RESEARCH

Research psychologists often measure a behavior under controlled conditions, as in a laboratory, then conduct statistical analyses to determine whether they have arrived at a finding that is significant for the subjects in the study. Early in the history of cyberpsychology, such researchers began developing standards for applying those methods in online studies (Reips, 2002).

Other psychologists, such as myself, took a different approach. Even though rigorously trained in the traditional scientific method, I found myself drawn to such approaches as Whyte's (1943) living within the Italian slums of 1930s Boston as a way to understand their subculture, Rosenhan's (1973) studying psychiatric hospitals by having his researchers get themselves admitted as patients, or my mentor Murray Levine's (1974) proposal of using an adversary model based on law practices as a way to verify research evidence. Taken collectively, these approaches are called *qualitative research* in which we examine the properties or attributes of people, ideally in natural environments, typically without the use of statistical analyses in a controlled research context. Some of the methods of qualitative research include interviews, case studies, focus groups, field observations, the researcher's own self-examination, and the analysis of logs, documents, photographs, and other visuals. In cyberpsychology, all these techniques can become a very unique form of "ethnographic" or "field research" because the place being studied does not necessarily require travel to and perhaps living within some area of a city, countryside, or rainforest, but rather accessing digital realms through our electronic devices without ever leaving our home or office.

Interviews and Case Studies

Interviews and case studies enable us to study people in depth, ideally arriving at an understanding of an individual as a holistic being in which any particular belief, feeling, or behavior operates within a complex constellation of beliefs, feelings, and behaviors that constitute an integrated personality greater than or at least different from the sum of its parts. Drawing on our objective knowledge as psychologists, while also relying heavily on empathic understanding, qualitative researchers believe strongly in a word often cited by cyberpsychologists when describing online experiences: *immersive*. We use interviews and case studies to immerse ourselves empathically into a person's subjective reactions to whatever happens in that individual's online lifestyle. Psychodynamic psychotherapists also rely on this strategy to understand their clients. As a psychodynamic psychotherapist myself, I am forever grateful for how well my training and practice prepared me for becoming a research cyberpsychologist.

Field Research

Field research helps us understand what actually happens in an environment by going there to observe it, rather relying on controlled laboratory conditions that might turn into somewhat artificial representations of events in the physical or online world. Experimental researchers are well aware of this problem. They think a great deal about how well their conclusions generalize to actual situations outside the confines of their labs. They refer to it as *external validity*. By venturing into cyberspace to observe carefully what people are doing there, experimental cyberpsychologists can estimate the limits of external validity.

Participant-Observation Research

Participant observation, which is often a component of ethnographic or field research, is a particularly fascinating and challenging aspect of qualitative approach, as illustrated by Spradley (1980) and Jorgensen (1989) in their books on this topic. It turns upside down the traditional scientific belief that researchers must remain objective in their work; that they should separate themselves from the people or phenomenon being investigated; and that they must hold at bay their own personal opinions, feelings, and expectations. The problem is that such objectivity is not easy to obtain, even in hardcore traditional scientific studies. Personal biases, often on an unconscious level, affect not only how scientists design their projects and interpret the results but also the very topics they choose to investigate in the first place.

Participant-observation researchers embrace their subjectivity just as they embrace the subjectivity of the people they study. In addition to stepping back in an attempt to observe objectively the situation they are investigating, they also immerse themselves into the relationships, groups, and activities that they hope to understand. Essentially, they become subjects in their own research, observing both themselves as well as others, which means their subjective reactions become part of the data about individual differences. They carefully examine their own thoughts, emotions, and behaviors, not just to determine how these reactions might bias what they see, but also to use those reactions as a tool in understanding what they see. When we oscillate between participating and observing in cyberspace, we learn as much about cyberspace and the people in it as we learn about ourselves.

Such research can be quite challenging. We must develop that ability to detect our own personal biases, including subtle or unconscious ones. We must be able to "decenter" from ourselves in order to understand those reactions objectively. What we discover about ourselves might not always be pleasant. Unconscious memories, feelings, and wishes often generate anxiety. Psychoanalytic training emphasizes this challenging type of self-understanding, mostly by analyzing *transference and countertransference reactions*, the various ways we misperceive each other based on past experiences, which I will discuss in Chapter 6, "Other Than You Think: Interpersonal Perceptions."

When it comes to experiences in cyberspace, where the rules of conventional social behavior mutate in unusual ways, we might revise Socrates' adage, "Know thyself," into, "Cyberpsychologist, know thy online self." If we have not done so in a sufficiently thorough manner beforehand, then we must do so while conducting our research, especially during participant observation.

Unlike other disciplines, even within traditional psychology, cyberpsychologists find themselves in the unusual position of being inevitably immersed into the very thing they are studying – because every cyberpsychologist is in cyberspace. Although they might not be engaged in the exact behaviors or situations they are studying, as in deliberate participant-observation research, cyberpsychologists at their computers cannot avoid the fact that they too are under the influence of the same powerful forces in cyberspace that shape how everyone thinks, feels, and behaves online. In a sense, all cyberpsychologists are doing participant-observation research, even though they may not realize it. To truly understand online behavior, cyberpsychologists of all types will do well to examine their own personal and occupational lifestyles in cyberspace, in addition to how those compare to their offline lifestyles. Once again, we might revise the old adage, "Know thyself," into, "Cyberpsychologist, know thyself, online and off."

APPLYING WHAT WE KNOW

As a clinical psychologist, I have always sought ways to apply the knowledge of my discipline to the challenges we face during everyday living, with the promotion of personal insight, growth, and mental health being a prime directive. In cyberspace, my applied emphasis led me to studying the inner psychological workings of everyday activities such as creating a text message, sharing a photo, looking for information, and constructing a personal profile, in addition to investigating clinical issues such as deviant behavior in cyberspace, online therapeutic activities, and overall well-being in the digital age. These endeavors fall under the umbrella of *clinical cyberpsychology*.

Given how complex cyberspace has become, we can organize the momentum of applied cyberpsychology around three general categories of experience. *Expressive experiences* include any activity in which people provide information about themselves or some topic while interacting very little or not all with other people, as in creating blogs, webpages, and videos without replying to viewer comments, if there are any. *Receptive experiences* are any activities in which a person consumes media without significant interaction with other people, as in simply viewing webpages, blogs, or videos without posting anything. As a clinical psychologist, my research focuses mostly on *social experiences* in which people interact with each other, both giving and receiving feedback. The popular term *social media* can apply broadly to any of these social experiences, although usually it refers to environments based on the concept of *social networking*, which is a web of ties among people.

I believe that even though basic research is important, cyberpsychology, like its parent discipline of psychology, will flourish only when it applies its knowledge to improve our well-being. Because computers and the Internet are tools that we use to enhance our lives, there is a built-in pragmatic dimension to cyberpsychology. It is the responsibility of cyberpsychologists to use their knowledge to improve quality of life. They must help prevent or intervene in any dangers that threaten our mental health. For these reasons, this book explores theory and research as a stepping-stone to offer practical ideas for cultivating a better online lifestyle. Apply the various guidelines I suggest in this book based on what makes sense to you, according to your unique lifestyle in cyberspace. Nicholas Negroponte, the founder of the MIT Media Lab, said, "Computing is not about computers anymore. It is about living."

Cyberpsychologists strive to understand how online and offline behaviors differ, but more importantly, to understand the widening overlap between online and offline living. How does the blending of these two worlds affect us in both negative and positive ways? What strategies can maximize the crossover of healthy behaviors from one realm to another as well as prevent or ameliorate the crossover of dysfunctional ones? It is our research into how the online and offline worlds can be effectively integrated to improve our lives – what I will describe as the *integration principle* in Chapter 3, "The Dynamic Digital Psyche" – that is the future of cyberpsychology as an applied science.

To ask how we can use cyberspace is to ask how we can use life. In our contemporary times, the two have become so intertwined that they now seem almost inseparable. With a firm grasp on the basic principles of cyberpsychology, we become empowered to change ourselves for the better. Consider this book a psychology 101 journey though the digital realm, with its comprehensive range of insights providing a platform to improve our lives, both online and offline.

AN EVOLUTION OF IMMERSIVE STUDIES

My applied research over the course of many years moved through various stages as I immersed myself into new online environments, often with the assistance of my students engaged in eQuest research projects (Suler, 2005), which I discuss in Chapter 15, "Electric Therapeutics." Here I hope a brief overview of these stages will give the reader a preliminary understanding of the foundation for this book. I describe these stages in more depth in Chapter 10, "One of Us: Groups and Communities." Many of my conclusions about cyberpsychology are deeply rooted in these experiences, including what people told me about these online spaces, what I observed, what my students reported in their research, my discussions with colleagues about their work, and what I realized about myself in these different digital realms. I discovered that my cyberspace travels parallel those of many other people, because we all move through similar computer-generated lands that make us question where we are, who we are, and what we hope to be as we interact with others.

Shape-Shifting at the Palace

My first highly immersive participant-observation field research occurred at the Palace, starting in 1995. It was one of the original communities where people could interact with each other via avatars that they moved through visual environments. Imagine creating your own collection of icon-size avatars from any images you want; clicking your mouse to navigate your avatar of choice through an imaginary mansion; interacting with other avatars, privately or publicly, via typed text that appeared in cartoon-style balloons popping over your head; and being able to change your avatar appearance at any time you wished as a way to express yourself.

In a nutshell, that was how life at the Palace worked. Even though technically primitive compared to the much more sophisticated avatar environments that appeared later, such as Second Life, the Palace fascinated me as a pioneering way to interact with other people not just via text, which was the norm at that time on the Internet, but also visually via your avatars that moved through a graphical space. I started out as a total newbie, awkwardly making my way through the Mansion, which was the hub of the Palace world. I gradually became familiar with the people and their culture. As someone who hung out at the Mansion a few hours every day for over a year, I eventually worked my way up to the ranks of becoming one of the "wizards" who supervised the community.

For me, the Palace became, in some ways quite literally, a fascinating playground for understanding how people experiment with their identities via avatars, how they interact and form relationships in these visual communities, and how complex the social dynamics could be in a seemingly simple, cartoonish environment. Since graduate school, my research focused on the role of visual images in creativity, meditation, and therapeutic change, so when I immersed myself into the Palace, I was amazed to witness the psychological power of communicating visually in a virtual world. When I launched the 1996 publication of my online book *The Psychology of Cyberspace*, a large section was devoted to "Life at the Palace," including articles about the history of Palace, the psychology of avatars and graphical space, gender switching, deviant behavior and how to manage it, and what it means to be socially "addicted" to a virtual community. Years later,

I ventured into Second Life, a much more technologically sophisticated version of an avatar world.

Encouraging Healthy and Educated Onliners

When I began my research at the Palace, I knew of no other psychologists who were studying cyberspace. That changed when colleagues found my online book and contacted me to express similar interests. Most were practicing psychologists who had quickly realized the potential of the Internet as a vehicle for offering psychological services as well as providing public information about mental health and psychotherapy. In 1997, our collaborations led to the creation of the International Society for Mental Health Online (ISMHO), where clinicians from around the world discussed these clinical and educational issues. Under the auspices of the organization, my colleague Michael Fenichel and I formed an online clinical case study group, which was the first of its kind in two respects: the topic we discussed and how we discussed it. We explored ways to adapt psychotherapy methods to cyberspace, as well as best practices for an online clinical case study group that operated via an email listserv.

After moderating discussion boards for professionals who belonged to ISMHO, I created educational groups about cyberpsychology for the public, including work in discussion board communities, such as Gil Levin's Behavior Online forums and Howard Rheingold's Brainstorms community. I also began integrating discussion boards and online activities into teaching my psychology courses at Rider University, what would later be referred to as "distance education" and "distance e-learning." Sensing how valuable cyberspace was becoming for this generation of students, I designed eQuest (Suler, 2005), a comprehensive research and personal growth program in which students found information, discussion groups, computer programs, psychological tests, and whatever online resources helped them better understand and address some psychological issue that was important in their lives.

The Soul of the Image

With the rise of digital photography and online photosharing, I returned to the topic of images that had always been an important feature of my research. Upon purchasing my first digital camera shortly after the turn of the millennium, I began to cultivate my lifelong interest in photography, which included learning how to edit images in Photoshop. When online photosharing groups appeared, I joined Flickr, which rapidly grew into one of the largest of these kinds of communities. Similar to my experiences at the Palace, I found myself once again delving into long-term, highly immersive, participant-observation field research, only this time in a community of photography aficionados and professionals who wanted to improve their technical and artistic skills while socializing through the use of images.

How do people express their personalities in their photography? How do they interact with each other in an online photosharing community? Are photography and online photosharing therapeutic? These were some of the questions I addressed in research concerning *Photographic Psychology* (Suler, 2008a, 2013b), which is the study of how people create, share, and react to images in the digital age. In *Qualitative Research Methodology in Photographic Psychology* (Suler, 2013b), I provided a comprehensive research framework for my students to investigate issues in photographic psychology that were personally meaningful to them. Similar to my research at the Palace, I also investigated the use of images along with text as the dynamic duo of communication in online photosharing groups.

In addition to these three distinct areas of my research, I spent quite a bit of time in other online realms, including Internet Relay Chat (IRC), the original America Online (AOL) discussion boards and chat rooms, Facebook, Google+, Instagram, Twitter, Blackboard, Canvas, Yik Yak, and many thousands of email exchanges. What continues to amaze me is the fact that all these adventures occurred via a device screen portal into another universe. Even though I conducted research that involved participating, observing, and conversing with people "in the field," this field was within reach from my desk chair, then later fell into the palm of my hand when mobile phones appeared. The new environment for cyberpsychologists to explore was no farther than a button-press away.

CITIES UNDER THE SEA

The information I offer in this book is the culmination of all these experiences over the years, but might I also offer in these pages my predictions of things to come in cyberspace? Despite the fascinating prognostications of some researchers and theorists, I find myself somewhat reticent about glimpses into the crystal ball of what lies ahead.

When I was eleven years old, my parents took me to the 1964 World's Fair in New York. In the very popular Futurama Pavilion created by General Motors, we glided on moving chairs through miniature three-dimensional (3D) scenes depicting what life might be like in "the near future." To my amazement, one of those dioramas showed people living in houses and towns constructed at the bottom of the sea. Of course, such cities were never built. But why not? Did we lack the technological know-how? Did such endeavors turn out to be too expensive or impractical? Perhaps not enough people were interested in living beneath the waves.

Whatever the reasons, I learned an important lesson. Our idealizing of technology sometimes leads to fascinating predictions that never see the light of day or to underwhelming outcomes. A perhaps more mundane example is the videophone, one of the earliest prototypes being AT&T's Picturephone, which became available in the 1960s. One giant leap ahead of the telephone, this device enabled people to see as well as talk to each other. No doubt AT&T believed everyone would love this more multimedia gadget, yet that technology never became popular. Even when video connections later became available via the Internet and cell phones, people used that technology considerably less often for everyday purposes than the comparatively simple phone call or text message. Apparently, people on phones prefer not seeing each other – or, more probably, not being seen. As we will discover throughout this book, cyberspace attracts us not simply because it offers many features for communicating. Its appeal also includes the option to eliminate some features. Sometimes less is more.

As the cyberspace universe grows in scope and sophistication, we see enthusiastic predictions about the future: the ability to take the vacation of your choice in a life-like virtual reality, or to program our identities into avatars that live online forever. This certainly has been the stuff of fascinating science fiction. Such predictions reflect our hopeful glorification of technology as a solution to all our problems, both practical and existential. Whether or not such predictions will follow the course of cities under the sea remains, as yet, unknown.

At times in this book I too might make predictions, although I will certainly keep the Futurama ride in the back of my thoughts. Mostly, I would like to focus on down-to-earth issues, the kinds of everyday experiences we all have online, while also discussing the unusual phenomena that have already occurred in cyberspace as opposed to anticipating fantastic outcomes of the future. Over the years, I have been interviewed by many journalists writing stories about the controversial or pathological aspects of cyberspace, such as Internet addiction, identity deception, and the blatant hostilities we often see online. Indeed, as we will see, such abnormalities are fascinating as well as important to understand. But let's not overlook the many compelling aspects of the now seemingly routine ability we have to communicate with any person or group of people, anywhere on the planet, for any purpose, in a variety of media, without leaving our homes or straying any farther than a phone in our hands. One of my mentors in graduate school, Murray Levine, said that we should never overlook the ordinary. Many insights hide behind the seemingly mundane. Nowadays we see no fireworks celebrating email – and yet, as we will see in Chapter 7, "Text Talk," it contains marvelous psychological nuances that we too often ignore.

Cyberspace was just born yesterday, but even in that very short period of time it has expanded into something quite overwhelming. We are only beginning to understand this new habitat we just created. And like some protean creature, it is still changing right in front of our eyes, which brings us back once again to the importance of evolution. If we humans so very recently in our existence synthesized an entirely new environment for ourselves, how well will we adapt to it? What if this new environment evolves into something we cannot handle? In his book *Evolution of Consciousness*, written even before the flourishing of the Internet, Ornstein (1992) suggested that our highly elaborate, rapidly changing, technological world challenges our minds to keep up with what might become a Frankenstein's monster. Without enough people raising their consciousness to fully realize how everything on our planet is interconnected, we run the risk of creating technology-driven problems that could permanently harm us all. Now that we have added cyberspace to the already mind-boggling complexity of global society, will this new environment help us realize that interconnectedness? Or will it just make our evolutionary dilemma worse?

Although many of us hypnotized by cyberspace want to hop on the bandwagon of new technologies, as well as speculate with wide-eyed wonder about what will happen down the digital road, we must not lose sight of what has already happened in cyberspace. We cannot see clearly where we are headed in our evolution if we do not fully understand where we have been. As the philosopher George Santayana said, those who do not remember the past are condemned to repeat it. For that reason, I place as much emphasis in this book on describing the beliefs and customs of times "long gone" in cyberspace as I do on examining what is happening now or on anticipating the future. Otherwise, in our weariness with technologies that seem old hat, along with our excitement about the Next Big Thing, we end up reinventing cyberpsychology wheels without even realizing it. Leaning on the proverb that the more things change, the more they stay the same, I will try in *Psychology of the Digital Age* to lay the foundation for the basic principles of cyberpsychology that will hold true no matter how fast or in what directions cyberspace evolves. Environments and communication tools will surely change, showing themselves to us with new names and promises, but many of their underlying cyberpsychological principles will remain constant. Edward Moffat Weyer, an editor of the *Natural History Magazine* for twenty years, once said, "The future is like a corridor into which we can see only by the light coming from behind."

1

Cyberpsychology Architecture

Technology is the knack of so arranging the world that we don't have to experience it.

– Max Frisch

Years ago I came across an advertisement from Tidal Wave Communications that introduced a new computer accessory called Orecchio. It was a headset, using the Telepathic Internet Data Exchange (TIDE) protocol, that enhanced email functionality by enabling you to send your most important thoughts directly from their source: your mind. "Imagine no more keyboards and achy hands. No more eye strain from the glare of the screen. Just visualize the message you want to send, followed by your send command, and poof! Your email is transmitted to our network for quick delivery to its destination." Enticed by the opportunity to connect my brain directly to the machine, I would have adopted Orecchio without hesitation, if not for the fact that the advertisement was, of course, an April Fools' joke. The telepathic headset was bogus, but not my realization that truth once again comes out in jest: our minds extend into cyberspace. Years later, research into brain-to-computer and brain-to-brain interfaces suggested that we might indeed control computers with just our minds and perhaps even communicate very simple thoughts and feelings directly between each other's brains via the machine.

CYBERSPACE IS PSYCHOLOGICAL SPACE

True to the literal definition of psychology as the study of the psyche or mind, cyberpsychology is the study of the cyber-psyche, the computer mind "out there" created by the fusion of humans and machines. We experience our online activities as occurring in a psychologically tangible space that mimics the sensation of space in the physical world. When people power up their computers and mobile devices, launch a program, write email, or sign on to their favorite social media, they feel that they are entering a particular place filled with palpable features and agendas. Moving about the Internet, they describe the experience as "going" someplace. Spatial metaphors such as "worlds," "domains," and "rooms" are common when describing online environments.

On a deeper psychological level, we perceive that territory on the other side of our device screens as an extension of our psyches, a space that reflects our personalities, beliefs, and lifestyles. In her groundbreaking book *Life on the Screen: Identity in the Age of the Internet*, Turkle (1995) noted how we have come to experience the boundary between our mind and that of the machine as slowly blurring. Applying a concept from Winnicott (1971), we can think of cyberspace as a *transitional space* that blends the individual's intrapsychic world with the electronic world – a space that is part me, part other – that provides a venue for play, creativity, and imagination. As we interact with other people online, we experience that exchange within an intermediate zone between self and other. Just as reading a book feels like joining the mind of the author, conversing online, especially via text, feels as if our minds have merged with those of online companions.

When we perceive cyberspace as this extension of our minds, as a transitional space between self and other, a door opens for all sorts of personal expectations, fantasies, and desires to be projected into this realm. As we will see throughout this book, some people use this space as an opportunity to better understand themselves. It becomes a creatively playful path for exploring their identity as it engages the identities of others. Unfortunately, other people simply act out their inner frustrations in an online domain they unconsciously created for that very purpose. Whether the outcome is positive or negative, it is impossible to choose, customize, and participate in any online environment, or to interact with anyone online, without that endeavor reflecting one's own psyche. As an experienced onliner once told me, "Everywhere I go on the Internet, I keep running into *me!*"

When we expand this realization, we see that cyberspace as a whole mirrors the collective human mind – its functions, knowledge, purposes, and hopes. How could it be anything other than a manifestation of the human psyches that inhabit it? That question makes us wonder whether cyberspace itself possesses a distinct personality that reflects its population. Old-timers, for example, lament how the character of the Internet changed dramatically once it became commercialized. The traditional philosophy of generously sharing resources gave way to proprietary ownership. As more people went online, the once tightly knit group of collaborating researchers from the early days of cyberspace melted into the much larger population of newcomers with varying and often competing agendas. As with the personality of any individual or group, cyberspace now consists of various subcomponents that merge, separate, collaborate, conflict, and change over time. Psychological concepts about the mind help us understand this dynamic world. Where can we find the id, ego, and superego of cyberspace? Does the Internet, or its subnets, consist of self-actualizing organisms? If cyberspace embodies a complex system of evolving links and associations – much like the human mind – might it attain its own independent personality, consciousness, and will, as predicted by science fiction writers and visionary computer scientists who speak about the "singularity"?

Connected and Distinct Worlds

Now that I have defined cyberspace as the psychological space mediated by computers and their networks, we face a rather interesting dilemma. What do we call the space in which we humans have lived for hundreds of thousands of years before we even invented the very first communication device? Onliners have referred to it as being "face to face" (FTF) or "in real life" (IRL). The problem is that video recreates the face-to-face encounter rather well, while applying the word "real" and "reality" to our traditional evolutionary realm implies that online activities are by comparison imaginary, fake, or somehow lacking substance – an idea to which many people, including researchers, would strongly object. I might choose to refer to this space as being "in-person" or similarly as the "physical world" because such terms imply our bodily presence in a mutually shared physical environment. Although haptic technology continues to flex its muscles in discovering how to transmit tactile sensations via cyberspace, it still cannot replicate all subtle ways we physically sense each other and the world around us. The holodecks of *Star Trek* are a very long ways off. If we wanted to avoid the dilemma of choosing a label that attempts to pinpoint the distinctive nature of our familiar evolutionary environment, we could simply refer to it as the "offline world" or "nondigital world" – but those expressions do devalue it by giving precedence to the notion of being in cyberspace.

Critics of what Jurgenson (2011) called "digital dualism" claimed that a false dichotomy has been drawn between the online and offline worlds, that what happens in social media in particular has become so enmeshed into the "real" world that it makes no sense to talk about online and offline as if they are separate domains. This is especially true when people interacting through social media tend also to know each other, or have known each other, in person – or when we use computerized devices in the moment to help us perceive, navigate, and understand the environment around us, what has been called *augmented reality*. Over time, life online and offline has become more intermixed, which is the *integration principle* discussed in Chapter 3, "The Dynamic Digital Psyche." Cyberspace has become deeply engrained into many aspects of our lives. But rather than thinking in terms of a "dualism" between online and offline, we can appreciate the "interactionism" between these two intertwining realms. As the subtitle of this book suggests, humans are becoming electric.

The environments created by computers and their networks have become so intricate, with such unprecedented levels of interactivity among people and those environments, that cyberspace has evolved into a new kind of reality. People do subjectively experience its digital realms as if they are specific, unique places – which is why they often use spatial metaphors when describing what it is like to "go there," "be there," or even "be on" a social media site as if one were appearing on a TV program. It is difficult to even talk about the Internet without relying on words suggesting that the digital realm is a place unto itself, even if it intersects the real world on many levels. People online can also act in ways that differ blatantly or subtly from how they act offline. Cutting-edge research about "presence" and "immersion" in virtual realities highlights even more the idea that cyberspace can be subjectively experienced as an environment completely separate and different from what one experiences when the virtual reality (VR) goggles are removed. From a practical perspective, we will see throughout this book that appreciating a distinction between cyberspace and the in-person world serves as a very useful tool in helping people improve their well-being online, offline, and in the intersection of these two worlds.

Despite debates about digital dualism, or about the pros and cons of the different terms that refer to online versus offline, I will rely on this distinction and these terms throughout this book. Whether I refer to this place where we humans originally evolved as reality, face-to-face, physical, in-person, or offline, people still seem to know what I mean, even if they do not particularly agree with the terms. Intuitively, we all know that this semantic predicament is a byproduct of cyberspace as an elusive extension of our own minds.

THE EIGHT DIMENSIONS OF CYBERPSYCHOLOGY ARCHITECTURE

Given that cyberspace is psychological space, what are the unique features of this realm? What are the building blocks that determine our psychological reactions to the different digital environments we have created? During my many years of participant-observation field research, I looked for answers to these questions, for a framework or model to help me organize and better understand the various elements of our experiences in the digital realm.

Here I will propose eight fundamental dimensions of cyberspace architecture (see Figure 1.1). Each one is a different facet or quality of the digital infrastructure that shapes our psychological experience of an environment. These interlocking dimensions also reflect how the human mind itself works. The essential question concerning any particular online environment then becomes this: what dimensions does it emphasize and in what specific ways? The history of the Internet has taught us that the power of cyberspace is its potential to isolate, minimize, enhance, manipulate, and combine these dimensions in surprisingly unique and useful ways. In different online environments, we see distinctive synergistic integrations of the dimensions, resulting in unique psychological infrastructures that determine what kinds of people will be attracted to a particular place, as well as how they will behave within it. Built on the concept of cyberspace as psychological space, these eight dimensions provide a foundation for a transdisciplinary theory of cyberpsychology, a theory that will guide us throughout this book.

We can also think of this architecture as a useful assessment tool. When examining a particular computer-generated environment, a particular activity in cyberspace, or simply when talking to people about their digital lifestyles, if we ask the key questions coming from each of these dimensions, we can form a very comprehensive picture of that environment, activity, or lifestyle.

In the sections that follow, I will briefly describe these dimensions, while noting how we will more fully explore them in the chapters throughout

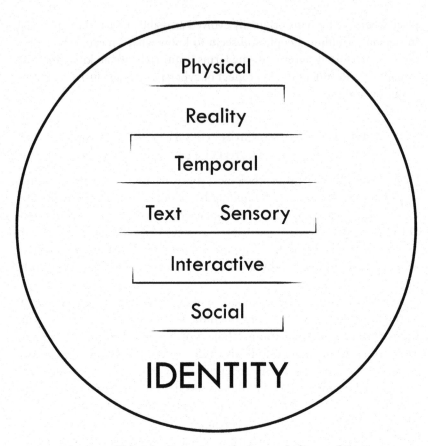

FIGURE 1.1. The eight dimensions of cyberpsychology architecture.

this book. At the end of each section, I include the key questions from that particular dimension, questions you can consider for better understanding your own online lifestyle.

THE IDENTITY DIMENSION: WHO AM I?

Identity, the sense of self, is the first dimension of cyberpsychology architecture, just as it is the foundation of all psychology. All of the other dimensions act as tributaries that feed into it. The identity dimension of an online environment is determined by the tools it provides for expressing who you are. How do people consciously and unconsciously use or avoid those tools? What healthy as well as pathological aspects of themselves do they disclose? The identity dimension also includes the intersection between the online and offline self – how the two parallel each other, differ from each other, and can be integrated when there are discrepancies. As we will see in Chapter 3, "The Dynamic Digital Psyche," it is the balance and integration of online and offline living that maximize well-being.

Deciding Who You Are

One of the most psychologically versatile aspects of cyberspace is how it allows every individual to express who he or she truly is, something less than who that person is, something more, or something entirely different. How much can you hide about yourself in a particular environment? How much can you transform yourself, in either a positive or negative way? Without having to reveal anything about their physical appearances or real-world lifestyles, people can start from scratch in establishing their online self. They can present particular facets of themselves but not others, and in an environment of their choice or creation. As one of my students said, "There's reality, then there's the cyberworld, where you can be anyone you want to be." Online realms offer the possibility of an ongoing process of creating, editing, and re-editing the presentation of one's digital identity (Attrill, 2015c).

The many diverse types of online environments offer pathways toward a decentered, dissociated, and multiplied expression of self, as Turkle (1995) described in *Life on the Screen*. Simply put, in different places people can convey different versions of themselves. Online environments also provide opportunities to reveal previously unrecognized aspects of one's identity, which can lead to *self-actualization* in the traditional sense of humanistic psychology, as well as to a more individuated, cohesive sense of self as conceptualized in contemporary psychoanalytic theory. "The invention of the computer and the Internet," another of my students commented, "made me the person I am."

Even when creating something as deceptively simple as a password, people already begin the process of determining their digital identity. Passwords always reveal how people think, what they find important, and what "secret" means to them. So too we see traces of our identity in where we go online, what we do there, and in the environment we create for ourselves on our communication devices, including the applications, images, sounds, music, and interface designs we select. Determined by what you do with it, your device becomes you. Erik Erikson (1968, p. 38) once said:

> In the social jungle of human existence, there is no feeling of being alive without a sense of identity.

Most social media offer wide latitude for creating personal profiles. People usually provide whatever text descriptions or pictures they want, even if it is partly or completely fabricated. They often have the option of picking whatever name they wish, a choice that reflects both conscious and unconscious attempts at image management. The particular set of profile information requested by the environment shapes the initial impression people will form of each other. Gaps in providing profile data, if the environment permits them, indicates people's defenses against revealing something about their identities. Any profile data that link to the real world – such as home addresses and places of occupation – provide a pathway for others to discover more information about someone. They can verify whether that person's online self matches his or her real-world identity or that person's identity as presented in another online locale. When administrators or hackers of an environment have access to the user's computer IP address, they have the power to investigate, use, and possibly exploit that person's identity.

Once people begin participating in an online community, they must grapple with the different alternatives for defining themselves. What are the options for typing text to express who you are? Are lengthy descriptions possible, or are you limited to 140 characters at a time? Can you upload pictures or video that show how you look, sound, and behave or that reveal your home or workplace for others to see? Do the norms of the domain dictate that you portray yourself in a way that accurately reflects your real-world self, as in traditional social media such as Facebook, or do they encourage you to adopt an imaginary identity, as in games? Violating these norms often leads to problems in the management of one's identity.

Being a Nobody or a Somebody

People can venture through some online habitats while remaining anonymous. Armed only with a generic or contrived username, or no name at all, they are free to behave in any way they want without constraints from their real-world identity. This anonymity, as we will see in Chapter 4, "The Disinhibited Self," encourages people to say or do things that they would not in the real world. In some environments, when not participating at all and when no evidence of their presence is displayed for others to see, people can disappear completely. They become invisible lurkers with no identifiable existence, a fly-on-the-wall phenomenon that we rarely experience in the physical world.

In describing the choices people make in creating their online identities, Walther (1996) referred to the *hyperpersonal self* that is strategically managed through selectively optimized disclosures, what psychoanalytic theory calls the *idealized self*. People create a version of their identity that is more socially acceptable, even exemplary. "Social media is a way to showcase your talents and accomplishments," one student said in a survey. People can materialize within cyberspace the intrinsic human desire for their own perfected individuality, which can then become a goal to motivate true personal growth, or simply turn into a pretence of unrealistic phoniness. People cannot easily tell the difference between the two. "We are not very good at recognizing illusions," Thomas Merton said, "least of all those we cherish about ourselves."

The more opportunities for identity expression, the more leeway exists not just for deliberate constructions of who we are or want to be, but also for unconscious disclosures of otherwise hidden feelings and needs that are not always benign. Without realizing it, people tip their hands while they experiment with different communication tools. They unknowingly leak the ingredients of their secret selves. As I will discuss in Chapter 3, "The Dynamic Digital Psyche," we must also take heed of warnings by such researchers as Turkle (2012), who in her book *Alone Together* described how the compulsion to connect online to others as a way to affirm one's thoughts and feelings might inadvertently backfire: by forgetting how to self-reflect in solitude, we lose track of who we are.

Chapters 3, "The Dynamic Digital Psyche," and 4, "The Disinhibited Self," are devoted to more in-depth discussions of the identity dimension of cyberpsychology architecture.

Key Questions from the Identity Dimension

- What do you reveal and hide about yourself in your different online activities?
- Which communication tools do you use or avoid when expressing yourself?
- How do you create an idealized version of your identity?
- What hidden, perhaps negative aspects of yourself sometimes slip out?
- When do you choose to be anonymous or invisible?
- How do your different online selves compare to the ways you are in-person?

THE SOCIAL DIMENSION: WHO ARE WE?

The social dimension entails the interpersonal aspects of an environment, that is, how it enables you to interact with friends, family, loved ones, peers, colleagues, and strangers. It encompasses one-on-one relationships; groups of all sizes, including the large communities of social media; and the culture that forms within a social environment according to its intended design or despite it. Because we arrive at a deeper understanding of ourselves within our relationships and groups, as psychologists have long known, the identity and social dimensions are intimately intertwined.

Relationships Chosen and Unchosen

In cyberspace, we can easily connect with dozens, hundreds, and even thousands of people from all walks of life. Using a search engine, we scan the vast online universe to zoom our attention onto particular kinds of people. While multitasking, we can juggle many relationships in a short period of time – or even at the same time, as in text messaging – without anyone being aware of our juggling act. By posting messages to a blog, discussion board, or social network, we create our own personal audience consisting of people who share even our most esoteric interests. Cyberspace has become increasingly more powerful in its tools for searching, filtering, and contacting almost any person or group we can imagine.

Why do we consciously choose to communicate with some people online but not others? Of course, we may intentionally select those who share similar interests and backgrounds or whose personality fits well with our own. We are driven by the intrinsic human need to belong to, identify with, and feel supported by relationships and groups. If we deliberately seek out people who are different from us, we have the opportunity to better understand the human condition and, in return, ourselves.

But not all choices are fully conscious. As we will see in Chapter 6, "Other Than You Think: Interpersonal Perceptions," the ability to sift through so many possibilities for developing online relationships invites transference reactions, which are biased perceptions of other people based on past relationships. We do not have as much mindful control over decisions based on transference. In addition to conscious preferences, people act on unconscious needs when selecting colleagues, friends, lovers, and enemies in cyberspace. Transference focuses them on predetermined social targets to address what their inner self expects. An experienced onliner once said to me, "Everywhere I go in cyberspace, I keep finding the same kinds of people!" Once a relationship is under way, transference continues to mold how we think and feel about the online companion, often in skewed ways.

Reading a webpage or playing a game of online solitaire involves a shallow social dimension because no other people are present. When we go to the Internet to get information rather than going to someone we know, we actually sidestep an ancient, practical motive for interacting with people. As compared to *expressive experiences* when we communicate with others online, these kinds of *receptive experiences* in cyberspace are clearly asocial.

In other scenarios, the social dimension is more intriguingly ambiguous. What if other beings are present but not human? Do artificially intelligent entities qualify for social encounters? In Chapter 14, "Synthesized Realities and Synthesized Beings," I will address this issue in more depth, including how the perception of "human" is complex because people possess a powerful ability to anthropomorphize almost anything. If Tom Hank's character in the movie *Castaway* plunges into grief over the loss at sea of Wilson, his soccer ball companion, then some people in cyberspace will easily attach interpersonal meaning to artificially intelligent beings, as demonstrated by computer programs that pass the Turing Test (Turing, 1950). As one of the building blocks of cyberspace architecture, the social dimension must take into account how computer-generated entities can and cannot serve as viable human substitutes in particular types of environments, for particular types of people, and for particular purposes.

Groups Are Us

The social dimension of online groups includes the wide range of issues we see in the traditional social psychology of in-person groups. What is the intended purpose of a particular social environment: gaming, socializing, matchmaking, education, professional development, artistic expression, personal growth? Who are the people drawn to it? What are its culture, history, and the different roles and statuses among its people? How does it create well-being or psychological problems?

Other issues in the social dimension are rather unique to cyberspace. Is the communication one-to-one, one-to-many, many-to-one, or many-to-many? What kinds of software tools does the environment provide for finding, gathering, and contacting others by public and private means? Do people realize who they are communicating with, or that a real group does or does not even exist? Are there people who possess more interpersonal power because they have greater technical knowledge and skills? In social media, people often find themselves in the position of weighing the need to create a large audience for whom they "perform" against the need to establish only a handful of intimate contacts. They might find themselves grappling with a plethora of performances by other people, a marketing mentality of everyone attempting to create their own personal "brand," competitions for attention, and what social scientists call *weak or loose ties* – all the while struggling to create some genuinely rewarding relationships.

The social dimension of cyberpsychology architecture must take into consideration the discrepancies between who is online and who is not. If the *digital divide* (Warschauer, 2004) persists, social media will be shaped by the privileged people who have access to the Internet. They bring their mental sets with them, ways of thinking very different from people who know nothing about cyberspace. Some people can go online, but have little or no interest in being there, or who eventually decide to abandon it. How does their absence affect the atmosphere of online cultures? The social dimension of a cyberspace environment is determined not just by the people who actively participate in it, but also indirectly by the people there who remain silent and by the people who never show up.

Chapters 5, "Electrified Relationships," 6, "Other Than You Think: Interpersonal Perceptions," and 10, "One of Us: Groups and Communities," are devoted to more in-depth discussions of the social dimension of cyberpsychological architecture.

Key Questions from the Social Dimension

- Why do you choose to communicate with some people online but not others?
- When do you perceive other people accurately or misperceive them?
- Why do you choose to participate in some online groups but not others?
- What roles do you play in your online groups?
- How do your groups affect you and others in positive and negative ways?

THE INTERACTIVE DIMENSION: HOW DO I DO THIS?

How well can you figure out, navigate, control, and modify an online environment? This is the key question concerning its interactive dimension. The more readily you can immerse yourself into an online domain, the more quickly it becomes an extension of your mind. The more customizable it is, the more you can express your identity, shape your experiences, and feel emotionally invested in that place. A purely informational website page would have little or no interactivity, although even the addition of links between sections of the site enables you to personalize your journey through the information. By contrast, very sophisticated gaming and avatar worlds produce complex interactivity in the many opportunities people have to create visual representations of themselves, to venture through all the lands within the world, and even to construct their own objects and dwellings. The interactive dimension also includes our attitudes toward cyberspace in general: how we feel we can control it, or how it controls us.

Climbing the Learning Curve

A highly interactive environment tends to be more complicated, requiring a steeper learning curve and greater skill. Does it demand particular motor, visual, auditory, reasoning, analytical, math, artistic, verbal, or interpersonal aptitudes? Is writing necessary, or working with images, or computer programming? These are the critical questions that come into play when we move from one type of environment to another, which I will discuss in Chapter 11, "Change and Excess." For complicated environments, a good "interface" between the person and the machine is critical. Here enters the discipline of *human–computer interaction* (HCI), as first described by Card, Moran, and Newell (1986), which entails the psychology of designing a software environment that is user-friendly because it parallels how humans intuitively perceive, think, and behave. As a very simple example, if you want to increase something, then a lever should go up to do so. If you want to convey the idea of danger or warning, use the color red. Other aspects of an interface simply require *standardization* to eliminate confusing alternatives. As many types of social media proliferate in the 2010s, people appreciate the fact that you can almost always find the log-out button in the upper right-hand corner of the screen.

Although low interactive environments that demand few skills might feel immersive, hypnotic, and even addictive – as in some online games – we humans tend to be curious, ambitious creatures who like an interactive challenge. A steep learning curve often leads to a sense of accomplishment when mastered. If an environment becomes excessively complex, especially when the interface is also complicated, users might become confused or frustrated, eventually abandoning that activity. No one likes to be confronted with a disorganized flurry of buttons, menus, options, and instructions, no matter how promising the environment seems to be. If people cannot figure out how to interact with something, they won't. Of course, people also vary in their motivation and persistence.

Machines That Betray and Control Us

We expect our devices to interact with us. That's the name of the game. Unfortunately, no matter how sophisticated our electronic tools become, they will sometimes fail to live up to their end of the bargain. There will be moments when software and hardware do not work properly, when noise intrudes into the communication, and when connections falter. There will be moments when our devices give us nothing, not even an error message. There will be moments when we have to fight the machine to get it to do something, or not do something, even something simple, such as not automatically correcting a word we do not want corrected. The frustration, anger, and even outright rage that people feel in reaction to these technical failures say something about our relationship to the machine and cyberspace, something about our dependency on them, as well as our need to control these electronic servants. The lack of response from the machine also opens the door for us to project all sorts of worries and anxieties onto it. Differences in the reliability of online environments are an important feature of the interactive dimension, precisely due to these psychological effects they have on us.

The interactive dimension takes into consideration not just how we approach the machine, but also how it approaches us. How well does it prompt us with notifications about what is happening in our online habitats? How well does it succeed in offering us suggestions about what we might want to do there based on its ability to recognize our preferences? How much does it force itself upon us as opposed to allowing us to decide what level of interaction we desire? What researchers have called *machine intelligence* are the software algorithms operating behind the scenes when we browse webpages or use search engines. A critical question in the interactive dimension is how these subtle forms of subliminal intervention shape what we see, hear, and do – how they benefit us, steer us in certain directions but not others, or even thwart us. The quality of the interactive dimension increases when an environment guides us toward higher, more enjoyable, and more easily controlled participation, either because the environment gave us an uncomplicated chance to tell it what we like or due to its ability to analyze our past behaviors effectively with the best of intentions for our well-being. "I hate technology but I still got sucked into it," one of my students said in a survey. "Be careful how you use it, or it will use you."

Chapter 11, "Change and Excess," explores other issues concerning the interactive dimension of cyberpsychology architecture.

Key Questions from the Interactive Dimension

- How do you feel about the interface of the online environments you use?
- What skills do you have, or lack, when participating in them?
- How do you react when your environments are not doing what you want?
- How do you react to the challenge of mastering a new environment?
- How much do you control your devices, and how much do they control you?
- How do you feel about cyberspace and technology in general?

THE TEXT DIMENSION: WHAT'S THE WORD?

The text dimension of an online environment entails how people communicate with typed language. In the early days of the Internet, everyone talked via text. Although this has changed dramatically with the rise of visual and audio features, text still prevails as one of the most powerful tools for conveying information, expressing oneself, and interacting with others. It surfaces in a wide variety of long and short forms: informational websites, blogs, email, texting, chat, and other short messaging systems as popularized with the appearance of Twitter. Drawing on different cognitive abilities than talking and listening, typing one's thoughts and reading those of another person in cyberspace is a unique method of presenting one's identity, perceiving the identity of others, and establishing relationships, which is why I like to give it the special title of *text talk*, while also devoting a whole chapter to it (Chapter 7, "Text Talk") based on my research into this topic (Suler, 2004b). Some researchers have used the term *computer-mediated communication* when referring to text communication. Chapter 7 explores this phenomenon in more depth.

When Words Fail

As the Internet evolved, many social media began to minimize text. Instead, people were encouraged to rely more on visuals, as in the early photosharing communities such as Flickr, where images dominated writing. Later, when sharing photographs became trendy via mobile devices, as in the very popular Instagram, text conversations fell to a bare minimum, even disappearing almost completely, leaving images as the primary vehicle for communication. While some people love text communication, others do not, which is often due to the fact that it requires more time, or more aptitude for typing, writing, and reading, skills that are not their forte. Such people feel uncomfortable or unskilled in expressing themselves through written words, an idea reinforced by the writer Elbert Hubbard, who said, "He who does not understand your silence will probably not understand your words."

The cognitive styles might differ between these people who avoid language and those who love to communicate with written words. The verbal systems of the mind, as in supposed "left-brain" activities, tend to involve thinking that is more conceptual, logical, factual, linear, and consciously controlled. As I will discuss in more depth in Chapter 7, "Text Talk," it is a unique skill unto itself, overlapping with but not quite the same as writing formal letters, reports, emails, and other traditional types of documents. Even people who love text might at times need a break from it. Visuals do have their appeal as a special form of expression, which we will explore in Chapter 8, "Image Talk." In that chapter, we will see how the integration of text and images provides a comprehensive, versatile mode of discourse that transcends either one alone.

Text communication does pose problems, even for people who are skilled at it. Lacking sounds and visuals, it is not a rich sensory encounter. You cannot see other people's faces or hear them speak. All the important interpersonal cues provided by voice, body language, and physical appearance disappear, which can dramatically alter how people relate to each other. Without those cues, it is easier to misunderstand the other person. Your online companion might be sick, drunk, or depressed without your knowing it. For some people, the lack of physical presence generated by the cues of voice and appearance might reduce the sense of intimacy, trust, and commitment in the relationship. Typed text feels formal, distant, unemotional, and lacking a supportive and empathic tone. In fact, without a visual and auditory connection, you can never be absolutely certain about the other person's identity. This absence of face-to-face cues, which adds a small dose of anonymity, encourages some people to behave inappropriately.

When Words Succeed

On the positive side, other people respond to the lack of face-to-face cues as an opportunity to be unusually honest and expressive. Some people claim that they naturally express themselves better through writing rather than talking, as well as understand others better by reading their text rather than listening to them speak. They experience writing as an opportunity to be more self-reflective, to more thoroughly sort through their ideas and emotions, as in keeping a journal. For people with social anxieties, not having to interact with others eyeball to eyeball offers disinhibiting relief.

Key Questions from the Text Dimension

- What types of text communication do you like and dislike in cyberspace?
- How do you express yourself with text compared to communicating in person?
- How do you react to other people with text compared to being in person?
- What are your feelings about using text versus photographs?

THE SENSORY DIMENSION: HOW AM I AWARE?

The sensory dimension of an online environment involves how much it activates the five senses: hearing, seeing, feeling, smelling, and tasting. Text by itself does not offer much direct sensory stimulation. During the evolution of cyberspace, the appearance of multimedia gaming, photosharing, video conferencing, podcasting, and Internet-mediated phone calls lifted online activities into a much more heightened sensory experience than text alone. However, cyberspace still pales in its sensory complexity compared to real-world situations. Although video communication comes the closest to an actual face-to-face meeting, the physical, tactile, olfactory, and spatial qualities of online activities – for example, handshakes, pats on the back, dancing, smelling perfume, going for a walk, feeling warmth on your skin, sensing things all around and behind you – are still very limited, or nonexistent, in cyberspace.

Imitating and Defying Reality

In Chapter 14, "Synthesized Realities and Synthesized Beings," we will see how researchers pioneering the technology of virtual reality are attempting to create environments that come as close as possible to mimicking the robust sensory experiences of the physical world. Great progress has been made in the realms of seeing and hearing, along with the generation of tactile sensations, the most basic example being a phone that vibrates. By comparison, the senses of smelling, tasting, and feeling the whole body stand as significant, if not impossible, barriers to cross in the attempt to fabricate truly lifelike encounters in cyberspace. Even if such rich virtual realities are someday possible – which is the very stuff of science fiction stories – we should not overlook the power of cyberspace to isolate, eliminate, and mix the five senses in different combinations. Even without my elaborating these scenarios, imagine what would it be like, and what would be the utility, of an online environment in which:

  – You can only feel bodily stimulation.
  – You can only hear and smell.
  – You can feel body stimulation, hear, smell, and taste, but not see.

The advantage of cyberspace is its potential to offer vivid sensory experiences that imitate the physical world, along with its ability to reduce or eliminate some sensory features of how the mind works while including and enhancing others. Cyberspace allows us to dissect and reassemble how we experience, interact with, and mentally construct "reality." Drawing on traditional research in cognitive psychology, we can examine in new ways how the various senses interact with each other. Similar to classic research on sensory deprivation and sensation seeking (Zubek, 1969; Zuckerman, 2007), extreme sensory experiences in cyberspace can give us unique insights into how the mind works. In its potential to push the limits of our five senses, virtual environments can also teach us about different types of sensory overload, when stimulation overruns the mind, which is an important topic in Chapter 11 "Change and Excess."

The Perceptual Feast

A rich sensory dimension can lead to rich psychological experiences. When interacting with other people, the multiple cues of visual appearance, body language, vocal expression, physical contact, and, in very intimate situations, smell and taste provide a very bountiful encounter with a person, with different cues affirming, enhancing, and at times contradicting each other, as when a person's body language does not match what the person says. "Lose your mind and come to your senses," the famous Gestalt psychologist Fritz Perls once said.

For some people, fuller sensory experiences generate a greater sense of presence, stimulate more emotions, and encourage a stronger psychological commitment to the situation. A hearty sensory environment provides more immediate clarity about where you are, who you are, what you are doing, and what specific meanings you find in that situation, as compared to the usually more ambiguous text environment. If you read, "You are in a toy store," you must rely on your powers of imagination to make that visit feel realistically alive. But suppose that you find yourself in a virtual toy store, with layers of shelves filled with toys of all shapes, colors, and sizes; laughing children running about the aisles; the sound of talking dolls, whistling locomotives, and music boxes; puffs of air from toy canons; bubbles popping on your skin; and the smell of candy. In the latter case, there is nothing vague about where you are or how you might feel about being there. Even my detailed text description of the toy store might pale in comparison to its virtually synthesized counterpart.

Bountiful sensory environments do have their disadvantages. Because they require more technology, they will cost more, demand more computer processing power, and break down more often. Nothing draws greater attention to how unconvincing a digital environment feels than when it makes dumb mistakes, lags in responding, or just stops working. Generating a specific experience through complex sensory stimulation might also prove to be a drawback when we want to encourage an individual's subjective interpretation of a situation, when we hope people will draw on their own memory and imagination to create an experience rather than provide all of it prepackaged for them. As one reader said about a book without illustrations, "I'm glad there were no pictures. I wanted to see it for myself."

Even though I have drawn a distinction between the text and sensory dimensions, I should point out that there is indeed a sensory component to text conversations – for example, in the visual styles of using smileys, spacing, capital letters, punctuation, and ASCII art, which I will discuss in Chapter 7, "Text Talk." Even the deceptively simple technology of rich text formatting (RTF) offers a wider range for self-expression by enabling us play with text alignment, font type, size, and color.

As any phenomenological psychologist will tell us, it is impossible for humans to experience reality without our senses. A pure text environment is no exception to the rule because we need vision to work with it. The more important question concerning the psychological impact of an online habitat is this: what types of sensory stimulation exist here, and what psychological effects do they have on us? To this we might add, when is more better, and when is less more?

Chapters 8, "Image Talk," and 9, "I, Avatar," specifically focus on the visual aspects of the sensory dimension in cyberpsychology architecture.

Key Questions from the Sensory Dimension

- How do you rely on seeing pictures in cyberspace, including photographs?
- How do you rely on hearing sounds and voices?
- How do you rely on tactile stimulation?
- How do you visually format text to express yourself?
- When do you prefer to eliminate visual, auditory, or tactile stimulation?

THE TEMPORAL DIMENSION: WHAT TIME IS IT?

The use and experience of time in cyberspace establish the temporal dimension. Often time in cyberspace differs significantly from in-person encounters. Each environment tends to have its own particular brand of temporality, which is partly determined by the technical design of its communication tools, as well as the social norms for their use. Elements of the temporal dimension include synchronous versus asynchronous communication, the acceleration of time, the suspension of time, and the intersection of cyberspace into real-world time. As we will see, time is far more psychologically complex than the steady march of ticking seconds.

Now or Later: Synchronicity and Asynchronicity

In synchronous communication, people are online at the same time, interacting with each other in the moment, in the "real time" that we associate with in-person conversations. Phone calls and live video are highly synchronous, with chat rooms and text messaging approaching the pace of face-to-face encounters. Even when the back-and-forth exchange of messages is significantly slower than conversations in the real world – as in delays of seconds to minutes – people might still feel that they are "together" in the same time frame. Many online environments can be used in either a synchronous or asynchronous fashion, resulting in shifts along a *synchronous/ asynchronous continuum*.

Asynchronous communication does not require people to be with each other in the moment, on their computer or mobile device simultaneously. Email, discussion boards, blogs, and social media posts are usually asynchronous. Responding to each other whenever they want, people interact outside of real time, with the subjective experience of togetherness continually surfacing and disappearing as their exchanges stretch out over minutes, hours, days, weeks, or even years. During synchronous communication, the person's immersion into the encounter tends to remain continuous and focused, but in asynchronous communication people leave the encounter, temporarily forget about it, then later reimmerse themselves. In some cases, there may be little or no sense of a time boundary at all. The perception of a temporally locked "meeting" disappears. Taking a moment to read a message or view an image may subjectively feel as if one has reentered a fluid temporal space with the other person.

Its flexibility in offering both synchronicity and asynchronicity makes cyberspace unique compared to the offline world. There are pros and cons to both types of communication, with the advantage of one often being the disadvantage of the other. A particular strength might also be a weakness:

Geographic location poses few problems in asynchronous communication, as long as delays between messages do no harm. A person on one side of the planet can conveniently use email to converse with someone on the other side. In synchronous communication, people from distant locations might have more difficulty talking with each other due to their incompatible time zones, or they must contend with the fact that each person speaks from a different place in his or her circadian rhythm. This is one reason why people use live video less often than simply texting. The temporal contexts between you and them do not match.

Spontaneity tends to be enhanced in synchronous communication, resulting in more uncensored, ad hoc, quickly paced, and revealing dialogues. Because the meeting is "live," people must react to each other in the moment, on the spot, which often leads to disclosures that might not happen otherwise. There is a point-by-point connectedness that elevates feelings of intimacy, presence, and "arriving together" at ideas. In asynchronous encounters, people tend to be more careful about composing what they say to each other. The interaction often feels more structured or even studied, as in an email message that mimics the format of the traditional postal letter. Sending images often includes some measure of asynchronous filtering, because only rarely do spontaneously taken photos, especially self-portraits, come out exactly the way the person hoped, ready to be sent on the first try.

Presence tends to be enhanced during synchronous communication, in part due to the increased feeling of spontaneity that imitates in-person situations, but also because people sense their mutual coexistence in the

moment, in real time. Encounters tend to feel more immediate and interactive. Making the effort to be with someone for a specific period of time
in a synchronous meeting is often interpreted as a sign of commitment.
"You are here with me right now!" Even though presence might feel greater
in synchronous contacts, we should not underestimate the potential for
heightened presence in asynchronous communication, especially when
using audio or video, or when writers are skilled in making themselves
come alive through text.

The absence of temporal cues in asynchronous communication can prove
to be a disadvantage. Pauses in the conversation, coming late to a meeting, and no-shows often mean something. Why did she hesitate when I said
that? Why didn't he show up for the live video chat we scheduled? Even
in asynchronous communication, the length of time between exchanged
messages, or changes in the pacing of the messages, might provide interpersonal insights. He used to send me an email every day, so why haven't
I heard from him for a week?

The zone for reflecting and composing is much greater in asynchronous
communication than in synchronous and in-person encounters. You are
not on the spot to reply quickly. Especially in email, discussion boards,
social media posts, and image sharing, you can reply whenever you are
ready, willing, and able, with time in between to think, evaluate the situation, and thoughtfully construct a response. You have the opportunity to
present yourself clearly, in the exact manner you wish. This zone for reflection comes in very handy during awkward or emotional situations. In texting and chat sessions, when people share that in-the-moment experience,
the time it takes to type, or lags in delivered messages, might offer some
zone for reflection and composing, although it tends to be minimal compared to very asynchronous communication.

Convenience and relevance are often inversely related in asynchronous
communication. People find it convenient to send and read messages at the
time that is best for them, according to their schedule. On the other hand, if
they delay too long in sending a message, it can become irrelevant or out of
date, which often poses a problem in rapidly changing situations, as in business or personal emergencies. Under conditions of urgency, asynchronous
communication often fails us. When using text, asynchronous methods are
usually more effective for conveying complex information. Trying to provide an in-depth description of your vacation via real-time texting on your
phone will be tediously difficult, if not impossible.

Communication attitudes determine one's reliance on synchronous versus asynchronous methods, leaving some possibilities that are never fully

explored. For example, even though asynchronous audio and video con-versations are possible, people rarely bother using them. We tend to asso-ciate such audio-visual contacts with real-time encounters. Even though researchers draw this distinction between synchronous and asynchronous communication, in reality the differences are subtle. The sense of being in the same time frame can become unclear in supposedly synchronous encounters, as when delays in receiving a text message make you wonder whether your companion is still there. Methods that we would typically consider asynchronous, such as email and discussion boards, can feel syn-chronous when people exchange messages rapidly: you sense the other person is with you in the moment. Regardless of whether we label a com-munication tool as synchronous or asynchronous, it is the person's subjec-tive expectation of when someone will respond that shapes the experience of temporality. People who are Internet novices, interpersonally naive, or under emotional stress might feel that it took "too long" if they do not receive a reply from someone when they wanted it. We do live in an age when many people expect instant results.

Accelerated Time

Time in cyberspace can feel accelerated, in part due to the fact that online environments change rapidly. Our subjective sense of time is linked to the rate of change in what happens around us. The more things change, the faster time seems to go. It requires little effort to move around cyberspace, so the people and groups we encounter differ from one moment to the next. If you are a member of an online community for just a year, you might be considered an old-timer. During addictive, highly immersive, and what Voiskounsky (2008) identified as online "flow" experiences, time seems to pass so quickly that it almost disappears. Everyone is familiar with the experience of intending to spend just a few minutes online, then two hours later realizing you far exceeded your limit.

Because cyberspace accelerates communication, it can speed up many types of social processes, including the formation of work relationships, friendships, romances, and social or political movements. Researchers speculate that online groups might progress more swiftly through the well-known stages of development proposed by Tuckman (1965): forming, norming, storming, performing, and adjourning. With the acceleration of many types of social activities comes the question as to whether they are also amplified by cyberspace, and whether such amplification thrives, leads to runaway explosions, or quickly fizzles out as swiftly as it surged.

For example, does rapid self-disclosure lead to a more fulfilling relationship or to embarrassment, regret, and withdrawal? As we will see in Chapter 4, "The Disinhibited Self," the *online disinhibition effect* fuels this acceleration and amplification, sometimes in healthy ways, and sometimes not.

Frozen Time

Online environments vary widely in how easily you can save whatever happens there, what I call its *recordability and preservability*. Even though the design, activities, and membership of social media might change over time, the content of what people posted usually remains intact. Email, video, audio, and text messages can be saved. When perfect preservation is possible, time has been suspended. Whenever you want, you can go back to reexamine those events from the past. In other situations, permanency slips between our fingers, even challenging our reality testing about whether something existed at all, as when an email that we seem to remember receiving mysteriously disappears from our inbox. The slightest accidental tap of the finger can send an otherwise permanent document into oblivion.

People differ in how and what they save of their online experiences. Some onliners consider texting or email as throwaway items of little significance. Although they might make more of an effort to save images and video, the overwhelming plethora of these items in our media-saturated lives detracts from their perceived worth. In the temporal dimension of an online environment, we take into consideration how people preserve their online lifestyles in an attempt to transcend the passing of time and the fading of memory, as well as the tools an environment provides to accomplish these ends. We also take into consideration what types of things people save, lose, and delete, how this selective preservation evolves over time, and the psychological ramifications of these fragmented archives. Your digital identity that evolves over time, that transcends time, perhaps for the benefit of future generations to witness, is the end product of what you save, delete, and lose.

What does all of cyberspace remember? What is recorded, by whom, and for what purposes? Some people say everything that has ever been uploaded is preserved somewhere in the massive archives of cyberspace memory, including all the information about who you are and what you did online. Your digital self lifts into eternity. More humbly, we might wonder whether some of that information about you will eventually be deleted or will become so lost in the vast ocean of online information that you forever fade into the background. Only time will tell how much the Internet will transcend time, as well as how cyberspace might allow us to attain some measure of immortality. In the meanwhile, we should consider how people pay attention to or ignore the potential power of cyberspace to preserve our personal information, despite the passing of time. For example, young adults applying for jobs should realize that their online childhood antics will come back to haunt them when employers decide to investigate their digital identities.

Ephemeral Time

Ironically, some forms of social media grew in popularity because they ingeniously reversed the ability to freeze time by deliberately making communication ephemeral, as exemplified so well in the phone application Snapchat. By enabling the transmission of text and images to someone who lasted on the screen for only a few seconds and then permanently disappeared (unless the recipient used a screen capture), the application became the perfect tool for playful communication in the fleeting moment. It was popular for surreptitious flirting and sexual teasing, at times generating romantic jealousy among couples when a partner used it to entice other lovers (Sonja, Nicole, & Cameran, 2015). Such environments illustrate how exaggerating one dimension of cyberpsychological architecture – in this case, the temporal dimension – can dramatically shape the psychological impact of the experience.

Intersected Time

Cyberspace time intersects the real time of our everyday schedules. People vary in when they go online: morning, afternoon, or night. They vary in how often they go online: a few times a day, every hour, or every few minutes. The temporal dimension of cyberspace architecture entails when these moments of online time cross over into the flow of everyday living, as well as how that crossover affects the experience of time in both realms. At what age during their history people first entered cyberspace might be considered another aspect of the temporal dimension.

Key Questions from the Temporal Dimension

- How do you use synchronous and asynchronous communication?
- When does time seem to go fast or slow in cyberspace?

- Why do you save or delete some things from cyberspace but not others?
- How do you feel about things that happen briefly, then disappear?
- When and how often do you go online?

THE REALITY DIMENSION: IS THIS FOR REAL?

Situations in the real world look, sound, and feel very … real. Over the course of our evolution, we humans have learned to define reality based on what we experience every day in the physical, sensory world. Some forms of online communication attempt to recreate these familiar situations. A video appears to be a reasonable representation of reality. A phone message sounds like how that person actually talks. Even though we do not communicate with typed text during face-to-face encounters, we still accept what people say in text messages as a matter-of-fact, realistic manifestation of who they are.

Other online environments deliberately strive to create scenarios that are much more imaginary, sometimes deviating just a little, and sometimes dramatically, from the real world. It does not matter whether the environment is generated in a virtual reality filled with rich state-of-the-art sensory stimulation or simply via plain text. Flights of fantasy can be as high in role-playing games driven only by typed words, such as the classic Dungeons and Dragons, as they are in sophisticated multimedia avatar worlds that gained prominence with Second Life and World of Warcraft.

When evaluating the reality dimension of an online domain, we ask how much it creates experiences based on imagination and how much it is grounded in the familiar everyday world. According to technical design as well as social norms, most games in cyberspace encourage make-believe. By contrast, most social media encourage people to be who they actually are, to convey factual information as best they can; otherwise, they are labeled as deceiving and even outright lying. Other environments, such as traditional Internet chat rooms, navigate the reality dimension in a more flexibly ambiguous fashion. With no visual references, communication tools, or community standards that specifically steer people toward reality or imagination, the place becomes what people make of it. The evolving social norms dictate the reality dimension. Those social norms might even override the reality variable intentionally built into an environment, as evident by the fact that some people in social media deceptively alter their identity, while people in fantasy role-playing games try to get to know who the other players really are. When evaluating the reality dimension of an online environment, we take into consideration its intentional design as well as how people actually behave there. It is ironic that as communication technology advanced, making it much easier for people to get to know each other and locate valuable information, the distinction between reality and fantasy progressively blurred, most notably in the "reality shows" and supposedly real-life videos on YouTube that actually turned out to be deliberately contrived.

Reality Is Illusive

As we will see in Chapter 14, "Synthesized Realities and Synthesized Beings," the subtleties of the reality dimension are many. Simply staring into your computer screen or mobile device, allowing the physical world around you to fade away, immediately opens the door to an altered state of consciousness. As we all rationally know but experientially forget, people are not actually living behind that screen. The images or sounds we see and hear are merely representations of the actual thing. They are portrayals of reality.

As an extension of the human mind, cyberspace is a realm in which our inner ideas, emotions, and needs shape what we experience. We interpret the environments we enter, and especially the people we meet, based on our past experiences that can distort our perceptions. Especially under ambiguous conditions, we might perceive others based on our unconscious expectations rather than on their actual identity, which are the *transference reactions* that I mentioned earlier in this chapter. When people filter or radically transform their online self compared to their actual identity, encounters become even more about fantasy than reality. Given their history of healthy relationships, along with their intrinsic psychological ability for reality testing, some people fare much better than others in distinguishing what online is real and what is not.

In their book *Infinite Reality: The Hidden Blueprint of Our Virtual Lives,* Blascovich and Bailenson (2012) described how the instinctual human mind cannot always distinguish reality from virtual reality even when the rational mind knows better. If you are immersed into the classic virtual pit scenario, with just a plank to cross a seemingly bottomless hole, your legs might freeze with anxiety. Your rational mind tells you that it is just a computer-generated simulation, that there is no real danger, but your instinctual brain feels otherwise. As philosophers have long stated, reality is a construction of the human mind, with its different parts sometimes disagreeing with each other. Drawing on what we have learned, as well as on the biologically determined patterns of human perception, our mind tries to decide whether something is real by comparing it to what the mind knows as real. If necessary, we attempt to alter our perceptions to fit the familiar patterns. By contrast, if we spend enough time in a computer-synthesized reality, no matter how unusual it might be, we can eventually adapt to it. The strangely unreal then becomes something rather recognizable, familiar, and therefore real. The reality dimension of an online environment entails how mind and environment interact to determine what seems realistic and what appears as fantasy.

Our human psyche operates along a polarity between reality and imagination. We need a grounding in the familiar, in what we have always known to be real. We need to know who people truly are. And yet, seemingly by its intrinsic nature, the human mind also seeks out imaginative states of consciousness, including altered perceptions of our own identities. We need these playful experimentations to discover new, more enriching, and adaptive opportunities for ourselves. When considering the reality dimension of an online environment, we recognize these parallel human needs for embracing both normal and altered states of consciousness.

Chapter 14, "Synthesized Realities and Synthesized Beings," focuses in more depth on these issues concerning the reality dimension of cyberpsychology architecture.

Key Questions from the Reality Dimension

- In what ways do your different online environments feel real to you?
- In what ways do your different environments feel like fantasy?
- How do you tell the difference between reality and fantasy in cyberspace?
- How do you react to places that are real versus imaginary?

THE PHYSICAL DIMENSION: IS THIS TANGIBLE?

In the beginning of cyberspace, people sat motionless at their computers while venturing around the world. Cyberspace felt like disembodied space. Our physical bodies and the real physical space around us seemed to have very little to do with our online endeavors. As technology advanced, we began to realize that cyberspace can, does, and must interact with physicality. Although some online activities are convenient, even powerful, because your physical location places no restrictions on you and even seems irrelevant, other online experiences deliberately capitalize on your physical location, as in applications that provide information about nearby restaurants or let you communicate specifically with people in your vicinity. As an anonymous text messaging system, Yik Yak became popular for this very reason, especially on college campuses: "I may not be sure about your name or identity, but I am sure that you're nearby." Knowing, perhaps knowing, or not knowing who people are adds fun, mystery, and even drama to the game-like social experience. Students in dormitories have also used Yik Yak as a signaling system, for such purposes as asking rowdy neighbors to quiet down or to alert them about resident assistants making their rounds.

We cannot escape the evolutionary fact that we humans developed in a physical world, are intertwined with it, are intrinsically blood-flesh-and-bones creatures. When evaluating the physical dimension of an online environment, we take into account how it involves the physical world and the corporeal body, including bodily sensations and movement, or the lack thereof.

One of the biggest mistakes in our love affair with the computer is the belief that we can sit at it for hours, accomplishing all sorts of things, without it having a negative physical effect on us. At this point in the history of computering, it comes as no surprise that it leads to health problems stemming from sedentariness, computer vision syndrome, and repetitive stress disorders such as carpal tunnel syndrome and musculoskeletal problems. "My body goes stiff when I'm online too long," one of my students noted, "and I don't even notice it's happening." Good ergonomic practices, although helpful, provide only band-aid solutions to online environments that require no physical activity. The simple truth is that evolution did not design us to sit all day in front of a glowing screen or to stare down into a phone. Mother Nature intended us to be physically active in order to be healthy in both mind and body. No matter how we might wax the poetic about shedding our bodies as we immerse our minds into cyberspace, in the final analysis the body cannot be ignored. Human beings are bodily beings.

Why Not Take All of Me? Dissociated and Integrated Physicality

The physical dimension of cyberspace architecture includes *dissociated and integrated physicality*. The dissociated type, which includes bodily movement that has nothing to do with the online activity, can pose significant problems, as evident to me when I witness students on campus staring into their phones and walking across the road right in front of my car. Physics tells us that two objects cannot occupy the same space at the same time. Now cyberpsychology shows us how one mind cannot easily occupy a physical and online space at the same time, unless one is very skilled at multitasking or using sophisticated *augmented reality* devices, such as goggles that provide visual overlays of information onto the scene around us. Some types of dissociated physicality present less obvious hazards, as when people walk a treadmill while doing something on their computer that has nothing to do with walking. The bilateral left/right movement of leg movements, in addition to the simple energizing effects of walking as exercise, might even enhance cognitive functions while computering, That mental boost might also apply to texting while walking, if we disregard the inherent dangers of not looking where one is going.

In integrated physicality, one's bodily movements coincide with the activity in cyberspace. Games that require hand skills or the physical mim-icry of real-world movements – as first popularized in the sports games of Nintendo's Wii – would be examples of integrated physicality, as would any virtual environment that changes in response to head and body motion; moving around a scene to take photos that are then shared online; and hap-tic technology that creates tactile stimulation via cyberspace. In all these cases, the bodily movement or sensation connects to the online experience rather than being mostly irrelevant to it.

Mobile devices involve physicality because people are often moving through different physical environments as they communicate. If they are not reporting on the changes in their location to their online companions, then at the very least the physical and psychological demands of their changing locations must in some way affect how they are communicating. Texting alone in your bedroom will not be the same experience as texting on a jostling, crowded subway.

The Things, Portals, and Sensors of Cyberspace

The physical dimension includes the psychological impact of where and how cyberspace enters into our concrete world. Where do the screens and controls for various devices appear in our surroundings and on our bod-ies? Where are the cameras and other sensors that transmit what we are doing into cyberspace? How do all these incursions of the digital realm into our physical environments affect us? With the introduction of wearable computers or even smart phones that people have with them all day long, how might we be evolving into cyborgs who are part body, part machine, part corporeal individual, part electronically merged with cyberspace consciousness? What is the psychological impact of any kind of robot that physically moves through our space while its "mind" remains connected to cyberspace? As suggested by Ashton (2009) in his concept of the *Internet of things*, all types of appliances in our physical world – cars, heating units, lighting systems, home security devices, and an endless variety of industrial machinery – will become arms of cyberspace. At this stage in the evolution of the Internet, we are just beginning to understand how cyberspace might manifest itself in the physical world, thereby changing it as well as our bodily selves that dwell there. To understand the physical dimension of cyberspace architecture, the once popular field known as environmental psychology must evolve into an environmental cyberpsychology.

The history of technology is the history of fluid, transcended space. In the age when walking served as the primary means of transportation, we were more acutely aware of the physical things along the way between where we were and where we were headed. With the invention of cars, trains, and especially planes, the spaces between here and there seemed less significant. Now, in the age of the Internet, we experience no physical space between the places we go online. By just clicking a button, we magically pop out of one location and into another. These online spaces then seep into our physical world through a variety of device portals, sometimes in places where we least expect or want them. If people wear eyeglasses with embedded devices, their companions might not know for sure whether this supposedly private encounter in the physical world is being broadcast to social media. Students staring into their phones during a lecture allow the social media space to infiltrate the classroom space. Cameras mounted in public spaces send images of us into cyberspace, often without our even knowing it. This interpenetration of our physical spaces with the elusively malleable spaces of the Internet might change our very perception of what "space" is.

Augmented Reality

The term *augmented reality* is often attributed to Boeing researcher Tom Caudell, who in 1990 used it to describe a digital display used by aircraft electricians who used goggles to blend virtual graphics onto a physical scene. In Zen fashion, we might wonder whether reality needs to be or even can be augmented, so other terms such as *computer-mediated reality* or *computer-interpreted reality* might be more appropriate. On a broad level, the term refers to any use of computer resources to provide additional information about one's physical environment or even one's physical body – such as enhancement of vision, hearing, touch sensations, changes in heart rate and respiration, or any kind of data about your surroundings and your physiological reactions to it (Craig, 2013). The computer assists the human in interpreting the situation based on predetermined criteria. Movies such as *The Terminator* illustrate this phenomenon as we look through the eyes of the cyborg, seeing not only the scene around him but also the computer's overlay display that offers both assessments of the situation along with possible decisions about it. A more mundane example is a global positioning system (GPS) application that tells you where you are and what is around you. In all these cases, cyberspace intersects with physical reality. Under ideal circumstances, it can enhance integrated physicality by using cyberspace to help us navigate the world around us.

The Boundary between the Spaces

Among all the eight dimensions of cyberpsychological architecture, the physical dimension plays a special role. It marks the most definitive, tangible boundary between cyberspace and this world in which we humans lived for so many millennia before the invention of electronics. We might call this world reality, the real world, the face-to-face world, or the in-person world, as I sometimes do in this book. However, the most accurate descriptor might be the "physical world" that embodies corporeal, concrete, and material entities, which cyberspace as psychological space does not. How cyberspace manifests itself in that physical world will be the challenge for future technology. How that infusion into physicality affects us humans – how we think, feel, behave – will be the challenge for cyberpsychology.

Key Questions from the Physical Dimension

- How does your use of a computer or phone negatively affect your body?
- When does your physical activity coincide with what you are doing online?
- When does your physical body disconnect from what you are doing?
- Where do you use your mobile device and how does that affect you?
- How do you use devices to interpret your environment and your reaction to it?
- Where do portals into cyberspace appear in your everyday environments?

APPLYING THE THEORY OF CYBERPSYCHOLOGY ARCHITECTURE

If we apply the eight dimensions of cyberpsychology architecture to everyday face-to-face encounters in the real physical world, we come to appreciate how different they can be compared to online environments. When sitting around a table talking to a group of friends, we do not communicate with each other via text. Stimulation includes the integration of all five senses. Talking is primarily synchronous, not asynchronous. As compared to digital realms, we have much less ability to turn ourselves or the situation into something highly imaginative. But we can get up from the table, hug people, cook, sing, and dance, a flexibility in sensory and physical experience that is much more difficult to achieve in any digital environment other than highly sophisticated virtual ones that have yet to be constructed.

In an attempt to offer a one-size-fits-all solution, many large online communities pack as much of the eight dimensions as they can into their platform. Striving for a big, multifaceted architecture, they offer synchronous as well as asynchronous communication, text discussions, images, video, the ability for varying degrees of real or imaginary identity presentation, possibilities for invisibility as well as presence, and a variety of opportunities for group in addition to one-on-one interactions. This jack-of-all-trades approach will work for some people, while others will find it confusingly complex, offering things they do not want or need. Instead, an environment with a specialized design that emphasizes some of the eight dimensions, but not others, can work more effectively for particular types of people with distinct interests. In my experience, for example, communities that were designed specifically for photography, such as Flickr, fared much better for the photosharing experience than multipurpose social media such as Facebook. The future of cyberpsychology is understanding the impact of the eight dimensions on how people think, feel, and behave so that it can assist in the design of integrated architectures that effectively address particular needs, with the ultimate goal of improving our collective well-being.

2

Presence

Be Here Now

We convince by our presence.
– Walt Whitman

After I signed onto Palace, I made my way down the hallway toward the study. As soon as I entered the room, I stopped dead in my tracks. What was going on here? I was standing in the middle of total blackness. Where were the comfy chairs, the chessboard, the bookshelves, the glowing fireplace? All I could see was my avatar owl standing in the middle of a featureless void. Was the Palace software suffering from some kind of glitch? Or was there maybe something wrong with my browser? I stepped back into the hallway. Reality popped back into existence. Everything looked normal there: the carpeted floor, the pictures on the wall. So I stepped back into the study. Sure enough, nothingness enveloped me once again. It was quite disorienting, as if I did not exist anywhere in particular. Then I noticed that the space was not a total vacuum. Along the perimeter of the emptiness I could see slivers of the room. Now I finally understood what was going on. Some mischievous person had painted black all over the walls, floor, and ceiling, while missing a few spots along the edges. "Clean" I said, invoking the command that wiped away anything users added to a room. Sure enough, the study reassuringly popped back into existence around me. Once more, it existed and I within it.

Be here now.

That is the advice from humanistic psychology on how to form meaningful relationships with others, to experience life more fully. Be right here, in this moment, wholly aware of this situation with your eyes, ears, nose, and skin, fully involved with both mind and body, thought and emotion – rather than placing one foot here while the other sinks into distracting ruminations about the past and future that fog our awareness of the here and now.

Be present.

That might be another way to put it. As Zen-like advice, it makes intuitive sense. But this notion was born in a time and place long before everyone started going online. So how do lifestyles in cyberspace address the principle of "be here now"? As early as 1980, scientists such as Minsky (1980) tackled that question in their research into what they called "telepresence." Other researchers use the term "immersion" when trying to understand how fully we feel we exist in a computer-generated environment. In research on virtual reality ranging from studies of games to investigations about psychotherapy, the most central and rather complex concept has been that of "presence" (Burdea, Grigore, & Coiffet, 2003; Diemer et al., 2015; Riva, Waterworth, & Murray, 2014; Schuemie et al. 2001; Steuer, 1992; Witmer & Singer, 1998).

In this chapter, to address that intriguing question about how to "be here now," we explore two very basic issues about our awareness of existence in a particular situation, while noting how cyberpsychology architecture contributes to that awareness:

I am present here.
Others are present here.

I AM HERE: ENVIRONMENTAL PRESENCE

How do we know that we have entered a place? How do we truly feel that we are somewhere in particular, that the setting at hand indeed engages us with some measure of meaning and consequence? We rely on at least four cues for perceiving presence within an environment.

I See, Hear, Feel It

The more robust the sensory dimension of an online environment, the more likely it strikes us as real and the more present we feel in it. If we can see, hear, touch, smell, taste in a panoramic experience, if we subliminally sense the subtleties of ambience, as we do in the real world, we know we indeed *are* somewhere. Cyberspace continually grows in its sophistication of visual, auditory, and tactile stimulation. Each degree of added complexity heightens our perception of environmental presence because the setting acquires more sensory character. Even at a very simplistic level, for example, you will probably have a greater sense of environmental presence **Here** ... than here.

We can feel present even within environments possessing low sensory character, such as no-frills text communication involving email, chat, texting, blogs, and discussion boards. When there are no pictures or sounds, a rudimentary sense of being "here" still arises from the very basic elements of text boxes, buttons, and webpage design. The simple browser window creates a visual sensation of place along with a perceptual invitation to enter it. Our use of the word "window" itself conjures up the idea of entering a different space than the one we are in, thanks to the insights of the original architects at Apple. However, as experts who design software interfaces well know, the particular visual features within a window can make it more inviting, more like a psychologically coherent and meaningful location. With its cushy chairs, chessboard, bookcases, and fireplace, all tucked neatly into my browser window, the study at the Palace seemed to exist as a real place, while a blanket of blackness felt like indeterminate nothingness.

It Moves and Changes Around Me

A well-constructed visual image, such as a painting, can draw the viewer into that scene. Adding movement, as in motion pictures, magnifies even more the sensation of experiencing a real place. As the Greek philosopher Heraclitus noted about our never stepping into the same river twice, the real world keeps moving without repeating itself. Movement means time, which introduces the temporal dimension that plays such an important role in our perception of reality. So too a cyberspace environment containing motion tends to be perceived as more lifelike. To "animate" is make things move, to give them life. In the early days of the Internet, one of the most popular additions to HTML code was text that blinked on and off. Then came animated gif images, followed by Java, Flash, and other tools to give cyberworlds even more action that attracted the eye and intensified the sensation of a unique, lively realm of movement. It if moves, it exists. Presence uses motion to wave at us.

Repetitious movement grows monotonous, resulting in boredom and a somnambulant dulling of the senses, including the sense of place. More complex, shifting patterns of motion have greater clout in creating the feeling of presence within a setting. The human mind rivets to unpredictability, even small doses of it, which is why we spend so much time talking about the weather. As in the river cited by Heraclitus, when we step into online environments that change over time, we are more likely to feel that wavering flow as evidence of lifelike presence.

It Interacts with Me

We reach a fuller level of presence when we can interact with the environment rather than simply witness it. The most basic form of interaction is our ability to enter, move within, and leave a setting. Any cue that heightens the sensation of going into and out of an environment enhances its presence as a setting distinct from other settings. A window that opens toward you when you click a button lets you know that you are entering that space. A voice saying, "Welcome," when you sign on reminds you that you have crossed a threshold from one area to another.

So too the ability to move within the environment – to see it from different perspectives – adds to its spatial quality along with your feeling present within it. In a multipage website, a navigation bar on each page creates the perception of being in one "room" among many possible rooms. In sophisticated three-dimensional (3D) graphical environments, the ability to look 360 degrees around a scene, or to move around an object to see it from various viewpoints, simulates lifelike perspectives and lifelike presence.

We know we are somewhere when we can have an effect on the setting, when it reacts to our actions. Reciprocal reactivity between you and environment enhances your sense of presence in that place. We might even add, as some philosophers have suggested, that objects reacting to other objects (including us) make them "conscious" in a petite way – conscious, and therefore present. Even a simple clicking on a button to make something happen enhances the feeling of doing and being in that place. As opportunities to interact with an online environment become more sophisticated and less predictably routine, the more fully present that environment feels.

To appreciate the power of movement and reciprocal interaction in creating presence, notice what happens when a program crashes. Everything on your screen freezes. You click on things, but nothing happens. The environment goes dead while your sensation of presence in it drops away. When interactivity comes to halt, so does the feeling of presence.

It Looks Familiar to Me

The unfamiliar and unknown tend to make humans feel out of place, anxious. We are not sure what to do, resulting in confusion that may cloud the feeling of presence, compelling us to leave. By contrast, we tend to feel at home, present, in a familiar setting. We have "been" there before, which makes it easier to "be" there now. Among the almost limitless choices of online environments to inhabit, we tend to stick to just a few, those familiar ones where presence has taken root in our consciousness. Any setting that looks confusing or unintelligible, that does not make visual or linguistic sense, or that offers no meaning to us, will tend to scramble our feeling present there.

We should not overstate the importance of familiarity, because novelty can pique our attention and curiosity. New environments create a challenge to explore, learn, and master them, thereby heightening immersion. The imaginative quality of some digital habitats also appeals to the unconscious: the human mind seeks out a dream-life. Although far from familiar, fantasy environments can stimulate presence by addressing the basic human need for an altered state of perception.

Balance is important. Settings that effectively blend the familiar with the novel – reality with fantasy – can be very powerful in stimulating attention, excitement, and the feeling of fully "being there."

OTHERS ARE HERE: INTERPERSONAL PRESENCE

How do we sense that other people are with us in a setting? How do we know that we are interacting with someone in particular, another human being with a unique identity and history, who thinks, feels, and behaves in a distinct way? In their book devoted to this topic, Short, Williams, and Christie (1976) referred to it as "social presence." As with environmental presence, we rely on at least four cues for experiencing the presence of other people.

I See, Hear, Feel You

The more sensory stimulation we receive about the other person, the more likely that person feels present and real. If we can see, hear, smell, and touch – as we do in the real world – we indeed know someone is here.

Throughout the life span, especially during childhood, humans rely heavily on the intimate stimulation of touch and smell in developing an awareness of significant others. Cyberspace has grown by leaps and bounds in the increasingly more sophisticated visual and auditory stimulation provided, with technologies for transmitting tactile and olfactory sensations beginning to emerge. Each degree of added sensory complexity heightens our perception of the other person's presence because the person acquires more sensory character.

Even without seeing or hearing them, we might feel very strongly the presence of people in the text communication of email, chat, texting, and social media posts. The history of literature, journalism, and personal correspondence clearly demonstrates our human capacity for "being with" someone via the written word. Some writers possess more skill at generating their presence with words, often because they understand the subtle psychological nuances of making themselves come alive in text.

You Move and Change Right in Front of Me

As with life itself, people move. They do. They change. Any place online that allows the person to move, change, and act will enhance that person's presence. Video shows fluctuating facial expressions, shifting body language, and physical motion. In communities and games where members use avatars to represent themselves, moving the avatar around the scene simulates body movement. Switching from one avatar to another also changes your visual appearance. Even in the text environments of chat, discussion boards, texting, and social media, you enhance your existence as a live entity by moving from one section of the environment to another, assuming other people can see you change locations. In any environment, the opportunity to add, remove, or change something boosts your presence in the minds of others who see your actions.

So too entering, leaving, and reentering an environment shows you coming, going, and being present. Similar to the peek-a-boo game that delights babies, cycles of appearing and disappearing reinforce your existence in the minds of others. When you vanish, other people's anticipation of your return sustains in their minds your being continuous over time, what psychologists call *object constancy*. Whenever you send an email or post to social media, your presence reemerges. You are felt anew by others. Only after a sustained period of no longer reappearing does your online existence begin to fade in the other's consciousness. Your posts remain, but your presence slips away.

You Interact with Me

We experience the presence of others more fully through their reaction to our presence. Human presence is reciprocally interactive. The more ways an online environment allows people to affect each other – that is, the more powerful its social dimension – the more present they will feel to each other. Conversing is one obvious method of interacting. When people respond to what we say online, their presence springs to the foreground, compared to the faded background presence of those who remain silent. Although limited compared to the real world, cyberspace does allow us to do things together other than just talk, such as playing games, sharing files, writing collaboratively, creating images, and remotely interacting with each other's device. Doing something together means being together, what psychoanalysts call a *twinning relationship* in which companions reinforce each other's identity. One evening in the Palace avatar community, several of us joined forces in planting a garden. It was a simple activity, with each of us just placing a picture of flowers onto the ground. Nevertheless, it made us feel, "we are all doing something, here and now." Even something as simple as clicking a "like" button lets others know that, "I was here."

If people do not react to your being and doing, your subjective sense of your own presence wanes. Described as early as 1902 in Cooley's concept of the *looking glass self* and decades later elaborated by psychoanalytic object relations theory (Greenberg & Mitchell, 1983), our identity is both affirmed and shaped through the eyes of others. When ignored, that sense of self-presence fades, perhaps resulting in feeling lost, powerless, frustrated, angry, lonely, or depressed. People whose presence is not acknowledged may avoid an environment or act out in negative ways to attain some kind of attention. Lacking visual contact, handshakes, and hugs, people in text-only environments might be more susceptible to feeling overlooked. If no one replies to your email or post, your very existence in that setting comes into question. You feel like a nobody. Your psychological commitment to others as being real and present might also fade, because *real* people respond to each other's presence. Truly present people express and react to each other's emotions. Maya Angelou said:

> I've learned that people will forget what you said, people will forget what you did, but people will never forget how you made them feel.

Everyone is a complex person. People feel more present to others – and even to themselves – when they are able to express the wide range of thoughts, memories, emotions, and motives that make up their identity An online environment providing tools that maximize these expressions of personal identity – that is, one that has a rich identity dimension – will enhance the experience of someone in particular really being there. A simple example is the opportunity in online communities to create a profile page. When people leave it blank, or provide minimal information about themselves, they miss the opportunity to pump up their presence. A more sophisticated example is the blog, where a person controls an almost limitless range of personal expression. Bloggers thrive on magnifying their presence, post by post.

The more people can give and receive feedback, sharing their lives and personalities, the more they sense each other truly being there. Within your own personal space in social media, you have greater presence than your visitors simply because it is your space – you are saying and doing more there. In order to equalize the social reinforcement of each other's presence, people in social media form clusters of contacts in which they visit each other's space to offer comments. If you acknowledge someone else's presence, even just by clicking a "like" button, you expect the same from them.

Our ability to interact with the presence of another person enhances our knowing not only that someone is here, but also *who* that someone is. Consider this scenario. A person is saying nothing, but you see their name in the list of people who are online at that moment, in the very same space where you are, perhaps a chat room. You feel uneasy about that person because you are not sure who he or she is, or even if that person is a he or a she when the username is gender ambiguous. If you do know the person, you might not be sure whether that person is actually present at all. A sense of the "uncanny" arises when we cannot be certain whether someone is here, and, if indeed they are here, who exactly that person is. Films about monsters draw on this sense of the uncanny because anxiety arises from this uncertainty about the presence, identity, and intentions of the other. Interacting with people to know more about them provides the remedy to that apprehension. The experience of the uncanny will also emerge in sophisticated cyberspace habitats that assess, adapt to, and even anticipate the needs of the particular person within it, what researchers call *ambient intelligence*. The environment itself becomes a mysteriously invisible but present "other," seemingly possessing its own powers of perception, mind, and will.

You Look Familiar

As with environmental presence, we tend to feel more at ease interacting with people we know. Upon meeting them again, we quickly slip into the sense of their presence because they are familiar to us. Just a few simple cues – verbal, auditory, visual – can trigger the memory of who they are. On the contrary, when we encounter people unfamiliar to us, especially when their behavior seems foreign, strange, erratic, or meaningless, we have a harder time forming a coherent impression of them. People detract from their presence when they choose to express themselves in a vague, peculiar, or chaotic fashion – for example, with unusual images, incomprehensible social media pages, or very terse and loosely constructed text.

Once again, we should not overstate the importance of familiarity, because novelty can pique our senses, alertness, and curiosity, while chronic familiarity leads to inattentiveness, boredom, and a dulling of presence. Relationships feel more alive as we discover new things about our companions. People seem more real when they occasionally act in ways we did not anticipate. This is why robots and other forms of artificial intelligence feel more present in the early stages of an encounter, but that feeling tends to fade over time. They run the risk of becoming too predictable, too mechanical, even predictably and mechanically confused, resulting in obvious interpersonal mistakes. As demonstrated by research on the classic Turing Test (Turing, 1950), some people are not at first able to tell the difference between an artificially intelligent machine and a real human communicating with them via text. But over time, very few programs can sustain the wide range of complexity, change, and interactivity that we interpret as human presence. A present machine, yes. A present human, no.

THE ARCHITECTURE OF PRESENCE

For all these factors that determine environmental and interpersonal presence, more is not necessarily better, while less is not necessarily worse. Too little sensory stimulation, change, and interactivity deplete presence, but an overwhelming dose blows it apart. Too little familiarity makes us anxiously uncertain, but too much puts us to sleep. We experience presence most fully, in this place with other people, when we reach an optimal level of sensory stimulation, change, interactivity, and familiarity.

As long as an environment is flexible enough to allow people to express the complexities of their identity – and as long as people use those opportunities – they can maintain as well as enrich their presence. People might apply the fantasy features of online games and avatar communities to spice up their identity in conventional social media with a pinch of imagination. It can be an effective balance between the familiar and new – between reality and inventiveness – that raises their presence to new levels. While presence tends to feel stronger during synchronous communication as people take advantage of that in-the-moment spontaneity, it also intensifies in asynchronous communication when they use the zone for reflection to create psychological nuance in what they say about themselves. With all the options for manipulating and combining the eight dimensions of cyberpsychology architecture – identity, social contact, machine interactivity, text, sensory stimulation, the shaping of time, reality, and physicality – digital environments offer different levels and varieties of presence.

ONE SIZE OF PRESENCE DOES NOT FIT ALL

People differ in how well they create the impression that they are here in the now. Some are skilled in making their presence known, in projecting themselves into an environment. People experienced in text communication know how to write clearly to express themselves, while also using creative keyboarding techniques that convey body language, subvocal thoughts, and underlying emotions, as we will see in Chapter 7, "Text Talk." In constructing their emails, websites, blogs, gaming characters, avatar collections, and social media pages, people differ in how well they implement sensory stimulation, change, interactivity, and the balance between familiar and novel. These skills often rest on an empathic attunement to the other person, on understanding how others might react to one's style of expressing presence. The savvy online communicator pays careful attention to the interaction between self and other that generates the synergistic feeling of being here together.

People also vary in their ability to sense the other person's presence. With only a small splash of text or a brief glance at an image, one person immediately knows that it is Joe, while another person has no clue. Empathic attunement to the identities and expressive styles of other people plays an important role in sensing presence, as does the desire to connect to another person. Prisoners isolated in their cells contact each other with muffled taps on a concrete wall. Despite this extreme minimalist communication, they sense each other's presence intensely. These same social needs, operating at many levels of intensity, surface in all online environments, whether they offer simple or complex communication tools.

Due to differences in personality and cognitive style, people select some online environments rather than others because they feel more able to express their presence, as well as sense the presence of others, the way they prefer. One basic difference is the predilection for communicating with text, pictures, or both. Hopefully, others in those environments are also well suited for that setting and the communication preferences of the people who live there. If any element is amiss in the optimal match between self, other, and environment, the quality of presence on all three levels might decay.

Psychoanalytic object relations theory describes how people vary in the extent to which they feel like a separate, unique person, distinct from other people. People who operate at a developmentally primitive level of object relations see others as an extension of themselves, as merged with their identity. In person or online, they do not sense the presence of the other person as a distinct being, but rather as a part of themselves. Some online settings – especially text communication that lacks the visual and auditory cues that help establish a separate physical being – can exacerbate this poor self/other differentiation. Narcissistic people in a discussion forum or email group might experience the presence of others primarily as a source of attention and admiration to bolster their self-esteem. They seek an audience rather than a shared emotional connection. That person may not experience others as distinct individuals with their own ideas, needs, feelings, and therefore unique presence. "Even in the presence of others he was completely alone," the writer Robert Pirsig once said.

For people with deficient object relations, presence of self and other means something very different than for people with well-established object relations. In what has been called *selfobject transferences*, others exist to mirror one's needs and feelings, to provide a twin that bolsters one's sense of self, or to serve as an idealized figure to merge with (Kohut, 1977, 1980). Text communication encourages a blending of the minds of self and other – a blending of presences – which magnifies the poor self/other differentiation that is a chronic problem for people with poor object relations. We will return to these issues in Chapter 5, "Electrified Relationships."

Even people at a developmentally advanced level of object relations may at times have difficulty establishing an accurate perception of the other person's presence. You correctly sense the existence of another unique, separate individual, but elements of that person's identity might be distorted by your own expectations, needs, and feelings. These kinds of transference reactions also tend to be magnified by the ambiguity of text communication. The mind-merging that sometimes occurs in text might even cause developmentally advanced people to dip into periods of selfobject transferences. Any person, with either mature or primitive selfobject relations, might under stress succumb to *depersonalization* and *derealization* in which they feel unreal, not quite alive, like robots, while the environment and others around them seem distant, hollow, as if everything turns into a stale, shallow cartoon. Under these conditions, the person's experience of presence declines on all levels.

WHAT IS HERE AND NOW?

Relationships in cyberspace encourage us to reexamine many of the traditional assumptions about presence implied in the "be here now" maxim of humanistic psychology. As we have seen, the very notion of "here" is called into question. The online environmental presence of "this place" always manifests itself, at least in our current state of technology, via a computer or mobile device screen. All of the many "Heres" we can experience in cyberspace emerge from that screen. Our actual physical location often is irrelevant to that psychological space inside the device, which points to the power of the mind to create and immerse itself into an emotionally real, meaningful environment. The "be here now" principle encourages us to let go of our mental distractions so we can experience the Here and Now more fully, more clearly – but as we stare into our screens, cyberspace reminds us that the Here and Now is more a state of mind than anything else.

Despite the powerful possibilities for presence online, we must remind ourselves that our physical body exists in a physical space, in front of a computer or mobile device screen, in a setting that is quite different from the online world precisely because it is physical. We may not even be consciously aware of that concretely tangible setting around us, or of our flesh-blood-and-bones body, which points to the role of both dissociated physicality and psychological dissociation in allowing us to experience presence online. To fully immerse ourselves into the environments and relationships of cyberspace, we must be able to minimize perceptions of the setting around us, at least for a time. If the phone rings or the dog barks to go out, we shift our attention back to our physical surroundings.

Despite staunch advocates of augmented reality and multitasking, who claim that online experiences and resources can be so smoothly integrated into our "real" lives that the distinction between those two realms become meaningless, the truth is that we cannot immerse ourselves fully into cyberspace and in-person presences simultaneously, any more than we can completely immerse ourselves into different online settings or relationships simultaneously. Just as physics says that two objects cannot occupy the same space at the same time, cyberpsychology tells us that a mind cannot be present in two spaces at the same time. For that reason, I can image Fritz Perls (1969), a vehement promoter of the "be here now" philosophy in the humanistic psychology of the 1960s, pulling a cell phone out of the hands of a person during a group therapy session and throwing it against the wall. If you are going to be here, be here fully.... Be here now! Echoes of his philosophy appeared in a comment by one of my students: "When I was vacationing in Florida, everyone brought their phones to the beach. I didn't. I sat there and enjoyed the physical company of those around me, and nature. Others were texting, calling, taking pictures, on Facebook, Twitter, Instagram. They weren't present. It annoyed me." By contrast, some students in my surveys report how their phones assist them here and now by serving as conversation pieces. "We run out of ideas to talk about," one student said, "so we look at our phones for a few minutes, then someone says something like, 'hey did you guys see this pic?'"

With practice, we learn how to manage a multitasking of presence. More so than ever in human history, our attention, particularly in social media, has become a precious gift, even a commodity, which we must learn how to apply wisely. We try to be here and now in one particular place online while keeping an eye and ear open for something that might call our attention to another place – either the real world or another online realm. Usually something changing in the other environment calls our attention to it. The machine assists us in that endeavor. While engrossed in texting with a companion, part of us notices a blinking icon for a social media notification, the call to the presence of another companion.

The Mindfulness of Now

Multitasking can easily turn into an attention span that is a jack of all trades but master of none. We thinly spread our awareness of presence across the board, without fully immersing it anywhere in particular. But some advocates of multitasking claim that under ideal conditions, a skillful multitasking of presence might resemble what has been called *mindfulness*: we focus the presence of our awareness fully on one thing, but also allow another part of our mind to remain open, silently noticing then shifting concentration to other presences in the periphery of our field of awareness. Rather than being one-dimensional, presence alters in magnitude, direction, and juxtaposition as we balance and redirect our awareness between here and there.

Mystics speak of an enhanced state of mindfulness in which we rise to a pure awareness of all aspects of reality simultaneously, without the distraction of thinking, analyzing, judging, or remembering, letting go of the distinction between "inside me" and "outside me," present to such an enhanced degree that even our performing some activity in this state of pure awareness loses its separateness as "me doing something." It takes many years of devoted meditation practice to reach this level of presence. Will a reality "augmented" by technologically multitasking devices attached to our bodies help us attain this state of mind? In his classic book *Zen in the Art of Archery*, Eugen Herrigel (1999) described how it required several years of dedicated practice under a master to learn how to let loose the arrow in this state of pure, fully aware presence. Can we speed up that process by wearing virtual reality goggles on our heads or by implanting sensors into our bodies that feed us information about our environment as well as our bodies? Devoting as much practice as Herrigel did to archery, perhaps some people might attain this advanced state of technologically mediated mindfulness.

Some humanistic psychologists advise us not to live in the past or future, but to be here in this very moment. The past and future are ghosts, only the Now truly exists as the physical, sensory, genuine reality. In the synchronous communication of chat and texting, we remain somewhat true to that idea, because synchronicity does tend to magnify the feeling of mutual presence between self and other. You are with me here and *now*. Some people claim they sense very intensely the companion's moment-by-moment presence even in the simple exchange of typed text. The humanistic psychologist might agree on that score, while objecting to the intangible "living inside one's head" quality of life online. True human encounters, they would say, involve seeing, hearing, touching, smelling, tasting, feeling with your whole body ... here and now.

Is presence less developed in asynchronous communication? When reading emails, blogs, or social media posts, do those other people seem less like they are with us *now*? We know that they probably will not react immediately to what we say, so interactivity is delayed and some might say weaker compared to synchronous communication. Yet in many other respects we sense that they are here now, just as writers of poems, stories, and essays create the feeling that they are with us in the moment. When we open an email message or enter social media, we might believe we are opening a Now that transcends the passing of time.

If applying the "be here now" principle of humanistic psychology to cyberspace tells us anything, it tells how the sense of presence arises from the cues of sensory stimulation, change, interactivity, and the degree of familiarity. It tells us that the impact of those cues is heavily influenced by the subjective interpretation of the individual, that the being here and now of presence resides in the human mind.

3

The Dynamic Digital Psyche

We know what we are, but not what we may be.
– William Shakespeare

Years ago, when I was writing a book on psychoanalysis and Eastern thought, I struggled with the question that has long troubled psychologists: What is this thing called "self"? Back then, the information superhighway known as the Internet was still brand new. If cyberspace marked the next stage in the evolution of the human mind and self, then why not consult it about this question? So I fired up the computer, aimed my browser at the Alta Vista search engine, and entered the keyword "self." After furiously scanning all of cyberspace, the engine came back with a reply: 2.5 million hits! Looks like the self is everywhere! Maybe that meant something. Or maybe I just needed to narrow my search. So I entered the keywords "true self." This time I got 11,000 hits. Better. I was on the right track. How about "essence of self"? The search engine hummed away and returned 245 hits. Now I was definitely zooming in on the target. I could tell this was the right path because a lot of the hits included websites devoted to philosophy, spirituality, and poetry – although it also turned up the American Legion Magazine and a webpage called "Understanding Diarrhea in Travelers." Maybe that was significant. After all, when asked what is the Buddha, a great Zen master once replied, "Dried turd." Or maybe anomalous search engine results meant that the hunt for the self leads to glitches and dead ends. But I wasn't going to let that stop me. Finally, I entered in the keywords "the true and essential Self." Once again Alta Vista went out into the vast Netherland of global electronified knowledge and came back with . . . zero hits. Nothing! The void! The True and Essential Self was nowhere to be found – well, at least not in cyberspace.

WHO ARE YOU?

Who are you in cyberspace? This is the key question in the identity dimension of cyberpsychology architecture. Are you the same person as you are in the real world? One of the most fascinating aspects of the Internet is the opportunity it offers people to present their identities in a variety of forms. You can alter your style of being just slightly, as well as indulge in wild experiments by manipulating your age, history, personality, physical appearance, and even your gender. The username you choose, the details you do or do not indicate about yourself, the information presented in your social media profile, the personae or avatars you adopt in an online community, the items you indicate you like and repost – all are important aspects of how people manage their individuality in cyberspace. Even something as simple as a change in your profile photo might reveal a dramatic shift in how you think about yourself. Just as traditional psychology has long recognized the complexity of personal identity as a crucial aspect of human nature, so too cyberpsychology searches the many intricacies of how people shape themselves online, what psychoanalytic thinkers would call an investigation into the "psychodynamics" of the digital psyche.

THIS THING CALLED SELF

Anyone well versed in theoretical attempts to define the "self" will tell you that it is the most elusive, complex, and yet important challenge in understanding what it is to be human. In my book *Contemporary Psychoanalysis and Eastern Thought* (1993), I described how theorists in both the East and West have tackled that challenge. Striving for a definition leads to complicated distinctions concerning the normal, pathological, and ideal self, as well as between the conscious and unconscious self. Cyberspace rubs our noses in these dilemmas whenever we talk about online identity. In the first part of this chapter, we will navigate through the paths of this maze called the "self."

The Molecular Me

The concept of the *self-as-structure* reminds me of the Tinker Toy set I had as a child. It was a box filled with wooden rods of various lengths and colors, as well as circular wheels with holes along the edges and sides. You would insert the rods into the wheels to make complex, interconnected structures of all different shapes, sizes, and colors. You could construct them into buildings or abstract shapes that looked like molecules.

So too the self-as-structure is a complex constellation of interconnected modules of memories, thoughts, and emotions. The self-as-structure is a nuts-and-bolts model of the self that has been very popular in Western psychology, no doubt inspired by concepts of molecular structure in classical chemistry and physics. We can think of the goal of psychotherapy, along with the evolution of the self, as the development of a sturdier and more elaborate, flexible, balanced, and cohesive constellation of memories, thoughts, and emotions.

This concept of the self-as-structure is implicit in many cyberpsychology theories about digital identity. All of the things that we do online constitute the nuts and bolts of our cyberspace self: our posts, comments, photographs, profile descriptions, everything we share, and all the places we visit. They reflect the many facets of who we are. Gathering them all up into one big bundle would be your digital self.

The challenge is discovering how well these various elements of self-as-structure fit together in cyberspace. Where do they overlap and reinforce each other? Are there discrepancies, missing pieces, or inaccuracies in what appears online concerning you? How accurately does the integration and comprehensiveness of the online Tinker Toy structure represent your identity in the real world? The more a person engages environments that maximize all eight dimensions of cyberpsychology architecture, the more wide-ranging the representation of this self-as-structure.

The Transcendent Me

The *self-as-transcendent* is the whole that is greater, or at least different, than the sum of its parts. We can think of that transcendent self as the superordinate glue, force, or container that holds the self-as-structure together, the fundamental organizing energy, the source or ground that gives rise to and unifies all elements of selfhood. Carrying that idea into the realm of mysticism, as Jung (1969) did in his theory of archetypes, we recognize this transcendent self as flowing from the larger Self (he capitalized the word) that embodies the individual self. A useful metaphor helps us understand this concept: your self is a wave on the ocean. It appears as a distinct entity, a little self, but it is a form that arises from, passes through, and eventually returns to the larger, formless Self beneath it.

Might cyberspace in its entirety serve as digital stand-in for this metaphysical grounding of the self as envisioned by ancient mystics, only now taking place inside wires, circuits, and microchips as the wellspring of the online self? This idea of an ethereal, all-encompassing, transcendent realm that serves as the source of all things in cyberspace surfaced in our collective consciousness when we began talking about the constellation of Internet servers as "the Cloud." Suspended in time and space, it sustains our digital selves.

The Manifested Me

The concept of *self-as-manifestation* spins off from the idea of the self-as-transcendent. The individual self is a representation, a manifestation of the larger, transcendent self. The transcendent self infuses or shines through the individual self. Sometimes only certain facets of the transcendent self emerge through each individual. Cyberspace has come to serve as the collective human mind while also providing a place for individuals to manifest themselves within it.

Cyberspace is an extremely complex realm of ideas and experiences that shows no limits in how much it will expand. Will it be a complete representation of the collective human mind, or partial? Is it a new stage in the evolution of human consciousness? How does the individual person choose to manifest his or her psyche in that collective cyberspace psyche? The term *avatar* comes from the Hindu word referring to the form gods choose to represent themselves on Earth. Now we see that term applied to the forms we create for ourselves while online, especially in virtual reality. Perhaps in cyberspace, we see a playing out of the divine process of connecting to a transcendent self while also finding new ways to manifest the individual self.

The Sentient Me

The concept of the *self-as-awareness* proposes that the true self is not a thing, object, or structure, but rather the phenomenon of observing, of being aware and conscious, of being sentient. An interesting turn of events in evolution occurred when we humans developed a unique type of awareness: self-awareness. We became conscious of ourselves, including the ideas, memories, and feelings of our self-as-structure. Psychodynamic psychologists call it the *observing ego*.

This self emerges in cyberspace when we use any computerized tool that helps us become aware of our online environment, the people who dwell there, and ourselves as participants in that space. The more tools for developing this consciousness – text, sounds, images, tactile stimulation – the more opportunities for the self-as-awareness to surface. If an online environment enhances our knowing where we are, who we are with, and what we are doing – in other words, "presence" – it enhances our self-as-awareness. Upping the ante to the question of self-awareness, how well are people attuned to themselves within their online habitat or in the real world? Does the online environment or any software application help us with that goal of knowing thyself, or undermine it?

The Willing and Doing Me

The concept of the *self-as-willing-and-doing* focuses on the self as a motivating force, an initiator of action with intention, direction, and meaning. It is the power that moves us along in life with a sense of purpose. A problem arises when we try to locate this "doer" within the psyche, as psychology has always tried to avoid the seemingly fruitless search for the intrapsychic homunculus, the entity inside one's head who makes things go. Instead, we might think of the self as the doing of something without reference to any hidden internal actor who is the source of the doing. According to Zen Buddhism, the realization of the self arrives when we act spontaneously, fluidly, in accordance to the moment, free from the burden of self-awareness that usually clogs the works.

An online environment actualizes the self-as-willing-and-doing to the degree that it encourages people to *do* something with the environment and the people there. In particular, how robust is its interactive and social dimensions? If we follow the Zen philosophy, we might add that an online habitat enhances this self-as-doing when it provides tools that encourage spontaneous, fluid expression with minimal interference from self-consciousness.

The Me That Is a We/Which Me Do We See?

In the self-as-structure, a single person's identity embodies multiplicity. There are different sectors within your personality, such as the numerous roles you play in your life: child, parent, student, employee, neighbor, friend. We have within us different agendas, moods, and beliefs. While online, do we fit these pieces together, or do we disconnect them? That is the question concerning the *integrated or dissociated self*.

Cyberspace offers separate niches for all facets of selfhood. Researchers talk about how we can deconstruct ourselves online and multitask our identities, or as Turkle (1995) stated, how we manage *distributed selves*. We do not have to present ourselves in toto – how we look, talk, and move, as well as our history, thoughts, feelings, and personality, all in one big package. Across different environments we can divvy up our characteristics to present them in packets of various sizes and content. Thanks to thousands of online groups – with each devoted to different professional, vocational, or personal topic – we can express, highlight, and develop specific parts of our identity while setting aside others: a movie group here, a competitive word game there; geologists, bicyclists, dancers, cat lovers, people who love to rant. Cyberspace provides places for us to perch all our identifications, places that are often separate from each other, each containing people who may know little or nothing about our other perches. Even in highly active social media, we tend to present some aspects of who we are, but not others. If that selective self-presentation progresses to the extreme, some people end up singing one-note songs about themselves in a particular online environment, focusing on just one aspect of their lives while dissociating almost everything else.

Dissociating the various aspects of who we are online might be an efficient, multitasking method for managing our complex lifestyles, especially when some of our social roles are not easily compatible with each other, as is usually the case with our professional versus personal modes of being.

During dissociation, something is always hidden. You do not have to mention to your stock trading group that you also hang out at the *Star Trek* fan club site. In social media, you decide what information you put into your personal profile and what you omit. You post a photo of yourself, but first crop someone out of the shot. If you want to see but not be seen, you can step back into lurking. In precarious situations, people dissociate parts of their identity that are sensitive, vulnerable, or possibly harmful to themselves or others. They express that part of themselves only in a place online that feels safe or where they think they can get away with it. Dissociation can become an outlet for psychological problems, as with people who create different online versions of themselves due to a multiple personality disorder (now often referred to as a "dissociative identity disorder").

This idea of self-multiplicity is not a new one in the history of psychology. In his studies of religious conversion experiences, William James (1902/2013), considered by many to be the father of American psychology, talked about how the mind operates in a field of consciousness where one's awareness shifts fluidly among different hot spots of ideas, memories, and feelings. Role theory in social psychology, proposed by such theorists as Mead (1934), described how we juggle our various social roles throughout the day, leading him to conclude that a multiple personality is in a certain sense normal. Cyberspace living is yet another manifestation of this consciousness shifting and social juggling act. It gives people unprecedented opportunities to cultivate something in particular about themselves in an environment designed for that purpose. It might even give people the chance to reveal parts of their identity that they never divulge in their real lives. No one at the office knows that Jim is a romantic knight in a medieval role-playing game. "We all seem to be bipolar or have multiple personalities," one student said in a survey, "because our lives online versus real life can be so different."

Despite the potentially beneficial aspects of compartmentalizing one's identity, we also have a basic need to unify the different parts of who we are. The psychoanalyst Kohut (1977, 1980) called it *self-cohesion*, the degree to which the different parts of our identity fit together. Combining the various components of both online and offline identities into one balanced, harmonious whole may be the hallmark of mental health, what I will describe later in this chapter as the *integration principle*.

When we evaluate our identity in cyberspace, we must ask ourselves two questions: How and to what degree is my identity dissociated or integrated? If I do compartmentalize those parts of myself, is this strategy working for me or hurting me? Given all those opportunities in cyberspace, we face a very basic choice. We can pick only one or two communities where we express a great deal about ourselves – or we spread ourselves out across many environments, usually with isolated or perhaps superficial expressions of our identities in each one.

The interpersonal significance of identity dissociation and integration becomes apparent in situations where people unexpectedly seem to know something about you that you did not realize they knew. During a video chat with a fellow researcher who had initially contacted me via email, I mentioned how he likes to bake cakes. He seemed surprised, even a bit embarrassed that I was aware of this fact. I pointed out that he had written about this hobby in his blog.

We might compartmentalize aspects of our identities into our various online habitats, sometimes even forgetting that we had done so. But other people who want to know more about us, to understand us better, hopefully with good intentions, will investigate and integrate those different features of who we are. In any particular online or offline environment, the self we think we are making known to others is not necessarily the self that they know. Feeling surprised, embarrassed, and even exposed in these situations points to discrepancies in how we consciously integrate or dissociate our identity as compared to how others integrate or dissociate it.

Good Me/Bad Me

We experience the different parts of our identity as either the *positive or negative self*. We associate shame, guilt, fear, anxiety, or anger with some aspects of who we are, while associating acceptance, appreciation, happiness, or love with other aspects.

People who act out in cyberspace, who hurt others or themselves, are often venting some negatively charged aspect of their psyche. Such purely cathartic behaviors often go nowhere, as in an insecure, passive-aggressive person who gets stuck in an endless stream of online arguments. In more extreme cases, unfortunately, cyberspace allows people with truly pathological traits to find similar comrades who reinforce their problem. Pedophiles and other predators are good examples, as are people who revolve their lives around hatred or crime. Funneling the "bad" self into an online habitat well suited for it often entails dissociation, for it is very possible that people never show that part of themselves anywhere else.

Some people online express what they believe is a negative self in an attempt to better understand and perhaps transform their attitude about it. Transgendered people who learn to accept themselves while participating in an online support group have changed their self-esteem from negative to positive. Cyberspace is interpersonally powerful because it allows people to find others who are just like them in some respect, but who feel about it in a very different but reparative way.

People strive to attain new, ideal ways of being while online. They explore the digital world as an opportunity to exercise their positive traits, or to develop new ones in a process that humanistic psychologists, such as Maslow (1943), called *self-actualization*. Putting one's best foot forward in cyberspace by only showing a good-looking self might simply be exaggeration or deception, as often happens on dating websites – but sometimes it reflects this attempt to self-actualize, to become that ideal self. Even online romances that clearly entail more quixotic fantasy than reality might be growth promoting.

Whether a personality trait is good or bad could very well depend on the social context, which is why people often have mixed feelings about themselves. "Suppose you struggle through to the good and find that it is also dreadful," C. S. Lewis once said. Different online habitats provide convenient testing grounds for exploring these pros and cons. Is it good or bad that a person tends to be quiet? In a discussion forum for professionals, a quiet member might better understand the advantages of hanging back as a way to see more clearly how the group behaves. In a chat room, that same quiet person might come to realize the delightful freedom of spontaneously opening up. What we think is bad about ourselves might also be good, and vice versa. It depends on where and when. Because cyberspace offers so many opportunities to engage new people and social situations, it can help us realize this fact.

Real Me/Fantasy Me

Our struggle with the perceived good and bad aspects of our identity often turns out to be the struggle between who we are and who we fantasize being. There is both a *real and fantasized self* operating within the psyche. Some online environments encourage that fantasy self, while others do not. In role-playing games, no one will object to your transformation into a superhuman with either malevolent or altruistic intentions – but in most social media, people expect you to be who you really are rather than pretend. Other environments fall somewhere in between reality and fantasy. People offer realistic portrayals of their identity, while fudging other things in order to appear different. While it is possible in cyberspace to free up a fantasized self as a way to actually take some of its traits into one's personality, the endeavor can also turn into unrealistic self-hypnosis. "We want to escape reality and become what doesn't exist," one of my students commented in a survey, "the people who hide behind false identities clearly have psychological problems." To which another added, "All of these things are wishes. It's a false happiness. Maybe people should just be happy with themselves and who they really are."

In and Out of Control of Me

How we present ourselves in cyberspace is not always a conscious, deliberate choice. We all have and need a *self-regulating self*, what psychoanalysts call the *ego*. But it sometimes fails us. Repressed wishes and emotions leak out in roundabout or disguised ways without our even knowing it. We are not always conscious of how we dissociate parts of our identity or even of the positive and negative feelings we attach to them. Often people select a username, upload a profile photo, or post a message on a whim, because it appeals to them, without fully understanding the deeper meanings of that choice. Or a person joins an online group because it seems interesting while failing to realize the motives concealed in that decision. The limitless variety of online environments, especially those that endorse anonymity and fantasy, gives ample opportunity for the expression of these unconscious feelings.

People vary greatly in the degree to which they are consciously aware of and control their identity in cyberspace. Some people who engage in imaginary role-playing scenarios report how the characters seem to take on a life of their own. They temporarily surrender their normal identity to the imaginary persona, perhaps later understanding the meaning of this transformation. "Trolls" who act out negativity by hurting others usually have little insight into why they are so cruel. By contrast, striving online to be a better person requires a conscious awareness of what the ideal self could be, as well as what unconscious emotional conflicts block the way. Some people, on their own, make a fully intentional choice about who they want to be in cyberspace. Some are only partially mindful of what they do online, but with help from others or through experience become more aware. Other people resist any self-insight at all. They live under the illusion that they are in control of themselves, even when others online clearly perceive that they are not.

None of us has complete authority over how cyberspace portrays our digital identity. As the Internet expands, more information becomes available about everyone. People post messages and photos about us without our awareness or permission. Our online behaviors are being tracked and recorded. We can lose control over these bits and pieces of our identity, which is very disconcerting when the information is distorted or incorrect. Even when the information is accurate, some people still consider it an impolite or outright intrusive violation of their privacy – and of their sense of self – when someone plugs their name into a search engine to gather data about them, what some people consider a type of "stalking." Advocates of privacy insist that people have the right to become invisible to search engines and computers that store information about their actions online.

Is it possible that cyberspace can assist us in becoming more self-aware, more in control of ourselves? We have access to all sorts of applications that will prompt us for information or automatically record something about us and then offer feedback in an attempt to make us more conscious of who we are and how we live – whether it is how many hours we sleep each night, what we tend to do online, or our personality style. We can even enter our own names into search engines to see how cyberspace depicts our identities. An interesting question is when, why, and how people take advantage of these opportunities for examining and regulating themselves. It comes as no surprise that people who are already more self-aware and in conscious control of their actions tend to be the people who are more willing to try self-improvement applications.

In an attempt to motivate people, software designers relied on what has been called *gamification*. By tapping the intrinsic need to achieve, compete, acquire status, and feel closure, a software application turns the attempts to improve such things as one's health, finances, and personal habits into a game where points are earned, rewards are attained, or comparisons to other people are made. Whether gamification entails competition or cooperation with other people becomes a critical question. If the purpose of the game is to gain insight into oneself, or to improve one's well-being, does it make sense to compete with other people to reach those goals? Most likely, cooperation would be the better option.

When using programs that supposedly tell us something useful about ourselves, we need to remain cautious about what psychology calls *reliability and validity*. How consistent is the program in measuring something? Is it even measuring what it is supposed to? In the "app happy" atmosphere that blossomed with mobile devices, overly enthusiastic designers created all sorts of self-assessment tools, but only rarely with a sophisticated psychological understanding of how to assess people. What technologists say about computer programs is equally true about these applications: garbage in, garbage out.

The Media Is Me

Any particular online environment is a media entity unto itself, with its own atmospheric style. Borrowing the idea from McLuhan and Fiore (1967) that the medium is the message, you shape your identity as a complex message within that environment. To create this *media-specific-self*, you chose a particular online habitat because it feels like the right match for your identity, because it has the kind of cyberpsychology architecture that allows you to construct the self you think you are or want to be.

People who chose text environments prefer the semantics of language, along with the linear, composed, rational dimensions of self that surface in the string of typed words. As described by such cognitive psychologists as Richardson (1969), they might be the "verbalizers" of the online world, in contrast to the "visualizers" who prefer the more concretely sensory, symbolic, and holistic qualities of expressing themselves with pictures. Some people choose synchronous communication – such as texting, chat, and phone calls – which reflects the spontaneous, free-form, witty, and temporally present self. Others are drawn to the more thoughtful, reflective, and deliberate style of asynchronous communication, as in discussion forums, blogs, and email. People who lack the ability or motivation to create text and images might rely on environments where they can repost other peoples' items that resonate with their own identities, which is a *self-expression by proxy*. They also rely on the clicking of a "like" button to reveal themselves, with the end result being identities that ride on a wave of likes and reposts as community members ally with particular people, attitudes, and causes.

While some people revolve their identities around flights of fantasy, others lean toward the practical. Some people need socializing to reveal who they are, while others prefer solitary activities to discover themselves. Some people actualize their identity by eagerly tackling the technical challenges of a complex environment, and others prefer being inside a simple interface. Whatever self we hope to manifest online, the dimensions of cyberpsychology architecture can usually provide the media environment that can make it happen. In turn, the media affect us in ways we might not have predicted. Marshall McLuhan said, "We shape our tools and then our tools shape us."

The True and Essential Me

In 1998, I gave a talk at a conference devoted to Eastern philosophy and psychology, with my presentation entitled "What Is This Thing Called Self?" After discussing the various concepts of self that I described in this chapter, I proposed to the audience, with tongue in cheek, that the answer to this question about the true nature of the self might be found online, in the information superhighway. So I told the audience about my attempt to find the "true self" in cyberspace using an Internet search engine – the humorous story that appears at the beginning of this chapter.

I decided to publish the talk on my "Zen Stories to Tell Your Neighbors" website. About a year later, I received the following email from a visitor, which drove home for me the idea that the self, though mysteriously difficult to conceptualize via intellectual discourse, is something always close to home. It is the subjective experience of the self that reveals its essence to us, if we just pay careful enough attention, regardless of whether we are walking about the world in our physical bodies or journeying somewhere through cyberspace:

> I was reading your essay "What is this thing called self." You say that on
> an AltaVista search you looked for "The True and Essential Self" and

found no hits, that this "True and Essential Self" is not out there .... Well, now it is, because if you try the same search again it will find 1 hit ... "The True and Essential Self" is in your essay!! It seems the answer has been closer to home than you thought all along ... now that is DEFINITELY zen! ... have a good day!

THE PERSONALITIES OF CYBERSPACE

The eight dimensions of cyberpsychology architecture shape how we respond to a particular environment, but that is only half the story. Our different personality styles determine the environments we choose and how we react to them. In fact, insights from cyberpsychology might lay to rest what Esptein and O'Brien (1985) called the *person-situation debate*: Is it our personalities that dictate our behavior, or is it the situations we find ourselves in? The cyberpsychologist's reply would be "yes." How could it not be both? The prolific universe we call cyberspace has given us the unique opportunity to witness how different people experience the variety of environments we have created. Cyberspace has become one big experiment in how personal identity and the environment synergistically sculpt each other.

How should we classify the types of people in cyberspace? We might focus on specific features of the user, such as the person's computer skills, goals for using the Internet; or demographic characteristics such as age, occupation, and social-economic status, which is often done in what researchers call "Big Data" analyses of online behavior. There also are several comprehensive theories in psychology that could help us understand personality types in cyberspace – for example, the Myers-Briggs system (Myers & Myers, 1995), the classic sixteen-trait model proposed by Cattell (1946), or the "big five personality traits" framework (Norman, 1963).

In this book, I emphasize the idea of cyberspace as a psychological extension of the individual's intrapsychic world. A personality theory that specializes in understanding this world would be especially useful in understanding the "person" side of the person/situation interaction. Psychoanalytic theory fits that bill very well. As a result of over one hundred years of research and clinical practice, it contains a very comprehensive understanding of personality styles. In her book *Psychoanalytic Diagnosis*, McWilliams (2011) effectively integrated this body of knowledge. For each personality type, she elucidates the characteristic emotions, temperament, developmental organization, defenses, adaptive processes, object relations, and transference tendencies. Summarized very briefly, these personality types are as follows:

- **Psychopathic (antisocial or sociopathic)** – motivated by the need to control and manipulate others, to "get over on" them; impulsive, self-centered, unreliable, and irresponsible; has difficulty experiencing social conscience and deep emotions.
- **Narcissistic** – motivated by the need to maintain a valued sense of self; has tendencies toward feeling privileged, special, grandiose, and self-centered; craves admiration and expects favors; inattentive to the needs and feelings of others.
- **Schizoid** – motivated by a need to preserve a sense of safety by avoiding intimacy with others; prefers being alone; has difficulty forming close relationships and showing warmth or tender feelings; has a tendency to withdraw into internal fantasies.
- **Paranoid** – motivated by a need to avoid feeling vulnerable and helpless; has tendencies toward being suspicious, guarded, irritable, cold, humorless, and argumentative; has a tendency to blame, criticize, or project onto others.
- **Depressive** – motivated by the need to grapple with feelings of somehow being bad; has tendencies toward gloominess, guilt, a lack of energy, difficulty in enjoying the pleasures of life, self-criticism, feeling rejected, and low self-esteem.
- **Manic** – motivated by a need to defend against underlying feelings of depression (the counterpart to depressive personality characteristics); has tendencies toward being elated, energetic, impulsive, mobile, distractible, self-promoting, highly social, witty, and entertaining.
- **Masochistic** – motivated by the need to endure pain and suffering for the purpose of attaining some greater moral good; has a tendency toward feeling depressed, but also experiencing resentment, indignation, and moralization on his or her own behalf.
- **Obsessive/compulsive** – motivated by a need to maintain emotional security and self-esteem; perfectionist, preoccupied with details and rules, more concerned with work than with pleasure; has a tendency to be serious and formal; has a need to be in control.
- **Histrionic** – motivated by a need for attention, love, and dependency; has tendencies toward being highly sociable, expressive of emotions, dramatic, attention-seeking, hypersensitive, and seductive; has a tendency to repress negative emotions and deny problems.

- **Dissociative** – motivated by a need to compartmentalize anxiety-provoking experiences by splitting identity into separate parts; has tendencies toward being resourceful, interpersonally sensitive, creative, sociable, susceptible to hypnotic states, and having a complex fantasy life.

I will refer to these personality types throughout the book, so you might want to bookmark these pages. Even these very brief descriptions might have succeeded in activating your memory of people you have encountered online. By applying McWilliams' system of personality styles, we can better understand how these people select and react to the different environments of cyberspace, how other people online respond to them, and the pathological as well as potentially beneficial aspects of what they do online. As compared to other systems, McWilliams' approach excels in its ability to explain the entire continuum of normal to pathological personalities, because all of the preceding characteristics surface in mild to extreme forms depending on the developmental maturity of an individual's sense of self: to what degree does he or she feel cohesive, continuous over time, and uniquely distinctive from other people? While pathological people tend to fall rigidly within the aforementioned types, relatively normal people might show a blend of characteristics from two or three of the types. For this reason, you might consider how you identify with these personality styles to better understand your own experiences in cyberspace and how others online react to you. Here is but a sample of the many interesting questions to explore about personality types:

- Does online anonymity and the power to manipulate environments encourage psychopathic personalities? Are they the malicious hackers of cyberspace? Out of a need to dominate people, do they become the "trolls" who deliberately stir up distress in others? Some people believe the Internet has become the playground of psychopaths.
- Do narcissistic personalities use cyberspace as a means to build an admiring audience? Do they create habitats where they display themselves while caring less about listening to others? Are they what traditionally was called the "newsgroup personality" – the person who always argued, who always had to be right in an online discussion?
- Do people with dissociative personalities tend to isolate their cyberspace lifestyles from their in-person lives? Are they especially attracted to the creation of multiple, compartmentalized online identities, as in online role-playing games?

- Are schizoid people attracted to the reduced intimacy resulting from partial or complete online anonymity? Do they tend to be lurkers?
- Do manic people take advantage of asynchronous communication as a means to send more measured responses to others, or do they naturally prefer the terse, immediate, and spontaneous conversations of chat and texting?
- Are compulsives drawn to computers and cyberspace for the control it gives them over their relationships and environment? Are they meticulous in how they manage their computers, online habitats, and relationships?
- Do histrionic people enjoy the opportunities for theatrical displays that are possible in social media, especially in environments that provide tools for creative and dramatic self-expression?
- Feeling vulnerable and helpless, do paranoid people take extreme measures in protecting their machines, security, and privacy in cyberspace? Are they the people who distrust the Internet, perhaps avoiding it completely?

People choose the online environments and communication strategies that are compatible with their personality styles. They slip into online relationships that feel comfortable to the intrinsic ways they think, feel, and behave. They use their habitat as a way to express the underlying motivations of their personality style.

It is also possible that some people choose their particular online activities as a means to stretch beyond their usual character style, as a way to resolve the problematic or limiting aspects of their personality in an attempt to be different. Given the multitude of flexible options for online living, cyberpsychology might resolve other longstanding questions among psychologists: when do people simply express who they are, including the problematic aspects of their identity; when do they unconsciously venture into environments that exacerbate their problems; and when do strive for beneficial changes in themselves? These are the kinds of questions we will explore throughout this book.

PUTTING ME ALL TOGETHER: THE INTEGRATION PRINCIPLE

So far in this chapter we have seen how any one person might manifest different selves in cyberspace, with or without conscious awareness and control. As fascinating and perhaps even productive as this dance of online selves can be, the history of clinical psychology and other professions devoted to mental health inevitably arrives at a different vision: the importance of an *integration principle*.

If there is any universally accepted axiom in psychology, it is this idea about fitting together and balancing the various elements of the psyche to make a complete, harmonious whole. A faulty or pathological psyche is almost always described with terms that connote forgetting, division, and fragmentation – such as repression, dissociation, splitting, and schizophrenia. By contrast, health is usually specified with terms that imply discovery, integration, and union – such as insight, assimilation, and self-actualization. Many religious philosophies also emphasize the attainment of connectedness and unity as the path for spiritual development. The whole is greater than the sum of its parts, as the concept of self-as-transcendent suggests. This greatness can be realized only when the parts are joined together.

As we have seen, there are two basic ways cyberspace might create divisions in identity. Firstly, some people separate their online and offline lives. They have companions, groups, and activities in cyberspace quite different from those in their in-person world. The two worlds are worlds apart. Other people communicate in social media with people they know or have known in the in-person world, but even in these cases people might act differently online than they do offline, sometimes in subtle ways.

Secondly, among the thousands of different groups and activities in cyberspace, with each one focusing on something in particular, people can easily join two, three, or a dozen of them to get information and support from likeminded people not available elsewhere. There might be no overlap at all among these various parts of their online lifestyles. How different from the societies of centuries past, when people lived in small villages. All your neighbors knew about all you. Your daily enterprises, the people around you, and the groups you belonged to were all interconnected.

As a general rule, integrating online and offline living, along with integrating our different online selves, builds a more robust identity. As in commerce, integration creates synergy. It leads to development and prosperity. Both sides of the trade are enriched by the exchange. If the goal of life is to know thyself, as Socrates suggested, then it must entail knowing how the various parts of thyself fit together to make that Big Self that is you. Reaching this goal requires our understanding and then taking down the barriers between the sectors of self. Barriers are erected out of the need to protect, out of fear. They are infused with unconscious anxieties that must be discovered and tamed, even if they are subtle anxieties about being

ignored, laughed at, or rejected. Maybe it would be a good idea for that corporation president to bring into the office his fondness for the online *Star
Trek* fan club. Maybe some good might come out of posting a photo from
one's pug group into the discussion forum for the PTA.

In an Internet addiction – or, for that matter, in any kind of addiction –
people isolate the compulsive activity from other aspects of their lives.
Overcoming the addiction means releasing and mastering the needs that
have been locked into that activity. It means reclaiming the sealed-off self
and folding it back into the mainstream of one's identity. If there is truth to
the idea that the self can benefit from deconstruction, it certainly applies to
the fact that the rigid, isolated, and dysfunctional compartments of identity need to be taken apart, digested, and reassembled into the bigger self.
What parts of yourself do you deconstruct into cyberspace, and how can
you reclaim those parts into the bigger you?

When people advocate what came to be called *augmented reality* and
computer-mediated reality, they allude to the value of online/offline integration, the effective blending of cyberspace into the physical world (see
Figure 3.1). We read online reviews of a restaurant as we look over the menu
the waiter just gave us. While at a lecture, we carry on a texting conversation about the speaker with other people attending. Whether it is a wearable computer, a phone, or any gadget that enhances our daily experience
of what is going on around us at that moment, we invite cyberspace to join

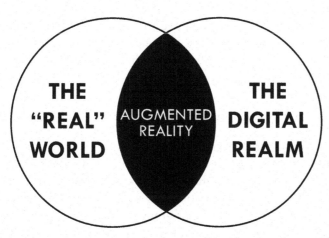

FIGURE 3.1. Augmented reality.

us in this in-person space. The two realms overlap. They begin integration, along with the selves we impart to those realms.

So how do we achieve integration, according to cyberpsychology? In this section, I will outline some possibilities. I will focus on connecting one's online and offline identities, but it is very easy to adapt these strategies for integrating the various compartments within one's digital lifestyle. Whenever we contact an online companion using a different form of communication – as when you email someone you previously only knew in public social media – we begin integration, along with promoting greater intimacy and bonding. Some sophisticated forms of social media encourage integration by offering a variety of communication tools and social activities, which might account for their popularity. That popularity suggests a self-correcting mechanism in how people want to use the digital realm to integrate rather than dissociate themselves.

Telling Online Companions about One's Offline Life

Lurking, imaginative role playing, and anonymous exchanges with people online can be benign activities, but if we want to enrich our relationship with online companions, we might consider letting them know about our in-person lives: work, family, friends, home, and hobbies. Those companions will have a much better sense of who we are. They may even be able to give us some new insights into how our offline identities compare to how we present ourselves online. Without even knowing it, we might dissociate some aspect of our cyberspace selves from our in-person selves. Online companions can help us see that. Even when people in social media communicate with others they also know in person, they might benefit from sharing something about their offline lifestyles that they never mention online.

Telling Offline Companions about One's Online Life

If we let family and friends know about our online activities, we invite them to see parts of our identities that we otherwise might not fully express in person. They can give us insightful feedback about our online lifestyle and companions. When communicating only with typed text, it is easy to misread the personality and intentions of the people we meet. Offline friends and family – who know us well – can give us some needed insight into those interpersonal distortions.

Meeting Online Companions in Person

As friendships, romances, and collegial relationships evolve in cyberspace, people eventually want to talk on the phone, chat via video, and ultimately meet in person. Most of the time, this is a very natural, healthy progression. The relationship can deepen when people get to see and hear each other, when they can visit each other's real-world environments. They also have an opportunity to realize the misconceptions they developed online about each other, because the mental image we form of our cyberspace companions often differs in some way from how they actually are. Realizing our online interpersonal misperceptions helps us understand ourselves. Because the expression and experience of oneself is always context-dependent, meeting someone for the first time in person can be awkward, surprising, and perhaps shocking, even if there were no online misperceptions. It is similar to meeting one's boss or teacher at the grocery store. Employer and employee, teacher and student, are not used to interacting with each other in a different environment.

Meeting Offline Companions Online

If we encourage family, friends, and colleagues to connect with us in cyberspace, as people often do in social media, we open a different channel of communication with them. We know what they are like in person, but how might they be different when conversing only via text, with photographs, in imaginary habitats, in a game, or within a group of people unlike your usual social circles? Because identity expression varies depending on which of the eight dimensions of cyberpsychology architecture an online environment emphasizes, we have an opportunity to experience our real-world companions in new ways. We can discover something different about their personalities while they can discover something different about ours.

Bringing Online Behavior Offline

River, an online friend of mine in the Palace avatar community, once described cyberspace living as "training wheels." People experiment with new ways to express themselves. If they then introduce those behaviors into their real-world lifestyle, they can better understand why previously they were unable to cultivate those parts of their identities in the offline world. There is a tendency to see online activities as little worlds unto themselves, dissociated from the rest of our lives, but discussing them with offline friends and family, people who know us well, almost always helps us gain a better perspective on what those activities mean to us.

Bringing Offline Behavior Online

Translating something about our identity from one realm to another often strengthens it. You are testing and refining it in a new locale. So if it is beneficial to bring online behaviors offline, then it is also beneficial to bring offline behaviors online. Cyberspace gives us the opportunity to try out our usual methods of self-expression in new situations, with new people.

Caveats about Integration

As I mentioned earlier, there is a caveat about this integration principle. Some aspects of a person's identity are a source of shame, guilt, or anxiety. They might be rejected by or be hurtful to other people. If acted upon, they might even be illegal. In the complex universe of cyberspace, there are many places where people can give expression to these problematic aspects of their identities. Should they tell people about it? Should they express these things in the real world? Should they carry into cyberspace a problematic behavior from their offline world?

There is no simple answer to these questions. Under optimal conditions, translating issues from one realm to the other might be helpful, even therapeutic. A person who learns to accept his homosexuality in an online support group may benefit by coming out in the face-to-face world. But a real-world sadist who goes online to carry out his intentions produces only harm. Research suggests that the norms and values of hacker subcultures cuts across the digital divide to shape relationships among hackers in both virtual and real situations (Holt, 2007). Offline/online "integration" leading to behaviors that hurt innocent people is never healthy. In fact, it is not psychological integration at all, which always involves self-understanding and personal growth. Healthy integration means resolving – and not simply acting out – the problematic aspects of one's identity.

Integration Means Balance

Implicit in the integration principle is the idea that we must find a balance between online and offline living. In our modern times, very few people, if anyone, can completely avoid connectedness to the digital realm. It is also obvious that constant immersion in cyberspace does not do anyone any good. To effectively integrate online and offline living means weighing the pros and cons of being online and offline. It means understanding when we benefit from looking into our screens and when we benefit from turning our devices and Internet connectedness off. As Crook (2015) said in the subtitle of her book *The Joy of Missing Out*, the future of our well-being in the digital age is finding balance in a wired world.

THE COMPROMISED AND RESCUED ME

In her early research documented in *Life on the Screen*, Turkle (1995), like other researchers and writers at the time, including myself, felt optimistic about the role cyberspace could play as an identity workshop in which people could learn new things about themselves in order to live a better life, online as well as offline. People celebrated cyberspace as the new frontier for human psychological development. Years later in her book *Alone Together*, Turkle (2012), along with like-minded researchers, began expressing worries about how cyberspace might actually be compromising our identities in troubling ways.

The Symbiotic Me

One of the problems arises from what psychoanalytic thinkers, beginning with Margaret Mahler, would describe as the disruption of *separation and individuation* as processes that enrich and solidify the self (Mahler, Pine, & Bergman, 1975). Especially with the advent of mobile devices, people seek out constant connection. They never have to be alone, separated from significant others and Mother-Internet herself. Being alone, Turkle noted, feels like a problem that needs to be solved. People sleep with their phones, even experience it as a bodily appendage. The *phantom vibration*, when we feel the phone vibrating with a notification when in fact it did not, shows how cyberspace has seeped into our physical being at a deep, unconscious level. The device as a connection to others can become an addictive *selfobject* – borrowing a term from psychoanalytic theory – that must be at hand in order to feel complete as a person. Without it, people fall prey to separation anxiety, a sense that one's self identity is dissolving.

Connecting to social media becomes a symptom of dysfunctional symbiosis in which people believe they must rely on feedback from others in order to feel real and alive – a dilemma I heard often in my surveys of students. "We need the Internet to tell us who we are instead of figuring it out for ourselves," one commented. "We rely on the Internet to feel important," said another, "No likes = no worth." In a looking glass self that has gone awry, people need a continuous supply of interpersonal mirroring and feeding that validates what they think and feel. "I share, therefore I am," and, "I want to have a feeling, so I need to send a text," surface as the mantras that guide their lives. When people receive compliments here and there in social media, seemingly unpredictably, an intermittent schedule of reinforcement creates a symbiotic connectedness to cyberspace that is difficult to break. "Getting positive feedback just gives you a temporary feeling of satisfaction that makes you want to go back for more," one student said.

As a result, Turkle (2012) stated, people lose the ability to be alone, to self-reflect in solitude, which plays such an important role in identifying for themselves what they feel and think, who they are, and who they want to be. "I go online, especially with my phone, when I'm in the bathroom or right before bed," one of my students commented. "These used to be times of reflection, but now I've lost perspective on myself so that I can like another picture on Instagram."

Although we must recognize that there are significant cultural differences in the emphasis on individuality versus social collectivism, we do see in science fiction stories a growing fear about what cyberspace could do to humankind. Will we become like the Borg of *Star Trek*, in which the symbiotic mass mind forged by computer networks sucks up every individual soul? Young people themselves, including my students, worry about this deindividuation. "Everyone posts the same types of photos and statuses to the point where the only thing different is the actual face in the photo or the name on the post."

When discussing cyberpsychology with my students, I invite them to participate in a guided imagery exercise in which they let their minds free-associate to the idea of how the Internet has affected their lives – a technique that encourages the surfacing of unconscious thoughts. Themes about anxiety-provoking symbiosis often emerge in the scenes they imagine, such as "freaking out" when seeing their phone literally glued to their hand; feeling out of control when envisioning a "huge chaotic mess of connections among millions of computers"; and experiencing images of different people, places, and things passing through one's body "as if I didn't exist." One student saw herself as part of "the cloud," sensing that her whole life was there, uploaded, never to be taken back. She felt herself "yearning for simplicity" and "wanting my innocence back."

Cyberspace has placed its inhabitants into a difficult existential dilemma. It offers many opportunities for self-expression and self-actualization, but perhaps too many. The choices are overwhelming. "You can be anything you want to be," said one student, "so why not make it simple and just go along with the crowd?" Another posed the question in an even simpler but just as profound form: "The real question is what we should do with all that we have."

The Shallow Me

A second problem arrives as a counterpoint to the loss of self via symbiotic connectedness. It entails the tendency toward creating dissociated, overly controlled, and superficial online relationships, which leads to a personal identity that fades in richness, complexity, and genuineness. In what Turkle (2012) described as the *Goldilock's Effect*, people multitask their in-person and online relationships so that they can be not too close, not too far, but supposedly just right in the degree of connection. They continually switch back and forth between in-person and online conversations, and among various online contacts, as a way to micromanage their attention, avoid boredom, bypass conflict, and even sidestep true intimacy, so much so that people get used to being shortchanged in conversation and interpersonal understanding. We create contacts with many people while keeping them all at a safe distance. The many little sips of tiny text messages, Turkle stated, do not add up to a meaningful gulp of human interaction. As the ultimate exercise in a technologically dissociated self, some people even brag about how to text while making eye contact in a face-to-face discussion.

In their carefully designed ideal self that they present online to others, people miss the opportunity to share who they truly are as revealed through spontaneity and the expression of their personality flaws, or what they believe to be flaws. Struggling with the intrinsic human ambivalence concerning a fear of intimacy versus a need to connect, some people opt for a static compromise in which they use cyberspace to create the illusion of companionship without the demands of authentic closeness. They want an admiring audience, but they also want to hide from deeper attachments. The remedy, Turkle suggested, is to reclaim messy conversations as we used to know them in the in-person world, complete with awkward pauses, stumbling to find the right words, and not saying exactly what you mean. Expressing oneself, along with the interpersonal relationships in which we do so, are intrinsically messy. It is when we grapple with and sort through the interpersonal confusion that we truly discover each other and ourselves.

For some people, the problem is not necessarily ambivalent anxiety about intimacy that leads to shallow, highly compartmentalized relationships in cyberspace, but simply not devoting the time and energy to develop any intimacy. Hypnotized by the online culture that heralds popularity through the accumulation of followers, view counts, and "likes," some people frantically stack up as many contacts as they can, while short-shrifting each one. Rather than enriching their identities in a few intimate relationships, they focus all their efforts on creating many superficial ones, in the hopes of building a bigger, applauding audience. In a culture where cyberspace seductively promises fifteen minutes of fame to everyone and anyone, online intimacy feels like a distracting luxury. Paying careful attention turns into a commodity afforded to very few, if anyone. In what turns into a *Tantalus Effect*, social media might entice some lonely people with the promise of fulfilling social relationships, but in the end falls short, leaving them feeling disappointed, disillusioned, and perhaps even lonelier than they felt when they sought out the community.

The Susceptible Me

When heeding these red flags about how cyberspace can compromise self-identity, we need to consider the various forces that moderate or perhaps remedy these problems. As indicated by McWilliams (2011) in her psychoanalytic theory of personality types, there are significant individual differences in the degree to which people experience a substantially or poorly individuated sense of self, apart from who they are online. People with a secure identity can resist the alluring pull toward constant connection as a way to continually feed their sense of self, while people with developmentally damaged or depleted selves might not, as in the so-called *borderline disorders*. Certain personality types will be more susceptible to micromanaging or dissociating their online selves, most notably the compulsive and dissociative types. When we consider the eight dimensions of cyberpsychology architecture, we see that online environments also differ in the extent to which they encourage or discourage a symbiotic, dissociated, or overly managed self. Phoning, real-time video, and even synchronous text messaging can be very messy affairs, just like real conversations, where many facets of the whole self are both intentionally and unintentionally revealed.

The Disillusioned Me

Cyberspace fails to give us interpersonal connections as often as it succeeds. Everyone is familiar with the scenario of posting a message to social media, only to receive little or no response – no comments, no likes, maybe no evidence of anyone paying any kind of attention. No one hears me. Doesn't anyone care? Am I not important? This is a type of *black hole experience*, which I will discuss in Chapter 6, "Other Than You Think: Interpersonal Perceptions." What happens to one's sense of self under these conditions, as well as in ongoing interactions where online companions selectively react to some things you reveal about yourself, but ignore your other self-disclosures – or when you see your self-esteem sag as you notice other people getting more attention, as evident in their higher number of views, comments, contacts, and likes? Doubting the value of what they revealed about themselves, some people feel unanchored, abandoned, unappreciated, or misunderstood. Their sense of self withers from the lack of feedback, or they resort to somewhat desperate attempts to selectively shape their presented identity so that their contacts do respond. Other people seize the paucity of feedback from their online audience as the opportunity to wonder why, self-reflect, and rely on themselves to acknowledge their own identity.

The Self-Correcting Me

Because cyberspace is such a new phenomenon in the course of human civilization, we are still learning how to use it. We are becoming much more savvy about how people tend to present an idealized version of themselves; about the very subtle interpersonal aspects of online communication that reveal what people are really thinking and feeling; about how our sense of self-worth does not have to ride on a wave of followers, view counts, and likes; and about how sometimes we have to actually talk to people in person to resolve online miscommunications and understand each other more deeply, as human nature intrinsically desires. I see this more sophisticated attitude when people receive favorable comments after posting a photograph in which they appear not like some perfected version of themselves, but rather downright bad – as if they are deliberately thumbing their noses at the online norm about creating an ideal self or, somewhat paradoxically, presenting themselves as the ideally natural person who knows that no one is always ideal. This sophisticated attitude entails a more fully conscious, responsible choice of what one decides to do in cyberspace. As one of my students wisely put it, "You choose how you present yourself in social media. You choose what websites you frequent. You choose how often you go online."

I like to believe that in our hundreds of thousands of years of evolution, we have developed self-correcting mechanisms in managing a healthy identity. Intrinsically we know that the integration principle can steer us towards a well-rounded self. It helps to bring together what we are online and offline. Integrating our identity in both realms helps bypass an overly dissociated, micromanaged, symbiotic, superficial identity. We also know intuitively that we should balance the amount of time and psychological investment we put into online versus offline living. If our minds do not warn us about an imbalance, then physical problems in our bodies will.

When people lose access to cyberspace because their connections are not available or break down, they might at first experience separation anxiety – what has been called FOMO, a "fear of missing out" – but almost always they settle into the realization that not being connected is rather nice. They appreciate the real world and themselves as unique individuals interacting with other unique individuals within it. I do not believe it is a coincidence that with our surging cyberspace preoccupations we also see a blossoming of interest in such practices as mindfulness meditation – popularized by people like Jon Kabat-Zinn (2005) – which teach us how to be present in the physical world here and now. Crook (2015) referred to this as the "joy of missing out," which includes the rediscovery of a quiet mind that seeks a peaceful connectedness to the world, while also bypassing the excessive distractions, drama, and pettiness too often witnessed in social media.

As we become wiser in our understanding of cyberspace, we will realize that a healthy self both integrates and balances online and offline living. We will reach the understanding that the very process of moving back and forth between the two realms can be our evolutionary step forward in the development of human identity, perhaps even in our understanding of this thing called "self." In the meanwhile, we need to rely on the wisdom of prior generations that remember what we were like before the birth of cyberspace. As the generations come and go, we will need to teach our children well.

4

The Disinhibited Self

It's what you do in your free time that will set you free – or enslave you.
– Jarod Kintz

I had spent several years very active in Flickr when one day my wife suggested that I try the new photosharing groups in Google+. I resisted the idea. I didn't particularly want to have to start all over in another social media. Nevertheless, because I was a cyberpsychologist studying online photosharing, and because Google+ was supposedly the Next Big Thing, I reluctantly gave it a try. Without really looking over recent posts in one of the groups that seemed active, I jumped right in to post my own message. I stated who I was, a cyberpsychologist specializing in online photosharing, along with a photo and image pointing to my online book about photographic psychology. The next day I received a message indicating that I had been banned from the community. What? That had never happened to me before. When I contacted the group moderator, he very briefly stated that I had inappropriately, right out of the gate, marketed myself. When I questioned his decision to ban me, he didn't reply. At first annoyed, I then reconsidered the situation. After all, in the real world, I would never pop into a room full of people talking and then announce myself without first finding out what was going on there.

THE ONLINE DISINHIBITION EFFECT

As cyberpsychologists such as Joinson (1998) and myself noted early on, people tend to say and do things in cyberspace that they would not ordinarily say or do in the face-to-face world. They loosen up, feel more uninhibited, and express themselves more openly. We called it the *online disinhibition effect* (Suler, 2004a). It is an important force that contributes to the acceleration and amplification of social processes in cyberspace, as well as helps explain the *privacy paradox*, how people express concern about their online privacy even though their behaviors do not reflect those concerns (Barnes, 2006). In this chapter, we will focus on the dimensions of cyberpsychology architecture that influence online disinhibition, particularly the identity, social, text, reality, and sensory dimensions.

In one of the earliest papers about this phenomenon, Holland (1996) attributed it to developmental regression. "Talking on the Internet, people regress," he begins the essay, "It's that simple." Drawing on traditional psychoanalytic theory, he considered the three major signs of regressive behavior in cyberspace: flaming; sexual harassment; and, curiously, extraordinary generosity and openness. He then traces these regressions to the transference reactions people have to the computer itself – unconscious fantasies about power, dominance, sex, narcissistic gratification, oral engulfment, and parental love. At the heart of the regression is the individual's tendency to confuse the person with the machine. Some people see the computer as human while viewing other people online as something less than human, resulting in a disinhibition of sexual and aggressive drives.

BENIGN AND TOXIC DISINHIBITION

Implicit in these kinds of observations is the fact that the disinhibition effect operates as a double-edged sword. Sometimes people share very personal things about themselves. They reveal secret emotions, fears, and wishes. They show unusual acts of kindness and altruism, even to strangers, as researchers noted in the free sharing of music through peer-to-peer systems such as Gnutella (Adar & Huberman, 2000). Although we could conceptualize these behaviors as a form of regression, we might also see them as an unleashed human need to better understand oneself, connect compassionately with others, or resolve personal problems. I call these kinds of actions *benign disinhibition*.

By contrast, the disinhibition effect can be anything but friendly. People explore the dark underworld of the Internet, places of hatred, violence, and crime that they would never visit in the real world. Or they spout rude language, harsh criticisms, anger, hatred, and even threats, a phenomenon that gained worldwide attention when online bullying and stalking grew into a serious problem. Rick Warren, an evangelical Christian, put it simply: "I just think the internet had made us ruder." In these cases, regression serves as an apt explanation, because such behaviors escalate into a developmentally immature catharsis of primitive impulses. I call these actions *toxic disinhibition*.

The distinction between benign and toxic disinhibition is as elusive as any categorical attempt to tell good from bad. For example, hostile language during text messaging could be a therapeutic breakthrough for those who chronically repress anger. In an increasingly intimate email relationship, people might open up with very honest self-disclosures, then later regret it, feeling exposed, vulnerable, or shameful. An excessively rapid, even false intimacy might develop that later destroys the relationship when one or both people feel overwhelmed or disappointed. In the very wide variety of online subcultures, what is considered antisocial behavior in one group may be considered very appropriate in another, which demonstrates that cultural relativity will blur any simple contrasts between disinhibition that is positive or negative.

We might define benign disinhibition in terms of *working through* as conceptualized in psychodynamic theory, or as the *self-actualization* proposed in humanistic perspectives. People attempt to grapple with and resolve psychological problems, to explore new dimensions to their identity. By contrast, toxic disinhibition is simply a fruitless repetition compulsion or acting out of pathological needs without any beneficial psychology change. In some situations, what the person is doing could be benign, toxic, or a mixture of both, as in online sexual activities otherwise avoided in the real world.

What causes this online disinhibition? What is it about cyberspace that loosens the psychological barriers against inner feelings and needs, regardless of whether they are benign or toxic? In this chapter, I will describe the factors that are at play (see Figure 4.1). For some people, one or two of them produce the lion's share of the disinhibition effect. In most cases, these ingredients interact with each other, supplement each other, resulting in a more complex, amplified effect. Depending on the person and the situation, disinhibition can be intense, mild – or completely absent, because some people online behave very much the way they do in-person.

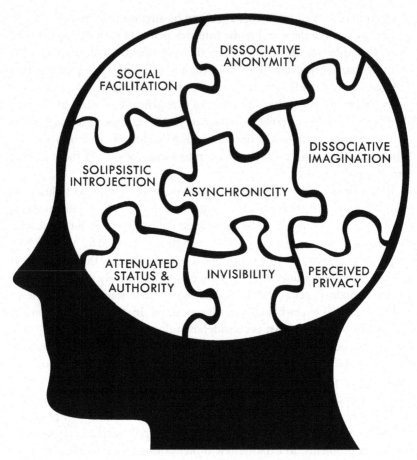

FIGURE 4.1. Ingredients of the online disinhibition effect.

YOU DON'T KNOW ME (DISSOCIATIVE ANONYMITY)

As we move around cyberspace, other people cannot easily determine who we are, even though they are aware of our presence. Usernames or email addresses might be visible, but this information does not reveal much about a person, especially if the username is contrived and the address comes from a large Internet service provider. Technologically savvy, motivated people can detect the location of a computer or mobile device, but for the most part others only know what we tell them. If so desired, we can hide some of our identity, conceal all of our identity, or completely change our identity. We can have no name, as the word "anonymous" indicates, or we can conceal our identity behind the mask of a contrived persona. In their research, Lapidot-Lefler and Barak (2012) also introduced the idea of *unidentifiability*, referring to missing information about one's identity, usually information that could not be discerned just by seeing and hearing someone, such as background, occupation, social status, and home or work address.

Even as common knowledge about technology rose to the level of everyone knowing that true online anonymity never exists, that our devices always leave a footprint of our identity in cyberspace, some people still operate under the assumption that others do not know who they are. Their needs and expectations in the moment override rational reasoning.

When people move through cyberspace via encrypted connections, as in the famous TOR (The Onion Router) network, they raise their level of anonymity to such a heightened degree that even technical experts have a difficult time determining their identity. It comes as no surprise that in these digital realms, often referred to as the *dark* or *deep web*, disinhibited behavior can skyrocket, leading to all sorts of antisocial behaviors and crime.

Anonymity is an important force contributing to the disinhibition effect. When people think their identity remains hidden, they feel less vulnerable about letting out what otherwise remains suppressed. Whatever they say or do will not be directly connected to the mainstream of who they are, or so they believe. Through dissociation, they do not have to own their behavior by acknowledging it within the full context of an integrated online/offline identity. The online self in that particular situation becomes a compartmentalized self. In the case of expressed hostilities or other deviant actions, the person can disown responsibility for those behaviors, almost as if morality and conscience have been temporarily suspended from the online psyche. People might even convince themselves that those online behaviors "aren't me at all." They belong to the artificial me projected into cyberspace.

As early as 1905, social psychologists such as Gustave Le Bon described how the *deindividuation* of a person in a crowd of people tends to unleash antisocial actions, which is largely due to the anonymity of blending in with the group. In other real-world situations as well, anonymity causes disinhibition, as when people let loose their opinions in a suggestion box or wear masks to hide their faces during a public demonstration. Applying the well-known effects of anonymity to online behavior is an example of how traditional ideas in psychology can be translated into cyberpsychology.

Seeing another person as anonymous also causes disinhibition. As social psychology has long recognized, the nameless, faceless stranger easily turns into a target for aggression and acting out. People who create destructive viruses, often as an expression of their underlying hostilities, do not know or see the victims of their assault. In social media, people who blatantly express political, religious, and racial beliefs often offend their contacts, including friends and family. By not making a conscious effort to remember exactly who makes up their audience, by allowing their audience to slip into a quasi-anonymous state within their minds as they blindly seek affirmation for their beliefs, they more easily fall prey to toxic disinhibition. People might also perceive the anonymously ambiguous other as a loving parent, a confident, or a rescuer to whom they open their hearts.

Disinhibition coming from an anonymous self can often backfire. While some people reply negatively to a toxically disinhibited person, others will simply write off, ignore, and even disown that person. People also rarely trust anyone who insists on remaining anonymous, even if that person's behavior seems benign. When people hide, chronically refusing to show who they truly are, why should they be accepted as "real" people?

YOU CAN'T SEE ME (INVISIBILITY)

In many online environments, other people cannot see you. As you browse through websites, blogs, and social media, people may not even know you are there at all, with the possible exception of technical experts who have access to software tools that can detect traffic through the site, assuming they have the inclination to keep an eye on you, one of maybe thousands or millions of users. This invisibility, or the belief that one is undetected, flying below the radar, gives people the courage to go places and do things that they otherwise would not. It is the type of invisibility that encourages deindividuation, when people feel that they can blend in with the gigantic crowds of users online, when they think that no one will notice them.

The power to be unobservable overlaps with anonymity, because anonymity is the concealment of identity. But there are some important differences. In text communication such as email, chat, blogs, and text messaging, others might know a great deal about who you are, but they still cannot see or hear you – and you cannot see or hear them. Even with everyone's identity known, the opportunity to be physically invisible might amplify the disinhibition effect. You do not have to worry about how you, or others, look and sound when you type something. Witnessing a frown, a shaking head, a sigh, a gasp, a bored expression, and many other subtle and not so subtle signs of disapproval or indifference can either slam the breaks on what people are willing to say or very subtly influence them. Moment-by-moment feedback in the form of facial expressions, body language, eye contact, and verbal utterances – often that we detect subconsciously – modulate what we are willing to say and do. Without it, we tend to go off on tangents, wandering into disinhibited territories.

In psychoanalysis, the clinician sits behind the patient in order to remain a physically ambiguous figure, without revealing any body language or facial expressions, so that patients have free range to discuss whatever they want without feeling inhibited by how the analyst physically reacts. In everyday relationships, people sometimes avert their eyes when discussing something personal and emotional. It is easier not to look into the other's face. Text communication in particular offers a built-in opportunity to keep one's eyes averted. In their research, Lapidot-Lefler and Barak (2012) found that lack of eye contact is an especially important feature of the online disinhibition effect. When we do not have to look into another person's eyes, we can minimize the inhibiting awareness that we are being observed.

SEE YOU LATER (ASYNCHRONICITY)

The temporal dimension of cyberpsychology architecture plays an important role in online disinhibition. During asynchronous communication, people do not interact with each other in real time. Others may take minutes, hours, days, or even months to reply. Not having to deal with someone's immediate reaction can be disinhibiting. In real life, it would be similar to speaking to someone, magically suspending time before that person can reply, and then returning to the conversation when you are willing and able to hear the response. Immediate, real-time feedback from others tends to have a very subtle, yet powerful effect on the ongoing flow of how much people reveal about themselves. In a continuous feedback loop that reinforces some behaviors and extinguishes others, moment-by-moment responses from companions will shape the ongoing stream of self-disclosure, usually in the direction of conforming to the social norms of the situation at hand.

In email, discussion boards, blogs, and many other forms of social media where there are delays in feedback, people's trains of thought might progress more steadily toward deeper expressions of what they are thinking and feeling, be it toxic or benign. Without an immediate response from others, we more easily get lost in our own ruminations, which encourages the kind of free association that bypasses the defense mechanisms that censor our words. Some people even experience asynchronous communication as form of running away after posting a message that is personal, emotional, or hostile. It feels safe putting it "out there" where it can be left behind. Munro (2002), one of the first online psychotherapists, aptly described it as an *emotional hit and run*. The quintessential example would be people who cannot overcome the anxiety of breaking up with a romantic partner face to face, so they hit their companion with a "Dear John" text message, then quickly disappear.

IT'S ALL INSIDE MY HEAD (SOLIPSISTIC INTROJECTION)

Absent face-to-face cues combined with text communication can alter our perception of self-boundaries. People feel that their minds have merged with the mind of the online companion. Reading another person's message is experienced as a voice inside one's head, as if that person magically has been inserted into one's psyche, what psychoanalysts call an *introjection*. If we not know what the other person's voice actually sounds like, we might assign one inside our imagination. We might even create a visual image of what we think that person looks like and how that person behaves. The online companion now becomes a constructed character within our intra-psychic world, a character that is shaped partly by how the person actually presents him or herself via text, but also by our expectations, wishes, and needs. Because the person might remind us of other people we know, we fill in the image of that character with memories of those other acquaintances, as in transference reactions. Transference encourages the shaping of this introjected character when similarities exist between the online companion and significant others in one's life, as well as when one fills in ambiguities about the personality of the online companion with images from past relationships or from characters in novels and film.

As the constructed character becomes more elaborate within our minds, we start to subconsciously experience the text conversation as taking place within our heads, as if it is a dialogue between us and this character in our imagination, as if we become authors typing out a play or a novel while the characters speak to us. Throughout the day, we carry on these kinds of internal conversations, regardless of whether the relationship we ponder is online or offline. People fantasize about flirting, arguing with a boss, or very honestly confronting a friend. In our imagination, where it is safe, we feel free to say and do all sorts of things that we would not in reality. During online text communication, a person's mind weaves these fantasy role-plays, usually unconsciously and with considerable disinhibition. All of cyberspace is a stage, and we are merely players.

When reading another's message, it is also possible that you "hear" that person's words using your own voice. We tend to subvocalize as we read, thereby projecting the sound of our voice into the other person's message. Unconsciously, it feels as if we are talking to/with ourselves. When we talk to ourselves, we are willing to say all sorts of things that we would not say to others.

A colleague of mine in Twitter once said, "I have always thought of Twitter as a sort of muttering-to-self service in which one might occasionally be overheard." In social media, solipsistic introjection operates when people experience their posts as a kind of disinhibited murmuring to themselves, with seemingly no one listening. When that internal conversation between parts of oneself is interrupted by the occasional visitor who does post a reaction to one's musings, that visitor's response might fit right into the imaginary play inside one's head, steer it in a new direction, or completely derail it.

IT'S JUST A GAME (DISSOCIATIVE IMAGINATION)

People might feel that the imaginary versions of themselves they create in cyberspace exist in a different realm, that one's online persona along with online others live in a not-quite-real, even dreamlike dimension separate from the demands and responsibilities of the real world. Some people see their online life as a kind of game with rules that do not apply to everyday living. Once they get up from the keyboard and return to their daily routine, they leave behind that game, along with their persona they created for it. They relinquish responsibility for what happened in a seemingly fabricated world that has little to do with reality. This *dissociative imagination* surfaces clearly in online fantasy games when a player consciously creates an imaginary character who undertakes fantasy adventures, but it also can infiltrate other online activities. During my interview with a man who regularly participated in an avatar community, he described how his wife accepted the fact that he used his avatars to have cybersex with other people. In the eyes of his wife and himself, his online sexuality was not "real." For similar reasons, authorities such as the police sometimes fail to understand victims who come to them with tales of having been abused online. In their eyes, what happened in cyberspace did not seem real enough to warrant concern or intervention. Fortunately, cultural attitudes about such online abuse are changing.

People who suffer from poor reality testing in general, especially those with psychotic conditions, will have a very hard time determining what is fantasy in cyberspace and what is not. But in this age of ours, when the media injects imagination into almost everything we see, including so-called "reality shows," everyone's ability for reality testing is being challenged. We frequently call into question the veracity of anything we witness in the media, with the outcome being the assumption that "anything goes."

Although anonymity amplifies dissociative imagination, dissociative imagination and dissociative anonymity usually differ in the complexity of the dissociated self. Under the influence of anonymity, the person moves toward invisibility, toward becoming a non-person, resulting in a significant reduction of identity. During dissociative imagination, the self that is expressed, but split off, tends to be more elaborately constructed.

JUST BETWEEN YOU AND ME (PERCEIVED PRIVACY)

In the news, we often hear reports about important people in business, politics, and entertainment who get themselves into trouble by sending text messages that clearly provide incriminating evidence of their misdoings. Even a modestly sophisticated Internet user realizes that such records can be accessed by those with the skill, and hopefully the legally sanctioned power, to do so. So why did these prominent people shoot themselves in the foot? What persuaded them to think their loose lips were somehow exempt from public scrutiny?

In addition to solipsistic introjection as an explanation, we see in these examples the power of *perceived privacy*. Some researchers apply this term to how secure people feel when they reveal personal information about themselves during online business, financial, and other official transactions. In a more general sense, the term refers to the fact that people – in either a very naive or dissociated manner – subconsciously experience themselves as being in a private encounter with companions in cyberspace, even when they rationally know better. Educated Internet users understand in the reality-oriented part of their minds that whatever they send out via their computers and mobile devices is being recorded on some company or government server. However, in another dissociated part of their minds, one ruled more by the emotions of the moment, they ignore the potentially very public nature of their disclosures. Especially during text communication, when we experience that blending of our minds with those of our companions, we subconsciously assume we are alone with those people.

It also comes as no surprise that people feel their privacy has been invaded when someone explores the various nooks and crannies of their social media accounts or conducts an Internet search to find out about them. Even when everyone knows that such information is wide open to the public, both the person searching and the person being searched might feel this is a type of stalking. The different online spaces that contain the many facets of a person's identity might be available for all to see, but that person might experience it as personal, private territory. Just as people in the physical world have an invisible zone around their body that they feel belongs to them, that should be occupied only by people they trust – what psychologists call "personal space" – so too people have their *online personal space*. You can enter it, but they might feel intruded upon. This is why advocates of online privacy insist that people have the right to become invisible to search engines if they so choose.

Device interface visually reinforces perceived privacy. When we look into our phones and computers, and into the little windows where we type our messages, all of our senses tell us that we are inside a box – in fact, a visual box inside the physical device box. It feels like a private, personal space. We see little or no evidence of anyone else being there, other than the people who reply to our messages. Everyone else is an "out of sight, out of mind" phenomenon. We might even think of perceived privacy in terms of evolutionary psychology. The more sophisticated, advanced, and rational parts of our brain tell us, "Someone else could see this." But the more simplistic, self-centric, and sensory part of our brain says, "There ain't nobody here but you and me inside this box."

Many people believe they have a right to privacy in digital realms such as email, text messaging, closed discussion groups, web browsing, and account records. This right to privacy will continue to be one of the most important legal and ethical dilemmas in the history of the Internet. Adamantly believing, even defiantly, that one's online activities *should* be confidential might amplify one's disinhibition. By contrast, our growing uncertainty, skepticism, and anxiety about how well our confidentiality is protected might reduce perceived privacy as well as the disinhibition it stimulates.

WE'RE EQUALS (ATTENUATED STATUS AND AUTHORITY)

While people are online, their status in the real world might not be known to others, or it might not have as much impact as it does in the real world. Authority figures demonstrate prestige in their dress, body language, and the embellishments of their settings. The absence of those cues in cyberspace, especially text environments, reduces the impact of their authority. If people online cannot see them in their surroundings, they do not know whether a person is the president of a major corporation sitting in an expensive office or is some ordinary soul lounging on the sofa at home. Even if people do know something about someone's offline status, that elevated position might have less bearing on the person's online presence. In many environments, everyone has an equal opportunity for self-expression. Regardless of status, wealth, race, and gender, we all start off on a level playing field. Although people's status in the real world will ultimately have some impact on their powers in cyberspace, what often determines online social influence is your skill in communicating (including writing skills), your persistence, the quality of your ideas, and your technical know-how. Unfortunately, some people interpret that ability to acquire power as a sanction to use it with hostile intentions, sometimes against the people they perceive as authorities whom they can "take down."

Due to a fear of disapproval or punishment, people are reluctant to say what they really think as they stand before an authority figure in the real world. While online, in what feels more like a peer relationship with the appearances of authority minimized, people are much more willing to speak out or act out. The traditional culture of cyberspace maintains that everyone is an equal, that the purpose of the net is to share ideas and resources among peers, what has been called *net democracy.* As cyberspace expands into new realms, many of its inhabitants see themselves as innovative, independent-minded explorers and pioneers, even as rebels. They develop an anarchistic "wild, wild West" attitude about their adventures. This atmosphere contributes to disinhibition and the minimizing of authority.

EVERYONE ELSE THINKS IT'S OK (SOCIAL FACILITATION)

The social environment can reinforce, amplify, or fail to dampen the disinhibition effect. Unfortunately, in some forms of social media, the audience witnessing the actions of a toxically disinhibited person might actually take delight in what they see, perhaps even resonating vicariously with the person as a voice for their own frustrations – what Anna Freud (1937) would call an *identification with the aggressor,* a phenomenon very evident in our cultural fascination for antisocial rebels and psychopaths. The unleashed ranting or attacks against someone or something transform into an online performance that others reward with comments of praise and such buttonized responses as "likes," a topic I discuss in Chapter 5, "Electrified Relationships." The toxic self of the disinhibited person becomes publically idealized. When other people join in to fuel the hostilities, a competition ensues in which the disinhibited people try to outdo each other (which can also occur with intimate self-disclosures in benign disinhibition).

In other situations, the audience passively observes the hostilities without interfering, perhaps out of fear that they too might become a target. Not wanting to get involved, or thinking that someone else will intervene, they relinquish their own sense of personal responsibility, implicitly giving the disinhibited person permission to continue – a phenomenon reminiscent of the *bystander effect* as described by the social psychologists Darley and Latané (1968). In a very different kind of scenario, couples in social media persist in openly expressing their amorous attraction to each other while uncomfortable or even annoyed bystanders say nothing, except perhaps thinking to themselves, "Get a room, why don't you?"

"There is something awe-inspiring in one who has lost all inhibitions," said F. Scott Fitzgerald – a feeling that probably contributes to the contagious nature of toxic disinhibition, but also to benign disinhibition, as when we see people online reinforcing each other's generosity and empathy.

BEING SUSCEPTIBLE OR RESISTANT TO DISINHIBITION

There is a tendency to conclude that cyberspace determines the disinhibition effect. When people do things online they would not do otherwise, they might even say, "Cyberspace made me do it" – an issue that comes up in legal cases involving men who, claiming they succumbed to the temptations of online disinhibition, attempted sexual activities with police officers disguised as minors. But the concept of person/situation interactions suggests that the phenomenon is more complex than that, as does research indicating that online self-disclosures are not always different from those that occur offline (Nguyen, Bin, & Campbell, 2012). Some people are disinhibited in cyberspace, some are not. Some people are disinhibited only in certain ways or in particular circumstances.

We must take into consideration how different traits and personality styles make some people more susceptible to the online disinhibition effect while others are more resistant to it. Individual differences play an important role in determining when and how people become disinhibited. The more intense the underlying needs of a particular person – be they benign or toxic – the stronger the push toward expressing them. The less a person understands the technical aspects of computer-mediated communication, the more likely that person will make decisions about self-disclosure based on misperceptions of perceived privacy. Differences in writing and image-creation skills account for carefully controlled expressions of self versus clumsily disinhibited ones. People who operate mostly in the receptive mode of their online activities, who watch what is happening online but rarely participate, tend to avoid the possibility of being disinhibited

The personality types described in the previous chapter provide a useful framework for understanding individual differences in online disinhibition. These personality types vary significantly in their reality testing, defense mechanisms, and tendencies toward inhibition or expression. People with histrionic styles tend to be very open and emotional; compulsive personalities show more restraint; schizotypal individuals are prone to fantasy; paranoid people are very protective of their privacy; and narcissistic people assume the privilege of saying what they want. Trust, extroversion, impulsivity, hypomania, guilt, and shame all emerge as personality traits that modulate disinhibition. Online disinhibition will interact with these personality variables, in some cases resulting in a small deviation from the person's offline behavior, while in other cases triggering dramatic changes.

People differ in how much they vacillate between feeling disinhibited versus restrained as they move in and out of the various locales of their online lifestyle. A person might be openly expressive in social media with friends, even more so than in the real world, but feel uncharacteristically guarded in an online workgroup. To varying degrees, people shift up and down along what we might consider a *disinhibition/inhibition continuum*. People will also differ in how they might feel simultaneously disinhibited and inhibited within a particular online situation. For example, people reveal intimate details about themselves to a cyberspace companion, but will not disclose their phone numbers, home addresses, or places of work. Relying on dissociation, they are trusting and suspicious at the same time.

LEAKS IN THE PERIMETER

Changes in self-boundary play an important role in online disinhibition and personal identity. Self-boundary is the sense of what is me and what is not me. It is the experience of a perimeter marking the distinction between my personality – my thoughts, feelings, and memories – and what exists outside that perimeter, within other people. The awareness of having a distinct physical body, the perception via the five senses of an outside world, the feeling of a psychological distinction between what I experience versus what others experience, and the sensation of the physical/psychological self moving cohesively along a linear continuum of past, present, and future – all contribute to self-boundary.

Life in cyberspace tends to disrupt this framework of self-boundary. Especially in text communication, the physical body and its five senses no longer play as crucial a role as in face-to-face relationships. In cyberspace, what others know or do not know about me is unclear. As we move back and forth through synchronous and asynchronous communication, the feeling of a linear past, present, and future becomes more obscure. As a result, these altered states of consciousness tend to destabilize self-boundary. The distinction between inner-me and outer-other becomes ambiguous, which accelerates solipsistic introjection. The person shifts to what psychoanalytic theory calls *primary process thinking*, in which divisions between the experience of self and other become more diffuse, while interpersonal perceptions become more subjective and emotion-centered. Within the transitional space of online social experiences, the psyches of self and other overlap. We allow the hidden self to surface because we no longer experience it as a purely inner self. This blending of the disinhibited inner self with the perception of other people can generate deep understanding and compassion – or the sense, sometimes vague and sometimes distinct, of a toxic intrusion into one's private world, resulting in suspicion, anxiety, and the need to defend one's exposed and vulnerable intrapsychic territory.

As with other aspects of personality, there are significant individual differences in the degree to which people experience the changes in self-boundary that lead to disinhibition. A person's developmental level of being able to relate to other people as distinct human beings – what psychoanalysts call *object relations* – will determine the susceptibility to the unimpeded feelings that surface in the psychological merging with online companions. Some people possess a healthy flexibility in lowering and reestablishing their self-boundary as a way to experience relationships more deeply; some people show a rigidity of self-boundary that blocks out other people; and in borderline and psychotic disorders, people lack the ability to differentiate themselves from others, which can lead to poor reality testing along with exaggerated, dysfunctional disinhibition.

THE TRUE SELF AS ILLUSION

On more than a few occasions in my interviews, people reported that they feel more like their true selves while online. For those who enjoy writing, they believe they express their inner being more honestly and fully than in their everyday lives. For others, the images they share in social media are a very intimate expression of who they are. Some researchers claim that the online disinhibition effect contributes to these articulations of the "true self." A woman with repressed hostility unleashes her anger in a social media post, or a shy man openly expresses his secret affection for his cyberspace companion. They seem to be expressing what they genuinely feel. If personality is constructed in layers, with a core true identity hidden beneath surface defenses and the seemingly superficial roles of everyday social interactions, then does the disinhibition effect release it?

Raising this question in cyberpsychology once again demonstrates how this new environment has become a laboratory for exploring longstanding questions about human nature. The very concept of a true self has been tempting in the history of psychology because it helps people articulate their subjective experience of what goes on inside them. In humanistic psychology, the concept also works well as a motivational tool for self-actualization, because people often talk about discovering who they really are. However, as we saw in the previous chapter, this thing called "self" is complex. The idea of a "true" one might be too ambiguous, arbitrary, and rudimentary to serve as a useful concept when investigating the online disinhibition effect.

The Inhibiting Self Is True

The concept of disinhibition can mistakenly lead us into thinking that what is disinhibited is more real or true than the part of us that inhibits. If we believe that peeling away repression and other defense mechanisms uncovers the real self, we overlook the fact that our inhibitions also define our personalities. Psychoanalytic clinicians believe that understanding defenses is crucial to the success of the therapy because it reveals how and why we suppress certain thoughts and feelings. Bypassing defenses to get to the supposedly true self bypasses the opportunity to understand the reality of the inhibiting self. In cyberspace, some disinhibited people reveal otherwise hidden parts of themselves, but they might not grapple with the unconscious reasons why they usually suppress these things. They miss the opportunity to discover something important about their true self.

Joe, who is shy in person, thrives socially in cyberspace thanks to the online disinhibition effect. He feels that what he reveals about himself online is the real Joe. But his shyness is also a true aspect of his personality. If online companions, who had formed the impression that Joe was outgoing, finally met him in person, they might very well conclude that Joe is "really" shy. They would also wonder what about his personality causes him to be shy in person but not online. It is an important part of his identity.

A True Self Here and There

While some aspects of one's personality are disinhibited online, other aspects might be inhibited. People show some parts of themselves, but not others. Online environments might encourage this compromise between some things being revealed while other things are kept hidden. In email, Joe reveals to Sue for the first time that he loves her, but she cannot see his hesitant voice and body language. The email reveals his desire to show affection while disguising his reluctance about it. These compromises point to the polarities that operate within all of us. We encompass ambivalent, sometimes contrary emotions, simultaneously. Sometimes we think, act, or feel one way, and sometimes the opposite. Neither one is more true than the other.

Inside all of us there are different constellations of memories, feelings, and beliefs that make up the various parts of our identity. We might even think of them as the different "selves" within us, with each one being true. Depending on its cyberpsychology architecture, each online environment allows for a different expression of these inner selves. The self expressed in one place is not necessarily deeper, more real, or more authentic than another. Each environment allows us to see the different perspectives of that complex thing we call "self."

5

Electrified Relationships

When I got my first television set, I stopped caring so much about having close relationships.

– Andy Warhol

On two separate occasions I got into a rather intense debate with experienced onliners who claimed that text relationships via email and chat were as powerful, if not more so, than those experienced in person. Both onliners talked about how they could more deeply express their true selves via text, how the merging of their minds with their cyberspace companions far exceeded anything possible in the real world, how one's physical appearance was not only irrelevant but an annoying distraction. I said that I understood their point of view, but also pointed out the important qualities of in-person relating, such as seeing and hearing people, and how we need physical contact, such as hugs and kisses. They staunchly objected, claiming these things were both primitive and superficial. Finally, I said to each of them, "If you had to choose between spending the rest of your life only in person interacting face to face, or only online interacting via text, which would you choose?" One of them fell silent at my question. The other said, "I'd stay online."

SKEPTICS BEWARE

When cyberpsychology first ascended as a new discipline, skeptics paid little attention simply because they viewed online relationships as superficial encounters at best, most probably a faddish illusion, possibly even a symptom of psychological deficiencies. If people like being with each other inside wires and circuits, there must be something wrong with them. They must fear the genuine intimacy of true human encounters. When cyberspace unrelentingly claimed its territory as a brand new sphere for human interactions – most notably when the term "social media" slipped into the repertoire of household words without a fuss – those skeptical attitudes began to fade out.

But not completely. Theorists, researchers, and everyday people alike continue to debate the pros and cons of online versus offline living, as we all well should. Although everyone would admit that cyberspace gives us some very captivating vehicles for socializing, everyone would also agree that being face to face in the real world, in our physical bodies, is more intrinsically natural. It must in some respects be better according to the wisdom of Mother Nature herself. The ongoing story of cyberspace includes an important sidebar debate where we continually compare cyberspace and in-person relationships. The fact that science fiction writers, along with some prominent computer scientists, believe we will someday upload our minds to cyberspace raises the debate to a whole new hypothetical level, one that breeds a new generation of skeptics. In this chapter, we will explore these interesting twists and turns in the social dimension of cyberpsychology architecture.

LET'S MAKE SENSE:
THE SENSORY DIMENSIONS OF RELATING

Long before technology, for several hundred thousand years, we humans related to each other via the five senses: hearing, seeing, touching, smelling, and even tasting each other. Those sensory pathways helped us interact and bond. Now that this apparently successful system for communicating has taken us to the age of cyberspace, how do online and in-person relationships compare on these five senses?

Can You Hear Me?

The human voice is rich in meaning and emotion. A sharp edge to someone's words can rouse your suspicion or anger. Just the sound of a loved one's voice is enough to create feelings of comfort and joy. Singing – one of the most expressive human activities – powerfully unites people. In cyberspace relationships mediated only by text, both obvious and subtle nuances in voice disappear. Singing is impossible, unless you consider the synchronous typing of lyrics with an online companion as singing, which I must admit I have enjoyed on several occasions.

As we will see in Chapter 7, "Text Talk," advocates of online text relationships do rebuke this criticism by pointing to the many subtle psychological cues embedded in text communication, as well as to the intimate melding of minds that occurs via text. In defense of cyberspace, they might also point to how one's voice obviously can be heard through phones that are now part of the Internet, as well as through a variety of other means to transmit voices. In fact, talking in cyberspace has some distinct advantages. Calls can be saved and conversations replayed. Using software programs, nuances in voice could be examined more carefully for subtle emotions and meanings – assuming, of course, people would ever want to use such tools. Programs also allow us to modify our voices. If you want to speak more deeply, more melodiously, as your favorite movie star or cartoon character, or to use the auto-tune technology that became so popular after the turn of the millennium, so be it. Or you can add in any music or sound effect you desire to embellish your words – *Pomp and Circumstance*, explosions, quacks. A unique feature of cyberspace relationships is this opportunity to apply imagination in presenting oneself to others, which might enrich a relationship.

Can You See Me?

The human face and body language are rich in meaning and emotion. Critics of text-only communication in cyberspace complain that all these visual cues are missing, hence making the relationship ambiguous and depleted. In retort, the advocates of text would again point to its many subtleties. They praise the level playing field of text relating. Appearances – such as gender, race, and whether you are attractive or not – are irrelevant. Everyone has an equal voice. Everyone is judged by the same standards: their words. Advocates claim that text talk carries you past the distracting superficial aspects of a person's appearance by connecting you more directly to that person's mind.

Cyberspace offers a variety of visual opportunities for self-expression. Sharing photographs became widely popular, which we will discuss in Chapter 8, "Image Talk." Video communication is a viable substitute for face-to-face contact, except the field of view often falls short of what we can witness during an in-person encounter. You can see only what the camera is pointed at, restricted to the boxy screen of your communication device, and eye contact is difficult.

Online relating has the advantage of supplementing social interactions with imaginary visuals. Those features might be simple, as in placing an "emoji" happy face icon into a text message, or much more complex, as in highly sophisticated avatar environments in which everyone's appearance, including the surroundings itself, can be creatively manipulated. Do you want to meet your friend at the bottom of the ocean, on a space station, or in the Oval Office, with each of you adopting bodies and attire to match your locale? You got it. The problem is whether people take advantage of these visual opportunities to enrich the relationship, or whether such imaginary visuals turn into relatively meaningless and possibly distracting novelty items.

Can You Touch Me?

Humans need physical contact with each other. Infants sink into depression and die without it. How parents interact physically with them becomes a cornerstone of their identity and well-being. Adults deprived of tactile contact for long periods will tell you just how depriving it feels. In day-to-day relationships, never underestimate the power of a handshake, a pat on the back, a hug, or a kiss. The poet and writer Margaret Atwood said:

> Touch comes before sight, before speech.
> It is the first language and the last, and it always tells the truth.

On this level of human relating, cyberspace falls short. In avatar communities, there are visual hints suggesting physical contact. You snuggle up your avatar next to someone else's. People give you a virtual "[[hug]]" in text relationships. As the first steps for infusing truly tactile sensations into online relationships, haptic technology has introduced the electronic transmission of vibrations, small electrical and heat stimulations, grasping sensations, and even erotic experiences such as teledildonics. Such technologically induced sensations are still quite crude compared to the subtle and powerful varieties of in-person physical contact. People might argue that you can psychologically embrace others through words alone, but the bottom line is that "holding" your loved one in cyberspace, along with all the deep emotions that accompany this sensation, will pale by comparison to doing so in person with your actual physical bodies. It should be noted, however, that some people will appreciate a lack of physical contact, as in autistic disorders.

In the physical, tactile, spatial world we also can *do* things with people, other than talk. We can play tennis, go for a walk, eat dinner, and have sex. Doing so creates bonds. It creates a history to the relationship. Are these things possible in cyberspace? To some degree, yes. Especially in sophisticated gaming and social media environments, we can meet people at some specified location, move with them from one area to another, as if we are "going places" with them. There are more than enough online games people can play together. Then, of course, there is cybersex, in all its various forms, which can very much feel like "doing" something with others.

Although enhancing a relationship, these online activities do not possess as powerful a physical, tactile, or spatial feeling as activities in the real world. Rarely do they include the experience of feeling the subliminal "energy" of someone's physical presence. Even in the most sophisticated avatar communities and gaming worlds, the representations of ourselves can engage each other in all sorts of fantastic ways, but usually our actual physical bodies are by themselves and rather sedentary. Almost anything people do together in cyberspace they also could do together in person, if only because they can sit side by side in front of the computer while they do it. But the reverse is not true. Everything you can do with someone in person cannot be duplicated in cyberspace – at least not yet.

Can You Smell and Taste Me?

The scent of perfume, hair, clothes, and skin – the sense of smell brings us very close to the other. It stirs up powerful emotional reactions. Just a whiff instantly triggers a memory of a place or person. The sense of taste brings us closer still. It is the sensation of lovers. One might say that smell and taste are rather primitive interpersonal experiences, yet both are the cornerstones of deep intimacy, perhaps because they are so primitive, so fundamental. It is the way infants relate to their mothers, the prototype for relationships later in life.

On this level of connecting interpersonally, cyberspace as we now know it falls flat on its noseless, tongueless face. Will the Internet ever be able transmit smells and tastes to another person a thousand miles away? Multisensory technologies are being developed to accomplish this feat through devices that electrically stimulate the tongue or release smells. But don't hold your breath waiting to share a tasty full course meal inside cyberspace with your online companion, or for the olfactory and gustatory presence of your lover.

All Together Now

Rarely during in-person encounters do we connect to the other person by one sense alone. At the very least, we see and hear simultaneously. During more intimate relating, we see, hear, touch, smell, and maybe even taste. The complex interactions among all that sensory input far exceed the interpersonal meaning we can extract from any one of them alone. Mother Nature was quite clever in giving us eyes, ears, skin, noses, and tongues, all interconnected in marvelous ways that science still does not fully understand. Those clusters of sensations make for relationships that are highly robust in emotion and meaning.

As Internet technology improves, auditory, visual, tactile, and perhaps even smell and taste sensations will be more effectively coordinated with each other. Yet even with unlimited bandwidth and highly imaginative code, will we ever see the five sensations fully integrated like they are in the real physical world? Are the robustly sensory interpersonal relationships as depicted in the virtual realities of science fiction movies possible, or do such experiences necessitate having a physical body in a physical world?

In cyberspace relationships, the five senses tend to be dissociated, which is a double-edged sword. On the one hand, the rich interpersonal qualities afforded by full sensory integration are lost, resulting in human encounters that might turn a bit stale compared to in-person situations. On the other hand, extracting some senses, or combining them in unusual ways, creates unique paths for interacting with each other. Do you want to hear but not see people? See but not hear them? Read their text, see them, but not hear them? Yes, we can do that online – and people definitely want it, as evident in the fact that they often choose texting over phone calls, and phone calls over video calls.

Can You Read My Mind?

Sometimes we humans connect to each other in ways that seem to defy the traditional laws of sense impressions. Call it telepathy, empathy, or intuition, we know what others are thinking or feeling without being aware of just how we know it. Some researchers believe we sense these things based on an unconscious detection of subtle qualities in voice and body language, or things said between the lines. Sensory information has a powerful subliminal effect on how we relate to each other.

Curiously, people report that even in the stripped-down sensory world of text communication, they sometimes sense what you are thinking and feeling without your actually having said anything about it. Did they detect your mood or state of mind from some subtle clue in what or how you typed? Are they picking up on some seemingly minor change in how you typically express yourself? Or does their empathy reach beyond your words on the screen? Perhaps they are in tune with your mind via some pathway that neither psychology nor computer technology can fully explain. If that kind of intuitive connection really exists, then the differences between in-person and cyberspace relationships might be less significant. On that mysterious level, human relating transcends our current understanding of sense organs and microchips.

TEXT VERSUS BODY

In the early days of cyberspace, online relationships consisted almost exclusively of typed text in email, chat, and discussion board posts. Even when phone calls and video chat became easily available through cyberspace, we still relied heavily on text. The question is, why? Why do people opt for text messages when they have a whole variety of visual and auditory tools for communicating? As we have seen, there are some distinct advantages of text relationships over in-person relationships.

The interaction can be asynchronous. It does not have to occur in real time, so you can respond to your companion whenever you wish, at whatever pace you wish. That gives you time to think about what you want to say, then compose your reply exactly the way you want. Rarely are you on the spot to reply immediately. Then there is advantage of being able to text quietly, unobtrusively when other people are around you.

The typed dialogues of online relationships involve different mental mechanisms than in-person talk. Writing entails a distinct cognitive style that enables some people to be more expressive, subtle, organized, or creative in how they communicate. Some people feel that they express themselves better in the written word. Surely, there have been truly great authors and poets who appeared bumbling or shallow during in-person conversation.

Text-mediated relationships enable you to easily record and save the messages. You can preserve segments of the relationship with your online companion, maybe even the entire relationship if you communicated only via text.

At your leisure, you can review what was said, cherish important moments, and reexamine misunderstandings and conflicts. During in-person encounters, you almost always have to rely on the vagaries of memory.

Because text relationships are especially susceptible to the online disinhibition effect, people tend to open up and say things that they normally would not say in person. Self-disclosure and intimacy are accelerated. Some people argue that one's inner self is more likely to surface online than in person, which theoretically should promote a genuine relationship.

While traveling in Europe, I noticed people on trains and in restaurants talking with each other in a variety of languages that were foreign to me. Even though I barely understood the content of their conversation, subtle changes in their attitudes were clearly visible in their tone of voice, facial expressions, and body language. How people communicate with these non-verbals struck me as a very important, universal aspect of human nature. I reflected on the points people make in defense of text communication, but I also realized we have to take very seriously the fact that these nonverbals are missing. "The human body is the best picture of the human soul," the philosopher Ludwig Wittgenstein said.

If we show a baby a highly expressive text message, what will the baby do? Perhaps suck on the phone? The email means nothing to the child. Sit in front of the baby, change your facial expressions, coo, raise and lower your voice, tickle and hug the child – and watch the baby respond immediately. We adults are no longer children, but we still rely heavily on this inborn reactivity to physical presence. Text smileys, shouted CAPS, and [[hugs]] are only abstract representations that have, at best, an indirect impact on the preverbal, nonsymbolic, and physical dimensions of how we humans react to each other. As research in developmental psychology shows, our human relatedness via nonverbal and preverbal experiences is neurologically wired into all humans. By contrast, text-simulated nonverbals are mostly learned as well as more subject to cultural factors.

"LOL" and "[[Joe]]" are text portrayals of a laugh and a hug for Joe, but they are not the laugh and the hug. What are the implications of interacting with text but not with the actual bodily experiences? How does the emotional impact of typing the abstractly raucous "ROFL" compare to the actual experience of rolling on the floor laughing? Does a text hug sink in the same way as actually feeling someone's arms around you? Most likely not. I am reminded of the Zen joke about typing up a description of a delicious dinner, printing it out, and then eating the paper. Or the famous Zen concept of the finger pointing to the moon. Just as the finger is not the moon, the text communication is not the actual experience; it just points to it.

In defense of text relationships, we should consider once again the fact that some people feel more comfortable in them. Those who are shy in person, or who lack face-to-face verbal skills, can thrive via text, as do people who wish to avoid showing their physical appearance if they suffer from an illness or physical abnormality. Some people have difficulty understanding face-to-face nonverbal cues or are overwhelmed by complex and emotional nonverbal signals from others. Text feels more predictable and safer. These problems often have inborn, neurological underpinnings, as demonstrated by research on autism, Aspergers Syndrome, and other difficulties in processing face-to-face social information. Trauma might also result in aversions to in-person contact. Finally, there is the simple fact that some people do not have the opportunity to develop good relationships in the "real" world. Finding "real" relationships online might be the right choice.

BUTTONIZED RELATING

In addition to all the text, visual, and auditory makings available to us, social media added another novel ingredient to the online fraternizing pie. Rather than using words, people could simply click a button to offer their approval of what someone else was posting. Facebook popularized it as the "like," while other social media used stars, pluses, hearts, and thumbs-up icons. Clicking the button seemed to be a relatively simple act of validation, a way to offer a small gift of appreciation. Reposting someone's message served a similar function, with the added benefit of spreading that person's ideas. As is often the case in the world of cyberpsychology, people have used these deceptively simple buttonized tools in a variety of unexpected ways. By clicking the like button or reposting a message, a person might be saying one of several different things.

All I Can Say Is "Wow"

People offer a like when something has a strong emotional impact on them. In the case of photosharing, that feeling might come from the purely visual qualities of an image that pops, although the emotions and meanings behind the image tend to be the more enduring factor compared to the shallow jolt of eye candy. The effect is usually an immediate, gut-level reaction, particularly in response to pictures. The "Wow Factor" in any type of social media post makes people think of how beautiful and inspiring it is, how it made them laugh, how it speaks to them, resonates with them, or touched them on a deep level. The button press might even feel like a disappointing understatement: they wish they could click the button ten or a hundred times. These types of likes and reposts help visitors express their appreciation when they feel the psychological impact but are not sure why, or cannot adequately verbalize why. In groups devoted to visual arts, such as photography groups, members who like an image only when it has a powerful effect on them tend to reserve such rewards for special occasions, when they feel other members have truly earned them.

I Support You

A person might offer a like or repost to support and encourage other people in their effort, whatever it might be. As a form of nonverbal behavior, the button click becomes an acknowledging smile, a nod of the head, a pat on the back, applause, or a sign of affection – which is why parents often gladly pin likes on whatever their children post. While some people offer such likes generously, others are more reserved or even outright stingy – differences that most likely reflect their supportive, demanding, or withholding styles of relating to others. People who reveal intimate things about themselves might receive more likes as an expression of social support from others who appreciate their honesty while hoping to alleviate their vulnerability.

I Feel Good

Some people find themselves offering more of these buttoned gifts when they are in a good mood. They altruistically spread their upbeat feelings with clicks. Others say doing so helps them feel better when they are in a bad mood. It is a well-known fact in psychology, as well as commonsense knowledge, that doing nice things for other people can make you feel good.

I'm Sorry

Among friends, family, and lovers, the like can be an attempt to resolve guilt about having done something wrong, to make up, without openly acknowledging the transgression – not unlike the man who offers flowers to the woman he disappointed. Psychologists call this defense mechanism "undoing." Paradoxically, people sometimes click a like button to indicate their sorrow for a post about a sad event. Of course doing so feels uncomfortable, which is why social media designers have considered adding a "sympathy" button.

Let's Make a Deal

In many forms of social media, likes and reposts serve as units of social currency. The more one has, the higher one's popularity, status, and visibility in the community. Within that economy, the like becomes a tool for social bartering. When people receive one, they often feel obligated to give one. When they give one, they hope or expect reciprocity. The value of these buttonized actions rests not only in their serving as a gesture of mutual appreciation, but also in the fact that increasing numbers of them boosts a person's visibility in the community.

This Is Easy for Me

The like and repost can serve as substitutes for leaving a comment when people cannot find the words to describe why something had an impact on them, when they do not have time to leave a comment, or, in cross-cultural situations, when they lack facility in the language being spoken. It is an easy, nonverbal way to express approval or even simply the fact that "I was here" in a benign fashion. In some cases, people consider it inconsiderate or outright rude when friends, family, or other close companions leave a like without an accompanying comment, especially when the post feels important to the person. Leaving a like is just a bit too easy and therefore emotionally distant.

Me Too

Social conformity often emerges in social media. People give likes to someone or repost messages because many others have already done so. They join the wave of venerating praise. For some people, this participation in the tidal wave of tributes buoys their self-esteem by feeling connected to the celebrities of the hour and their followers in a transference reaction that idealizes others. In other cases, the like or repost is simply a way of saying "ditto."

I Disapprove

Some people deliberately hold back on a like or repost when someone has already received many of them, perhaps out of a sense of envy, not wanting to be just another person applauding, or because they feel the person has already received enough attention. Not offering a like can be a deliberate insult, withholding disapproval, competitive belittling, or an unconscious act of passive-aggressiveness.

I Like You

People give likes to friends as a somewhat distant gesture of affection, or to acquaintances and strangers in hopes of establishing an amiable relationship. As a type of social grooming among companions, offering one shows enthusiasm about a person, mostly because it is the friendship that is important and not necessarily the quality of the person's post. Some people feel more inclined to reward friends with a like rather than acquaintances and strangers because they consider it a gesture of camaraderie and intimacy. Others use it as a comfortable way to approve of a stranger while trying to keep the relationship superficial, as this member of a photosharing community pointed out:

> At first I was enamored of the community, but now I see it as taking too much time. So I've avoided adding new contacts, avoiding commenting on even photos that I think are worthy of praise, so as not to begin another relationship. It's really tempting though – you see a photo that speaks to your heart, the person who posted it looks like someone you'd like – but you know that if you comment, you may create expectations of a relationship that you don't really have time for. So you just like it with no comment, as a way of reminding yourself that this person is doing something interesting, and you can go back and check their progress without attracting attention.... Am I an ogre? A misanthrope? Unfriendly and unsociable? I don't know. I like keeping up the contacts I have, but I don't want to add more.

LOST IN THE BUTTONIZED ECONOMY

With the concept of *social currency* in mind, many designers of social media hoped that buttonized relating could work as a viable tool for quantifying the value of a person's online presence. How do you measure someone's influence online, the influence they have on other influencers, and the activity they spark in cyberspace? The number of button presses associated with them could provide important data.

Ideally, when people stimulate the social economy with their posts, what they offer is worthwhile, whether it be comments, information, pictures, or stories. If many people like it, it must be good. Unfortunately, some rather big flies have spoiled the ointment of this assumption, forcing us to question how valid they are as indicators of quality rather than simply quantity of online activity. As we have just seen, people give likes for a variety of reasons other than how "good" something is, so what does a high pile of them actually mean? Many people rely on likes as a source of self-esteem, self-worth, and social status, which drives up the stakes to get more as a badge for feeling good and looking better than other people. With the like or repost sounding like a hand clap, some people clamor for louder applause from their audience. In an attempt to micromanage their social status, some people even quietly remove posts that received no clap.

Unfortunately, the end result can be a competitive game, with losers falling behind the winners – winners who sometimes came out on top not because they offered higher-quality posts, but because they succeeded at devising clever strategies to drive their numbers into a skyrocketing range, perhaps even resorting to button presses from pay-per-service bots or click farms of low-paid workers whose job is to dole out button presses. Modifying Mark Twain's famous saying, some disillusioned people in social media conclude that there are three types of lies: lies, damned lies, and likes. The marvelous online opportunity to offer quick-and-easy clicked replies to people's posts can warp into a frustrating, uncomfortable, and disappointing *compare and compete mentality*. Narcissitic people are more susceptible to these woes, for as Baltasar Gracian, the Spanish Jesuit, once said, "The envious die not once, but as oft as the envied win applause." While the upside of buttonized relating is its versatility and ease of use in conveying subtle but important interpersonal intentions, the downside is a social climate based on rating systems, contests, polls, or popularity votes that feel very arbitrary, and therefore at least a tad meaningless.

When social media includes both "up" and "down" ratings of posts, the environment can sink into even deeper negativity. Getting no likes might feel like disappointing abandonment, but receiving buttonized feedback that resembles a "thumbs down" turns into outright rejection or even condemnation. With up and down votes reflecting the predominant values or even the momentary whims of the viewing audience, the scenario resembles the Colosseum of ancient Rome, with not actual life or death as the outcome, but the rising or falling of one's self-esteem.

These problems are part of the larger dilemma in social media that Festinger (1954) would have described in terms of his *social comparison theory*. People evaluate themselves through comparisons to others. Social media accelerates this phenomenon by enabling people to make many dozens of such comparisons in a matter of minutes. Seeing other people getting more followers, likes, comments, and praise – especially when their posts focus on accomplishments, happy occasions, or idyllic versions of themselves – can punch holes in the self-esteem of anyone who feels inferior by comparison. Being ignored or receiving negative feedback rubs salt into those wounds.

A SHOWDOWN BETWEEN IN-PERSON AND ONLINE RELATIONSHIPS?

If we entertain some kind of comparison test, or even a showdown, between in-person and cyberspace relationships, as some people still do, which one wins? Is it the buttonized, time-stretching, distance-shortening, efficiently managed, and potentially imaginative realm of online interactions, or the in-person world that offers rich physical sensations, the complex integration of all the senses, and a more robust potential to "do things" with others? People can and will continue to argue for their side of the debate. For perspective, I sometimes offer the acid test question that I described in the story at the beginning of this chapter. If given a forced choice, would you spend the rest of your life interacting with people only online or only in person? Cyberspace certainly provides us with a wonderful supplement to in-person relationships, but in the long run, for most people, we should question its validity as a substitute for real-world encounters, especially when it comes to our most significant others.

Fortunately, we rarely have to face such a dichotomous choice. As the prominence of the Internet grew in our culture, people pursued a variety of ways to develop their relationships, both online and offline. They interacted with some people only online. They interacted with others only in person. In many important cases, as with family and friends, they socialized in person as well as in cyberspace, using various online communication tools, hopefully combining the best of all worlds.

The question is not whether online or offline relating is better. It is what types of relating work best for what kinds of relationships and endeavors. Cyberspace encourages us to rethink our concept of what constitutes a relationship, how it can be broken down into its component qualities as indicated by the eight dimensions of cyberpsychology architecture, and which dimensions can be combined to maximize the purpose of the encounter with others.

The temptation to focus on some kind of showdown between in-person and cyberspace relationships often comes from expectations about interacting in an intimate, comprehensive, and honest way with others, as opposed to shallow encounters. Which realm wins that contest? Of course, there is no simple answer to that question because cyberspace is not one monolithic environment, but many different types of environments as determined by their cyberpsychology architectures. Cyberspace does teach us that intimacy and bonding among people tends to increase according to the *integration principle* – when we begin to encounter each other across different environments; when we combine, in various ways, synchronous, asynchronous, visual, auditory, tactile, and text communication; and when we get to know others both online and in person. Because we express ourselves differently depending on the media, we learn more about each other and thereby enhance the quality of the relationship as we add new ways of communicating, when we cross the boundaries of different media to meet each other. Any time we reach out to someone using a different communication environment – whether it is text, pictures, voice, private as opposed to a public contact, or any other method – we are extending an invitation to know each other better, in a new way.

Interacting with someone both in person and online, or within different online habitats, can lead to separate, slightly different tracks in how you relate to each other. It might even be a conscious or unconscious attempt to dissociate parts of the relationship. It is not unusual for people to discuss a sensitive topic online, usually via text and triggered by the online disinhibition effect, but they never mention it when face to face. That type of dissociation must be overcome to achieve a more complete, integrated experience of each other.

We should always consider how individuals differ in their preference for in-person relationships or online relationships in the wide variety of environments that are now and will be possible in the future. People with schizoid or paranoid personality styles might prefer text. Histrionic people might like the immediacy and performance versatility of a face-to-face encounter. People with physical handicaps might want online relationships in which their bodies pose few problems, as in text talk, or cyberspace environments that give them capabilities for relating what they lack in the physical world – like being able to speak or to dance using an avatar. In these cases, cyberspace offers a valuable service. It would be equally rewarding if we lived in a world where physical handicaps and appearances were not critical factors determining how comfortable people feel with each other or how well they treat each other. Ideally, cyberspace can help us learn such lessons rather than provide a convenient vehicle for bypassing the necessity of eliminating stereotypes and prejudices.

6

Other Than You Think
Interpersonal Perceptions

The single biggest problem in communication is the illusion that it has taken place.

– George Bernard Shaw

Shortly after I published an article online about the psychology of body language, I received an email from a man who expressed an interest in the topic. Given the generic username in the email address and his not indicating anything about himself, I had no idea who he was. He asked if I would watch a YouTube video in which journalists interviewed the Apollo 11 astronauts who had returned from the first moon landing. He wanted to know what I thought of their "strange" body language. Curious, I clicked the link he provided and viewed the video. The astronauts appeared a bit uncomfortable, but more interesting to me was the discussion that ensued among the other visitors to the page. Many of them firmly believed in the conspiracy theory about the first lunar landing, how it never actually happened but was instead staged by the U.S. government. Many of them agreed that the astronauts looked very guarded, that they were clearly lying. In my email to the man who had contacted me, I stated that the astronauts appeared a bit nervous, perhaps due to the fact that they were not used to being in the media spotlight. Here is what he said in his email reply:

oh PLEASE! ... Nervous. These are men that are from highly specialized backgrounds, and with high influence, at least one was a 33 degree mason. They would be used to TV. It goes much deeper than what you suggest, which is reflected in their body language.

No, what you mean is, you refuse to "look." As is very typical with the establishment of psychology, you jump at the chance at labeling the "little person," but HIDE when asked to expose the body language of those part of the power structures and its propaganda.... See?? – i can read you like a book.

MOM, DAD, MACHINE

To begin this second chapter devoted to the social dimension of cyberpsy-chology architecture, let's try a quick exercise. Think about your spouse, a romantic relationship, or a close friend. Focus on some important characteristic of that individual's personality – a characteristic or trait of that person to which you have a strong emotional reaction, positive or negative.

Now think about one of your parents. Does that parent possess the very same characteristic? Are the reactions you have to that aspect of your parent similar to those concerning your current close relationship?

The phenomenon of transference is one of the cornerstones of psycho-analytic theory. Rows of bookshelves could be filled with what has been written about it. The basic idea is that we tend to recreate in our current relationships the patterns of thinking, feeling, and behaving that were formed early in our life, most importantly in the relationships with our parents and siblings when we were children. We often do this unconsciously, so you might not have been able to answer the questions in that exercise. As Fred Rogers, the educator and television host, said:

Parents are like shuttles on a loom.
They join the threads of the past with threads of the future
and leave their own bright patterns as they go.

Critics challenge this idea by accusing psychoanalytic theory of dwelling too much on the effects of childhood and family dynamics on the evolution of one's identity. One's personality does change throughout the course of one's life as a result of our colleagues, friends, lovers, and new life experi-ences. It is not solely determined by how our parents raised us as children. Although such qualifications must be considered, the fact remains that our parents, or other highly influential parental figures, did indeed spend a great deal of time with us during those formative years, when our minds were young, impressionable, and eager to learn about how we humans relate to each other. Based on our relationships with them, we created men-tal templates about the expected ways in which people behave toward each other. We formed basic impressions about the kinds of needs, wishes, and fears that shape relationships and our concept of ourselves in those rela-tionships. Often we do not realize these templates are our own, that they might in fact be very different from those that formed in the minds of other people. Think of a time when, as a young person, you went to a friend's house where you were surprised, maybe even shocked, at how differently that family behaved as compared to your own. To them it was "normal." As we grow, up we take these templates with us into adulthood. Often operating at an unconscious level, they affect the choices we make in the kinds of people we get involved with, as well as how we experience those people once the relationship is under way. Think about how your first boyfriend or girlfriend might have been similar to one or perhaps both of your parents. How often have companions said to each other, "You're just like my mother/father!"

Later in this chapter, we will apply this concept to online relationships, but first let's back up a step. What might it be about our relationship to the machine itself, the computer or mobile device that mediates our interactions with other people online? It is well known among psychoanalytic clinicians that these transference templates also shape how we experience things in our lives that are not human, but so closely touch our needs and emotions that we tend to imbue them with personality characteristics. We humans cannot help but anthropomorphize the elements in the world around us. It is in our blood. We use our internal templates to humanize our experience of cars, houses, pets, careers, the weather, as well as our computers, mobile devices, and "cyberspace" itself.

The vehicles that connect us to cyberspace are prime targets for transference because they are complex machines that have been designed to operate in ways that mimic how we think and behave. Unlike TV, movies, or books, they are highly interactive. We ask them to do something and they do it – at least, they usually do, because like humans they sometimes disobey, disappoint, frustrate, and surprise us. With new generations of highly visual, auditory, tactile, and customizable operating systems and software applications, we have a machine that can be tailored to reflect both who we are and what we expect from a close companion. The more sophisticated a device becomes in its powers to notify and guide us to something that is happening online or offline, the more it strikes us as an entity that possesses its own willful mind that interacts in complex ways with our own mind that we try to impose on it.

When our devices appear humanlike, complex in ways we do not always understand, but emotionally neutral, they might strike us as mysteriously ambiguous companions. How does that affect us? Psychoanalysts discovered that if they remain ambiguous in how they behaved with their clients, the clients begin to mold their perceptions of the analyst according to their internal templates from childhood. This transference often is unconscious. We might react to our intelligent but enigmatic machines in the same way.

When designers intentionally create devices with human personality traits built into their artificially intelligent interfaces, those machines could very well encourage specific kinds of transference reactions. Some people will perceive a seemingly caring and supportive operating system as like a mother. A demanding, matter-of-fact, emotionally distant device will remind others of a father. If computerized devices are constructed with such particular personality styles, those designs could very well reflect the transference reactions of the designers. When they decide how the device reacts to the user, what it says and the kinds of questions it asks, the designers might very well have their fathers, mothers, or any significant other in the back of their minds, without even realizing how those mental templates are influencing their creation.

So now we can return to the exercise at the beginning of this chapter. Only now we substitute in "computer" or "phone" for husband, wife, lover, or friend. How do we unconsciously experience the machine as being like our mother, father, or sibling? Keep in mind that I am not saying that we think the communication device *is* our parent or sibling, but rather that we recreate in our relationship with it some aspect of how we related to our significant others.

Some people might insist that their computer or mobile device is nothing like their mother or father. Here is where we need to examine the phenomenon of transference more carefully, for there are curious twists and turns that make it considerably more complex than what I have explained so far.

In the descriptions that follow, I will outline some of the most basic types of transference reactions. We will see that the same pattern of relating to a family member can be played out in various ways in one's relationship to the communication device. I will focus mostly on relationships with parents, while keeping in mind the fact that these transference phenomena also could have their roots in perceptions of other family members or important people from the past. After we explore these ideas about the relationship between a person and the machine, we will see how they apply to interactions between self and other in cyberspace.

The Machine as Your Parent

This is the most obvious type of transference, the type implied in my descriptions so far. You experience the other as being like your parent while you see yourself as the child you once were. As an example, let's say Leonard was raised by a mother who had many rules for how he should behave, but the rules always seemed to be changing. Even though he tried to figure out and obey his mother's requests, he never quite succeeded, never quite satisfied her. As a result, he felt frustrated, helpless, and defeated whenever he tried his best, but ultimately failed in the eyes of his mother. As an adult, Leonard experiences his computer in the same light. He is intimidated by it, never quite sure how to please it. When he tries to accomplish something, the computer does not seem to like what he does. It will not respond. He gets error messages. He has failed once again. His computer makes him feel frustrated, helpless, and defeated. Maybe he even tries to avoid it, just like he did with his mother.

Jenny had a father who was frail, not quite competent as a person. She loved him, took care of him, and was very attentive to his needs. Perhaps she sometimes sacrificed her own needs in order to attend to his. As an adult, she perceives her computer as fragile and vulnerable. She is very careful about how she uses it because she does not want to cause damage. She is very conscientious about running diagnostics and antivirus programs. The well-being of her machine, she feels very earnestly, is in her hands. Some might even say she is bit overprotective of it.

Leonard and Jenny are just two examples. This first type of transference can take many different forms. Traditional psychoanalysts of the Freudian type often described it in terms of sexual wishes and fantasies toward the parent. Later, after resolving the conflicts associated with these wishes, the child learns to identify with the same-sex parent. In one of the earliest articles written about online transference, Holland (1996) focused on these types of reactions towards computer. It is seen as a seductive sex object, a satisfier of desire, a symbol of sexual power and prowess. Consider this real conversation from a cyberspace chat room in which the members are discussing how one of their friends, "Suzy," was flashed by an exhibitionist during their video chat:

DAISY: so all she sees is a big penis on her screen! lol!
HAWKEYE: lol
DAISY: I can't figure out why he wanted to see *Suzy's* penis!
DRAGON: next ur gonna say she has a 15 inch monitor, right?
DAISY: 20 inch, Dragon
THR: geez and black and white haha
MR. TOPS: 17 in rotating
DAISY: hahahahhahah
TWEETY: bigger is ... bigger!
DRAGON: wow, no wonder you gals like macs so much
DAISY: doesn't have to be bigger, just better
DAISY: and rechargeable
TWEETY: or plugged in the wall ...

HAWKEYE: what about bigger AND better?
MR. TOPS: it's not the size of the monitor, but the driver behind it
TWEETY: with loads of amps
HAWKEYE: as one of my friends like to say, "How hard is your big drive?"
DAISY: lol!
DRAGON: more importantly, Hawkeye, is it compressed?
DAISY: more importantly, is it unzipped?
HAWKEYE: and how often do you optimize it?
LOLA: or is it backed up?
DRAGON: only in san francisco
DAISY: LOL!

No doubt Freud would have a great deal to say about this conversation. It is not too difficult to detect themes about phallic power, penis envy, castration fears, and a miscellaneous collection of heterosexual and homosexual issues. But I do not want to dwell on the idea of computers as sex objects. This type of transference applies in some cases, but certainly not all. I am not even convinced that it is a prominent type of transference. The language of classical Freudian theory also tends to be rather sexist and culturally biased.

In the unconscious, sex is not always about sex per se, but about the many powerful emotions we associate with it. Most important about the erotic transference toward computers is the perception of them as something powerful, just as children see parents as powerful. This perception is obvious in the dialogue from the chat room. The computer can think faster than us; has a more massive and accurate memory, can perform tasks that we could not do alone; and guides us through a vast, wondrous world called cyberspace. These qualities stir up feelings of admiration, awe, fear, and competition, not unlike the transference feelings toward any authority figure.

You as the Parent to the Machine Child

In this type of transference, a person's mind reverses the roles played by child and parent. For example, by adopting in adulthood the role of someone who is powerfully in command, a person might be trying to master childhood feelings of helplessness and anxiety. The person becomes the dominating parent who once exerted control over the child. In his classic 1915 paper, Freud described these kinds of reversals as *turning the passive into the active.*

Some people might abuse their computers just as they might have been abused within their family of origin. Once controlled, dominated, and manipulated – sometimes as if they were not really people at all, but just objects to be used – they might very well as adults treat their computers in the same manner. Anger and outright rage at the machine, when it does not behave the way one expects, can be a symptom of this kind of transference. Infuriated people literally throw their phones to the ground.

By contrast, the machine can be perceived, almost lovingly, as one's baby. Becoming the good parent that they had as children, people attend to the computer's needs, nurture the machine, and help it develop and grow by adding software and hardware. Not unlike Jenny, who assumed a parental role toward her father, they feel protectively responsible for the computer's well-being. They become invested in its achievements, even feeling pride in the new things it can do. With delight and wonder, they feel as if they have taken part in the creation of an individual with unique abilities and a personality that reflects its admiring parent. Quite unlike real children, this electronic substitute might never become independent and leave them. For some people, that is a very attractive proposition.

The Machine as the Wished-for Parent

Many people wish, consciously or unconsciously, that their parents could have been different in some way, a wish that shapes their perception of the communication device as possessing those desired characteristics.

Sam's mother showed unpredictable behavior and emotions. One moment she would be caring and loving and the next harsh, critical, and punishing. Never being able to tell what was coming his way next, Sam became a hypervigilant, anxious child. He always needed to keep a lookout for subtle cues indicating how his mother would behave. He tried to anticipate her moves, but often was not successful. Feeling helpless and angry, he experienced life as unpredictable, dangerous, and beyond his control.

As an adult, Sam takes comfort in his computers. They are the way he wished his mother had been – predictable, reliable, and nonjudgmental, with no unexplained emotional outbursts. If he applies his hard-earned skills at analyzing the subtle details of how his communication devices behave, almost all of the time he can control what they do. He holds only vague feelings of intimacy or affection toward them. This is perfectly acceptable to him. Those emotions only got him entangled in problems with his

mother. In fact, he takes some pleasure in his distantly intellectual authority over the obedient machine. People say his compulsive personality really
shines in how he treats his devices.

Lorna experiences her phone quite differently. She sees it as a benign
presence. It is always there, with her, waiting for her. It pays attention to
what she wants, always providing immediate feedback. It allows her to
express her thoughts, feelings, and creativity. She sees it as a very responsive, compassionate companion who recognizes her value as a person. It
helps her develop her individuality. How different it is compared to her
parents, who were so busily preoccupied that they failed to show any kind
of real interest in her life. She was the neglected child.

You as the Wished-for Parent to the Machine Child

In this last type of transference, a reversal once again occurs, only this time
the person acquires the wished-for parental qualities, while the computer
assumes the role of the child. Often people strive to adopt the benign qualities that were missing in their parents. This can even amount to a simple
matter of reversing some characteristic of the mother or father. Sometimes
that reversal goes too far. If the parents were too strict, people become too
liberal with their children. If the parents were uninvolved in their lives, they
intrude a bit too much in the lives of their children.

Becoming the wished-for parent of one's computer follows the same
pattern. In benign cases, people strive to be good to their devices in ways
that their own parents were not to them. They are conscientious about taking care of it. But in some cases, they carry that effort too far. Growing up
with extremely strict parents, Sam is too lackadaisical about managing his
machine, to the point where it falls apart. Linda is so worried about viruses
and possible damage to her devices that she refuses to explore cyberspace,
grows wary of installing new software, and rarely lets anyone else use it. Bill
takes interest in what goes on inside the mind of his computer, just like a
good parent should, but Larry drives himself crazy trying to understand all
its technical details.

You Are Me, I Am You, We Are All Together

Kohut (1977, 1980) described a type of transference that he called a *selfobject
transference*. Selfobjects are external things, including people, that complete
one's sense of self and enhance its normal functioning, but they are not
experienced as separate from oneself. They fortify identity by being part of

one's psyche. Selfobject transferences take three basic forms: *mirroring, idealizing,* and *twinship transferences.*

When parents admire their children's paintings, acknowledge their thoughts about a TV program, or empathize with their feeling anger, sadness, or delight, the identities of the children are strengthened through this mirroring. If a boy imitates his father mowing the lawn, or a girl plays with Mommy's briefcase, this idealizing identification with the parent enhances their self-esteem and sense of self. In a twinship relationship when siblings play or work with each other, the feeling that "we are doing this together" satisfies their thirst for knowing who they are by what they do with their alter ego. For all three of these selfobject transferences, there is a blending of oneself with the other, so that the other person is not necessarily experienced as a separate person, but as part of oneself. One feels calm, unified, and confident in that psychological merging.

Our communication devices can stimulate these selfobject experiences. Some people rely on their computers or mobile devices to clarify and strengthen their identity. The machine attentively accommodates to their needs. It mirrors them. As users customize its hardware and software, it becomes more and more like a responsive reflection of their wants, feelings, and ambitions. It is part of them, a likeness of who they are, a world created from within themselves. By idealizing it, by participating in all the amazing, powerful things a computer can do, people strengthen their confidence and feelings of success. By spending so much time together with their mobile device, it becomes a reassuring extension of their motivations, personality, and inner psychological life – like a good buddy, a sibling, or a twin.

Although selfobjects can assist us in maintaining a healthy identity, there is a danger in relying too heavily on the computer as a support for one's sense of self. Placing all your eggs in one basket is never a good idea. The system crashes at exactly the wrong moment. The Internet connection drops. Files disappear. For any of a wide variety of reasons, the treasured machine fails the person. The rug has been pulled out from under one's feet. The person feels betrayed, abandoned, and lost, resulting in anger or depression. The more intense the selfobject transference, the more severely pathological the reaction can be, as in rage reactions blasted at the machine, such as throwing one's phone against the wall or when in 2015 a thirty-seven-year-old man in Colorado Springs hauled his problematic computer into the back alley where he shot seven holes into it.

All computer transferences entail some blending of the person's mind with the cyberspace inside the machine, with that psychological realm that arises as a computer-mediated extension of one's intrapsychic world. The communication devices create the *transitional space* – an intermediate zone between self and other – where identifications, internalizations, and introjects interact with each other. Cyberspace is a realm where the big and little bits of our parents and siblings that we have taken into our own psyches become free to express themselves, to play, work, fight, and, ideally, make peace with each other.

MOM, DAD, AND PEOPLE ONLINE

All of the transference reactions described so far also apply to how people interact with each other in cyberspace. Cyberpsychology architecture will influence the intensity of such reactions. Communicating only by text results in a somewhat ambiguous environment where we cannot see or hear people: they become shadowy figures, a screen onto which we may launch any of the variety of transference perceptions. Environments that encourage experimentation with reality and personal identity stimulate the acting out of fantasies in the types of imaginary others people choose to engage, as well as in the personae people create for themselves, all of which can stem from transference needs. The more an online habitat emphasizes robust sensory value, along with true-to-life depictions of identity and reality, the more reduced the transference phenomena.

Unconscious motivations emerging from transference can affect the filtering process that determines the choices people make in establishing new online relationships. They tend to zoom in on others who touch some hidden transference need within them. They may be surprised to discover that the close friends they make online all seem to be the same types of people, even though this was not immediately obvious at the start of the relationship. This unconscious homing device can be quite sensitive, powerful, and sometimes totally misleading, as is often the case with transference. A common example involves twinship transferences in which people with shared interests and agendas join forces online as they grow convinced of their deeply meaningful bond, only later to witness their relationship dissolve or even explode when they discover their supposed alter ego has needs and feelings that are incompatible with their own.

Transference to the "other" online includes our psychological reactions to cyberspace in general, and to the specific environments we choose within it. When people immerse themselves into their favorite social media, it might satisfy or frustrate the needs from important relationships in their past.

The Out-of-the-Blue Message

Some social media posts and incoming email are prepackaged with transference, along with a heavy dose of online disinhibition, even though the person is a complete stranger to you. If you created a professional or personal website or have any kind of online audience for your posts, or if any information about you is available online, people can form inaccurate impressions of you that they launch your way via an "out-of-the-blue" message. They may idealize you, detest you, or something in-between. If you are any kind of authority or parental figure, you are a prime target. These kinds of transference reactions often are deeply ingrained, prepackaged responses in the person that are ready to leap out at any opportune moment. Occasionally I receive email from people whom I call *spoon-feeders*. There is no greeting or name indicated, just a terse request or even a demand for something. Another common transference reaction is the *chip-on-my-shoulder email*. People who have antagonistic conflicts with authority figures feel free to send a flaming email to someone they perceive as a parental figure. In a very different scenario, the person reaches out after perceiving a twinship neediness in the other person, as if saying, "We're going through the same thing, aren't we?" The bottom line with these kinds of unrequested messages is this: You do not have a relationship with them, but they think they have a relationship with you.

In the vignette at the beginning of this chapter, I described the incident in which a stranger from cyberspace asked me what I thought about the media interview with the astronauts who first landed on the moon. His request that I watch the YouTube video seemed somewhat benign, but when I failed to corroborate his hidden agenda – a paranoid need to believe in the conspiracy theory – his rapid retort confirmed for me the power of online transference. In his mind, I was a fearful, insincere person who yields to dominating authority figures while victimizing the weak. Such unexpected, inappropriate comments from strangers is a telltale sign of their transference reactions.

The Other through the Device

Because we experience online others through our communication devices, it is also possible that transference to people interacts with transference to the device. Our attitudes about the communication tool can spill over to, amplify, or be contradicted by the perception of the online other. As an example, let's say that if William perceives the computer as a passive thing to be manipulated – similar to how his father manipulated him – he extends that perception to other people he meets online, treating them as weaker beings to be controlled. If they happen to say something that sounds passive, or if their personality style is indeed a bit passive, William significantly amplifies in his own mind how submissive they seem to be. As a result, his reactions to them are inappropriate. If others do something that grossly contradicts his perception of the computer as obedient, if they act assertive or independent, he reacts with severe disappointment or anger at the perceived betrayal.

So too our attitudes about cyberspace itself can color our perceptions of other people online. As evident in science fiction as well as news stories, transference to cyberspace often takes one of two forms. Some people idealize it as a technology that will save humankind. Others see it as the evil vehicle of our own destruction. How could such attitudes, in their extreme as well as milder forms, not influence how we react to each other online?

WHO IS DOING WHAT TO WHOM?

Just as in the real world, healthy online relationships are those in which we realize how our interpersonal perceptions can be inaccurate. Once we fully understand that the computer, others online, and social media are not our mothers, fathers, sisters, or brothers, we free ourselves to enjoy cyberspace in the ways that we wish, with fewer unconscious strings attached. Other people are other people, not extensions of our childhood memories or ghosts in the machine. Given the complexities of transference, this realization can be a challenge. Psychological reactions to the computer, online companions, and people in general are often a complicated combination of some or all of the types of transference previously described. Mother, father, and sibling transferences interact with each other and change over time. One minute we perceive others as the father figure, then a mother figure, then a sibling, ourselves as the child and then as the parent. When thinking about transference in online relationships, we might ask, "Who am I to you, who are you to me, and how are we treating each other?" Psychoanalytic clinicians ask themselves a similar question when working with their clients in psychotherapy. "Who is doing what to whom?"

Perceiving Your Misperceptions

So how do we know when we are experiencing transference? There are some telltale signs, such as unrealistically intense emotional responses, like shouting into the screen or wanting to throw the computer against the wall. The transference alarm rings when people say that someone "makes them" feel a certain way; when they feel lonely and empty because they have not had enough time to spend online; when they want to be with their communication device more than they want to be with family and friends; or when their family and friends complain about their obsession with the computer, phone, and online companions. Transference rears its head whenever one feels addicted to the computer and online relationships. Such addictions often mean that the person is attempting to use cyberspace to satisfy some strong internal need related to transference, but the strategy never quite works because cyberspace – either the machine itself or the people who live inside it – have become inadequate substitutes for a genuine relationship.

When people who communicated only via text eventually exchange photos, call on the telephone, or finally meet each other, they often are surprised at how the real person does not always match the image they had previously developed in their mind. Meeting face to face challenges and helps correct the transference reaction. In return, the mental constructs we create from our in-person encounters of people then help regulate how we experience them online. We read their text messages and see online images of them through our memory of what they actually are like in the real world. The mental templates we create of people in one online environment also shape how we experience those people in other online environments.

Growing up into a mature adult is a gradual process of realizing how the mental models from our childhood mold our relationships. Sometimes these models steer us in the right direction, toward the right people and activities, thereby enriching our lives. Sometimes they do not. We need to challenge, develop, or outright abandon some of them. In all cases, the enlightening path is to see these mental models for what they truly are: our own intrapsychic templates about how we expect people to be as opposed to how they actually are. As in the quote from the experienced onliner I mentioned at the beginning of this book, we must grapple with the realization that, "Everywhere I go on the Internet, I keep running into ... ME!"

REAL AND IMAGINED ONLINE LOVERS

Contrary to the claims of skeptics who believe that genuine relationships cannot develop in cyberspace alone, especially in the sparse realm of text-only correspondence, people do frequently report how they have found deeply rewarding relationships with their online companions. Because everyone has access to numerous people in cyberspace, that filtering process occurs

in which a person narrows down – based on both conscious and unconscious needs – the range of potential contacts, eliminating those that feel
superficial, unsatisfactory, or irrelevant, then finally selecting someone with
whom to develop a more rewardingly intimate bond. Although transference inevitably creeps in, as it does in all forms of human contact, friendships and even romances in cyberspace became widely recognized as not
just commonplace, but also promising in their authenticity. As one of the
most psychologically powerful forms of human relating, love relationships
in particular afforded cyberpsychologists a unique opportunity for understanding intimacy in cyberspace, including intimacy based on transference.

Early in the history of cyberspace, the exotic quality of an online lover
attracted some people. In the course of human history, using computers was
a very novel, intriguing way to develop an intimate relationship. Because it
occurred through this powerfully mysterious thing called the Internet, the
love connection felt exciting to some people. It seemed magical to experience the lover's presence entering into your home or office without the
person physically being there. As we moved further along in the history of
cyberspace, especially when online dating services boomed and everyone
became more used to cyberspace relationships in general, the exotic quality
of finding online love diminished. On a more practical level, people were
drawn to cyber-romances for the same reasons they are drawn to in-person
romances: either they do not have a love relationship at the moment, or
there is something missing in their current one. In cyberspace, people hope
to find what they are otherwise lacking. Sometimes, ruled by wishful fantasy
and transference reactions, they delude themselves into thinking they have
discovered genuine love online. And sometimes they actually do find it.

Playing at Love

In their book about online romances, Whitty and Carr (2006) relied on
the idea that cyberspace serves as a realm for identity experimentation.
In online dating sites in particular, people play with love, sexuality, and
the presentation of themselves as the ideal romantic partner, often based
on their own transference needs while also activating the transference
needs in the other person looking for that kind of perfect companion.
The degree to which people engage in such playing at love varies, most
likely depending on the person's susceptibility to idealizing and twinship transferences. Those who go overboard in creating a perfect but
very false persona face the risk of having to "live up to your profile." Or
as Muhammad Waseem said, "I don't miss you. I miss who I thought

you were." To navigate dating sites successfully, Whitty and Carr argued, people must be cognizant of this playing-at-love experimentation, both in themselves and others. They also emphasized how romantic relationships develop differently in dating sites as compared to other online environments, a phenomenon that I would explain by how the various dimensions of cyberpsychology architecture affect one's presence as a real person seeking a real relationship.

Genuine Love

As evident by the many online romances that turned into successful marriages, genuine love indeed can blossom in cyberspace. A great deal of intimacy is possible simply by communicating with someone through typed text, which should come as no surprise given the fact that throughout history love has flourished via letter correspondence. Within the text relationship, some people believe that they are more directly encountering the mind, heart, and even soul of their lover because they are not distracted or misled by physical appearances, as in real life. Of course, there is also much to be learned about someone by seeing them and, even more importantly, by being with them in person. Not only is physical presence an important feature of nonverbal communication, physical contact is a basic human need, an essential element of human intimacy. This is why almost all people who fall in love online eventually feel that they must meet the lover in person. Although some people will wax the poetic about embracing the lover psychologically and spiritually within cyberspace, the truth remains that you cannot physically hold your lover, as the human psyche so desires. In the early stages of an online relationship, cyberspace excels at helping people find potential lovers who share compatible interests and personalities, but later on the relationship develops more fully when they join together in the physical world.

Preferring a Fantasy Lover

There are some people who never want to meet the online lover face to face. In these cases, people might prefer living with the fantasy that they constructed about their companion, a fantasy often based on transference needs. The couple might be collaborating in the creation of mutually satisfying personae that portray themselves in ways quite different from how they truly are in reality. They may not want to meet each other face to face because the fantasy would be destroyed by the hard facts of reality.

Although we might find it tempting to condemn such relationships, who can say whether they are inherently wrong or dangerous? Many people afford themselves the luxury of fantasized love, either through books, TV programs, or movies. Most people do not confuse this fantasy with reality. In some cases, cyber-love might indeed become a pathological self-delusion that ultimately leads to disillusionment, disappointment, and hurt. For others, it serves as a mutually accepted fantasy, almost like a game, only much more interactive and therefore exciting than the conventional methods of indulging in love fantasies.

Inspired by the title of a 2010 documentary, the term *catfish* referred to people who fabricate online identities to trick people into long-term romantic relationships. In the documentary, a photographer eventually discovers that the nineteen-year-old woman that he fell in love with through Facebook conversations, as well as her artistically talented younger sister who amazed him with paintings she sent via email, were actually the fantasy creations of a homebound mother who had given up her career to take care of her disabled sons. Feeling desperate for an escape from her life, she created the paintings and pursued the imaginary relationships with him. To help explain the dilemma, the woman's husband tells the story of how fishermen shipping cod in tanks discovered that adding catfish into the tanks kept the cod active and alive, thereby ensuring their quality. So too there are people in everyone's lives who keep them on their toes, thinking, energetic, feeling. The woman needed her fantasy selves to hold onto a zest for living, but the photographer also needed those fantasies to feel alive through the mystery of romantic love in cyberspace.

Cybersex

That most lovers will prefer the physical intimacy of an in-person encounter does not negate the possibilities for online sexuality. Being the inventive creatures we are, humans have found ways to have sex via cyberspace ever since the invention of the Internet. At first, erotic encounters involved sexy discussions via text messages, what came to be known as *sexting*. Soon thereafter, sexting incorporated sexual images, including nude or partially nude self-portraits that fell under the more general category of what people later called "selfies." Cybersex via audio communication was also an option, not unlike traditional phone sex, later to be followed by sexual video trysts. By undressing and manipulating avatars in computer-generated graphical worlds, people could also conduct erotic acts with each other in visually imaginative styles, bodies, and locales. The limitation of these activities was that partners could not physically stimulate each other, a handicap overcome by the fact that, as one person told me, "I've gotten good at typing with one hand." With the invention of such technologies as *teledildonics* – sex devices that can be controlled remotely by a partner via the Internet – the physical dimension of cybersex entered a new realm where erotically stimulating sensations could be transmitted between lovers. Any of these forms of cybersex might appeal to romantic partners who are separated by distance or prefer to avoid in-person sex, either due to physical handicaps, anxiety about physical intimacy, or worries about sexually transmitted disease. Lovers who want to explore sexual fantasies often enjoy the flights of imagination that are possible via sexting, in which they are free to describe anything they desire, as well as by using sexual avatars in erotic online locales where they are not restricted by the limitations of a real physical environment, body, and identity. There can be no doubt that computers and mobile devices, among all their other functions, have also turned into very powerful sex toys.

Futuristic Online Romances

What might we predict about online romances in the future of cyberspace? If we assume that people will want to keep a comfortable distance, at least at first, or that they want to allow ample room for fantasies created inside their own heads, then communications systems based mostly on text will endure as a viable option. If we assume that lovers will want the fullest possible sensory experience of each other, we must consider how, as I will discuss in Chapter 14, "Synthesized Realities and Synthesized Beings," the construction of online environments can follow two distinct paths. The first will be very sophisticated imitations of real-world interactions that employ visual, auditory, spatial, and tactile technologies. Appearing and sounding as they actually do, lovers stroll together through a park just like the real thing. In the second, more intriguing scenario, people will interact with each other using similar technologies that emphasize the sensory dimension, but in sophisticated environments that stretch the identity and reality dimensions into the realm of imagination. Adopting the appearance of their favorite movie stars, lovers travel together to a distant, exotic planet. Less sophisticated versions of these two scenarios already exist in the form of video conferencing versus imaginary avatar worlds. They represent two alternative but not mutually exclusive needs: to truly know each other and fall in love by discovering who they are in the real world, and by discovering who they are through their shared fantasies.

THE HE THAT PLAYS A SHE: GENDER SWAPPING

Brad first met Natalie in a text-based fantasy game. He was a college senior at an Eastern university, she a junior on the West coast. They got to know each other better by corresponding through email. Over time, he felt very close to her. Maybe, he thought, he was even falling in love. When he finally suggested, then insisted, that he give her a phone call, the truth came crashing down on his head. Natalie confessed to being a fifty-year-old man.

Our identities are rooted in our physical bodies, with gender being one important feature of that mind/body correlation. In the evolution of our biological and psychological selves, what could be a more basic issue than gender? And what could be a more intriguing phenomenon concerning gender than people who want to change theirs?

Cyberpsychology has joined forces with traditional studies of gender by showing how some people need to push beyond fixed stereotypes about male versus female. One benefit and sometimes misfortune of cyberspace is how it provides the chance for people to experiment with their male/female identity, regardless of their physical bodies. In a text-only environment, the first step is simply to change one's username. Highly visual habitats such as avatar communities, as well as social media that include profile pictures, offer the additional challenge of creating an opposite sex avatar or photo to represent visually the newly gendered self. The choice of name and picture create the initial impression one wishes to cast: Bambi wearing skimpy lingerie; Rocky with sunglasses; Sheila in leather and chains; Lyle playing guitar; Hera in a long, white robe. After selecting a new name and appearance comes the more challenging task of trying to play the role of the opposite-sex person.

Gender swapping in cyberspace is quite commonplace (Zaheer & Griffiths, 2008). Everyone familiar with life online has heard about or even experienced the kind of dilemma faced by Brad. Based on what I have seen, it seems that more males switch gender than females, a conclusion confirmed by some research studies on role-playing games. If this accurately reflects the population of cybercitizens as a whole, why are males so interested in experimenting with a woman's identity? The answers go far beyond cyberspace. They point to larger social-psychological issues, including needs based on transference. The following sections present a few possibilities that have been suggested to me by people I interviewed.

To Develop One's Femininity

Due to the pressure of cultural stereotypes, it is difficult for some men to explore within themselves what society labels as feminine characteristics, such as being emotional. These males rely on the anonymity of cyberspace to express their feminine side that they otherwise hide. Some of these males strongly identify with women.

To Attract Attention

Adopting a feminine role can be quite effective in drawing more attention to oneself, especially from males in a male-dominated environment. Getting noticed is not always easy in distracting or busy places. Displaying a female name and/or picture, especially an enticing one, makes a person stand out. The gender-switched male might even enjoy the feeling of power and control over other males that goes along with this switch.

To Understand Male/Female Relationships

Some males adopt a feminine identity to investigate how males and females respond to each other. They test out various ways of interacting with males in order to learn, firsthand, what it is like from the woman's point of view. Hopefully they use that knowledge to enhance their relationships with females. By contrast, some look for ways to gain power and control. In online games where participants assume imaginary identities, being a female might be advantageous. Sometimes males lend more assistance to females, so they progress faster in the game.

To Explore Homosexual or Bisexual Feelings

Disguised as a female, a male looking for intimacy, romance, or cybersex from another male might be acting on conscious or unconscious homosexual feelings. Transsexuals – people who feel, psychologically, they are the gender opposite to their biological sex – might also feel drawn to online gender switching, as might transvestites who crossdress for sexual arousal or as an identification with females. In more rare cases, gender swapping could be a sign of gender confusion, a psychological disorder in which a person's identity as a male or female has not fully developed. Early in the history of cyberspace, when many users were male, one reader of my online article about gender swapping offered this comment:

> I think I can sum up a factor about genderhacking by repeating a line I saw someone type in a chat room once: "Won't someone at least pretend to be female?" Lets face it, the majority of users of the Internet are still male, and in such an ambiguous environment as the Internet, the ability to lose one's inhibitions is quite strong. With a great many horny computer nerds out there, and no counterpart women on the net, I think some men pretend to be women – not because they have any desire to have sexual experiences with men themselves, but because they wish to perpetuate some form of cyber experience. It is as if they are an actor, manipulating the puppet of a women (just as they might in their own mind, during a sexual fantasy) but in this case, they are sustaining the puppet for some other stranger at the end of another modem to play with. Once this cyberstory then exists, it doesn't really matter who wrote the woman's lines or who wrote the man's. For both can enjoy it from whatever perspective that they choose.

Wanting or trying to switch gender is by no means a new social phenomenon. Theories in psychology abound on this topic. As Anselmi and Law (2007) demonstrated in their book *Questions of Gender*, the influence of "male versus female" on one's sense of self is complex, illusive, and at times paradoxical. In the long history of gender experimentation, the online version of it is unique because cyberspace makes it so easy. It provides a conveniently attractive opportunity to experiment, abandon the experiment if necessary, and safely try again, if one so desires. More people experiment with gender switching online than in the real world. Cyberspace provides researchers with an unprecedented opportunity to study how and why people flip the male/female switch.

Unfortunately, the wide latitude for online gender swapping also makes situations like those of Brad much more common. Even though exploring the anima/animus of the human psyche can be enriching, healthy, or just plain fun, hurting other people is not an acceptable outcome. There is a very thin line between the right to experiment with one's gender and violating the rights of others by deliberately deceiving them. At some point in an online relationship, in order to protect their feelings and even their sanity, people sometimes find it necessary to test the companion to see whether that person is faking gender.

THE SHE WHO PLAYS A HE

One reader of my article about gender switching – a "straight, happily married mother" – emailed me to say that it validated many of her own experiences in cyberspace. She had participated in fantasy role-playing, except she was a woman assuming the persona of a man. She only played the roles for a short period of time, usually one evening a week. "I found the characters tiring to keep up and had to stop. Usually I found myself shifting into a feminine, softer mood and had to quit before I got my character in serious trouble. I got too empathic and too flirtatious with males buddies. I knew my cover was slipping and my true proclivities leaking out and so I had to kill the character." She listed a number of reasons why she played those male roles:

To Find Out How Other Females Act with Men

This was partially competitive and sexual on her part, she noted. "How do other women entice men? Are the other women better than me at it?" She usually concluded that this was not the case. She felt other women were somewhat "silly and boring." Also, men seemed to have more pressure on them to be entertaining.

To Practice as a Seductive Male

She was interested in romance novels, especially how they are constructed with a heavy emphasis on the hero. The object of the story, she explained, is the capture and/or discovery of the hero, who must be a well-defined personality. In her online gender switching, she experimented with hero personalities to see how they affected women. She felt her character was much more attentive and romantic than the average male. She acted the way she would have liked a male to court her. Her important realization was that the projection of power and competence can be very seductive. "I hadn't truly appreciated how much a guy has to constantly maintain the facade of strength. One slip of weakness and the women crush you like a walnut."

To Run a Clan

In some games, a clan is a group of players who compete with other clans. While some of the clans were led by females, she had difficulty gathering followers as a female persona. Once she switched to a male character, she immediately became more successful in building and running her group. She also discovered that being a clan leader draws more female attention, and that women are very competitive in fighting for the position of the clan master's wife. She found it much easier dealing with the competition from male underlings jockeying for position.

To Experience More Power than in Real Life

As a very quiet adolescent, she felt dominated by strong-willed boyfriends, which affected her development in ways she was still trying to understand. "Donning a male identity allowed me to freely express certain aggressive and powerful actions that I don't seem able to project when perceived as a female. I say perceived, because this was all about how others saw me. All during the time, I felt like myself and female. It was just the male side of me that I was allowed to show, but had always been there." Here it is interesting to note a finding by Huh and Williams (2010) in their research on gender swapping in an online game. Men who played female characters did not act in stereotypically female ways, but women who played male characters did display a degree of hypermasculine behavior. When considering the various opportunities for power that explain why females gender-switch to males, we might consider what Oscar Wilde once said:

> Women have a much better time than men in this world;
> there are far more things forbidden to them.

Another reader of my article who contacted me described what happened when she adopted the username "The Doctor" in a chat room. She originally intended it to be gender-neutral. Consistently, however, she was judged to be male, forcing her to correct her companions' perceptions. The perception was so persistent that she herself came to think of the handle as a male persona. On one occasion, when she initiated what she felt was a very benign gesture toward a vulnerable female teenager, the girl instead interpreted her behavior as the advances of a "dirty old man." This unexpected reaction suddenly reversed her own perception of what she had done. She was as horrified as she would have been if she had witnessed some dirty old man acting sleazy toward a young girl. She instantly dropped "The Doctor" as her primary username. The only times she reverted to it were when she felt hurt or vulnerable in an online relationship. The more intellectual, male persona helped her gain distance, objectivity, and clarity, "to get my head together when my heart was feeling shattered." Why she adopted a male persona to accomplish this is, as she put it, "a mystery of socialization in a patriarchal society."

> "He" was much shyer than my normal real or cyber self, if also older, and presumably wiser, and I could often see him in my mind's eye, wiping his glasses, which I also do not wear, as he hovered as observer on the fringes of a chat, before committing himself to considered opinion. This is very unlike my primary (Aries) identity, which tends to jump in first, boots and all, and ask questions, and, if necessary, apologize for tactlessness later! I wonder if I am an oddity, or are there other women out there who use male personae for similar reasons? I see "The Doctor" as a little like your (John Suler's) grey owl avatar at the Palace! But this could also be interpreted as a wholly feminine image, i.e. the grey owl of the goddess Athene!

Eventually, she felt she did not need "The Doctor" anymore. She learned that when she felt threatened or vulnerable, she could simply retreat into a lurking mode as a way to get the same effect. Even with what she regarded as a "feminine-enough" username, many males still assumed she was male, which she attributed to the fact that as a strongly opinionated woman, she seemed to be expressing her own inner masculine energies. "However, it does serve as a handy weapon, when they think they have me all sewn up, to come back with, 'All that may or may not be true, but you at least have got the sex entirely wrong,' usually accompanied by a protruding tongue, as in playground battles!"

RESOLVING ONLINE CONFLICTS

Some of the ideas I described so far about online relationships imply that they might easily go awry. What begins as a small difference of opinion or misunderstanding can escalate into a bigger controversy, so much so that early in the history of cyberspace people invented special terms for it: *flaming* and *flame wars*. What is it about online communication that seems to ignite these blazes and make them difficult to put out?

The lack of visual and auditory cues in text communication often contributes to the misperceptions that culminate in conflict. When we cannot see those facial expressions and body language, or hear the tone of people's voices, what we think the person means, especially when they use ambiguous words, is left up to the imagination of our transference tendencies. Someone saying, "Do you understand?" while shouting and jabbing a finger at you comes across very differently from speaking those words with gentle kindness. In text communication, you cannot see that distinction. All we have are the words on a glowing screen and how we hear those words in our head. "There is a lot of miscommunication in text," one of my students commented in a survey. "Most of the time I find it hard to share how I truly feel because there is no way to show my face, or the sound of my voice. The smileys don't do it for me."

Although people who know each other well have a better chance at avoiding such misunderstandings, even they might fall into arguments online that would not occur in-person. Sarcasm is particularly problematic because it relies heavily on subtle voice cues. Even when people know that someone tends to make sarcastic remarks, they can easily misread it as genuine hostility in text conversation. As a rule of thumb, avoid being sarcastic in cyberspace.

Transference reactions – along with any tendency to project our expectations, needs, and feelings into the way we perceive others – influence our interpretations of almost all interpersonal situations, but especially ambiguous ones as in text communication. How we hear the voice of the other person inside our heads says as much about us as it does about the other person. When people anticipate criticism, that is what they will see in an email from their boss. If someone feels rejected, a very terse email from a friend seems to confirm that emotion. People with effective writing skills combined with psychological maturity will succeed more often at clearly communicating their thoughts, while people with effective reading abilities along with psychological maturity will more often accurately decipher an ambiguous message. However, even under ideal conditions the power of transference and projection can override the best of efforts.

The online disinhibition effect contributes to interpersonal battles, in part because it tends to encourage transference and projection. When people become disinhibited through anonymity, invisibility, and equalized status, the thoughts and feelings that surface often are unleashed hostile ones that generate conflict. Solipsistic introjection accounts for the angry voices people hear inside their heads as they read a seemingly negative text message. While asynchronicity allows for an "emotional hit and run" in text messaging, dissociative imagination might lead people into mistakenly believing that the conflict with another person is just a game, not to be taken too seriously, even though the other person might take it very seriously.

Recognizing these ingredients of miscommunication that lead to hostility in cyberspace, Kali Munro (2002), an experienced online psychotherapist and member of the Clinical Case Study Group of the International

Society for Mental Health Online, proposed several tips for resolving online conflicts:

Do Not Respond Right Away

When you feel hurt or angry about a message, do not respond immediately. Your first reaction to a message or post is affected by how you are feeling at the time. You might compose a reply to give expression to your thoughts and feelings, but do not send it. Take advantage of asynchronous communication. Wait until the next day – what I call the *Mañana Principle* or the *24-hour rule* – so you get a chance to sleep on it. Then reread the messages – theirs and yours, if you composed one – before you consider sending a response. Some people take advantage of the zone for reflection offered by the Mañana Principle. Others, acting more spontaneously or impulsively, do not.

Read the Message in Different Voices

Reading a message later, and a few times, can give you a new perspective on it. You might even experiment by reading it with different tones (matter-of-fact, gentle, noncritical, etc.) to see whether could have been written with a different attitude than the one you initially heard.

Discuss the Situation with Someone Who Knows You

Ask people what they think about the message and the response you plan to send, ideally someone who knows you well. Having input from others who are hopefully more objective can help you to step back from the situation to understand it better. Try discussing the situation with these people in an environment that is different from the one in which you are having the potential conflict. For example, if it is a text message that is the source of the problem, call a friend or family member or talk to him or her in person.

Choose Whether or Not You Want to Respond

You do have a choice. You do not have to respond. You might be too upset to respond in the way that you would like, or it may not be worthy of a response. If it is an accusatory or inflammatory message from a person who tends to be aggressive or bullying, the best strategy might be to ignore that person.

Assume Good Will

Assume that people mean well, especially with people you know, unless they have a history or pattern of deliberate aggression. Everyone has bad days, gets triggered, reacts insensitively, and writes a message without thinking it through completely. It does not necessarily mean that they lack good intentions. Due to your transference reactions, projections, and bad days, you might be the one who is reacting inappropriately.

Beware of Trolls and Bullies

Some people are mean and pick fights no matter how kind and patient you are with them, behavior that was traditionally called *trolling* but also falls under the category of *bullying*. They distort what you say, quote you out of context, criticize you, and make all sorts of accusations with the purposeful intention to antagonize, demean, and vilify you. Do not take the bait by engaging in a struggle with them because they will never stop. Sometimes the best strategy is to ignore and avoid them. If necessary, report the incident to authorities.

Clarify What the Person Meant

Due to transference, projections, and bad days, we all misinterpret what we hear and read, particularly when we feel hurt or upset. It is a good idea to check out whether you understood people correctly. Ask them what they meant when they said something that felt upsetting. Often what we think someone said is not even close to what that person actually intended. Give people the benefit of the doubt, the chance to be clear about what they are thinking and feeling.

Think about What You Want to Accomplish

Consider whether you are trying to connect with this person, understand him or her better, or be understood yourself. What is the message you hope to convey? What is the tone you want to communicate? Think about how you can accomplish those goals in what you say. For example, you might say such things as, "I want to understand what you mean.... I feel hurt by some things that you said.... I want to talk about it in a way that we both feel heard and understood.... I want to find a way to work this out.... I know we don't agree about everything, and that's okay.... I hope we can talk this through, because I really like you.... I don't want to be argumentative or blaming."

Use "I" and Feeling Language

As illustrated in the preceding examples, use "I" language to focus on your experience rather than blame the other person, which will only escalate the situation. Feeling statements also clarify how you felt hurt, sad, scared, angry, happy, guilty, remorseful, and so on. For example, rather than saying that the other person attacked you, state that you felt attacked.

Choose Your Words Carefully

Do so especially when you are upset. You are not physically present with the other person to clarify what you meant. During text communication, he or she cannot experience the kindness in your eyes or voice. People must rely entirely on your words to interpret your meaning, intent, and tone. You can still be real and honest while being selective about what you say.

Place Yourself in the Other Person's Shoes

Think about the other person when writing your message. What is his or her personality like? How might that person hear you? To avoid unnecessary conflict and hurt feelings, put yourself in his or her shoes in order to anticipate the various ways that person might react to your response.

Use Emoticons or Images

Given the limitations and ambiguities of text communication, a smiley or a friendly image embedded in your reply might provide the extra bit of information that helps clarify the emotional intentions of your message.

Start and End your Reply with Positive Statements

Say what you agree with, what you understand about how the other person feels, and any other positive statements at the beginning of your message. This helps set a constructive tone. End on a positive note as well. If you like the person, say so. Having a conflict or misunderstanding does not mean that you now hate that person, but people often forget that reality.

Connections and Disconnections

The elements of the online disinhibition effect that intensify online conflict can also contribute to peaceful resolutions of them. Absent visual and auditory cues, anonymity, invisibility, delayed reactions, and neutralizing of status all free us to express negative thoughts and feelings, but they also free us to try out new, more positive ways to communicate, including genuine attempts to resolve conflict.

According to Atwood and Stolorow (2014), productive changes take place in relationships when we recognize and repair *intersubjective dysjunctions*, which are those situations when a breakdown in mutual understanding occurs between people. You and I simply do not see things the same way. Our experiences of ourselves, each other, and the relationship are incompatible. Because resolving these kinds of interpersonal conflicts coincides with a deeper knowledge of self and other as well as a deeper relationship, cyberspace might offer many valuable learning experiences in its tendency to encourage misunderstandings that can then be resolved. People disconnect, then reconnect. Intersubjective dysjunctions are part of everyday life, part of who we are and how we come to recognize our individualities. "If you understood everything I said," Miles Davis once commented, "you'd be me."

People differ in the type of online environment they prefer for connecting to others. Depending on who the online companion is, some people like texting, others prefer phone calls, still others rely on photographs. Such differences reflect how they vary in their personalities, lifestyles, and skill sets. This *incompatibility in preferred environments* might lead to a conflict, because if one person wants to talk via email while the other greatly prefers phone calls, each can see the other as not being cooperative or communicative. While some people adapt to their companion's preferences, others cannot or will not, which might indicate an intersubjective dysjunction not simply in how they prefer to communicate with each other, but in their relationship in general.

It is fairly easy to end a conflicted online relationship. Whenever they want, people simply disappear or actively terminate the connection to the other person. As social media developed, people began to "unfriend" or delete a contact with others who hurt or offended them, sometimes even family members and formerly close friends. This negating of the person's presence – even, unconsciously, of the person's very existence – might be the byproduct of an unresolved conflict, such as a need to protect oneself or an act of hostility. Disconnected people might not realize they have been shunned. Even when there is no dissension, when people simply lose interest in the relationship, they can avoid the discomfort of saying their goodbyes by allowing the relationship to fizzle out as their messages become few and far between. The social connection slowly dissolves.

BLACK HOLE EXPERIENCES

In the online version of *The Psychology of Cyberspace* that I first published in 1996, I include in the table of contents a link to an article entitled *The Black Hole of Cyberspace*. When readers click that link, they land on a page that contains ... nothing – just a field of black filling their browser window. The curious visitor who did not immediately click out of the page due to an unfulfilled need for instant results, but who instead scrolled downward, discovered the beginning of the actual article:

> So what crossed your mind when you first landed on this page and saw nothing? Were you a bit confused, frustrated, annoyed – not sure what was happening, or where you were – maybe for just a split second? Did you doubt yourself, maybe thinking you had made a mistake with your browser? Or did you doubt me, thinking I had made an error in designing this page? Maybe you guessed I was intending to play some kind of trick on you. Maybe you weren't sure.

This is one type of *black hole experience*: those moments in cyberspace when we do something but receive nothing. There is no reaction; no feeling of having an impact or presence; not even an error message. It is as if our intentions were completely gobbled up by some mysterious beast akin to those pits in outer space that swallow anything that comes their way, letting nothing escape. The black hole completely defies what everyone praises about computers: interactivity. In the black hole, there is no interactivity. It is just you and the yawning void. The black hole yanks the interactive dimension out from the cyberpsychology architecture, so all the walls go tumbling down.

It can surface in many forms. The definition might include scenarios in which the machine itself has clearly failed, as when turning on the device only to be greeted by a blank screen, or when clicking a button that is supposed to do something but does nothing. The device crashes. These scenarios might easily activate the transference reactions we often have to the machine as the parent or companion who is supposed to react to us, but does not. It is the dilemma of the neglected child.

Other black hole experiences surface in the social dimension, in our online relationships. You discover that a person who was a contact or friend in your social network is no more. Did they deliberately disconnect you? A more common and perplexing situation is when you send an email or text to someone but receive no reply. So what happened when you pressed the button that supposedly delivered your message, with the electrons you personally configured flying out of your device into cyberspace – and then hours, days, or weeks go by with no response from the other person? What happened to your message? You do not know for sure. You might never know. Even the most sophisticated network guru could only suggest possibilities. It is a complete uncertainty that would make even Heisenberg's head ache.

This is the critical psychological feature of the interpersonal black hole experience: uncertainty, including the uncertainty as to whether the problem is interpersonal or instead mechanical. That ambiguity gives rise to many questions, self-doubts, and second-guessing. Did the message get lost somewhere in cyberspace? Should I resend it, or would that just annoy him, or make her feel guilty, or put pressure on him, or make me look like I am overly eager? Did the message indeed get to her, but she has not read it yet? Or it was accidentally deleted, filtered into junk? Maybe he is away on vacation. Maybe she has lots of messages and failed to spot mine. Am I that unimportant that he would read all those other messages before mine? Maybe she is in trouble or hurt! Maybe he did read it but has not had time to reply. But why not? Don't I deserve a timely reply? I'm busy too, you know. Maybe she is mad at me. Did I write something that would make him that angry? Or maybe she wants to keep me sitting on the edge of my seat. Maybe he is just toying with me. How dare she! Did I forget to send the message? I better check my device.

The black hole is the quintessential projective test, like Rorschach's inkblots. It draws out whatever is on our mind – a blank screen onto which we project our anxieties, worries, and insecurities. It is the ultimate arena for transference reactions. Deciding what to do about the unrequited message requires that we grapple with and resolve these projections and transferences. But at least the inkblot looks like something. The black hole has no texture, color, or shape. It is completely formless. It might surface unpredictably, which grates against the intrinsic human need for some consistency, especially in our relationships. It is not giving us what we need to feel connected, empowered, and grounded. At a deep unconscious level, it might even stir up primitive fears of being negated or engulfed.

In many cases, when we finally do get the reply along with an explanation, we realize our worries and anxieties were unjustified. We have the opportunity to see them for what they are and how they reflect our attitudes about that relationship. The lack of response from other people might have involved no negative intentions at all on their part. Otherwise, in a more unfortunate scenario, the lack of response might indicate their indifference about the relationship, guilty avoidance of you, or the hostility of people with passive-aggressive personality, who hold back on responding as a way to express anger, without realizing what they are doing. Under ideal conditions, if toxic emotions did motivate someone to delay his or her reply, those feelings can be aired and the problem worked through. In rare cases, we never get a reply from someone, which leaves us hanging on, in that black hole, indefinitely.

7

Text Talk

There is creative writing as well as creative reading.
– Ralph Waldo Emerson

I had been wandering around the Internet for a while, but this was my first time in America Online (AOL). I sat back and wondered what I should do there first. There were all those discussion boards devoted to topics that I enjoyed, such as psychology, of course, but also Eastern philosophy, martial arts, and music. But maybe the first thing I should do was send an email to my friend and colleague Rick, the only person from my real life who was also online. AOL was easy to use, but I wasn't exactly sure how to compose my message. Like a regular postal letter? I told him how I had decided to join America Online, that this was my first email, and I clicked the Send button. About half an hour later, he replied, welcoming me aboard. Amazing! I had just carried on a conversation with a friend using mail, but without envelopes, stamps, the U.S. postal system, or a delay of at least several days. It was all happening inside my computer, right now, inside this thing called "cyberspace."

A NEW KIND OF RELATIONSHIP

In the course of human history, the written word emerged as a powerful technique for communicating across distances. In addition to books and other types of manuscripts, personal letter writing between individuals dates back to antiquity. Publishing houses and modern postal systems expedited text communication, but the advent of the Internet raised the game to a whole new level. Not only did cyberspace enable more people to communicate using text quickly, efficiently, and across time and space, it also led to unique styles of talking among individuals and groups. Some researchers refer to it as *text speak* or *computer-mediated communication*, while I prefer the term *text talk* because it implies both an individual's attempt to communicate as well as conversation among people. More so than ever before in human history, we have entered a prolific age of text-driven relationships, even though we now take it for granted. For these reasons, I include text in its own category as one of the eight dimensions of cyberpsychology architecture, and have devoted this chapter to it.

TEXT TALK SKILLS, STYLES, AND ATTITUDES

Similar to speaking, text talk is both a skill and an art, yet it is also quite different from speaking. Proficiency in one does not guarantee success in the other. A person's ability to communicate effectively via text obviously depends on writing abilities. Because people who hate to write or are poor typists will most likely avoid text communication, self-selection shapes the population of text-talking people. Those who enjoy it take delight in words, sentence structure, and the creative opportunity to craft subtly exactly how they wish to articulate their thoughts and moods. During asynchronous communication, they enjoy that zone for self-reflection where they ponder different ways to express themselves. This asynchronous text talk is usually a less spontaneous form of communicating than speaking in person and online synchronous communication, such as chat and real-time text messaging. Unlike verbal conversation – where words issue forth and immediately evaporate – writing also places one's thoughts in a more visible, permanent, concrete, objective format. An email or text message is a tiny packet of preserved self-representation that we launch off into cyberspace. Some people see it as a piece of themselves, a creative work, a gift sent to their online companion. They hope or expect it to be treated with understanding and respect.

People also differ in their reading skills. Some are more sensitive than others in detecting the meaning and mood expressed "between the lines" of text talk. This is a type of interpersonal empathy unique to text relationships. It entails an aptitude not simply for a rational understanding of what was written, but for a deeper intuitive sense of the underlying needs, feelings, and motivations embedded in the text.

The quality of a text relationship relies on these writing and reading skills. The better people can express themselves through writing, the more they understand each other so the relationship can progress. Poor writing and reading abilities lead to misunderstandings, transference reactions, and possibly conflicts. A disparity in writing ability between people can also be problematic. The equivalent in face-to-face encounters would be one person who is very eloquent and forthcoming, talking to another who speaks awkwardly and minimally. The loquacious person eventually may resent putting so much effort into the encounter while taking all the risks of self-disclosure. The quiet one may feel controlled, ignored, or misunderstood. As in face-to-face relationships, people might need to modify their writing techniques – even basic elements of grammar and composition – in order to interact more effectively and empathically with an online companion.

We tend to think of writing abilities as a fixed skill, a tool for expressing oneself that is either sophisticated, unsophisticated, or something in between. It is also possible that the quality of one's writing interacts with the quality of the online relationship. As a text relationship deepens – and trust develops – people tend to open up to using more expressive language. They become more willing to experiment, take risks, not just in what specific thoughts or emotions they express, but also in the words and compositions used. The companions develop their own private language of abbreviations, symbols, and phrasings. Writing style can advance when people feel safe to explore; it regresses when they feel threatened, hurt, or angry. Those changes reflect the developmental shifts in the relationship. Writing is not just a tool for developing the text relationship. Writing affects the relationship, and the relationship affects the style of the writing.

Text Talk Personalities

Concrete expressions, emotional and abstract phrases, complexity of vocabulary and sentence structure, the organization and flow of thought – all reflect one's cognitive and personality style. They influence how people react to each other. The discipline known as *computational stylometry* uses computer algorithms to identify the unique patterns of someone's writing, the text talk "fingerprint" that identifies what kind of person he or she might be. People with compulsive personality styles usually strive for well-organized, logically constructed, intellectualized messages with sparse emotions and few, if any, spelling or grammatical errors. Those with a histrionic flair might offer a more dramatic presentation, where neatness takes a back seat to the expressive use of spacing, caps, unique keyboard characters, and colorful language. Narcissistic people might write long, rambling blocks of paragraphs. People with schizoid tendencies might be pithy, while those who are more impulsive dash off a disorganized, spelling-challenged message with emotional phrases highlighted in shouted caps. Different writing/personality styles can be compatible, incompatible, or complementary to other styles.

A person's past experience with writing also plays an important role in the text relationship. The demand to produce a composition conjures up memories from the school years of one's childhood, sometimes good and sometimes bad. One's self-concept and self-esteem ride on those memories. In the course of text communication, those issues from the past can be stirred up, sometimes filtering their way into the online relationship.

When entering a text relationship, it is a good idea to estimate the companion's skills and attitudes about reading and writing. They very well could be different from your own. What does reading and writing mean to the person? What needs do these activities fulfill? Are there any known physical or cognitive problems that will limit the ability to read and write? In a long-term text relationship, it might even be helpful to discuss these issues with the person. Keep in mind that reading and writing techniques will evolve with the relationship itself. Because synchronous and asynchronous text talk are quite different, we might also determine the online companion's attitudes regarding each. How does the person feel about the spontaneous, in-the-moment communication of chat as opposed to the opportunity to compose, edit, and reflect, as in email?

People have known throughout history that writing is not simply a matter-of-fact communication tool. It offers psychological benefits. When people express themselves in prose, they tap and strengthen a variety of inner resources. Writing encourages the ability to self-reflect; gain insight into oneself; work through difficult emotions; install positive ideas into one's mind; and, especially in longer or ongoing text forms, therapeutically construct your life story, as in journal writing and memoirs. Socially anxious people might appreciate text relationships as a way to desensitize their apprehension so they can build interpersonal skills. Emails, webpages, blogs, and even social media posts can become a form of self-directed psy-chotherapy, true to the spirit of what the psychologist James Pennebaker (2004) called *writing therapy*.

Novice to Pro Text Users

For *avid text users*, their communication device is a major feature of their interpersonal and professional lifestyles. The online world has become deeply ingrained into their psyches, with text talk as an important tool for navigating that world. With a steady flow of incoming messages all day long, they check their devices constantly. It is the first thing they do in the morning and the last thing they do before bedtime, not uncommonly while they are in bed. They adeptly take advantage of the fact that text talk, more so than other types of communication, allows for a multitasking of several relationships. A technical failure resulting in a disconnection from cyber-space is big problem for them. They feel cut off, out of the loop.

Regular text users read and respond to messages, especially email, a few times each day, usually at a prescribed time. That scheduled session becomes a special psychological space in which they leave the face-to-face world to immerse themselves momentarily into their text relationships. These rela-tionships can become a very significant feature of their lives, as with the avid user, although their text worlds do not take on the same continuously ongoing intensity as with avid users. Being temporarily disconnected from cyberspace does not feel like an emergency.

Newbie or *casual text users* do not fully understand the rules of the road. They may breach etiquette, such as by typing all in caps, which is the text talk equivalent of shouting. They do not fully understand the complexities of text communication, or its potential for developing relationships. Some of them might think of it as a curiosity, a toy to play with, or an amusement for leisure time. They might enjoy tinkering with it as a way to establish ongoing connections with family, friends, and colleagues, but text talk has not become an important feature of their interpersonal world.

Difficulties may arise when regular and avid users communicate with newbie or casual users. There might be a disparity in the perceived impor-tance of developing a relationship via text. The avid or regular user expects more frequent, detailed, or expressive messages, but does not receive them. Experienced users quickly recognize this disparity and adjust accordingly. A problem arises when casual users misrepresent themselves: "Sure! I text all the time!" People with psychopathic personalities may toy with or try to take advantage of the naive newbie, while narcissistic people might use the opportunity to enlist the unskilled user simply as a sounding board for their thoughts.

The impact text communication has on your social life increases as you become more intensely involved. It is an upward-spiraling process: the more you email, text message, or post to social media, the more relationships you develop, the more you need to keep going in order to stay connected to your family, friends, and colleagues. With that ever-expanding text lifestyle comes increased skill in composing, reading, and organizing one's messages. You become sensitized to the nuances of text relationships, which makes that interpersonal world even more enticing, challenging, and rewarding.

TEXT TALK IS BLIND AND DEAF

It always helps to keep reminding ourselves that the absence of face-to-face nonverbal cues creates ambiguity in a text relationship that can lead to misperceptions and transference reactions. As a text relationship develops over time, these misperceptions come and go. When we first communicate via text, transference tends to be minimal since we do not know the other person well. We have yet to develop a strong psychological investment in the relationship. Transference reactions surface more quickly when emotional attachments begin to form, but we still do not have a good "feel" for the person due to that lack of face-to-face cues. Peak moments occur when emotional topics come up, but we are unable to pinpoint exactly where the other person stands on the issue. Under ideal conditions, as we spend more time conversing with a person via text, we begin to understand and work through our misperceptions so that we can see the other person as he or she really is. Even under the best of circumstances, some aspect of our mental image of the other person rests more on our own expectations and needs than on the reality of our online companion. We may not even be consciously aware that we have formed that impression until we meet the person face-to-face or talk to them on the phone, only to discover, much to our surprise, that they are in some important way very different from what we expected.

People differ in how they react to the absence of face-to-face cues. For some, the lack of physical presence reduces intimacy, trust, and commitment. Typed text feels formal, distant, unemotional, or lacking a supportive and empathic tone. They want and need those in-person cues. Others will be attracted to the silent, less sensory-stimulating quality of text relationships, as is often the case in social anxieties or conditions such as Aspergers. Those who are ambivalent about intimacy might be drawn to text communication because it is a paradoxical blend of allowing people to be intimately honest while also maintaining their distance. Then there are those people who prefer text because it enables them to avoid physical appearances that they find embarrassing, distracting or irrelevant to the relationship. Without the complications of in-person cues, they feel they can connect more directly to the mind and soul of the other person. Text becomes the extension of their mind that blends with the extension of the other person's mind, that transitional space between psyches. Consider this woman's experience with her online lover:

> Through our closeness, we are easily able to gauge each other's moods, and often type the same things at the same time. We are able to almost read each other's thoughts in a way I have rarely found even in ftf [face-to-face] relationships (only my sister and I have a similar relationship in this respect) .... It is in the cybersexual relationship where the most interesting aspects have developed. We are now able to actually "feel" each other, and I am often able to tell what he is wearing, even though we live more than 6000 miles away. I can "feel" his skin and smell and taste senses have also developed during sexual episodes. I have only seen one very small and blurred picture of this person so I have no idea what he really looks like, but I'm able to accurately describe him. He is able to "feel" me too. I'm sure that in the main it is just fantasizing, but to actually and accurately describe the clothing and color and texture of skin is really something I have never experienced before.

TEXT TALK BENDS TIME

Because text talk falls anywhere along the synchronous/asynchronous continuum, it creates fluidity in how we experience time. In text messaging, we can respond to a person immediately, which generates an atmosphere of being with the person in real time, in the spontaneous now. We can also take can take minutes, hours, days to respond – in email maybe even months – which elongates the temporal feeling of the relationship or even takes it outside the experience of time. If you reply right away, you are engaging, enthusiastic, or impulsive. If you wait awhile, you might appear reserved, distracted, or hard to get.

Due to this *adjustable conversing speed*, the pacing of exchanged messages will vary over the course of a text relationship. This changing rhythm parallels the ebb and flow of the relationship itself. Today you are rapidly texting back and forth in a freeform, spontaneous style, while a week later there are long delays between your messages. Significant shifts in this cadence can indicate changes in one's attitudes about the relationship. As a general rule, the more frequently people contact each other, the more important and intimate the relationship feels to them. Bursts in the intensity of the pace occur when hot topics are being discussed or when recent events in one's life need to be explained. Declines in the pace indicate a temporary or long-term weakening of the bonds between people, either due to a lagging interest in the relationship or distractions from other areas of one's life. Drastic drops in the pace, or an apparent failure of the partner to respond at all, throws us into a *black hole experience.* Is the person's silence a sign of anger, indifference, stubborn withdrawal, punishment, laziness, or a preoccupation with other things? We easily project our own worries into the ambiguous no-reply.

Most forms of synchronous texting entail message-by-message exchanges in which a button is clicked to transmit the fully composed message. In the less common form of chat called *real-time texting,* everything that both parties type can be seen as it is being typed, including typos, backspacing, and deletions. By letting you "see" inside the person's head as you witness their moment-by-moment creation and altering of the message, real-time texting takes the spontaneity of the relationship to a whole new level. In all types of texting, the act of typing does slow down the pace of the interaction, thus making the conversation a bit asynchronous compared to face-to-face conversations. Technical factors, especially transmission speeds, also determine just how closely a supposedly synchronous text encounter approaches the tempo of an in-person encounter. Delays due to busy networks slow down the conversation, resulting in temporal hiccups of several seconds or even minutes. This creates a small zone for reflection, which can be useful, especially in delicate emotional situations.

During synchronous text talk, especially chat and instant messaging, it is not always easy knowing when to wait to see whether the person will continue to type, when to reply, or when to change the topic of discussion. A conversation can accidentally become crisscrossed until both partners get in sync. Savvy people create incomplete sentences or used dot *trailers,* also known as *ellipses,* at the end of a sentence fragment ... that lead the companion into the next message. To allow the other user to express a complex idea, you may need to sit back into a listening mode. In traditional chat rooms, some people would even type "listening" to indicate how they were waiting for their companion to complete a thought. Some people have a better intuitive sense of how to pace the conversation, when to type, and when to wait and listen. They possess an empathic understanding of temporality in synchronous texting.

Many forms of text communication, especially email, can easily be saved. Unlike real-world interactions, we have the opportunity to keep a permanent record of what was said, to whom, and when. Many email users create filters and a special folder to direct and store messages from a particular person or group, thereby creating a distinct space or "room" for those relationships. Some email services automatically save and organize email exchanges into threads that resemble the traditional discussion board. Mobile devices also save conversations with individuals and groups within designated spaces, although people tend to perceive text messages as more discardable than emails. They serve an immediate purpose and are then forgotten. With the exception of emotionally significant messages, the shorter the text talk message, the more likely it will feel like a throwaway item that served only a temporary purpose.

If we have communicated with a particular person only via text, never having met him or her in the real world, we may even go so far as to say that our relationship with that person *is* the messages we exchanged, that these relationships can be permanently recorded in their entirety, perfectly preserved in bits and bytes. At your leisure, you can review what you and your companion said, cherish important moments in the relationship, reexamine misunderstandings and conflicts, or refresh a faulty memory. The archive of messages offers people an opportunity to examine nuances in the relationship as well as how it changed over time. It provides a tangible sense of continuity. "Saving conversations to look back on can be both convenient and harmful," one of my students said in a survey. "Words can be read, bringing back all the feelings involved, for better or for worse." Even in synchronous texting, there is a flow of messages preserved right in front of our eyes, which enables us to participate in the relationship while also backing up to examine ourselves and the other person in it.

People differ in how much of a text relationship they save. The person who saves less – or maybe none at all – might have a lower investment in the relationship. He or she may not be as self-reflective about relationships as people who wish to reread and ponder what was said. People who think of texting or email as superficial, throwaway conversations might create a self-fulfilling prophecy: if they think it is superficial, that is how they use it. Other people simply have less of a need to capture, preserve, or control the relationship. Preferring to "live in the moment," they do not feel a need to store away what was said, which does not necessarily indicate less of an emotional attachment.

When people save only some of the text, they usually choose those chunks of the relationship that are especially meaningful to them: emotional high points, moments of intimacy, important personal information, or other milestones. They are shaping how they want to remember the relationship. Comparing the text saved by one person to those saved by the partner could reveal similarities and discrepancies in what each of them finds most important about their time together. One person might savor humor, practical information, personal self-disclosures, emotional recollections, or intellectual debate – while the other may not. Saving mostly one's own messages, or mostly the other person's messages, reflects a difference in focus on either self or other. The area of significant overlap in saved messages indicates the common ground of interest that holds the relationship together.

Unless we are simply searching for practical information (e.g., a phone number or address), our desire to reread preserved text indicates something significant happening in the relationship or our reaction to it. What motivates us to go back to look at a message – doubt, worry, confusion, reassurance, nostalgia? The curious thing about rereading old text – even if it is just a few hours old – is that it can sound different than it did the first time around. You might see the old message in a new light, from a new perspective, or notice nuances that you overlooked before. It can help reduce errors in recollecting what was said. You might discover that the emotions and meanings you previously detected were mostly reflections of your own state of mind.

LONG TO SHORT TEXT TALK

A wide variety of text formats have blossomed since cyberspace first came to life. True to its concept, e-mail (electronic mail) followed the style of traditional letter writing, eventually becoming so popular that many people dropped the hyphen from its name. Serving as one of the original forms of social media for one-on-one relationships and group discussions, as in the traditional *listserv*, email shared the spotlight with other formats, most notably chat and discussion/message boards. The blog (a truncation of the expression "web log") arrived on the cyberspace scene later, offering a unique chronologically organized sequence of posts by a single author that an audience of followers could read and discuss. Later text messaging via phone offered the novel opportunity for text talk on the go, although the writing techniques of such "texting," as it was later called, date back to the traditional methods of online chat. Based on the concept of the short messaging service (SMS), social media such as Twitter became a popular synthesis of the audience concept in blogs and the pithy interactive text of chat, which is why people referred to them as "microblogs." Although we can point to Morse code as the original form of pithy electronic communication, its service as a social medium paled by comparison to much more prolific and versatile forms of terse text via cyberspace.

We might classify the different types of online text communication along a continuum from long to short forms. Blog entries and webpages tend to be longer, while chat and texting tend to be shorter, with emails usually falling somewhere in-between. How people conduct their interpersonal relationships via long or short form is not determined simply by the length of the message, but also by the fact that the writing techniques differ, sometimes quite dramatically, between long and short forms. As we will see later in this chapter, concise text talk of all genres requires special skills to maximize its social effectiveness, with longer forms similarly requiring their own special skills as well as longer efforts. The fact that shorter forms require less writing stamina contributed to the blossoming of texting as the one of the most popular formats for communicating via typed words. Some people treated it as an art form, like poetry, while others fell to the temptation of letting short form become quick, easy, and superficial. By contrast, the long form, which requires more ongoing self-reflection as one composes the message, might serve as a useful antidote to the symbiotic need for instant feedback that we often see in mobile device texting.

THE ANATOMY OF TEXT TALK NUANCES

Over time, the popularity of the traditional email seemed to fade as cyberspace gave birth to newer, quicker types of text communication, such as texting, social media posts, and the popular microblogging of Twitter. As one student said to me, "My parents do email." However, the reports about the demise of email have been greatly exaggerated. As a mature technology, it is beyond the early phase of exciting newness and now resides in the "plateau of productivity" as described in the *Gartner Hype Cycle* (Linden & Fenn, 2003). According to a Pew Research Center study, email continues to be a primary mode of communication for people in the workforce (Purcell & Rainie, 2014).

Let's take a moment to appreciate the elegant sophistication of the email. There was some wisdom behind the thousand years of evolution leading to the format of the classic postal letter. So accustomed to its structure, we tend to overlook the many psychological subtleties embedded in it.

The body of the message is what most people consider the actual message itself. It is the most lengthy and complex part of the conversation among email companions. The other components of the message are tiny gems of communication that sophisticated email users pay careful attention to when expressing themselves as well as "reading" their text companion. In our analysis of the various features of an email message, we see reflections of what happens in many forms of online text communication, because these other text environments, including social media, often include components of the traditional email.

The Sender's Name

Once people create their username, they usually leave it that way. It reflects the ongoing identity that one wishes to present online. The name chosen might be one's real name, a pseudonym, or sometimes in email a combined name, for example "Bill and Martha Smith." Using one's real name indicates a wish to simply be oneself. It is a straightforward, honest presentation. Pseudonyms are more mysterious, sometimes playful approaches that can express some nonobvious, underlying, or otherwise unknown aspect of the person's self-concept: Onenerveleft, Dreamboat, AngelnotSlut, TheDoctor, Blithering Genius, Urethra Papercut, Julius Sneezer, OttoCad. They may reveal unconscious motivating fantasies, wishes, or even fears about one's identity. A combined name is a way of letting it be known that you have a partner, that the two of you are sharing the account, although it might not always be clear to other people who is actually sending and receiving the messages. For example, I have seen people using a combined name who send extreme political opinions via email without indicating their own name in the message, leaving the recipient guessing as to which person in the couple sent it, almost as if it indicated a symbiotic relationship or an attempt to disguise personal responsibility. When people change their username, it reflects a shift in how they wish to present their identity, perhaps even a significant transition in their self-concept. Moving from a pseudonym to one's real name expresses the wish to drop the "mask" (albeit a meaningful one). Changing the combined name to a single name is a move toward separation and individuation that invites more private, one-on-one dialogue.

The Message Title

The subject line or title of an email, discussion board, or social media post is a tiny microcosm unto itself. Often people use it simply to highlight the major idea contained in the body of the message. Experienced users also understand the more subtle techniques for communicating meaning in their message titles. The subject line can elaborate a particular idea in the message, ask a definitive question, shoot back a categorical answer, joke, tease, prod, berate, shout, whisper, or emote. Sometimes its meaning blatantly or discreetly contradicts the sentiment expressed in the body of the message. A creative application of caps, commas, slashes, parentheses, and other keyboard characters adds emphasis and complexity to the ideas expressed in the subject heading. Here are some examples illustrating these ideas:

HELLO SAM!
And now for something completely different
What should I do?
The solution is ....
Loved it!
Jim! help, Help, HELP!!
Offensive
I'm so impressed (yawn)
Even more/sorry
Thanks for your compliment and support, really!
Please read
????
OK folks, settle down
It's been fun, boys & girls;-)
Apology
&**%$#))(*@#%%$
HUGZZZ
Bob / battles / techniques / bullshit
Sigh ...

In an email archive or discussion board, examining the list of subjects is like perusing the headlines of a newspaper over the course of months or years. It reflects the flow of important themes in the history of the relationship or group.

Even the appearance and disappearance in email of the "re:" as a prefix to the subject line can be meaningful. When people eliminate it and create a new title, they take the lead by updating the heading for the discussion, as if creating a chapter title that announces the next stage in the ongoing story.

It might be an attempt to conceptualize, summarize, and highlight what the person perceives as the most important feature of the evolving conversation. It shows a sense of responsibility and ownership for the discussion, in some cases maybe even an attempt to control it. Simply clicking the reply button without creating a new message title – which results in the appearance of the "re:" – indicates less reflection on the discussion and more of a spontaneous reaction. For how many messages did the "re:" endure? Might it reflect the emotional intensity of the ongoing issue being discussed or simply a passive indifference or inattention to the relevance of the title.

The Greeting

Similar to writing letters or meeting someone on the street, the conversation in email and other private messaging usually begins with a greeting of some sort. Different greetings convey slightly different emotional tones. The greeting sets the mood for the rest of the message, sometimes even contradicting its tone. Over the course of a batch of exchanged emails, the back-and-forth modifications in the greetings turn into a revealing little dance, sometimes playful, sometimes competitive. Who is being more polite, friendly, intimate, enthusiastic, or emotional? Here are some examples:

Dear Pat: This formal opening originated in letter writing. People new to email often fall back on this familiar way to start off a correspondence. Rarely have I seen experienced users begin with "Dear" – except when approaching a stranger or a person of status for whom respectful formality feels appropriate. In most cases, it is a bit too polite for the casual atmosphere that many associate with cyberspace, even when corresponding with work associates.

Hello Pat

This causal, friendly greeting, with a hint of politeness and respect, makes for a very handy, all-purpose opener.

Hi Pat

A slightly more casual, friendlier greeting than "Hello," this is probably not appropriate for the first email exchange with a stranger, unless you immediately want to set the tone of "friendliness among peers."

Hi Pat!/Hello Pat!!

This is a more enthusiastic salutation, almost like hugging or slapping the person on the back. There also can be an element of surprise or delight in the exclamation point, as if you just called the person on the phone and can hear in their "Hi!" how they happily recognize that it is you. The more exclamation points, the more enthusiasm, although a long row of exclamation points might be perceived as phony or contrived overkill.

Pat!!!

This one conveys an even higher level of enthusiasm, surprise, or delight, so much so that only the companion's name gushes forth from one's consciousness.

Pat

This is a very matter-of-fact, "let's get to the point" opening. Sometimes there is an almost ominous tone to this greeting, as if the sender is trying to get your attention in preparation for some unpleasant discussion.

Hey There!

This very informal greeting is usually reserved for friends. Although the recipient's name is omitted, it is assumed that the sender knows it is you.

Greetings!

This greeting provides a possible sign that spam is coming at you, or perhaps a message from a colleague or friend who is trying to be a bit humorous by offering a tongue-in-cheek "formal" hello.

Hi/Hello

Whereas the "Hi" is a bit more casual than the "Hello," both of these greetings lack the intimate touch of including the recipient's name. They come across as a bit flat or impersonal. Commercial spammers, people sending the same message to several recipients, and others who are basically indifferent to who you are will begin the message with this lackluster salutation.

No greeting at all might indicate senders who are passively indifferent, who have included you in their mass mailing, or who lack any personal connection to you. In some messages I have received of this type, I felt almost as if the person perceived me as a machine ready to respond to their needs, with no identity or needs of my own. On the other hand, no greeting can indicate the opposite sentiment. The sender indeed feels connected to you, so much so that a greeting is not required. He assumes you know that it is indeed *you* who is on his mind. Or she never felt like she psychologically left the online conversational space she inhabits with you, so why inject a greeting into the message? In an ongoing, back-and-forth dialogue, there may be no greetings at all throughout a string of exchanged emails. In the face-to-face world, you do not say "hello" in the midst of an energetic discussion. In cyberspace, the same principle holds. Although each email message might be a discrete unit of correspondence that traditionally starts off with a greeting, in many cases it is perceived as a segment of an ongoing conversation.

The Message Body

The body of the message is its most complex component. Messages can vary widely in length; organization; the flow of ideas; the quoting of text; spelling errors; grammar sophistication; the spacing of paragraphs; the use of caps, tabs, smileys, and other unique keyboard characters; and the overall visual feel of the text. The structure of the message body reflects the personality style of the individual who creates it.

A meticulously constructed message tends to lack spontaneity. It is possible to overthink and micromanage it to the point where it sounds a bit contrived. Short messages with some obvious spelling errors, glitches, or a slightly chaotic visual appearance can be a sincere expression of affectionate friendship, as if the person is willing to let you see how they look hanging around the house, wearing an old T-shirt and jeans. Such messages can be a genuine expression of the person's state of mind at that moment: "I'm in a hurry, but I wanted to dash this off to you!" Unless formality is required, the most effective message is often one that strikes a balance between spontaneity and thoughtfully clear expression. In the course of an ongoing text relationship, there will be an engaging rhythm between spontaneity and carefully composed messages that parallels the ebb and flow of the relationship.

Text empathy plays a crucial role in the success of the relationship. Does the creator of a message pay attention to and anticipate the needs of the recipient? Empathic people will specifically respond to what their text partners have said. They ask their partners questions about themselves and their lives. They also construct their messages anticipating what it will be like for the recipient to read it. They write in a style that is both engaging and readily understood. With appropriate use of spacing and paragraph breaks, they visually construct the message so it is easy to read. They estimate just how long is too long. Essentially, they are good writers who pay attention to the needs of their audience. People with narcissistic or impulsive tendencies tend to have difficulty putting themselves into the shoes of the recipient. They may produce lengthy blocks of unbroken text, expecting that their partner will sustain an interest in scrolling, reading, scrolling, and reading for seemingly endless screens of long-winded descriptions of what the person thinks and feels. Paradoxically, the narcissistic person's need to be heard and admired can result in the recipient hitting the delete key out of confused frustration or boredom.

Creative Keyboarding

Humans are curious creatures. When faced with barriers, we find all sorts of creative ways to work around them, especially when those barriers involve communication. Experienced text users have developed a variety of keyboard techniques to simulate vocal and kinesthetic experiences, what some researchers would consider a form of *paralanguage*, as well as a benign example of the *generativity principle*, which is how people find inventive ways to use technology unanticipated by its designers (Zittrain, 2009). Experienced text users' conversations are less like postal letters and more like a face-to-face, physical encounter. Many of these strategies can be traced back to the original Internet chat rooms. They offer an almost infinite variety of creative expressiveness to a text message. In addition to developing skill in these techniques, a person might have to fight or turn off automated correction programs that insist on typing that conforms to conventional prose, which creative keyboarding often does not. Such automated "help" illustrates how some design features of the interactive dimension can unintentionally interfere with effective communication.

Parenthetical expressions entail thoughts and feelings embedded into parentheses or brackets. It is a kind of subvocal muttering to oneself, as if you are thinking out loud, tipping your hand, allowing other people to peek inside your head. The parenthetical icing added to the message can clarify or amplify it, add subtlety, and sometimes even sarcastically contradict the message. There is an honest, even vulnerable quality to such expressions because you are letting the other person in on something that otherwise might remain hidden. Actions placed in parentheses indicate body language, an attempt to convey some of the face-to-face cues that are missing in typed text encounters. Options range from a simple grin, [g], to more complex, personally tailored descriptions as indicated in the preceding examples, sometimes indicating actions that might be impossible for the person in real life (like a backflip). Of course, people have more conscious control over these parenthetical actions than they do over body language in the in-person world. Sometimes it is an intentional effort to convey some subtle mood or state of mind. In a way, one implicitly is saying, "Hey, if there is something hidden or unconscious going on inside me, this is it!" Here are some examples:

Thank you so much! (happy, happy, happy)
That's fantastic news (doing a backflip)
Ah, shucks ... That was so nice of you to say! (blushing)

[feeling insecure here]
I completely forgot! (slapping myself on the forehead)
Hi (yawn) everyone.
I know exactly what I'm talking about (scratching forehead)

Sidebar text, similar to a parenthetical expression, provides a supplemental commentary on a person's post in social media. Sidebars appear in such forms as the *hashtags* that originated in Twitter and *keywords* that were used in photosharing communities. By design, both were intended as a way to categorize or label the content of the post, so it could be found by search engines as well as grouped with other posts of similar content, providing a thread of conversation related to that topic. But people also began using them as a kind of sidebar remark, a subvocalization, an aside, a whispering in other people's ears, or as surreptitious communication with some particular person or group of people, often for the purpose of humor and inside jokes. Even when funny and idiosyncratic, sidebar text often pointed to a universal psychological theme of some sort, something that could resonate with many people. Here are some examples:

#someonepleaseshootme
#Marysdilemma
#anotherbadhairday
– incredible, spectacular, amazing … not -
– hail, hail, the gangs all here -
– if you believe that, there's a bridge I'd like to sell you –

Voice accentuation can be accomplished using caps, asterisks, underlining, brackets, bold type, and other keyboard characters. Exclamation points add to the effect. It is an attempt to mimic the changes in voice emphasis that you might hear in the face-to-face world along with the emotions accompanying that emphasis. Accentuating a **single** word in a sentence sometimes drastically alters its meaning and impact, depending on which **word** is emphasized. Rather than highlighting voice, the last two preceding examples illustrate an *action accentuation*. Similar to parenthetical actions, it expresses physical action, but in a more amplified manner:

I'd love to hear about *your* opinion
I urge you to PLEASE PLEASE PLEASE keep everything you have!
I will **NOT** do it!!!
On the other hand, if it _IS_ true, then we have to do something.
big smoochies

Trailers, a series of dots also known as *ellipses,* can be used creatively in a variety of ways. Usually they mimic a pause in one's speaking. That pause might be applied dramatically, to lead the person into or psychologically prepare them for the next idea, sometimes even a "you might want to sit down for this" warning. Trailers can also simulate a pause to breathe (as in text singing), a transition in your thinking, and a temporary lapse or faltering in your train of thought. The addition of the "um" and "uh" in that one example mimics the sense of confused hesitation in a faltering line of thought. It resembles in-person speech patterns. *Dashes* indicate a transition between thoughts, similar to trailers, but in a more straight-line, darting fashion, as if one is literally dashing from one idea to another, as one often sees in hypomanic personality styles:

> Speaking of which....
> Happy birthday to you.... happy birthday to yooooouuuuu!!
> That's for sure.... On the other hand, I may be wrong.
> I would say that ... um.... uh....
> Wow, what a stressful morning – off now to go shopping – then a
>   quick dinner
> Yep – totally – I'll do it.

Emoticons are faces created from text characters that people usually tag onto the end of a sentence to clarify its emotions. Although creative keyboarders devised hundreds of emoticons, the most frequently used have been the smiley, the frown, and the winky. They can amplify the feeling expressed in the sentence, add a subtle emotional spin to it, or even contradict its sentiment. The smiley can be used to clarify a friendly feeling when otherwise the tone of one's sentence might be ambiguous. It also can reflect benign assertiveness, an attempt to undo hostility, subtle denial or sarcasm, self-consciousness, and apologetic anxiety. The winky is like elbowing your companion, implying that you both know something that does not need to be said out loud. It is also a good way to clarify sarcasm, which people otherwise misinterpret in text communication. Although at first created only via text, emoticons later surfaced as prepackaged visual icons called *emojis* that could be inserted into a message:

> I disagree with you Bill:-)
> I have complete faith in you:-)
> My, aren't we defensive:-)
> Gotta go:-(
> This is really upsetting:-(
> Know what I mean?;-)

We'll show him a thing or two.;-)
He has SUCH a magnetic personality;-)

The *LOL* (laughing out loud) – which originated in chat rooms – has served as one of the handiest tools for responding to something funny without having to actually say, "Oh, that's funny!" It feels more natural and spontaneous, more like the way you would respond in a face-to-face situation. The following sequence of listed acronyms indicates increasing levels of mirth, beginning with the weak, perhaps even perfunctory "lol," then rising up to the unrestrained "rolling on floor laughing" (ROFL) and "laughing my ass off" (LMAO):

LOL
LOL!!!!
ROFL!!!!
LMAO!!!

Exclamation points enhance the effect. Over time, the LOL yielded to the newer generation of *hahaha*s, which mimic the sound of laughing. Increasing the length of the "haha" suggests a bigger reaction, with misspellings revealing spontaneity, perhaps even due to a tiny mirthful disruption of motor control:

Haha
Hahhahahahha

Exclamation points tend to be used much more freely in online text relationships than in traditional and formal styles of writing. Unless the sentiment of the sentence is clearly negative, they lighten up the mood by adding energy, excitement, and enthusiasm. Like spice in cooking, there are dangers of excess as well as omissions. Leaving out exclamation points entirely, as in the first of the following examples, can result in a message that appears emotionally bland, ambiguous, or overly serious. Without even a hint of enthusiasm, some people might wonder if the sender is suppressing some hostility. On the other extreme, too many exclamation points can result in a message mood that feels contrived, shallow, or even uncomfortably manic. A message peppered lightly with exclamations, at just the right spots, can give it a varying texture of energy that helps regulate the reader's reaction:

Hello Sam. I didn't know that you felt that way. Let's talk more about it.
Hello Sam! I didn't know that you felt that way. Let's talk more about it!
Hello Sam!! I didn't know that you felt that way!!! Let's talk more about it!!!

Quoted Text

A useful feature of some email and discussion board programs is the ability to quote what people said in a previous message, usually indicated by colored text, vertical lines, or arrow marks (>) that appear next to the text when you click the reply button. Adding your response at the top or bottom of the quoted message will feel appropriate to your companions when their messages are short. However, inserting a reply at the top or bottom of a long quoted message could be perceived by your partner as something less than thoughtful, as if you simply clicked the reply button, typed your response, and launched it. The person might not be sure what part of the long message you are responding to. Sticking a reply at the end of the lengthy quoted message can be annoying because it forces people to scroll a long ways to find it.

The alternative to quoting the whole message is to select and respond individually to segments of it. Some email programs allow users to place vertical lines or arrow marks next to specific blocks of text they wish to quote. If not, users can manually place arrows at the beginning and end of the segments to which they want to respond (>often like this<). Some people use "[snip]" to indicate that what follows is quoted text. It takes more effort to quote and reply to separate segments of a message rather than the whole thing, but there are several advantages. People appreciate the fact that you put that effort into your response. It makes your message more to the point and easier to follow. It conveys your empathic attentiveness because you are specifically identifying different things your companion said and then responding to each one individually. You are letting recipients know exactly what from their message stood out in your mind. Replying to several segments can create a rich dialogue in which there are several threads of conversation occurring at the same time, each with a different content and emotional tone. For continuity and clarity, several back-and-forth exchanges can be captured by embedding quoted segments, resulting in a multilayered conversation within one message. Here is a simple example of Nancy's email to Sam:

>> I know what you mean, Sam. He said the same thing to me.
> What was your reaction, Nancy?
I didn't know exactly what to say, Sam, but it annoyed me.
>> On a lighter note, we went on vacation last week and had a great time.
> You deserve a vacation, Nancy. Where did you go?
We went to the mountains. It's been a long time since we've been there.

>> Oh, I forgot to ask, Sam, did you get that package I sent you last week?
> Yes, I did, Nancy! Thank you so much. I'm going to put it to use immediately!
You're more than welcome, Sam. Anything for an old friend.

In flame wars, people quote selective fragments of what opponents said, using it as ammunition to launch counterattacks. A series of point-by-point retorts to the quoted fragments verbally slices up one's foes, as if reflecting an unconscious wish to destroy them by ripping apart their messages. The attacker wants to legitimize his or her arguments by appearing to cite the opponent's exact words. The citations supposedly stand as concrete, unquestionable evidence. "This is precisely what you said." Unfortunately, it is very easy to distort meaning by taking sentences out of context, to misread their emotional tone completely, or to cleverly juxtapose several segments extracted from different parts of another's message as a way to draw a false conclusion from that forced composite of ideas. My colleague Michael Fenichel aptly called this a *cut and paste reality*.

Rich Text

Some email and text-messaging programs enable the person to control font type, size, color, centering, left and right justification, and bold and italic styling. These options provide another dimension for expressively formatting the message. Bold print comes in handy for voice accentuation. Color can highlight mood – for example, red text can convey anger while multicolored text shows jubilation. However, as in cuisine, overly rich text can make the reader queasy. A heavy mixture of fonts, colors, styling, and indentations becomes confusingly unpalatable. All creative keyboarding techniques require a light hand, a delicate balance of expressive versus straightforward communication.

Not all communication programs or Internet servers will be kind to rich text creations because they do not recognize the special formatting. A paragraph creatively formatted by the sender appears riddled with meaningless glitches in the reader's window – or that part of the message might simply disappear. Essentially, the machines at both ends – and in between – speak different languages, resulting in these annoying *message translation errors*. Before attempting rich text, it is wise to send a sample message to the recipient, to test out what can and cannot be deciphered correctly.

The Sign-off Line and Name

Whereas the greeting is the way people say hello and sign in, the sign-off line is the way they exit from their message. As with the greeting, the sign-off is a fingerprint revealing the status of the person's mood and state of mind – sometimes obvious, sometimes subtle. "Here's where I'm at as I say goodbye." A contrast between the greeting and the sign-off might be significant, as if writing the email altered the person's attitude. Across a series of messages, the sign-off lines may be a string of repartees between the partners that amplifies, highlights, or adds nuance to their dialogue in the message bodies. The progression of exchanged sign-off lines can itself become an encapsulated, Morse code–like dialogue between the partners. "Sincerely," "Regards," or other similar sign-offs are rather safe, all-purpose tools borrowed from the world of postal mail. They are formal, polite ways to exit. Some avid email users apply them sparingly because they suggest a snail-mail mentality, a lack of appreciation for the creatively conversational quality of email. Here are some examples of sign-off lines that are a bit more revealing of the person's state of mind:

HUGZZ,
take care,
an unusually annoyed,
thanks for listening,
Live long and prosper,
peace,
just my 2 cents,
stay cool,
have fun!
still confused,
looking forward to hearing from you,
enough for now,

Almost invariably, the sender's name follows the sign-off line, which demonstrates how intrinsically connected the sign-off line is to the identity of the sender. Simply otyping your real name is the easiest, most straightforward tactic. If the email partners both belong to the same online community, they must make a conscious choice about whether to use their real names or their online usernames. The online name can be entertaining and revealing, but changing from that imaginary handle to your real name shows a gesture of honestly and intimacy, a kind of "coming out." Creatively playing with your sign-off name is another effective way to express your state of mind, some aspect of your identity, or your relationship with your email companions. Usually this type of play feels appropriate only with friends and family, or it indicates that one wishes to be friendly, disinhibited, and imaginative. Here are some examples of playful sign-off names:

Ed!
Kat:-)
Busy Guy
Sam (aka SupraSuds)
Weary2
BirthdayGal
The Frozen Man
BigBro
Cyberhappy

Leaving out the sign-off line and/or name is an omission with meaning. It might suggest a curt, efficient, formal, impersonal, or even angry attitude about the conversation. The ending could appear especially bureaucratic or impersonal if people insert their signature blocks and nothing else. Friends leave out a sign-off line and name as a gesture of informal familiarity. "You know it's me." They assume that the conversation is ongoing, as in an in-person conversation, so there is no need to type anything that suggests a goodbye.

The Signature Block

Many email programs offer the option of creating a signature file or "block" that automatically appears at the bottom of the message. People usually place factual identifying information into that file, such as their full name, title, email address, institutional affiliation, and so on. It is a fingerprint profile, a prepackaged stamp indicating "who and where I am." What a person puts into that file reflects what they hold dear to their public identity. Some programs offer the feature of writing alternative signature blocks, which gives the person the opportunity to create several different fingerprints, each one tailored for a specific purpose. For example, one may be formal and factual, another more casual and playful, perhaps including a favorite quote. Each signature block is a slightly different slice of the person's identity.

Because all signature blocks have a nonspontaneous, prepackaged feeling to them, people often make a conscious effort to turn the feature off when writing to a friend or family member. You are dropping your status and title while also assuming the person knows your address, phone number, and so on. The first message in which the signature block is eliminated reflects the sender's attempt to be more casual and friendly. As with the sign-off line and name, a change in a person's signature block reflects a shift in his or her identity or in how that person wishes to present that identity.

An Email Makeover

What follows is an example of a "before" and "after" message. The two are similar in the content of what Susan says to Joe. However, the second one employs creative keyboarding, quoted text, and a more visually appealing formatting of the message. As a result, it is a significant improvement over the first version.

Joe,

Quoting text in email isn't hard. If your email program doesn't automatically set up a new message with the quoted text in it, here's a way to do it. Create a new (blank) email to send to me. Copy segments of text from my email that you want to reply to. Paste those text segments into the new email message. Place arrows > < around each segment. Then reply to each separate segment. Have a great time on your vacation. We were supposed to leave for vacation last week, but our car broke down. Something to do with the transmission. It's at the dealers now being fixed. It will probably cost an arm and a leg. But that doesn't matter. You know us. We have lots of money.

– Susan

Hello Joe!

> Working on ideas for the paper together through email is a great idea. My trouble is that I don't know how to insert responses to different parts of your email, like I've seen you do with my messages. I'm such a dolt! <

LOL! Quoting text in email isn't hard. If your email program doesn't automatically set up a new message with the quoted text in it, here's a way to do it:

– create a new (blank) email to send to me
– copy segments of text from my email that you want to reply to
– paste those text segments into the new email message
– place arrows > < around each segment
– then reply to each separate segment.

> Otherwise all is going well here. We're headed to the beach for our vacation next week. We're looking forward to it. We need some time off from work. <

Have a GREAT time!:-) .... (feeling jealous).... We were *supposed* to leave for vacation last week, but our car broke down. Something to do with the transmission. It's at the dealers now being fixed. It will probably cost an arm and a leg. But that doesn't matter. You know us....we.... uh ... (cough) ... have LOTS of money.;-)

hands in holes in pockets,

Susan

Simply Susan
ssmith@newnet.com
"Life without art isn't life."

FROM CHAT TO TEXTING

In my early research on text communication, I was intrigued by the traditional chat environments, such as the original America Online chat rooms and one of the earliest forms of text talk, Internet Relay Chat (IRC). Although they yielded to the domination of large social media, chat rooms later regained some of their former popularity, especially among young people looking for their own place to hang out with peers and still intrigued by the feeling of presence and spontaneity in live encounters. The fact that millions of people downloaded chat room apps for their phones showed that, as with email, the reports of chat's death were highly exaggerated. This style of synchronous text talk originating in chat rooms also endured in the form of real-time online classroom discussions as well as live texting via phone, including group texting. Although the pace of short-form texting can stretch across the synchronous/asynchronous continuum, it resembles traditional chat in many ways.

Chat and texting are an austere, even in some ways pure, form of communication, without sounds, voices, facial expressions, or body language, that takes place inside a very minimalist visual environment. All you see is a downward flow of typed words inside boxes. Some people find that experience too sparse. They feel disoriented, disembodied, and adrift in that screen of silently scrolling dialogue. Other people thoroughly enjoy this Spartan style of text talk. They love to see how people creatively expressed themselves despite the limitations. They love to immerse themselves in the quiet flow of words that feels like a direct, intimate connection between one's mind and the minds of others, as if the others are inside your head, or you are talking with parts of yourself. Without any of the distracting sights and sounds of conventional social media, the sparse quality of chat and texting promises a freer space for the flight of imagination.

The banter in chat rooms and synchronous group texting can seem quite chaotic, especially when there are many people talking, or you have just entered a room to dive into the ongoing flow of overlapping conversations. There are no visual cues indicating what pairs or groups of people are huddled together in conversation, so the lines of scrolling dialogue seem disjointed. You have to sit back and follow the flow of the text to detect the themes of conversation, to see who is talking with whom. Creating mental filters helps you focus your concentration on particular people and discussions by sifting through the background "noise" of other users and conversations. You become immersed in one or two strings of dialogue while filtering out the rest, although your peripheral awareness remains open to noticing other interesting comments. With experience, people develop an eye for efficiently reading group chat. Some people are more skilled at this cognitive-perceptual endeavor than others.

Let's pop into a segment from an ongoing chat room conversation. See whether you can figure out what is happening in this seemingly buzzing confusion. Here are a few hints: there is an intellectual discussion between Symmetry and TipTop; the greeting of a user (YieldNot) whom people have not seen in a while; some mutual ribbing between Avenger and Barney; and a new user (Newbie) who is having a hard time edging his way into this conversation among more the experienced users.

CHILL: good to see JH back
THEBRAT: Why do ya ask ... Chill?
SYMMETRY: my life is out of balance ... this computer stuff is far to consuming
BELLE: good I hate to think you became a woman on me
YIELDNOT: hehe
BANDIT: Its TheBrat!
BELLE: hi JH
YIELDNOT: good to be back
NEWBIE: hello everybody
BARNEY: NO more crotch jokes, Avenger.
CHILL: good to have you back JH
TIPTOP: we don't keep our sanity ... that's the problem!
THEBRAT: ??????????????????? It made no sense ...
SYMMETRY: reading a book about humor and disabilities
AVENGER: I love you too Barney, not.
CHILL: that's yer sister calling
YIELDNOT: thanks everyone!
BANDIT: Hah! Busted JH!
NEWBIE: what's up everyone?

CHILL: I wondered that too:-)
SYMMETRY: my interest in sociology of time and space
TIPTOP: interesting topics!
YIELDNOT: hmmm ...
TIPTOP: I love that kind of stuff
TIPTOP: and philosophy too
YIELDNOT: Chill ... gotta show you my server some time!
SYMMETRY: Interesting ... how cultures think about time
CHILL: having trouble with my typing and log

What I find interesting about these log excerpts is that they are more diffi-cult to understand than actually being there at the time. This is partly due to the fact that during a post hoc reading of a log, you tend to proceed at your normal pace for traditional prose, which is too quick for absorbing the banter of synchronous chat and texting. While online, the lag created by people typing and busy Internet servers forces the conversation into a slower pace. You have a few moments to scan backward and forward in the dialogue while you ponder what to say next. There is more time for those cognitive filters to operate. There is also more time for a psychological con-text to evolve in your mind, a context that helps you follow the nuances of meaning that are developing in the dialogue.

We might expect that the lack of face-to-face cues in chat rooms and group texting, along with multiple conversations occurring simultaneously, would intensify the interpersonal misunderstandings we tend to see in text communication. After searching through my archive of logs, I found no obviously blatant examples of this. Indeed, there are moments when people are not exactly sure what someone else meant. Usually situations involving humor and sarcasm are the culprits, because that smile, chuckle, or wry tone of voice are missing. But these misunderstandings are usually cleared up quickly. An expeditious explanation accompanied by a simple smiley or winky efficiently resolves the confusion. What is fascinating about text talk is that experienced users mostly do understand what others mean, despite the lack of visual and auditory cues.

In and Out of Sync

Due to lag in network connections, messages do not always appear on the computer screen at a steady pace, which causes temporal hiccups in the pacing of the conversation. People also may be fumbling with their key-boarding, typing a long message, pausing to think – but you cannot see that, so it is a challenge knowing when to wait to see whether someone will continue to talk, when to reply, or when to change the topic of discussion. A conversation sometimes becomes crisscrossed until both partners get in sync. Users skilled in chat and text messaging create incomplete sentences or ideas that lead the companion into the next message, often by using trailers (…). To allow the other user to express a complex idea, you may need to sit back into a listener mode. Some chat users will even type "listening to Joe" to indicate their quiet attentiveness.

Staccato to-the-Point Speak

Chat rooms and texting assume a staccato style, including the use of acronyms such as BRB (be right back), which vary from one online subculture to another. Most of the time, people express what they have to say in a brief sentence or two or in sentence fragments. At his typewriter, tapping out his free association of sentences and questions, then studying text length more systematically, the engineer and technology consultant Friedheim Hillebrand determined that 160 characters sufficed to express almost any complete thought for a text message. It became the guiding principle for the short messaging system (SMS), with Twitter emerging as living proof that a complex social media could thrive on just 140 (with 20 left over for the username). As an art form, even as the haiku of text talk, such pithy messages require skill in concise thinking and writing. This crisp style also works well when people are brainstorming or joking with each other, often in what turns out to be a playful game of "can you top this?" It usually does not matter whether people's messages arrive on your screen out of order because no specific logical sequence is necessary. It is more like a group free association with ideas bouncing off each other. As Twitter demonstrated, ideas and relationships between people evolve into clusters. In the following excerpt from a chat room, people are discussing online romances:

> SUSAN: You can make the other person look anyway you want them to
> POLLY: mental love is powerful
> SUSAN: I think the internet is a very dangerous place for some marriages
> JEN: a few friends argue that cyberaffairs aren't a problem to their marriages
> JEN: i think they may be deluding themselves in some cases
> POLLY: if you are looking, you can find love anywhere
> JO: some say cybersex isn't really adultery
> AL: give me ambiguity or give me something else
> WISK: i don't think you can really love someone in cyberspace

JEN: hmm is this the topic we started on?
WISK: until you've spent time with them in person
JEN: can you say "infatuation"?

These terse styles of text talk can lead to either superficial conversation or a very honest to-the-point discussion of personal matters. One does not have the verbose luxury of gradually leading the conversation to a serious topic. Self-disclosures can be sudden and very revealing, with the various features of the online disinhibition effect enhancing the results. In the following excerpt from a chat room, both superficial and very personal conversations occur simultaneously. Sensing the seriousness of Helen's distress, Dan and Diamond try to address it. On the other hand, LostBoy speaks inappropriately because he is unable to detect the seriousness of the discussion, partly due to the fact that he cannot see or hear Helen's depression and perhaps due to his youth or lack of interpersonal sensitivity, a dilemma exacerbated by missing face-to-face cues. Arriving in the middle of the discussion, Yabada also cannot sense the serious atmosphere in the room, which in the real world most people would detect almost immediately. Rather ungraciously abrupt by real-world standards, although acceptable in cyberspace, he decides to leave when he finally realizes what is happening and what Helen wants: an understanding stranger to listen to her anonymous self-disclosures about her problems. It is a need that draws some people to chat rooms.

DAN: Helen, you sound depressed
HELEN: I am forever depressed.
LOSTBOY: If you traveled back in time and killed yourself, you wouldn't be alive now so you could go back in time to kill yourself.
    A paradox!
DIAMOND: I was like that a lot ... now I am doing better thanks to prosaic
DAN: Helen, why are you depressed?
HELEN: my heart hasn't healed from life yet
DIAMOND: I have a family of depressed people
YABADA: hi folks!!
DIAMOND: and ... like I said ... am doing better
YABADA: hi Diamond!
LOSTBOY: Helen, I have no self confidence ... but I never let it get me down.
DIAMOND: hi Yabada
YABADA: I pale to see myself typing this ... but how old are you Helen?
LOSTBOY: Yabada, are hitting on poor Helen?
DAN: Helen, did you just break up?

HELEN: no, he's being very nice
LOSTBOY: I have never officially had a girlfriend before
DIAMOND: I am in therapy now
HELEN: I have a psychiatrist
LOSTBOY: Never been on a date. Never done the hunk chunk
HELEN: actually a good listener is all I need right now
YABADA: Gotta go. See you all later.

Just between You and Me

Quite unlike in-person situations, people can send private messages to another person in a chat room or during group texting, a message that no one else can see. Very few or no messages might appear on your screen, but the room might not be quiet at all. There may be numerous private exchanges among the other people. In face-to-face situations, the equivalent would be a silent room filled with telepaths or people surreptitiously texting each other. In the real world, during a lecture or performance, it has become quite common for members of the audience to talk privately, "telepathically," to each other or to anyone else in cyberspace.

If you are engaged in a private text conversation within a public online or offline environment, as well as conversing openly with everyone else in that space, you will find yourself in the peculiar situation of carrying on dual social roles: an intimate you and a public you, simultaneously. Even more challenging is when you attempt to conduct two or more private text conversations, perhaps in addition to a public conversation. You might be joking privately with Joe, conducting a serious personal discussion with Alice, while engaging in simple chitchat out loud with the rest of the room. This complex multitasking requires *dissociation*, the ability to separate out and direct the components of your mind in more than one direction, the same mechanism that becomes pathologically exaggerated in a multiple personality disorder. It takes a great deal of online experience, mental concentration, interpersonal skill, and keyboarding talent to pull it off successfully.

Deep Text

Texting, especially when we use the word "chat," suggests a superficial mode of relating. Indeed, the brief exchanges in a chat room or in any short messaging system can be something less than deep. But as we have seen in the log excerpts so far, the conversation can also be very meaningful. Despite the staccato style and the potential for buzzing confusion in chat rooms, discussions might be very fluid, sophisticated, and intimate, as in the following excerpt. These three people are discussing whether the Palace avatar community is a "real" community:

> BIGTHINK: do you think Palace is a "community"?
> JOAN: yes i do
> BIGTHINK: question is ... what is "community"
> BALANCE: there are some members that depend on it
> BIGTHINK: but that doesn't necessarily mean it's a community
> JOAN: hmmmm ... interesting
> BALANCE: there are repeated interactions
> JOAN: it's a group of people with commonalities
> BALANCE: certain people care about each other ... look for each other
> BIGTHINK: is that community?
> JOAN: as much as any other "community"
> BALANCE: or more so
> BALANCE: there are "relationships" beyond the sum of the individuals
> BIGTHINK: if people hang out at a bar regularly ... is that a community?
> JOAN: this is not just a bar, BigThink
> BIGTHINK: I'm playing the devil's advocate
> JOAN: ah ... and doing well at it;)
> BIGTHINK: hehe
> BALANCE: some people here call each other, see each other in "real life"....
> BALANCE: help each other, so there are commitments ...
> BALANCE: if that isn't a community, what is?

TEXT TALK GOES MOBILE

Even though the traditional chat rooms declined in popularity, the preoccupation with short forms of text talk did not. People still enjoy its minimalist format, the challenge of creatively expressing themselves given the barest bones possible, and the beauty of a simple, quiet, controlled stream of words in tidy little boxes. That alone has sufficed for ensuring the preservation of text talk derived from traditional chat. But another advancement in technology sealed the deal: mobile devices. The fact that people could travel with their miniature computers to different locales made a very big difference in how people used and experienced terse text talk.

Mobility, immediacy, and immersion became the enticing trifecta of the phone texting phenomenon. Because people had their devices with them all day long, everywhere they went, then felt compelled to report on the moment-by-moment happenings of their lives, to stay in touch with others who did the same. The immersion into cyberspace happened more spontaneously, more frequently, and, as a result, with more disinhibition. The fact that communication devices were literally attached to one's body magnified the feeling that cyberspace is an extension of oneself, bringing human evolution even closer to the concept of the "cyborg." Every experience, thought, and feeling could be shared on the spot, with whomever one wanted. In the ultimate form of solipsistic introjection, friends and family rested in your hand and head from morning to night. The opportunity to send a message at any moment creates a comforting feeling that the companion is always there, always present, which eases the feeling of separation. It allows us to articulate thoughts and feelings in the ongoing stream of our lives, immediately during or after some important event, rather than having to wait for the next in-person meeting. For these reasons, researchers such as Turkle (2012) began to worry that people might not even be sure about their own thoughts and feelings unless they validated them via text messaging with others. As if transforming into telepaths, people could even text talk to each other in the same room at the same time without anyone else knowing.

The Woes and Pros of Texting

A high frequency of texting can lead to problems. Social pressure mounts to respond quickly, to always be available, resulting in stressful multitasking. The impulse to open the message as soon as it arrives is strong, regardless of what else is happening at the moment. Some people feel that if they do not respond immediately, they will be perceived as rude, disinterested, or sadly out of the social loop. Constantly monitoring one's messages and responding as quickly as possible then amplifies the frequency of exchanges, resulting in a positive feedback loop, an ongoing vicious cycle. The social environment created by such text talk can grow unrelentingly nonstop. This dependence on constant contact evolves into a double-bind in which people feel overwhelmed by the continuous demand of staying in touch, but disoriented and alienated when the contact stops. Texting escalates into a relational vortex where messages fly fast, furious, and out of control with emotional outbursts. Messages typed quickly or while distracted result in typos, ambiguities in meaning, and excessive disinhibition that causes problems in one's relationships. Red warning flags fly high when people text while drunk, when driving, and in bed trying unsuccessfully to go to sleep.

Researchers and everyday people alike find themselves dismayed by the urge to sacrifice living in the here and now to the gods of mobile texting. Out to dinner, at parties, or at family gatherings, many people keep their phones very close at hand so that they can respond to the incoming flow of messages from people who are not physically present. Teachers find themselves talking in front of classes where inattentive students stare into their laps, smiling and giggling even though the teacher has not said anything funny. Rather than grappling with difficult, unpleasant, or awkward social situations in person, which is often the most effective method for clearing up misunderstandings and resolving conflicts, people instead take the easy way out by relying on texting to do the dirty work for them, as in the quintessentially unclassy attempt to break up a romantic relationship with a hit-and-run text message. Even the simple phone call may take a back seat to the more controllable, safer, and convenient launching of a typed-out thought.

Of course, it would be narrow-minded to focus only on the problems associated with mobile text talk. Text messaging does serve as a very useful substitute for voice calls and in-person conversation in situations where those kinds of communication are impossible or undesirable. It can be a very functional way to get straight to the point about a matter, and even to deepen a relationship with a short but emotionally expressive message. Who would want to completely abandon the ability to contact friends, family, and colleagues at any time, using a method that quietly and conveniently slips into the flow of the day? The ease of connecting to a significant other anytime and anywhere can alleviate separation anxiety at moments when that relief is sorely needed. In long-distance relationships, especially romantic ones, a text message can create a surprising sense of connection because it feels so immediate. Your companion spontaneously feels present with you. "You never know how a quick text message can make someone feel better," one of my students noted.

While researching websites that offered advice about texting, I found that their recommendations often took into consideration its positive as well as negative aspects. Curiously, many of these sites focused on tips for males in pursuit of females, which suggests that texting plays a very crucial role in the modern mating ritual. The suggestions offered by these websites fell into a few broad categories that address the concise quality and potential ambiguity of text talk in general, but especially the immediacy of mobile text messaging.

Not Too Fast and Not Too Slow

Much of the online advice about texting tries to find a happy medium between pressured versus lackadaisical responding. Respond as soon as reasonably possible; otherwise, people will assume they are being ignored. You will create a *black hole experience* for them. If you have no time to reply, say something like "stuck in a meeting," or "can't talk now, will get back to you." When answering a message later on, a "sorry I just got this" might ease the other person's concerns. On the other hand, do not send too many texts too quickly, which might overwhelm the other person. In the case of a male pursuing a female, it might appear too desperately needy, especially when she is not replying. If she does reply, avoid reciprocating too quickly: follow the *Fifteen Minute Rule*, which even some websites recommend. No doubt, such advice reflects cultural attitudes about successful courting behavior, although the *rule of reciprocity* applies more generally to all forms of text messaging: strive for a balance with the other person in how many and how often messages are sent. Following the *send and forget strategy*, you might also dispense a message, then put it out of your mind rather than continually checking the phone.

The Clear Text Message

Avoid guessing. If a message is cryptic or vague, you might need to wait until you can talk with the person to ask what he or she meant, rather than attempt to clarify it via a flurry of exchanged messages, which can become frustratingly awkward. Do not abbreviate too much, which can create ambiguity and confusion. Stick with terms and symbols that most people are familiar with, rather than trying to create new ones that seem creatively expressive but might only perplex people. Do text sweet nothings to a lover and other messages that simply touch base with significant others. It is an easy, efficient way to reestablish and clarify the emotional connection to the person in what otherwise might be a hectic, multitasking day for everyone.

Beware of Emotional Texting

Avoid angry or rude texting. One might express general frustration with a "grrr" or a "humph" or an "ugh," but pick up the phone, use a video call, or meet in person to work through the situation. Text fighting inevitably leads to misunderstanding and escalating conflict. So too breaking bad news should be avoided via texting, as well as excessive flirting, which can spiral into inappropriate banter that can offend people, attract an unwanted admirer, or unrealistically raises a person's expectations, only to feel hurt later on. In our hyperconnected culture, it is relatively easy to get a bad reputation for any of these unacceptable forms of texting.

DIFFERENT CULTURES, DIFFERENT CUSTOMS

People around the world have different customs for conversing and developing relationships, including text relationships. Some of the ideas discussed in this chapter will be culture-bound. A good rule of thumb in conversing with people from other lands is to be appropriately polite, friendly, and as clear as possible in what you write. Stretch your text talk empathy muscles. Unless you are very sure of your relationship with the person, avoid colloquialisms, slang, humor, innuendos, and especially subtle attempts at cynicism and sarcasm, which are difficult to convey in text even under the best of circumstances. Starting off polite and later loosening up as the relationship develops is safer than inadvertently committing a faux pas, then awkwardly trying to patch up the damage. If the other person says something that feels hostile, insulting, or somehow inappropriate, follow the rule that often turns out to be a very effective, all-purpose bit of advice: assume good will.

8

Image Talk

Pictures must not be too picturesque.
  – Ralph Waldo Emerson

Long before selfies became popular in social media, I and many other members of Flickr, the largest photosharing community at that time, experimented with the longstanding tradition in photography of creating self-portraits. A popular but technically challenging genre was the "clones" self-portrait, which are multiple exposures merged together in Photoshop so that several versions of oneself appear together in the picture. Because I often used photography to illustrate concepts in psychology, I decided to create one to depict Freud's tripartite model of the psyche. Wearing a black shirt, with fists clenched tight, the id version of me stares angrily at the superego version of me, wearing a white shirt, looking complacently self-righteous, with a finger raised in the air. In between them sat the ego-me, wearing a gray shirt, with his hands calmly spread outward, as if trying to make peace between the two antagonists. I thought it was a rather humorous conceptual image, but little did I know that it would rapidly receive widespread attention as one of the most popular photos in Flickr, in fact becoming one of my signature pieces. I was also surprised to see how much it resonated with people, as evident by comments such as these:

Freud isn't dead. He is very much with us just like Newton.
So which one usually gets the better of you?
I hate to think of 3 versions of me – the mind boggles at what each of me would be doing and thinking.
I think we're all Freudians – it's one of those belief systems that no one can get out of their minds once it's learned, like being an ex-Catholic or an ex–Chicago Cubs fan.
The battles within the mind you've so expertly portrayed are something everyone experiences every day.
I've seen this image in my head waaaay to many times. Thanks for visualizing it for me:)
By the way, what is the true me?
And the soul is free of all three.

As Internet connection speeds increased, people no longer communicated by text alone. Visual images became increasing popular as a tool for self-expression. In fact, it was the evolution of the Internet from text-only to text-plus-images that catapulted it from a place inhabited mostly by academics and technology aficionados to a world that encompassed almost everyone. And for a good reason: images capture ideas in ways that words cannot. In imaginary virtual communities such as Second Life, people created complex visual habitats consisting of houses, streets, towns, and cities, complete with furnishings, landscaping, products, and avatars to represent their physical bodies. YouTube skyrocketed to fame as a place where members uploaded videos on almost any topic one could imagine. With the boom of digital photography, people began sharing their visual creations in social networks devoted specifically to images, beginning with such communities as Flickr and Webshots. Even traditional social media that originally relied primarily on text communication hopped on the bandwagon to make pictures and videos a part of their repertoire, which everyone eagerly adopted.

As a highlighted feature of the sensory dimension of cyberpsychology architecture, this shift toward visual communication provided a unique opportunity for psychologists to study interpersonal interactions. At no point in human history was it easier for people from around the world to converse with each other via images. The synergistic combination of digital photography and cyberspace made image talk relatively simple, powerful, global, and intercultural because writing skills and language discrepancies posed little or no obstacles. *Photographic psychology* (Suler, 2013a) is the branch of cyberpsychology that focuses on this aspect of the sensory dimension of cyberpsychology architecture – on how people create, share, and react to images in this new age of digital photography in cyberspace.

INSIGHTS FROM PHOTOSHARING AFICIONADOS

People in all forms of social media can learn important lessons about image talk from groups devoted specifically to photosharing. Much of my research occurred in Instagram, Google+, and especially Flickr, which was one of the first and most popular photosharing communities. Compared to the more all-purpose social media, such as Facebook, people in these photosharing communities were more serious about the technical, interpersonal, and artistic aspects of photography. For a photo to get attention, it was not enough simply to depict an interesting subject. The photo's professional and creative qualities mattered, sometimes a great deal. In Facebook, pictures of food, young couples, people partying, pets, babies, and parents with babies almost always received a positive response, sometimes due to implicit social pressure, for how could you not click "like" in response to a shot of someone's baby? In photosharing groups, these types of photos would not necessarily receive widespread acclaim because people were looking for more insights into photography than simply a "fun" or "cute" picture.

Many of the insights I will share from these photography groups gradually spread to a wide range of people online, because the interest in photography has never been stronger than in this age of digital technology. People want to know how to improve the photographs they share. By learning about the art and science of photography, people can avoid the dilemma of using photographs as a lazy substitute for words. They can evade the temptation to take pictures as a way to sidestep having to recall something with their own memory, so they do not have to notice anything or truly experience what is happening, but simply capture an event in knee-jerk fashion, then proudly display it online. Instead, understanding photography can help them see more clearly, experience things more deeply, remember more fully, and convey their lives more effectively when sharing their photos.

IMAGES VERSUS WORDS

How do images and words differ as psychological experiences? How can images and words enrich each other? These questions rest at the heart of this chapter.

Psychology proposes that language and visualizations are two basic ways our mind manages memories and processes information. Richardson (1969) described them as separate but interacting *verbal and mental imagery systems*. Inside our heads, we often think with words. We indulge in all sorts of internal conversations. In our mind's eye, we also see pictures, as in recalling a childhood memory or imagining some scenario. While language resides in the left side of the brain, complex visual imagining occurs in the right. These two cognitive systems coincide with the two basic ways humans have expressed themselves throughout history: by speaking and writing, or by creating visual images to share. The interpersonal use of words becomes internalized inside our minds as part of the verbal system, while communicating with each other via pictures fuels internal mental imagery.

The verbal system tends to involve thinking that is more conceptual, linear, conscious, and factual. Words are abstractions that refer to things that bear little resemblance to the words. The word "tree" does not look like a tree. We sequence words into sentences so we can communicate a specific series of ideas. That effort of the verbal system requires considerable conscious control. Because we developed language to convey complex ideas and experiences to other people, the verbal system tends to be more concerned with the factual demands of reality that we all together must address. It is the vehicle for expressing practical ideas as well as abstract but useful concepts.

The mental imagery system tends to be more sensory, holistic, and personal. Images easily arouse the senses, including the sensations of sound and touch. They contain individual elements that the mind can isolate, but the mind also reacts intuitively to the impression of the image as a whole. More so than words, mental images can be the stuff of imagination, fantasy, and symbolism. They quickly arouse our feelings and personal memories. As dreams show us, they are easily influenced by the unconscious. Because infants process their experience of the world via images before they learn language, we might even consider the imagery system as the more fundamental method by which the human mind works.

Images enable you to communicate experiences that cannot be captured easily by words or that might in fact be distorted by conscious attempts to verbalize them. They contain symbols that point to things unseen, to deeper layers of the mind. Like dreams, they are highly creative constructions that convey a wide range of emotions, memories, needs, and wishes. We say a picture is worth a thousand words because many ideas can be condensed into a single image, making it a powerful way to express oneself. A photograph or any visual creation can be a concrete, external representation of what you are, fear, or want to be. It offers a seemingly more real, tangible form for internal experiences that otherwise might elude you. "You don't take a good photograph," Ansel Adams, said, "You make it." To which Henri Cartier-Bresson, the master of the decisive moment in taking photographs, added, "For me, the camera is a sketch book, an instrument of intuition and spontaneity."

Most people rely on both the imagery and verbal systems for cognitive functioning, but some people are better visualizers while others are better verbalizers. Visualizers are drawn to and skilled with such things as photography and visual design, as well as mental images within their own imagination. They tend to think visually and prefer to express themselves that way. Their verbal system might not be as fully developed. They might have a hard time talking about images, including their own. They take wonderful photographs without being able to verbalize how they do it or why those photos feel good to them. Instead, they intuitively sense the visual aspects of their surroundings, while also knowing how to capture it effectively. Other people may be strong verbalizers who love conversation, writing, reading, and thinking with words, but they might not understand the visual language of a photograph. They have a hard time creating a good photograph or appreciating one shown to them.

Visualizing and verbalizing can enhance each other as a powerful duo for reasoning, creating, and communicating. Integrating them combines the best of both cognitive worlds, but doing so effectively requires some skill in understanding how images work. We can learn how to create pictures from a verbal concept as well as talk about them in a way that clarifies or expands on the visual experience. Unfortunately, traditional education in many countries emphasizes the development of language skills, but not so much the cultivation of visual ones.

When it comes to visual images, it is possible to talk too much as well as not enough. An image does not necessarily dictate an overlay of language to be appreciated. Some people, especially those of Zen persuasion, would even go so far as to say that attempting to describe the impact of an image ruins it because doing so causes us to lose sight of the fundamentally immediate, immersive, holistic, and emotional reverberations of the visual experience. As the Zen master said to the student who felt compelled to comment on the beautiful mountains surrounding them, "True, but how unfortunate to have to say so." Although verbose commentaries can indeed become boring, useless, or irrelevant to the emotional experience of an image, not talking at all might bypass some important insights. It did, after all, require words to tell that Zen story.

Even though our educational system offers little training in sophisticated skills for creating and evaluating visual images, digital photography has made them very easy to produce, easier than writing a block of text. One picture of a party, a vacation spot, or oneself could say a whole lot more than what most people were willing to describe in writing. Visual material also catches the eye and can be perused more quickly than most typed words. For these reasons, there was a steady trend in cyberspace for people to communicate with more images and fewer words. In many forms of social media, especially those devoted specifically to photosharing, boxes for text became smaller, more hidden, and more difficult to use, while images popped up all over the page in both stream and tiled formats. Videos became an ideal way to combine images, motion, spoken words, and sound, thereby elevating the sensory dimension of cyberpsychology architecture to new heights, along with raising the bar for the kinds of skills needed – because truly good videos require talent in the art and science of cinematography. Along with photography, video production, and its appreciation, especially as a feature of social media, is not something emphasized in our education system.

IMAGES AS SELF

I've always approached photography, my kind of photography, as a documentation of my time. I am quite vain and believe I am the most important person on earth and therefore I want to leave behind a legacy of my time and how I spent it, as visually as possible ... so I would be very afraid indeed to know that what I am missing tells a lot more about me that what I shoot.

As this quote from one of my interviews with a member of Flickr indicates, images on their own, without any accompanying text, can be a powerful vehicle for self-expression. People might say that they photographed something simply because it was appealing to them – but without their realizing it, that image echoes their identity. Every picture we take is a self-portrait because we only take shots of things that interest us, which says something about who we are. When a person reposts someone else's photograph without asking permission, it might feel like a violation not only of ownership, but of oneself.

The image can give expression to the unconscious dimensions of one's character. It is a creative representation of oneself that is not the actual self as usually experienced, but rather an experiment that gives expression to some underlying anxiety, wish, or ideal. The person then establishes a relationship to that image as a way to establish a relationship to some emerging aspect of his or her identity. For all of these reasons, the flow of images people upload to social media acquires a specific visual and thematic style for each person, distinct from those of other people, whether the person consciously intends this or not.

Going Public with Your Self

The posting of photographs to social media is an act of "going public" with this visual shaping of oneself. It is a process of making the intrapersonal interpersonal. When we share photographs, we hope others will validate the facets of our identities that we embedded in those images. Knowing others can see the picture gives it more emotional power. Feedback from others makes it feel more real. As in art therapy, creating an image can be a therapeutic process of self-insight, emotional catharsis, the working through of conflicts, and the affirmation of oneself. Going public with the image enhances that process. Photosharing groups devoted to specific psychological problems – such as depression, self-harm, and bipolar disorders – illustrate these therapeutic qualities of image creation and sharing. This is why, in all forms of social media, photos that depict the struggles of one's life – such as the dilemmas of work and family – often receive positive feedback, especially when wrapped in humor. It illustrates the phenomenon of misery loving company, as well as the therapeutic quality of attempting to master a problematic feeling by giving it a specific visual form that others can acknowledge.

When people post photos of someone else, they take charge of the online public image being created of that person. They manipulate the establishment of that person's identity in cyberspace, which may or may not be to the person's liking. To regain some jurisdiction over the portrayal of their online self, people have relied on such tools as "untagging" themselves in social media photos, which limits the number of people being notified of their presence in an image. When very uncomfortable about how their identity is being depicted, people request that the uploaded picture be removed – whether the photo artificially created some inaccurate impression of who they are, or whether it revealed something true that they did not want revealed.

The Wow Factor

Due to the time restraints many people feel while trying to cope with the busyness of social media, they quickly browse pictures with an eye open for those that catch their attention. In photosharing groups, members describe how some images instantaneously grab them, what they call the "wow factor." They might feel speechless, unable to verbalize why or how the image affects them. They immediately sense a connection to the photograph as well as to the person who posted it. The image draws them in, encourages them to spend more time visually exploring it, while other images go barely noticed. A powerful image speaks for itself, although viewers also project their own personal meaning into it, so that it becomes a nonverbal space shared by the viewer and the photographer, with its meaning partly created by the viewer, partly by the photographer. Sometimes an image shocks, frightens, annoys, or disgusts people, causing them to immediately leave that page, never to return.

The Subject Matters

Traditional categories in photography are useful to classify the basic types of subjects captured in a picture, such as people, portraits, nature, landscapes, cityscapes, abstracts, architecture, sports, animals, fashion, and food. People tend to create images that fall within only a few categories that reflect the dominant themes of their lifestyle and personality. Young parents frequently post shots of their children, travelers offer photos of their vacations, and somewhat narcissistic people mostly upload self-portraits, which became so popular with the advent of phone cameras that people affectionately nicknamed them *selfies*. Unfortunately, if people in social media receive positive feedback on only certain types of pictures, but not others, a subtle process of reinforcement takes effect. Sometimes without their even being consciously aware of what is happening, they continue to post more of the same types of pictures, in the hopes of getting more positive feedback, while perhaps neglecting to post images that reflect other important aspects of their identity and lifestyle. Very self-conscious people even delete photos that received no "likes." They erase a part of who they are.

The Psychological Picture

We can also identify images by the basic psychological issues portrayed in them, such as self-concept, interpersonal relationships, childhood, achievement, conflict, spirituality, health, and illness. These issues often transcend subject matter as traditionally defined in photography. For example, photos of children could portray any number of different psychological themes, such as innocence, learning, joy, disappointment, or hurt. Of particular importance would be the feelings depicted in a picture, as classified according to the seven basic emotions identified by Ekman (2007): anger, sadness, fear, surprise, disgust, contempt, and happiness. Even when images contain no people, they can still portray human qualities via symbolism, atmosphere, and our tendency to project our thoughts and feelings onto almost anything we see. People focus on specific kinds of psychological and emotional issues in their social media photos: silly drunk, angry with politicians, victorious at sports, in love with the cat, overwhelmed by work. It says something about who they are and how they live their lives.

It's All about Appearances

How the final uploaded image looks depends on the type of camera and lens, the methods used to take the shot, and its *editing* or *post-processing*, which are terms that refer to the techniques applied in programs like Photoshop to alter the appearance of the image coming out of the camera. Cameras with a wide-angle lens produce big vista scenes or wild distortions of things nearby, while a telephoto lens enables the photographer to zoom right in on subjects far away. Females fond of selfies often hold the camera slightly above their heads, which highlights their eyes while making them appear petite. Low camera angles instead make people appear big, powerful, and even ominous.

At first, editing techniques remained exclusively within the domain of serious photographers because programs such as Photoshop demanded a steep learning curve. With the advent of easily applied filters – especially in the widely popular phone application Instagram – that all changed. Everyone enjoyed altering the appearance of their photos using a variety of effects well known in traditional photography, such as soft-focus blur, sepia, black and white, vignettes, texture overlays, warming and cooling tones, and all sorts of effects given nicknames such as "vintage," "urban," or "dreamy."

People tend to rely on a specific set of imaging tools and techniques, which reflects their personality styles. For the histrionic person, it might be colors; for the paranoid, the distance of a telephoto lens; and for the compulsive, the precision of black and white. A person's visual style can be understood according to well-known psychological tests that employ visual stimuli, such as Exner's (2002) system for interpreting responses to the Rorschach inkblots, including how people react to form, movement, color, shading, texture, reflections, symmetry, and vista. How is a person who creates soft focus, faded photos different from someone who prefers high contrast with surreal colors? What are the moods or intentions behind these different visual styles? Given the increasing number of tools that can dramatically transform their photos, people have the special effects power to create within cyberspace their own subjective versions of reality, including an idealized selfie with smoothed complexion, brightened eyes, and a carefully reshaped body.

THE SECRET LIFE OF SELF-PORTRAITS

What could be more intrinsically human than self-portraits? They represent what makes us unique among all creatures on this planet: our highly developed self-awareness along with the desire to capture it in a work of art. At a deep philosophical and psychological level of analysis, the phenomenon is wondrously introspective, paradoxical, and even mystical, which is why photographers have been enamored with this genre ever since the invention of the camera. "The portrait I do best is the person I know best," Felix Nadar once said. This is why studying self-portraits is an especially important topic in cyberpsychology (Suler, 2013c).

Because our brain intrinsically rivets to the qualities of the human face, seeing yours will make you feel more real to others online, more so than your simply providing text. Self-portraits are a very effective way to get one's visual identity out there while maintaining control over that personal image, a process that helps some people feel better about themselves. You deliberately create an objective representation of the subjective you because the self-portrait allows you to see yourself as others might see you. It allows others to see you as you see yourself or as you wish to be seen.

Did I Shoot Myself?

The *objective self-portrait* creates the illusion that someone else might have taken the photo. That illusion is magnified when people place the camera on a surface or tripod to take a shot of themselves from a distance or when they use a "selfie stick." The farther away the camera, the less likely the viewer will assume that the subject in the picture is the photographer. If people have their eyes closed, avoid looking into the lens, and can shed that very subtle self-conscious look on their faces, it might appear as if they do not know they are being photographed, which also leads the viewer to assume someone else took the shot. These kinds of self-portraits create the impression of objectivity, as if pretending, playfully or quite deliberately, "this is how someone else captured me." By creating the illusion of someone else's presence, the objective self-portrait suggests a relationship between the person as subject and that imaginary photographer who took the shot. Consciously or unconsciously, the person might be referring to and posing for someone in particular, in many cases anticipating the reactions of online companions who will see the photo.

In the *subjective self-portrait*, the viewer knows that photographers took the shots of themselves, as when we see or sense their outstretched arms pointing the camera at themselves or when they shoot into a mirror. We are aware of the presence of the lens. When photographers look into the camera, the sensation of self capturing self is magnified. These subjective self-portraits tend to be much more common than the objective types, especially in generic social media, where the self-conscious need to tell one's ongoing life story is much stronger than in the more serious photosharing communities, where objective self-portraits prevail as a form of artistic expression. Subjective self-portraits are also easier to take on the go with phone cameras, which makes them more amenable to the spontaneously immediate feeling of sharing one's life stories that people cherish in social media. Well-executed objective self-portraits ease impressions people might have of the photographer as self-absorbed, whereas subjective ones, especially such obvious poses as taking a shot of oneself in a mirror, tend to amplify that sense of self-preoccupation.

Why Not Take All of Me?

Self-portraits differ in how much photographers reveal about themselves. Some shots focus on a particular part of the person's body, usually the face and especially the eyes, but sometimes on another body part, such as the legs, hands, feet, and hair. These types of self-portraits tend to be common in social media, in part because they are easier to take with a phone camera. In wider angle shots, the person expands the field of view, showing all of themselves, things in their hands, and their surroundings – what photographers call *environmental self-portraits*. Body language, clothing, nearby objects, and one's location always reveal something important about a person's identity. What people include or exclude reflects the aspects of their lives they wish to reveal or hide, as well as determines the complexity of the story they tell. Turning a photo into a self-portrait by cropping someone else out of it shows how the photographer wants to eliminate that person from the "me" being shared. It might even reveal the hostility of wanting to cut that person out from one's life.

Me Observing Me

When people post self-portraits, they are commenting on and seeking feedback about something in particular: their past, present, or future self; their positive or negative emotions; their strengths and weaknesses; the memories and experiences that make them who they are; their selves as they wish others could see them; their important relationships, interests, and roles in life that define them; the beliefs they hold to be true or false; or the aspects of their identities that are weak, confused, outdated, unexplored, or misunderstood

Even though they seek feedback about these things, they often are not consciously aware of everything their self-portraits reveal about them. The more they study these photos, the more they might understand what those images say about them. Taking a self-portrait and then posting it to social media can place you into a more objective viewpoint about your identity. It stimulates the *observing self,* that part of us that can step back to look at ourselves in a more detached way, as if through the eyes of others. It might serve as an experiment in understanding how others see you or as a bridge between their perceptions of you as compared to your own self-concept. Photographers sometimes talk about a self-portrait as if the subject is some-one else. They might even experience that subject as another person. People find it easier to talk about the thoughts and emotions of the person in their self-portraits as a transition to talking directly about themselves.

A Glimpse into Johari's Window

Johari's window is a concept in social psychology developed by Joseph Luft and Harrington Ingham (1955), who used the letters of their names to con-struct the term. It is a diagram that depicts the four possible combinations of what is known and unknown to self and other in an interpersonal situ-ation (see Figure 8.1). By applying Johari's window to self-portraits shared online, we see four possibilities.

(1) There are "open" things about you that both you and other people know from looking at the photo. This situation confirms who you are: you and other people share the same perception of your identity.

(2) There are "hidden" things about you that you know from looking at the photo, while other people do not. In this scenario, you would need to reveal the undisclosed aspect of yourself for others to under-stand the photo, and therefore you, better.

(3) There are things unknown or "blind" to you about yourself that other people realize from looking at the photo. In this situation, you learn more about your blind spots in self-awareness if the other person shares what they see about you in the self-portrait.

(4) There are "unknown" things that might be revealed about you in the photo that neither you nor other people realize. This fourth scenario

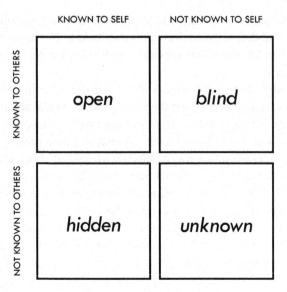

FIGURE 8.1. Johari's window.

reminds us that some things about us are deeply unconscious, unknown to ourselves as well as others. By discussing the self-portrait with other people, by proposing hypotheses with them, we might discover these underlying aspects of our personalities, which shows how useful it can be to invite other people's interpretations of our self-portraits.

People's Opinions of Me

What is it like to put self-portraits online when many viewers are complete strangers or barely know you? Some photographers say they feel freed up when visitors do not personally know them. They enjoy showing their true colors, just being themselves, without need for approval. Because visitors do not know who they are, photographers go ahead and create whatever image of themselves they want. Whether it is anonymity, thinking of their online images as extensions of their own thought-space, or just being uninhibited, some people in online photosharing communities do seem incredibly candid in their self-portraits, without worrying about how people react. They bare their souls to strangers, so much so that visitors might feel uncomfortable leaving a comment that intrudes on the photographer's seemingly vulnerable self-reflective space.

Other photographers cannot help being influenced by the comments strangers make, by whether they "like" the self-portraits or not. The photographer might dwell on posting specific kinds of photos due to the acclaim they receive for them while ignoring or avoiding other expressions of their identity. "My audience seems to like me best when I am the loving parent, the jokester, the athlete, or the lonely sensitive introvert," some photographers think, "so that's what I'll keep posting."

Sometimes, even unconsciously, we create a self-portrait with particular people in mind, such as a romantic partner, family members, or good friends. We subconsciously perceive privacy as we post it to social media when it actually does not exist. Awkward, embarrassing, annoying, or otherwise problematic situations arise when someone for whom we did not intend the photo sees it or comments on it. Photosharing communities do offer features for restricting access to selected images. Nevertheless, some photographers, with a dash of hesitation and anxiety, take the risk of posting their sensitive self-portraits for the whole world to see.

People like the opportunity to post self-portraits as a way to bypass or override the social impact of photos that other people take of them. Whenever a person takes a shot of you, it represents their perspective on your personality, their feelings about who you are, their commentary on their relationship to you. The results can be flattering or not – but in either case you have little control over how it affects other people's opinions of you once the photo is posted. For this reason, it is not uncommon for displeased people to ask a friend or relative to delete from cyberspace a photo they had taken, or for people to post unpleasant or intimate photos of someone else as an act of hostility. On a widespread scale, our culture has grown more suspicious about what photographers might do with their shots. Wary potential subjects dodge the camera at parties, while cautious street photographers only take shots of subjects with their faces hidden.

The Spontaneous or Carefully Composed Me

On the spur of the moment, you hold the camera out at arm's length to quickly snap a shot of yourself. It was a split-second decision. You were not even sure why you did it. You like the shot, then immediately post it to your favorite social media. That is about as spontaneous as a self-portrait gets. Such impromptu shots can provide insights into one's personality that would be difficult to achieve in a carefully staged picture.

Serious photographers say that while they are working on a self-portrait, they take their time in setting up and composing the shot. They think about how they want to express themselves in that particular picture, how they want "to be" in that moment. By taking this opportunity to reflect on themselves, they might attain a better understanding of their personality traits being depicted. The process of controlling the image might even help them manage problematic feelings rather than act them out. Sometimes deliberately exaggerating a feeling or attitude for a posed shot enhances this feeling of mastery.

Spontaneity and planning are not necessarily antagonistic or mutually exclusive elements of self-portraits. People who become skilled in this type of photography learn how to balance the two. They come to realize that while new insights spring from spontaneous actions, thoughtful planning helps improve them. Spontaneity and controlled design synergistically enrich each other. This holds true for life itself.

The Superficially Narcissistic Selfie

Sharing self-portraits online eventually became so popular that a nickname was invented for it – the *selfie*. Why did it become so ubiquitous, so quickly? The invention of digital photography and the Internet had already recruited millions of people to the joy of taking, editing, and sharing photos with everyone around the world. Then the emphasis in social media on narrating one's life led to the self-portrait as an essential feature of that storytelling. When very portable mobile phones included cameras with dual-view screens, the ongoing visual autobiographies catapulted to new heights. People could take selfies whenever and wherever they wanted, simply by holding out their hands to aim the camera at themselves, staring into the screen as if it were mirror, a feat much more difficult to accomplish with traditional cameras. Aficionados professing an expertise on creating selfies convinced so many people about the "right" way to take them that those styles proliferated like viruses, such as holding the camera slightly above one's head to shoot down toward the face. As one of my students said, "Everyone posts the same types of photos to the point where the only thing different is the actual face in the photo."

Critics claimed that the blossoming of selfies in the early 2010s unveiled an age of shallow exhibitionism. Yielding to the pressure of cultural ideals, people wanted to perform in a reality show of their own making, where they were the stars. It was pure narcissism, the critics claimed – an act of self-indulgence, a competitive comparing of oneself to others, a needy quest for attention, an obsession with validation, a product of social dependence, and a desperate crusade to counteract low self-esteem. If people are not supposed to brag about themselves, according to traditional social norms, then the proliferation of selfies was a thumbing of one's nose at such conventions. Staring at oneself in the LCD screen, like the mythical Narcissus staring at his reflection in a pond, amplified the loop of self-absorption. Nude or otherwise sexually provocative selfies, a sure-fire way to attract an online audience, especially for females seeking male attention, sprouted as a source of empowerment, even if people realized the superficial nature of what they were revealing about themselves. "Social media is a shared delusion of grandeur," Michael Naughton said.

The word "selfie," constructed in a diminutive form, suggests affectionate familiarity for a small bit of oneself that is being expressed in an immediate, impermanent, and insignificant way. People are just playing with it, having fun, perhaps making light of themselves. It simply documents oneself at that moment in time, idle proof of having been in some situation, without offering anything else of real substance. Ironically, when people are more concerned with presenting to the world how they look at that moment in that particular locale, making multiple attempts to get the shot perfect, they actually take themselves out of that moment, experiencing the situation only superficially or simply as a stage for performing.

Many people are tempted to post only idealized versions of themselves in social media. They take many versions of the same picture in a careful attempt to capture the Perfect Me. When Instagam introduced post-processing filters for phone cameras that made it easy to cover up flaws and otherwise glamorize a self-portrait, people adopted them with great enthusiasm, especially those who used photosharing as a way to invite sexual and romantic partners. Because everyone was doing it, everyone recognized that highly attractive self-portraits were not realistic, or realistic only in a very contrived way. Enlightened people began to see that friends and family responded as favorably, or even more favorably, when you upload shots that show the real you, flaws and all.

We often appreciate someone who shows honesty and vulnerability. On the other hand, when people truthfully reveal the upsetting problems in their lives, especially when such self-disclosures are an ongoing feature of their social media posts, others might respond with mixed reactions: pity, sympathy, distress, the desire to be supportive, or relief that their lives are going okay by comparison.

The March of Selfies

When people first create and share a self-portrait, they often feel somewhat apprehensive. They worry about appearing narcissistic, feel uncomfortably self-conscious about their appearance, or fear negative feedback. If they receive positive reactions, or if they are not particularly concerned about criticism, they might become more creative, spontaneous, and even care-free about their self-portraits, which reflects increasing confidence and self-acceptance. Literally and figuratively, they show different angles on themselves. They take a closer look at what they like and dislike about their lives. In one self-portrait they might reveal a particular side to their per-sonality, while in later ones they depict something quite the opposite, as if recognizing their internal conflicts and the polarities in their personal-ity styles. Patterns surface that point to underlying, perhaps unconscious dimensions of personal identity that are not clearly evident in any one photo. The online collection of self-portraits eventually becomes a kalei-doscope of beliefs, emotions, and behaviors that reveal a more complete, multifaceted representation of who the photographer is. The more people do self-portraits, the more they might think, "How much should I and am I revealing about myself?"

For photographers who create self-portraits on a regular basis, such as those who participate in 365 groups, where members post one photo every day for a year, the process becomes an ongoing visual journal that identifies transitions in moods, beliefs, and activities. Like a thermometer, the self-portrait takes one's psychological temperature on a daily basis. It enhances one's sense of self-continuity and cohesion over time. Some peo-ple say that it gives them a chance to decide who they want to be on a partic-ular day, even if they cannot express that directly in their actual life. When asked about their motivations to undertake a 365 project, people always say that it is a big challenge – the challenge of asking oneself, every day, "How am I feeling? Who am I? How will others react to me?" It is an ongoing quest in understanding what changes about oneself, as well as what stays the same.

In some respects, self-portraits become easier the more people do them. Their skills in using the camera, posing, and editing the photos improve. In other respects, they become harder. People hit creative blocks. They run out of ideas. They get stuck on particular types of self-portraits because they run into a psychological dead end. They are, literally and figuratively, stuck on a certain kind of self-perception, perhaps because they value it, need it, or are conflicted about it. The stalemate might be due to the fact that their audience needs, applauds, and therefore reinforces them for producing that particular type of self-portrait, which prevents photographers, consciously or unconsciously, from expressing other things about themselves. At times like these, people might need to take a break, to allow other life experiences to rejuvenate their motivations and insights, to look past what other people want from their photos so they can concentrate on what they themselves want to express.

When pursuing the self-reflective process of creating self-portraits, peo-ple are not always sure where they are headed. They are not sure what they are becoming in their stream of photos. It can be a slow, complicated process with unexpected twists and turns. In that sense, it is a lot like life.

THE VISUAL FLOW

The many dozens of images that pass before our eyes every day in social media usually present themselves in the form of streams, tiles, collections, and slide shows. Flickr introduced the term *photostream* for images that flowed vertically down the page, one after another, following the chronological order in which they were uploaded, a strategy used in other forms of social media that emphasized the idea of day-by-day journaling. Later, in their push to display more images with less text, communities devoted to photosharing moved to the tile configuration, where images were packed tightly together in a rectangular design. Photos could be organized in collections according to the photographer's preferences rather than necessarily in the order they were uploaded. Slide shows presented images in sequence, one at a time.

When scholars study the periods of great artists, they discover how the creative styles, personalities, and lives of those artists changed over time, as well as what essential things about them remained constant. We can gain the same insights about people in social media by examining the photos they post over months or years. We see a photographer post cityscapes, then shots of people on the streets, then black-and-white self-portraits. We see an infant held by a tired but joyful mother, then a baby crawling below a hovering father, then a child feeding herself as the proud parents look on. Any particular image is best understood when viewed in the context of the images that came before and after it. The meaning of a photo can be mis-interpreted or overlooked when viewed out of its position in the sequence over time.

A stream of images is a stream of consciousness. It can change direction, pick up speed, slow down, or run shallow or deep. The stream is ongoing, with each image linked to those before and after it in psychological ways not visible in the individual pictures. The spaces between the photos hint at the underlying thoughts and feelings that stimulated the transition from one photo to another, or to the distractions of life that interfered with the effort to keep the flow going. The human psyche itself consists of memories, ideas, and emotions, all linked to each other in complex chains of associations. A series of photos provides a glimpse into how that intrapsychic constellation fluctuates over time. In generic forms of social media, people usually do not take the time to examine how the photo sequence reflects these changes in a person's psychological reality. That happens more often in groups specifically devoted to photography, as reflected in this comment from a member of Flickr:

> What I enjoy more than any individual image, is to soak in the atmosphere of people's individual photostreams. All of them are so different and reflect the owner's personality and interests. I love being able to visit these wonderful micro-worlds, so much to learn and absorb.

Organizing Oneself

People differ significantly in their desire and the extent to which they organize their photos into collections. Meticulous photographers might create a very complex archive with nested categories. Compulsive personalities might even feel anxiously compelled to construct a "perfect" system. At the other extreme, free-wheeling people barely organize their images at all, which feels perfectly acceptable to them, although they might have a hard time finding things.

The way people organize their photos says a great deal about them. If you compare the collections of people in social media, you will quickly notice the differences. Their distinctive classification strategies reveal how they label the experiences in their lives, what life issues are important to them. Their state of mind shows itself in whether they focus on travel, parties, family, friends, work, pets, flowers, or silly shots; in how they broaden or narrowing the range of photos they take; and in the kind of pictures they never take or take but never share online.

Swimming the Image Stream

How do we react to the ongoing flow of pictures in cyberspace? What captures our attention, and what does not? If we spend just a few moments glancing at a handful of images, what about them registers in our minds? In his book on subliminal stimulation, Dixon (1971) describes the debates in psychology about how much information outside our conscious awareness actually affects us. Researchers such as Loftus and Klinger (1992) also wondered just how smart or dumb our unconscious might be when it deals with such stimulation.

These are the kinds of questions that intrigued me as a psychologist who studies the impact of images in online photosharing communities, where photographers scroll past hundreds of pictures in a matter of minutes. And so I set out to conduct a research study that might shed light on these questions about the psychological impact of image streams (Suler, 2011).

In several of my undergraduate psychology classes, I presented a slide show of two hundred numbered photographs at the rather rapid pace of five seconds each. The wide variety of images included landscapes, animals, architecture, street scenes, still life, abstracts, groups of people, and portraits. As they watched the slide show, the students wrote down the numbers of any images that stood out for them, to which they found themselves having a significant positive or negative reaction, for whatever reason. Once the slide show ended, I asked them to close their eyes, relax and clear their minds, then allow one of the photos from the slide show to surface into their awareness – a technique of recalling images that encourages unconscious reactions. After giving them a few moments to focus on the photo they recalled, they wrote down their responses, including their replies to several questions used in the form of psychotherapy that Weiser (1993) called *phototherapy*. What thoughts, feelings, or memories come to mind about this image? If you could go into this photo, what would you say or do? What would you change about this picture? What message might this photo be giving you?

Our Conscious Mind Goes Numb, but Not Our Unconscious

The number of photos that stood out for the students as they watched the slide show decreased over time. When we are flooded with images in cyberspace, we become a bit numb to it all, similar to watching movies chock full of special effects. We start off thinking "wow," but by the end of the film we find ourselves yawning. However, the images the students recalled after the slide show ended were randomly distributed throughout the whole slide show. Even though the conscious mind tends to grow numb during a steady flow of pictures, the unconscious mind remembers images that could have appeared anywhere during it. The unconscious does not fall asleep. It is ready to notice something interesting in a stream of visual stimulation, even when conscious awareness grows tired.

High and Low Responders to the Flow

Some students listed many photos as standing out for them during the slide show, while others listed very few. Some people respond more strongly, or at least more frequently, to an ongoing stream of images. The low responders reacted to the photos they recalled afterward with feelings of worry, anxiety, fear, a need to withdraw into sleep, or a desire for relaxation. Perhaps the numbness some people develop to the flood of pictures in cyberspace is penetrated by images that trigger anxiety and the need for relief from it, images that might linger in their unconscious mind. By contrast, almost all of the high responders who listed many standout images during the slide show later recalled a photo that triggered ideas about happy and loving situations with friends and family, which rarely happened among the low responders. Perhaps a history of fulfilling relationships encourages people to respond more readily to the variety of life experiences depicted in the images that fill cyberspace.

Individual Differences Trump "Pop"

The visual design of the photographs in the slide show ranged from average to excellent, with some portraying congenial scenes (e.g., a path curving through woods) and others depicting slightly unpleasant or strange situations (e.g., a clown in a graveyard, holding a duck in one hand and a camera in the other). Curiously, differences in the "pop" of visual design and concept did not make a difference in what images the subjects recalled after the slide show ended. For example, despite the fact that the graveyard clown was one of the top images that stood out for the students as they watched the slide show, only one person recalled this photo afterward. In fact, there was very little overlap in what specific images the students remembered, with only half of the top twenty images that stood out during the slide show being recalled later once the slide show ended. This finding suggested that the pop of visual design and concept has an immediate conscious impact on what stands out for people as they view an ongoing stream of images, but what they later recall, what lingers in their minds, and most probably in their unconscious, is determined more by their individual personalities.

We Long for Oneness and Tranquility

The most common theme in the images recalled by the students was a desire for such feelings as "peacefulness, joy, contentment, love, relaxation, comfort, security, oneness, rejuvenation, synchronization, immersion, and pure tranquility." They longed for a release from the stresses of our forever-busy modern lifestyle, hoping for simplicity, clearness of mind, and presence in the here and now. Paradoxically, cyberspace continually bombards us with a never-ending stream of fantastic, supercharged, and exciting images, when what really attracts people are ideas about returning to a state of oneness and tranquility. Even more paradoxical is the fact that some people seek out cyberspace because it offers the possibility of a comfortable merging with others while also bombarding them with overwhelming stimulation.

Dream Images Trigger Negative Feelings

After the slide show ended, only a handful of students recalled a photo that stirred exclusively negative emotions. Three basic themes emerged: being attacked by a threatening figure; experiencing the loss of a loved one; and being restrained or trapped, either by some external force or by one's own limitations. All of these images were not realistic looking photographs, but rather surrealistic, dark, or blurry scenes, much like those we experience during dreamlike states of consciousness, as in nightmares. Perhaps in cyberspace we defend ourselves against remembering images that arouse negative feelings, but if an image does break through those protective barriers, it will more likely succeed when it simulates unconscious, dreamlike modes of perception, or it will succeed for those people who are more susceptible to these dreamlike styles of thinking.

It Is Meant to Be Like This

Of all the questions posed to the students about the photos they remembered after the slide show, I found most intriguing their reactions to this one: "What would you change about this image?" Many people did not respond to this question, and if they did, they almost always said that they would change nothing, even when the image triggered negative emotions. A few people remarked that if they could enter the picture, they would provide help to the person in it who appeared distressed, yet they would still not change the image itself. "It's meant to be like this," one student said. As a psychologist who studies photography, I found this quite profound, because it supports what many photographers say about their work, including their photos that capture a moment of suffering in the human condition. This is the way it was, and for that moment, this is the way it was meant to be. We might wonder how often the images in cyberspace generate these kinds of reactions in its citizens.

Mayer (2009) and McKevitt (2011) described how researchers who study education, similar to researchers who investigate artificial intelligence, agree that integrating language with images can accelerate learning. Words and pictures are a dynamic duo. Unfortunately, people in social media and even groups dedicated to learning photography often default to sharing photos while using minimal text talk, or none at all, mostly because posting and perusing images is much easier than trying to write something during a busy online lifestyle. Cyberpsychology should carefully examine how online relationships are affected by communicating via images only, text only, and various mixtures of images plus text, and how these two dimensions of cyberpsychology architecture influence each other. It should also raise public awareness about the importance of combining pictures and words.

Creating a Title for a Photo

Creating a title for an image serves a practical purpose. Without one, how would you refer to one particular picture among many, some of which are similar? You could say, "It's the shot of the bicycle, not the bicycle in the playground, the other one, after it, the bicycle on the grass, shot from below, through the spokes up at the sky." The title "Spoked Sky" would be much easier. Although people rarely create titles for their images in the all-purpose forms of social media, they frequently do so in groups devoted specifically to photography.

Some famous photographers left their works untitled or created very generic ones with the expectation that viewers would generate their own meanings when confronted with the mystery of the purely visual experience. As artists, they say that they do not want to overly control the person's interpretation of the work by providing a specific title. Instead, they invite viewers to project themselves into the image, creating their own meanings for it.

While some photographers in photosharing communities share that artistic agenda, others realize that creating an interesting title can fuel insights into the intended meanings of an image. We might use it to steer the viewer toward ideas we really want to convey, to draw them into a more accurate understanding of our motives in posting the picture. We use photos to share our thoughts, feelings, and lives with others. If a title helps people appreciate what you hope to express, then create one, although avoid blatantly humdrum titles, like "Sunset" or "My Car." Instead, the title might add a layer of meaning that is not immediately obvious in the photo, like "Long Day Done" or "Hell on Wheels." It can even be playful or provocative by contradicting something in the image, as in a shot of someone sitting alone at a large table, entitled "Me and All My Friends." For these reasons, when browsing someone's collection of photographs, do not simply focus on the pictures. Pay attention to the titles too. They might help you better appreciate photos that you would otherwise overlook.

Some titles will pop into your mind right away. You know exactly what you want the image to say. In other cases, you will need to reflect on the ideas you are trying to express. That process can be very valuable. You know you like the photo, but are not entirely sure why. Searching your mind for a title might clarify that for you. It can help you uncover the subconscious feelings, memories, and fantasies that you associate with it, which might be why you took the shot in the first place, even though you were not fully aware of those motivations at the time. Coming up with a good title can also help you refine the photo. The title gives you a direction for editing the colors, focus, and contrast. It is an excellent exercise in bringing the qualities of the photo in line with what you are trying to portray.

Famous quotes and lyrics from songs serve well as titles. If you are examining one of your photos, a word might come to mind – "fishing," for example. If you are intrigued by the idea of using a quote for a title, enter "quotes about fishing" into a search engine, then go to one of the websites that offers a list of famous quotes about that topic. As you read through the list, you will most likely find one that fits the picture, and you, perfectly. "Many men go fishing all their lives without knowing that it is not fish they are after," I entitled one of my photos in Flickr, thanks to Thoreau.

Whatever method you use, you know when you have a good title. It feels right. It sticks. Weeks, months, and even years later, you will remember it. It is a perfect wedding of words and image.

Creating a Description for a Photo

When posting a photo to social media, we often find ourselves having to decide whether we want to say anything about it. Should we explain it, or offer a description to help people understand what we intended? Whether or not we offer that accompanying text, and what text we provide, undoubtedly affects the impact the image has on its viewers. In groups devoted to photography, people sometimes present their photos without any accompanying text as a way to maintain some measure of privacy, especially when the image reveals something very personal about themselves. As a compromise formation, the image exposes aspects of their identity, beliefs, and lifestyle, while the absence of text helps protect their confidentiality. Photos without any accompanying description leaves it up to the sometimes puzzled viewer to find an explanation, especially when the photo also has no title. In social media with friends and family, where the agenda is letting people know about one's life, people usually do offer some type of explanation for the pictures they post.

Descriptions come in various shapes and sizes. They might explain how the picture illustrates something about oneself, as in, "I thought raising kids would be a joy, until I had to deal with situations like this," under a photo of a child with a food-smeared face, sitting in a room littered from wall to wall with toys. Descriptions might clarify something about the shot, as when something is dark or blurry, or when the viewer needs to know who the people are, or where the shot was taken: "Those legs sticking out of the barrel belong to my friend Bob, who was trying to grab something he thought was a dollar bill." A description might be a conversation starter: "That beer, or that exercise bike? Your choice?" Some people use a photo as a springboard for a social, political, or philosophical statement. The photo might even be a "seeing is believing" reinforcement of the person's commentary. "Don't you agree that angry public protests like this are counterproductive?" As puzzlers and jokes, the description can present the image as a riddle or game that the viewer is challenged to tackle. "If you look closely enough, you'll see three versions of me in this shot." Another creative strategy is to create a dialogue that gives voices to the people, animals, or even objects in the image, not unlike the script that would accompany a scene from a movie. A description puts the words, "Wow, aren't I great at hip-hop!" into the mouth of a man on the dance floor at a club, while it suggests his female partner is thinking, "Maybe people don't know I'm with him."

Words Create Relationships More So Than Images

Although images all by themselves have a powerful impact on people, it is the combination of the image with a title and description that launches the potential for a meaningful relationship between the people posting and their visitors. Seeing someone's photos can be inspiring, but it is not easy to form a relationship via pictures alone. People become more real, their presence is more deeply felt, when text is effectively integrated with images. "Alternate descriptions of the same reality evoke different emotions and different associations," said the psychologist Daniel Kahneman. Text invites people to spend more time considering the picture, to show more commitment in understanding it as well as the photographer. It stimulates conversation. For this reason, people often feel misunderstood and alienated when visitors obviously have paid little or no attention to the description, as when a visitor offers the comment "Beautiful Sunset!" on an image that the person described as a sunrise. The viewers' neglect in understanding the image and the photographer might even come across as callous or toxic when they offer comments indicating that they obviously overlooked the photographer's personal self-disclosures in the title or description. If someone presents a shot of a dog along with a description about mourning that pet's death, a viewer's comment, "You've got such a cute dog!" is not going to sit well with the person. The interpersonal price of not paying attention to text is clearly illustrated in this situation:

> There's one woman, one of whose photos sadly I did not click on when it first appeared in my photostream, because it was a picture of a dead animal and as such did not appeal to me as an image at all. However, because I did not take a look at it and comment on it, it may have cost me a friendship. Why? Because had I read the description, I would have learned that this person had just suffered from a bad accident! So I lost big time emotional points with her because whereas other people were right there immediately offering support (which I would have been more than happy to offer too, had I only known!), I was ignorant to her situation and this was quite probably interpreted as coldness. I've since commented on that photo and offered support, but it might well be seen as too little, too late.

Commenting on a Photo

People usually offer very terse, complimentary comments, such as "Nice photo," or, "That's great." These kinds of remarks are pleasant to receive, although they might feel rather generic and unsatisfying to photographers, especially when they put a lot of work into creating an image or it expresses something very meaningful to them that visitors do not seem to understand. People usually give such benignly generic comments because it is hard for them to verbalize exactly why they like the shot, or because they have a very limited amount of time as they browse dozens of posts. Short and positive comments tend to be the norm in many online groups. Because everyone seems to be doing it, others follow suit. People's social status and sense of worth often revolve around how many comments appear under their images, so the terse, complimentary comment becomes an efficient form of social barter: if I give you one, you give me one. People who feel uncomfortable writing, lack skill in writing, or attempt to write in a language that is not their own might resort to these concise remarks. It is simply their way of saying, "I was here. I saw this. I approve."

One strategy is to comment on something in particular that you like about a photo. It might be something about the colors, shapes, or textures, the camera angle, the people or subjects in the shot, or the idea, feeling, or sensation that the image creates. Just comment on anything you notice and what it means to you. The advantage to simply saying what you like is that there is no right or wrong to it. What does it remind you of? What does the image say to you? How might it relate to your life? People usually like that kind of feedback about their photos. They enjoy hearing about the different ways people interpret it. This is what makes photography valuable as a tool for conversation and developing relationships.

Rather than giving a comment that is a statement, you can also ask a question. What did the photographer like about the shot? How did he shoot it? What does it mean to her? What was it like being at that scene? People are usually happy to reply to these kinds of questions. To them it shows you are interested, that you want to know more. It opens the door to the photographer talking about what went into the creation of that picture. People often feel as excited about how they took the photo and the situation involved as they are about the shot itself.

What should you do if there is something you dislike? Should you say so? Very possibly, people might feel offended or hurt or react defensively, especially if you say you dislike it without explaining yourself, and especially in groups that are not devoted specifically to learning photography. For serious photographers, their photo is like their child. They might feel hurt about negative feedback, but they also might appreciate honesty if it helps them improve their skills or, at the very least, gain a better understanding of how people vary in their photography tastes. People appreciate constructive feedback as long as it is offered in a genuine spirit of helpfulness, without being harsh. Criticisms or suggestions for improving a shot should not be presented as if they are objective truths. Although there are some traditional rules about good photography, all the rules are meant to be broken. In many cases, it is just your opinion and personal taste, which reflects your approach to photography that might simply be different from someone else's and not necessarily "better." Rather than presenting a critical statement, you could describe how you might have done the shot differently. You might suggest alternatives. That way you are opening a dialogue with people about how your photography compares to theirs rather than making some kind of blanket statement. Henrich Heine, the German poet and journalist, said, "He only profits from praise who values criticism."

What should you do when you truly hate a photo? Exploring that strong reaction could lead to some interesting insights into yourself, as well into the personality of the image, which an open-minded photographer with artistic interests might like to understand. But avoid being overly negative in your comments. I find that if I look at shot for a while, I always find something about it that I like. I also try to keep in mind the fact that photographers took a shot because something about it was worthwhile, important, or interesting to them. That is what makes it interesting to me too.

When interacting with people dedicated to improving their photography, you might comment on the composition or some technical aspect of the shot, such as the use of colors and focus. The more you learn about these technical issues, the more feedback you will be able to give. Photographers who pay careful attention to technique usually appreciate this kind of comment. They might even see something in their photo that they did not realize before. One precaution is to not go overboard with a heavy-duty technical analysis that feels burdensome, like beating a dead horse.

If you want to offer sophisticated psychological rather than technical comments, this is a skill that can be developed. When you first look at a photo, a thought, feeling, memory, sensation, or image will very quickly flash through your mind. It happens at an almost subconscious level. Your unconscious is speaking to you. It is very easy to overlook that reaction, let it slip away, or dismiss it because it might not immediately make sense to you. But if you catch that fleeting response, reflect on it, then share these thoughts with the person, you will see that it is your subconscious mind communicating with the person's subconscious mind. Because you might not fully understand what happened inside your own psyche, you could say to the other person, "I'm not sure what this means, but here's my immediate, gut-level impression of your photo." More often than not, once a dialogue gets going, light bulbs will start popping for you as well as the other person. Keep in mind that your comment based on this kind of empathic attunement might unlock something personal for the other photographer that he or she might not feel comfortable discussing, especially in public. It is also possible your subconscious reaction to the photo does not connect accurately to the person's psyche. Your comment based on a spontaneous impression of the photo might say more about you than it does about the photographer.

Occasionally in photosharing groups, a person turns off the feature that allows visitors to comment. Why would someone do that? Obviously, those who turn off the feature are indicating they do not want comments, even though they are making the photo available. They want to say something with the picture but do not want to hear anyone else's thoughts on it. Perhaps they want to avoid being influenced by comments that might alter their artistic explorations. Perhaps, in a Zen-like fashion, they are suggesting that their image points to an experience that cannot be captured by words, a suggestion reinforced if the photographer also does not provide a title or description for the image. They think the photo is better without words at all. They seek silence. Words simply destroy the pure visual immersion into the photo. Or maybe they want to circumvent hearing anything negative. They do not want to face the possibility of feeling misunderstood and rejected, or the disappointment of receiving no comments even if they did enable that feature. The image might reveal something vulnerable about their lives, so preventing comments helps protect them from hurtful responses. Such situations are a good example of an online environment rich in the development of the identity dimension of cyberpsychology architecture, but underdeveloped in the social and text dimensions.

PHOTOS AS THERAPY

Can images be a form of psychotherapy? Mental health workers certainly believe so, as Weiser (1993) demonstrated in her classic book about *phototherapy* that is conducted by professional clinicians, along with *therapeutic photography* that people pursue on their own. We can define something as therapeutic if it enhances insight into oneself, promotes the awareness and expression of underlying feelings, and moves one's identity into new, more rewarding directions. "When I have a camera in my hand, I know no fear," commented Alfred Eisenstaedt. All of these things are possible when people take, edit, reflect on, and discuss photos. All of these therapeutic activities can be amplified and accelerated thanks to digital technology and cyberspace.

 Weiser describes how the potentially therapeutic effects of photography fall into five basic categories. *Shots taken of you by other people* help you understand how others see you, what they value about you, and the nature of their relationship to you. *Photos taken or collected by you* illustrate what you think is important in life, as well as give you a sense of mastery over those things that you capture. *Your photo albums or collections* reflect your attempt to organize your experience of yourself, your significant others, and your life activities. *Your reaction to any photo* reveals your individuality, because no two people see the same photo in exactly the same way. Each of us projects his or own personal feelings, memories, and meanings into a picture. Everyone's perspective is valid. Accepting this means accepting each other, which is a very important lesson.

As discussed earlier in this chapter, the last category, *self-portraits*, clearly serve as representations of your identity. They encourage you look at yourself from an objective viewpoint while also expressing your real self, your ideal self, or what you fear about yourself. Creating a self-portrait is constructing a tangible, external representation of who you are. It gives concrete shape to experiences that previously felt ambiguous, inaccessible, or unknown. It generates a feeling of mastery over formerly vague or even threatening aspects of one's identity. By representing such things as depression, anxiety, helplessness, disability, self-injury, loss, and death, the self-portrait helps objectify emotions so the person can more clearly witness and control them rather than be controlled by them. So too a hope, goal, or ideal self in the potential future feels more real and possible when it takes a clear visible form in the self-portrait, just as an old self-portrait serves as a concrete reminder of who you were in the past. The important question about self-portraits shared in social media is whether other people contribute to these therapeutic effects or undermine them, either by unjustly criticizing or ignoring the photo.

Some photosharing groups are the newest manifestation of the support group and mutual-aid movements that began in the 1960s. It is not difficult in the larger social media communities to find smaller subgroups devoted to particular types of mental health issues. Although the images are sometimes disturbing – such as depictions of self-harm – groups devoted to depression and bipolar disorder explore these issues through photographs, including self-portraits. When successful, such groups are grassroots illustrations of image therapeutics. Unfortunately, as with all types of self-help organizations, a group sometimes develops blind spots, acts on misinformation, or succumbs to dysfunctional interpersonal dynamics that do more harm than good.

Given the explosion of activity in taking, editing, sharing, and discussing photos across a wide range of people – thanks to digital photography and the Internet – cyberpsychologists can help people realize the therapeutic qualities of images in cyberspace, as well as the potentially harmful consequences of revealing oneself through images. The many people dedicated to photography in photosharing groups sooner or later discover the pros and cons on their own. With the help of insights from cyberpsychology, everyone can maximize the benefits while minimizing the potential hazards. In my interviews with members of Flickr, one person commented on these issues:

> I find flickr rewarding and frustrating. If I post a shot I really like and it gets little interest I find that very disheartening and frustrating. It makes me feel like a bit of a failure. When a shot is well received it is obviously nice to see that it has had many views and has received lots of positive comments. I see that some people really do use flickr as a form of therapy. One of my contacts is very open and honest about the various aspects of their life – what gets them down, their emotional problems, highs and lows and so on. They use their images, narratives and tags to express this, and they do get a lot of feedback, sympathy and support from people, and this does act as a very real and meaningful form of therapy for them. I'm not like that. I occasionally reveal little snippets of my personal life through flickr but I'm not into airing my personal issues/problems in this way.

The psychological power of revealing oneself and discovering others through the sharing of visual experiences does not end with photographs. In the next chapter, we will see that image talk also ventures into more unusual realms, into the creation of purely imaginary versions of oneself called avatars.

9

I, Avatar

Appearances are a glimpse of the unseen.
                                    – Anaxagoras

When I entered Harry's Bar, the social center of the Palace Mansion, my friend River immediately whispered a warning to me, "Watch out! Nightmare is trying to steal our avatars." I quickly noticed that everyone in the room had taken the form of the generic smiley face rather than their own custom-designed avatars. Except Nightmare. He looked exactly like River should: a disheveled cartoon character with bug eyes and spiky red hair, except the username hanging around his neck said "Nightmare" rather than "River." For a second I felt disoriented, then annoyed. I quickly switched off my own primary avatar, a small gray owl, so I could automatically default to the generic smiley, just as everyone else had done to protect themselves. Unfortunately, it was too late. Nightmare had already captured my owl image and turned himself into it. I added my aggravation to everyone else's. We told Nightmare that this was unacceptable behavior. People took their avatars very seriously. They should not be snatched, no less worn, without permission. But our objections had no impact on him. Adding insult to injury, he duplicated my owl, littering copies of it all around the room, which I promptly erased using the "clean" command. Later that night, I found more lifeless clones of my owl hanging on the walls in the Armory. I indeed felt that something important had been taken cavalierly from me – that my visual manifestation, my identity, had been violated.

GMUKS AND SECOND LIVES

Of all the many ways people might express themselves in cyberspace, the most embodied experience is the avatar. It is a very unique fusion of the identity and sensory dimensions of cyberpsychology architecture. In Hinduism, the term refers to deities who have "descended" or "crossed over" to manifest their presence on Earth, typically in a human or animal form. The writer and game designer Neal Stephenson adapted the term for his science fiction novel *Snow Crash* (1992). It was a perfect term to capture the unique online experience that began in the late 1980s, when inventors of digital media constructed graphical worlds in which people could create and maneuver visual representations of themselves as a way to interact with the environment and the people in it. Unlike other forms of image talk, such as sharing photos, the avatar serves as a very tangible embodiment of the person, consciously created as a projection of self and infused with the power to move about a visual space, like a willing puppet of the person who owned and lived inside it. It does indeed feel as if you are a deity who had descended or crossed over to another world, giving birth to a stand-in being who behaves according to your overseeing will, serving as a handy vehicle for a twinning transference that enhances your sense of self. Many online fantasy games revolve around the goal-directed missions of one's avatar in an imaginary world, with the term "avatar" also referring to the original text-constructed version of oneself in the games of the early multi-user domains (MUDs). In this chapter, I will focus on the visual, open-ended social environments where there is no particular game to play – at least not one that is obvious.

These forms of social media function like a visual chat room, sometimes referred to as *multimedia chat;* graphical multi-user conversations (*GMUKS*); *habitats,* a term coined by Randy Farmer, one of the first designers to invent them; or simply *virtual worlds.* Rather than limiting people to text-only communication, these worlds entail highly visual environments that simulate the sensation of space, movement, and physicality. People living through their avatar bodies, in addition to talking to each other, can walk, run, jump, dance, and even fly through picturesque scenes. The inclusion of environmental sound effects, music, and talking to others via audio connections all round out the multimedia experience. The result is a whole realm for self-expression and social interaction dramatically different from the text-only environment.

One of the earliest programs for creating these worlds was called the *Palace.* It included three visual components: the backdrop or room in which people socialized with each other; the avatars they wore; and "props," which were objects that could be created and moved about the environment. Dozens of Palace sites surfaced across cyberspace, each with its own unique graphical theme – a bowling alley, a futuristic cybertown, a haunted house. The original and most populated site was the Main Mansion, or simply Main, which consisted of approximately thirty rooms, including a bar, a game room, bedrooms, a study, a beach, a moor, and several surrealistic scenes, such as the orbit of an alien planet and an underground cave that looks like Hades. People could move freely within and between the rooms. Like characters in comic strips, they communicated with each other via typed text that appeared in balloons popping out from the avatar's head.

A decade later, successors to the Palace significantly raised the bar in the technical sophistication of these worlds, allowing much greater flexibility in creating and maneuvering one's avatars, with more complex physical surroundings, activities, populations of people, and social structures, as documented in books about Second Life and similar types of virtual realities, including elaborate fantasy games using avatars, such as World of Warcraft (Castronova, 2008; Guest, 2008; Malaby, 2009; Meadows, 2008).

Years after completing my extensive research at the Palace, I decided to explore Second Life. Several journalists who had interviewed me were excited to hear my opinion about this new generation of avatar worlds. I spent many hours tackling the steep learning curve of building my avatar, learning how to move about, navigating the seemingly endless number of locales, talking to people, and visiting such places as the Reuters Building, Amsterdam, and a dance club. I was experiencing things that never existed at the Palace, including exotic possibilities, such as flying through clouds above an endless ocean, along with more mundane ones, like being spotted instantly as a newbie because I could not walk my avatar in a straight line or deciding how I should spend the few Linden dollars that were automatically given to me as a new member of a monetary-driven culture. Despite the marvels of how technically advanced this environment seemed compared to the Palace, I nevertheless had a distinct "been there, done that" feeling. The basic psychological principles of avatars living in a graphical space did not seem all that different (Suler, 2001).

Although we usually associate avatars with these kinds of imaginary social environments, or with gamers in role-playing worlds, we might also consider the pictures or icons people use to represent themselves in social media as a type of avatar. Whenever people post to various areas of the community, their avatar appears with it, as if their personal manifestation moves from one place to another. Whether they change their profile picture, as well as how often they change it and what they change it into, says something about their avatars as a shifting self-representation. Research on virtual reality also relies on avatars to study human behavior in cyberspace. In fact, some researchers envision a future in which almost all social media will entail our wearing goggles to immerse our avatar selves into multimedia rich communities.

AVATARS THAT HIDE, REVEAL, AND TRANSFORM

Imaginative avatars function as compromise formations that simultaneously hide and reveal one's identity. Inspired by Scott McCloud's concept of masking in comics, Jim Bumgardner, the creator of Palace, believed such avatars give people a partial anonymity that allows them to loosen up a bit, what cyberpsychologists now describe in terms of the online disinhibition effect. It is similar to attending a masquerade party. Concealed behind their masks, people feel freer to say and do what they please. Wearing a costume at a real-life party does indeed filter out many of the physical features of your identity. You are somewhat anonymous. At the same time, the costume also symbolically highlights aspects of who you are – something about your interests, some facet of your personality or lifestyle, something you desire, or perhaps even a dark side to your psyche. People either deliberately choose their avatars for these expressive reasons, or their mask reveals these features of their identity without their consciously realizing it.

In addition to reflecting who you are, avatars might also change who you are. In a series of research studies on virtual reality, Yee and Bailenson (2007) found that subjects with attractive, tall avatars showed signs of acting with more confidence, both in the virtual environment and afterward in real-life social situations, as compared to subjects with less attractive, shorter avatars. The researchers called this phenomenon the *Proteus effect*, based on the Greek god Proteus who possessed the power to change his physical form. People sometimes change their behavior, and perhaps even their self-concept, in order to conform to the personae they adopt in cyberspace. It might be possible to integrate one's artificially idealized self into the real world. These ideas echo what psychotherapists discovered about using mental imagery to transform one's personality. If you can vividly imagine yourself as something, you start to become it. Under ideal conditions, we might accelerate that process of self-transformation by enlisting the help of our new and improved avatar selves in cyberspace. As marvelous as this possibility might seem, we would be wise to question whether such changes are deep and long lasting.

ALL SHAPES AND SIZES

"Avs," as Palace members affectionately call them, fall into two general categories. The standard circular face "smileys" were available to everyone as a feature included in the Palace program. Inspired by text smileys, they came in a set that displayed basic human emotions and gestures: happy, sad, angry, winking, sleeping, blushing, head-nodding, and head-shaking. People could also change the color of the face or add to it one or more props, such as hats, wigs, scarfs, devil horns, a halo, a glass of beer, a bicycle, and so on. Because the faces and props could be mixed and matched, people had at their disposal a wide array of combinations to express themselves. You might drink a beer with a frown on your face or poke someone with a pitchfork while laughing. Because you could easily shift among different smileys to convey your emotions, some people preferred them as their avatars of choice.

Most longstanding members of Palace avoided or even hated the smileys. "They're dorky," one member told me, "I wouldn't be caught dead wearing those tennis balls." His remark reflected a pervasive attitude among many Palace members. The standard avs were associated with newbies, whom some considered a lower class in the Palace population. They were usually fresh arrivals who did not understand the Palace culture, nor had they established their identity and status within it. As is true of all avatar worlds, technically primitive or sophisticated, adopting a generic appearance that places you within the masses of similar looking entities proves that you have not emerged as a unique, full-fledged member who has mastered the art and science of creating your own personal avatar.

Here enters the second major category of avatars: those created, often from scratch, by the members themselves. This is the key to what is perhaps the most fascinating dimension of the avatar worlds. Visually, you can be anything you want. Only your technical skills and imagination limit you. Early in the development of Palace, most members preferred their customized appearances over the more generic smileys. The technical and artistic ability one demonstrated by creating them was an important source of self-esteem and social status. If you spend time in any avatar world, you will witness an endless parade of colors, sizes, and styles that point to the boundless diversity of the human psyche. If you peeked into the collection of any dedicated member, you might see many dozens of avatars, with each one serving a particular social function or as a different manifestation of that person's identity.

To make sense out of all these visual expressions of the human psyche, we might categorize them, perhaps using a preexisting classification system. For example, we might explain customized avatars according to the personality types proposed by McWilliams (2011), as described in Chapter 3, "The Dynamic Digital Psyche." What kind of avatars would belong to a narcissistic person who dwells on power, status, perfection, and the desire for admiration and praise? What avatars would be chosen by the schizoid person who feels detached and indifferent, who has difficulty feeling warmth and tenderness, or who prefers being alone? Would we expect a masochistic person to create avatars that depict self-destructiveness and low self-esteem? In answering these questions, we would have to consider whether avatars reflect the way people are, the way they wish to be, or the way they fear they might be. As a cyberspace buddy, the avatar might also fulfill twinship transference needs.

Another approach would involve classifying avatars according to their thematic style as a way to discover the psychological issues embedded in those categories. Here I will outline several different types, but by no means is this list definitive or exhaustive. There are many ways to slice the avatar pie. In some cases, the psychological issues conveyed in each category overlap with the characteristics of the aforementioned personality styles. Most of these categories also apply to the icons or other pictures that people use to construct their profile information in many forms of social media other than avatar worlds. Whether they are highly multimedia-driven beings in an imaginary virtual world or simple pictures representing oneself in social media, these different types of avatars are seen as expressions of identity, as well as reflections of the various archetypes that shape the human psyche.

Animal Avatars

Animal avatars are popular. Some people come as their pets. Because animals symbolize character traits in classic mythology as well as popular culture – for example, strength, loyalty, grace, independence, cunning, and transcendence – people choose a particular animal form to manifest a real aspect of their identity, some characteristic they admire, or something they fear and hope to master. Thinking in the tradition of the Native American, we might even regard an animal avatar as an individual's totem, a symbol of one's essential nature or potential.

Cartoon Avatars

The balloons popping from one's head when speaking at the Palace was a carryover from the world of comic strips. This cartoon ambiance fostered a playful regression among members. Jim Bumgardner wanted people to feel like they were "getting away with something" – which surely is a familiar theme in comic strip plots. As a result, it was no surprise that cartoon avatars proliferated at the Palace, as they do in many avatar worlds. While younger people might be more inclined to don cartoon costumes, older people use them as well. The psychological significance of the cartoon character determines why a person chooses it. People select characters with whom they identify or admire. Some cartoon characters have very specific cultural meanings, often harking back to archetypal personality styles – for example, Bugs Bunny as the confident trickster or Aladdin's genie as the powerful but benevolent friend. Rather than relying on childhood characters, some people wear cartoon avs of a more sophisticated style – for example, the colorfully vibrant forms of Japanese *anime* that might appear more seductive, whimsical, supernatural, or mysterious.

Celebrity Avatars

Celebrity avatars follow trends in popular culture, which means they might quickly become epidemic, then disappear. People use them to express personality traits or social issues associated with the celebrity's image – for example, sensuality, intelligence, power, corruption, or rebellion. The person might identify with, desire, or be poking fun at these attributes. Living inside the image of their admired celebrity might even bolster one's self-esteem. Some people simply wish to display their knowledge of current events in pop culture. Celebrity avs also advertise one's particular interests in entertainment as a way to find like-minded people: "Hey, I like Groucho! Anyone else out there like Groucho?"

Evil Avatars

Some say that humans have a dark or "evil" side to their personalities. The definition of evil varies from person to person, although usually it has something to do with malicious fantasies or feelings concerning sin and guilt, as we might see in depressive personality styles. Note how many Halloween costumes fit this category. As a form of sublimation, evil costumes allow people to express their dark side safely and even creatively. While some people wear an evil avatar as their manifestation for the day, others quickly flash it as an almost subliminal signal to others. At the Palace, if a misbehaving member challenged one of the "wizards" who served as the overseers of the site, the wizard might quickly morph into an evil form as a warning that they were annoyed, that they were getting close to disciplining the unruly member. On one occasion, I witnessed a male attempting to seduce an attractive female avatar. When her attempts to brush him off failed, she very briefly transformed into a nefarious skull that stared at him. He immediately backed away. Deliberately or unconsciously, some people use evil or aggressive avatars as a way to alienate themselves from other people, which might indicate their anxiety about intimacy.

Real Face Avatars

Unlike conventional social media, most people in imaginary virtual worlds do not use actual pictures of themselves as their primary avatars. They prefer the partial anonymity of expressing only limited aspects of their identities in the masks they wear, or they simply enjoy the creative fun of using avatars to experiment with new identities. In more rare cases, people find their real faces to be an uncomfortable, dissociative experience. "I have a picture of myself in my av collection but I really don't like to use it any longer than it takes for me to show it to a new friend," said River, a wizard at the Palace. "It's a little disturbing to sit here at home and see myself speaking in cartoon balloons in a nonreality." By contrast, some people develop an entire set of real face avatars.

When people present a picture of their actual appearance, it often serves as a gesture of honesty, intimacy, friendship, or even romance. Showing one's real face can be a very poignant experience. Several members of the Palace described to me encounters when an intimate conversation culminated in their companion transforming into their real selves. "That moment will stay with me for a long time to come," one person stated. "The value I placed on that particular moment was, friendship, trust, a sense of oneness." On special occasions an entire group of people might feel compelled to use their real faces, what Palatians affectionately referred to as "face nite." The intimacy level reached a point where people wished to step out of their masks. They wanted be as real as possible.

Idiosyncratic Avatars

These avatars become strongly associated with a specific person, as if that av is the person's trademark. In some cases, the avatar is unusually creative, but other times it is quite simple. Regardless of the level of sophistication, its association to the particular individual is so strong that others experience it uniquely as that person. Although trading avatars is a common practice, the owner of an idiosyncratic av rarely gives it away. It would be like awarding one's identity to someone else. Conscientious members also do not steal an idiosyncratic av in order to use it as their own. They respect its integrity. If someone were to attempt such an impersonation, the owner would inevitably confront the person. The community might even ostracize the thief.

Environmental Avatars

People construct these avatars to visually match a particular environment or function in a specific way within it – for example, an avatar might be designed to be airborne or swim in water. They reveal how the visual qualities of the environment are much more than a simple backdrop. The visual surroundings significantly influence, even inspire behavior, although some people are more sensitive to the graphic features of the environment than others. Because creating avatars to match and interact with the habitat can be a challenging technical as well as creative endeavor, they serve as status symbols. By displaying them, a person demonstrates a sophisticated awareness of the visual culture, in addition to an advanced know-how in creating avatars.

Power Avatars

Some people, such as those with narcissistic personalities, have conscious or unconscious fantasies of omnipotence. Who would not want strength and invulnerability? In some cases, the power theme is benign. If not, these avs are a variation of the evil avatar. Because competition invariably accompanies displays of power, some people vie with each other in constructing the most formidable being. Such competition tends to be more common among adolescent males. People who only use ostentatious power avs might be troubled by underlying feelings of helplessness and insecurity, with their avs serving as a defense mechanism, what psychoanalytic thinkers would call a *reaction formation*.

Seductive Avatars

Frontal nudity, including uncovered breasts, was not permitted at the Palace. Offenders were first warned by wizards; prop-gagged (forced into the standard smiley); and, if necessary, disconnected from the server. Adapting to these house rules, some people created avatars of partially naked or scantily clothed figures. Mischievous members sometimes pushed the envelope by wearing avs that tested the limits and ambiguities of the rules. Supreme Court justices had a hard time defining pornography, so the task is not any easier for the officials who run avatar worlds. Even though the rules can become very specific about what body parts cannot be visible, borderline cases always pop up. At the Palace, female seductive avatars were more common than male, although these female manifestations were sometimes manned by male gender-switchers. Palace members generally assumed that males were more likely to dress up as females, especially seductive females, than women dressing up as males.

People usually wear seductive avatars to attract attention, a strategy that works quite well. At the Palace, males quickly flocked to a sexy female form. Owners of seductive avatars might be interested in harmless flirting or advertising their availability for cybersex. When frustrated at work, one member would think to himself, "I need a Palace break." He would then sign onto the Palace dressed as a sexy female in order to lure other men into bedrooms. Some people wearing seductive avs wish to be admired as an attractive, sexy individual, without necessarily being interested in flirting or cybersex. "I have some very sexy stuff given to me by friends (all men!)," said one woman at the Palace. "What do they say about me? Not quite sure, except that I would love to be younger and more beautiful and some of my avatars are that indeed."

A seductive, sexy, or simply attractive avatar has a powerful impact on other members, which is why people often compete in creating them. One Palatian described how his cartoon animal did not seem to be getting him much attention from females. Most of them would not even talk to him. Curious about whether he could change his fate, he found a picture of Brad Pitt that he turned into an avatar. The result? Lots of attention. If he happened to be wearing his cartoon av only to find that a woman was ignoring him, he would move to another room, change into Brad Pitt, and then return. Or he would switch to Pitt right in front of her. As if he had waved a magic wand, the woman would strike up a conversation even if he had not said a word. He even established a relationship with someone who eventually wanted to meet him face to face. "The pic got her attention," he concluded, "but in the end it was me that won her over." Curiously, everyone knows an attractive person does not necessarily reside behind an attractive avatar, but a seductive appearance nevertheless possesses tremendous drawing power. Perhaps some people enjoy the illusion of interacting with and hopefully winning over an attractive person. Perhaps, as many critics of contemporary culture claim, some people cannot resist the temptation of superficial appearances, despite knowing better. Or perhaps they are just curious, "Who *is* that person behind that sexy av?" As Marilyn Monroe once said:

> Boys think girls are like books. If the cover doesn't catch their eye they won't bother to read what's inside.

Other people wear seductive avs simply to gain admiration for their skill in knowing how to create one. Because some avatar worlds feel like an ongoing party where people flirt, playfully compete, jockey for attention, and strut their stuff, it is a cultural prerequisite that every experienced member owns at least one seductive manifestation. Of course, there are exceptions to every rule. As one Palace member said, "I don't really think sexy avs are for me, it just wouldn't be a true representation of what I'm about."

Odd and Shocking Avatars

These avatars are strange, sometimes downright bizarre pictures, perhaps revealing people who like to surprise, play jokes on, startle, or even upset others: a face with no eyes, a knife stabbed into a bursting heart, disgusting road kill. Truly weird pictures might make you wonder about the person's grasp of social appropriateness or even their mental health, as is sometimes the case with schizotypal personality styles. Such very unusual avs tend to be popular among adolescents, for whom extreme behavior is a way to express independence and individuality or to test the limits of social conventions.

Clan Avatars

Members of the same social group might wear similar avatars to demonstrate their group identification, in some cases not unlike "colors" in gangs. These avs tend to be similar in basic design with slight variations to differentiate individuals. Members announce their allegiance to the group by adopting its collective visual appearance while also maintaining some measure of individuality. Clan avs are popular among adolescents who seek out peer groups as an important stage in their psychological development. Similar to clan avatars, *paired avatars* are designed to accompany each other, often in complementary ways, therefore indicating a bond between two people. The avatars might resemble each other visually, or they might fit together like puzzle pieces to create a whole that is more than the two individual parts. His avatar sits on one side of a seesaw, while her avatar sits on the other side.

Inanimate Avatars

One's manifestations are not limited to animal or human forms. *Abstract avatars* that show shapes or patterns might be used by people who enjoy symmetry, nonverbal conceptual thinking, or artistic visualizations. *Billboard* avatars entail political, philosophical, social, or religious messages by people who have something to say and are not reluctant to display their beliefs by adopting a sign as their body. *Lifestyle avatars*, which are quite common and varied, depict some significant aspect of a person's life, usually something to do with one's occupation, hobby, or personal habits, such as golf clubs, cars, flowers, or sunsets. It might be a way to attract like-minded individuals. Although inanimate avatars do help people express something about themselves, they tend to fall short as effective interpersonal beings. We feel perfectly comfortable talking to manifestations that look like people, and even animals and cartoon characters – but conversing with a motorcycle or a pair of shoes will eventually strike us as something less than personal.

In the category of inanimate avatars, we might include machines, computers, robots, cyborgs, and all varieties of technological images resembling human forms. Such avatars obviously reflect an identification with technology, perhaps even the idealization of or anxiety about that ambiguous zone between humans and inanimate machines.

Animated Avatars

Although the technology is advancing rapidly, especially in the world of immersive games, you still cannot move around in an avatar like you can in your own body. In the social virtual realities that became popular, such as Second Life, simple behaviors – such as walking, picking up objects, and sitting down – were usually included in the basic software package for participating in the community. More complex behaviors – such as dancing – might have to be built into the avatar by the users themselves, which means they must first decide what physical action they desire for their avatars, and then either create code for that behavior or acquire it from someone else. Avatar cultures revolve around this sharing, bartering, and purchasing of avatar behaviors as well as physical forms for one's avatar collection.

How sophisticated you look and behave helps determine your social status. Clumsy, repetitive actions such as robotically waving your arm to say hello will not impress fellow avatars as much as sophisticated dance steps in rhythm to the music. Given the challenges in acquiring new behaviors, the choices made reflect one's priorities and personality. Would you rather dance, climb a tree, ride a bicycle, or do backflips? What does that say about you?

Similar to the animated avatar was the animated graphical image format (GIF) that appeared on many websites and in many forms of social media. It was a relatively simple picture that repeats some movement over and over again. People use human and animal versions of animated images to express a particular attitude, emotion, or state of mind that would be more difficult to express in words. For example, to show disagreement, one might post the classic Oprah Winfrey, "Uh uh, no way" GIF in which she tersely shakes her tilted head while rolling her eyes.

AVATAR EVOLUTION

Jim Bumgardner did not design Palace as a game with imposed plots and rules, but as an open social environment in which people would "make of it what they will." The culture evolved according to the motivations of the people who made it their home. Because members had complete control over their appearances, avs served as signposts of the developmental ebb and flow of Palace life. In my interviews with Bumgardner, he compared the history of avatars to biological evolution:

> This last week I read "Naturalist," a memoir by the biologist Edward O. Wilson. My intent was to read something completely unrelated to the Palace, to take my mind off it, but I found Wilson's descriptions of island ecologies particularly relevant. In some ways one can compare avatars to Plumage. More interesting, attractive (or I might even say "powerful") avatars tend to propagate, while less interesting, ugly ones don't. Some avatars have incredible staying power – were created a long time ago and are still around, while others have had relatively short cycles. In addition there has been a marked evolution in the quality and size of avatars. A typical scene in Harry's Bar this evening is quite different from a typical scene two months ago. You see more large, elaborate avs, and more sexy avs. There was a big influx of sexy lingerie-clad female avatars at the Valentine's party, and interestingly those have continued. Where competitive principles come in is that the overall quality of the avs has been rising with time, as people keep up with the Joneses, and teach other how to make better-looking avs.

Survival of the fittest rules avatar evolution. Those with staying power successfully capture archetypal ideas, needs, and feelings. As in biology, the overall trend toward more diversity and subtlety in avatar design points to a basic human need that these imaginary worlds satisfy: the need for the species to seek variety, to push the envelope, to advance. This momentum is boosted by the desire of individuals to express their unique identities within the archetypal forms. As Sammy Davis, Jr., said, "I gotta be me." The end result is a seemingly infinite variety of differences within and across whatever avatar categories we propose.

TAKING IT PERSONAL

Avatars often reveal something about people that otherwise is not immediately obvious, maybe not even obvious if you met those people in real life, and maybe not even obvious to the owners themselves. One's unconscious needs direct the choice of avatar. When people say they are wearing a particular av simply because "I like it," friends or family members often recognize the psychological significance of the chosen appearance.

On a few occasions at the Palace, I suggested to the group that we play an avatar game. One at a time, people take turns standing before the group while they shape-shift among their favorite manifestations. The rest of group tosses out ideas about how each avatar looks, its emotional connotations, its possible symbolisms. Those free associations often uncover something interesting about the player's personality. The avatar is like a Rorschach inkblot, or the Draw-a-House/Person/Tree technique in psychological assessments, or any work of art. People project themselves into their imaginative creations – who they are, who they wish to be, what they fear, what moves them. By free-associating in the avatar game, the other members help unpack the possible meanings condensed into the avatar. It is very much like interpreting dreams. In some cases, people project their own state of mind into how they interpret someone else's avatars, which might reflect transference. In fact, due to their imaginative, dreamlike quality, avatars become ripe targets for stirring up the unconscious emotions that fuel transference reactions.

Palatians enjoyed the avatar game, probably for the same reasons that they were attracted to Palace as the haven of avatars. It was a creatively entertaining arena for self-expression, for better understanding oneself and others. In many avatar worlds, people intuitively play the game as they socialize. They shape-shift into their different forms while giving each other feedback about what they see. It is a form of play, which as Winnicott (1971) pointed out is a valuable way to explore one's identity. "You can discover more about a person in an hour of play," Plato noted, "than in a year of conversation."

While playing, you do not steal someone else's toys. An indication of people's emotional attachment to their avatars is their reaction when someone takes one, especially if it is an idiosyncratic avatar, one that they put a lot of work into, or their primary avatar that they spend most of their time wearing. If newbies simply made a naive mistake, they realize the error of their ways when confronted by the owner. Sometimes a friend assumes your form as a lighthearted joke. Otherwise, it is an act of aggression. Your identity is tightly packed into these precious nuggets. That is how people recognize you as unique. If someone abducts your body, they are snatching your individuality. One Palatian struggled to create a new primary avatar after her original had been stolen. She tried out different visual styles, but eventually gave up and returned to her old design, with some modifications to make it feel new.

In all avatar worlds, people skilled at avatar creation feel committed to the themes of personal expression in their artwork. They want to cultivate their own personal style. That style makes them one of a kind in the eyes of others. It provides continuity to their identity, even though they may be switching among many manifestations. For one specialist, it is flying *anime* figures; for another, it might be hockey players. An artist at the Palace, who built her own avatars from scratch, commented on how she worked within specific parameters that made her stand out. "I know with my art, if you don't have gimmicks you can go unnoticed or easily copied." She also noticed similar tendencies in other members. "When someone stumbles upon those self-induced parameters that get them noticed, they invariably stick with that persona and build on it."

THAT'S ME ALL OVER: AVATAR COLLECTIONS

You can tell a great about people by examining their collection of avatars and how they use them. Each avatar reflects a distinct facet of the individual's personality and lifestyle – whether it is a mood, a hobby or interest, a social role such as mother or student, one's attitudes and values, or a wished-for state of being. The avatars in a collection represent the archetypal sectors of one's personality. During my participant-observation research at the Palace, I myself could not resist the temptation of constructing my own collection or speculating about why I created those particular avs.

The Small Gray Owl

I spent the majority of my time inside a small gray owl named AsKi. I specifically chose this picture for several reasons. It was nonthreatening. I never hid the fact that I was a psychologist conducting research at the Palace, in addition to enjoying a social life there, so I wanted to appear as benign as possible. The small size of this av made it innocuous, as well as easy to fit into a crowded room. An owl is observant, nonintrusive, and wise – characteristics that I hoped would positively shape people's reactions, and that I would like to claim as the real me. Also, the gender of the owl was unclear. My intention here was to allow other members to perceive AsKi as male or female according to their own wishes, although I always revealed my gender when asked. Curiously, as I moved about the rooms of the Palace, I noticed myself looking for comfortable perches for AsKi. Often I found myself sitting above and on the outside of a circle of people socializing, perhaps on a chair near the door or atop a picture frame. Was I acting like an outsider – observant, quiet, benign, perhaps a bit distant? People who know me well would say I tend to be like that in the real world. Sometimes I would have to catch myself defaulting to this detached posture. I did not just want to do research. I wanted to socialize and have fun too.

The Earth

This was next in line as my most frequently used avatar. It was an environmental av. Several of the rooms at the Palace were actually outdoor scenes, such as a beach, the moor, and the front yard of the mansion. In these locales, I placed myself in the sky. I was inspired to create this avatar when I first visited Nrutas, an outer space scene where computer geeks hung out. The first time I sat silently in the Nrutas sky, a new member said to a fellow Palatian, "I don't remember the Earth being there. Is that new?" I found it amusing that my presence would be mistaken for the environment itself. Perhaps I am the kind of person who likes to blend into the situation. I value ecology, spirituality, outer space science fiction, and, as a boy, very much wanted to become an astronaut. All of this, and probably more, was condensed into that avatar.

James Taylor

This picture of James Taylor dancing with his guitar was from his album *New Moon Shine*. When in my partying "let's get down" mood, I would dance as JT across the carpet in Harry's Bar. Even introverted people let their exhibitionist side out once in a while, especially with the force of the online disinhibition effect at their back. JT was a good example of a "wannabe" avatar, a representation of an ideal or wished-for self. I play guitar and piano, with average skill. If I could magically inherit anyone's musical abilities, James Taylor would be one of my choices. Most people have a wannabe avatar of some kind in their collection. It reveals their potential push toward self-actualization. Using this avatar also drove home for me the fact that avs can be very effective signposts for attracting like-minded people. If not for this one, I would have missed the opportunity to connect with several other JT fans.

Freud Wearing a Propeller Beanie

For the sake of humor, I transformed myself into this persona when people asked me questions about psychology, or if someone in the room, not knowing I was a psychologist, said something to the group like, "Maybe we should ask a shrink about that!" My silly appearance helped eliminate tension, which some people feel around psychologists. I wanted to let others know that we, including psychologists, should never take ourselves too seriously. On a few occasions, I switched to this av when obnoxious guests were harassing people in the room. I tried to find out why they were being so insulting in the hopes of either talking them down or, if necessary, encouraging them to leave.

Dressed to the Nines

This silhouetted figure of a man dressed in a formal tuxedo was my mildly seductive avatar. I assumed this form – on rare occasions, I might add – to interact with women who wanted to flirt. It was my attempt to assume the persona of a sophisticated, debonair man-about-town – perhaps another wannabe avatar? It also came in handy for those nights when everyone in the room was in the mood to dress formally.

Hercules Taming Cerberus

This was my power av. What could be more commanding than Hercules wrestling down the multiheaded dog that guards the gates of hell? It was symbolic, among other things, of the need to master instinctual impulses, which is the stock in trade of any psychologist. Because power avatars are often large, I attempted to make this one as big as possible. Some people were impressed while others were put off by its size and aggressive quality. So I wore it only occasionally for fear of offending people or intruding on their personal space. This was the most difficult of my avatars to construct. It was my competitive attempt to demonstrate that I possessed the technical skills to make complex avs.

The Home and Experimental Avs

Many people cherish one of their original avatars in their collection because it represents their birth identity in the community. For me it was AsKi. It was an old, reliable friend. Many people also have a primary, all-purpose manifestation that they use most of the time. It is the familiar home base, the image they feel most identified with and most comfortable wearing. Because active members are always creating new avs, their collections are a balance of new and old persona, a harmony between experimenting with new selves while holding onto the more familiar and stable ones. The variations within a collection indicate the extent to which the person explores personal identity. Some people have a secret avatar that they use when they want to conceal themselves, as well as one they wear when with friends, an appearance that readily identifies them to their companions, often that birth or primary avatar. When people create an avatar that they truly like but are not sure why, they present to themselves a puzzle about some hidden facet of their individuality.

SOCIAL GREASE

Avatars make socializing easier by serving as meaningful conversation pieces. If you can think of nothing else to say, express an interest in someone's avatar. It greases social interaction, especially when you are meeting someone for the first time. It is a very acceptable and common topic of discussion in virtual worlds, like discussing the weather, except people are more emotionally invested in their avatars than the climate. You will also learn more about their personalities than by speculating about sunshine or rain. This suggestion holds true for the profile pictures people use in any type of social media, although people rarely talk about them. If you do ask about these pictures, people will mostly likely feel pleasantly surprised by the interest you have taken in them.

Avatars facilitate communication, relationships, and states of mind. When people shape-shift through their avs, they convey changes in their moods and intentions without having to speak. According to the *Proteus effect*, being inside a particular av modifies how people feel and behave, as well as how others react to them. When you wear a seductive avatar, you will feel more attractive, in part because people will show an interest in you. If you feel vulnerable, turn into an elaborately designed Superman and hear others say "Wow." To motivate himself into a jovial mood, one Palatian would transform himself into an avatar that leaped about the room. Another member, when deciding to sign off, changed into his white dog carrying a stick with a bandana sack at the end. Immediately recognizing what this meant, his friends would bid him farewell for the evening. What follows is a dialogue illustrating some typical flirting behavior, in this case lubricated by avatar play. The word "play" seems quite appropriate, as these scenarios often unfold as an amusing, impromptu performance. The participants are SweetyPie, whose well-dressed female avatar is positioned in the sky at the Palace front gate; AsKi, affording himself a small luxury from the participant side of participant-observation research; and Misty, who assumes the role of a one-person Greek chorus:

SWEETYPIE: I look like a bride, I need a groom

MISTY: dont look here hahaha

ASKI: (changes to the dress-to-the-nines avatar and joins SweetyPie in the sky) Will you marry me, SweetyPie!

SWEETYPIE: yes dear yes

MISTY: Wow ...SP ... a proposal online in 5 mins

SWEETYPIE: my groom!

MISTY: that's power

ASKI: (changes to the Earth avatar) A match made in heaven!

MISTY: I will sing at the wedding

SWEETYPIE: yes

MISTY: hahaha

SWEETYPIE: He is now the world to me (changes to star-shaped av)

MISTY: hahahaha

ASKI: and you my shining star!

SWEETYPIE: A brand new world!!!!! (plays a "kiss" sound)

ASKI: (changes to a lips avatar – plays "kiss" sound)

SWEETYPIE: now he is all lips (plays "kiss" sound)

SWEETYPIE: oh my groom

ASKI: SweetyPie, we can't go on meeting like this, people will find out!

MISTY: swooning....

SWEETYPIE: ahhh yes well what can we do, love is in the air

SWEETYPIE: hahahaha

ASKI: (changes to flying bird) you are the wind beneath my wings

SWEETYPIE: lolol
SWEETYPIE: awwww so cute
ASKI: aw shucks

Some planned social events revolve around themes designed for avatars. People specifically create new bodies for themselves to attend the celebrations, as in the St. Paddy's and Valentine's Day parties at the Palace. Other gatherings – for example, our Hawaiian luau – emerge spontaneously like improvisational theater. Showing off, trading, and talking about avatars is an important part of the festivities. The ever-changing visuals of such events make them quite captivating. When the creator of a new Palace site once asked me how he could draw people to his place, a few solutions seemed obvious: avatar contests, games, and parties. Costume affairs in cyberspace do not have to wait until Halloween. They are an ongoing, cherished feature of the avatar culture.

ABERRANT AVS

Whenever an online environment provides interpersonal tools, people will find ways to abuse them, sometimes in very devious ways. Like all aberrant behavior, deviant avatar behavior at the Palace ranged from mild to severe. As Jim Bumgardner intended, people did try to "get away with something" by playing jokes on their fellow Palatians. Newbies were prime targets. Sometimes it was just a good-natured prank, but in other cases the aggression was obvious. In these aberrant avs, we see deviant behaviors carried over from the real world. We also see unusual, even dreamlike scenarios unique to the world of avatars. In Chapter 13, "The Digital Deviant," I will return to some of these issues about the obvious and subtle forms of online abnormality. Here and in that later chapter we see the early historical examples of behaviors that have become chronically serious problems in cyberspace.

Graffiti

By painting on the background room image, hostile pranksters adorned the walls with obscene or hateful drawings, words, or just plain gibberish. Other mischievous members – whom Freud would be tempted to label as anal expulsive personalities – smeared black over an entire room, or filled the space with props, thereby destroying one's sense of orientation and presence, leaving inexperienced users totally confused as to where they were or what was happening. Jealous, insecure people want to destroy what others create.

Spoofing

By "spoofing," you could throw your voice to make it appear as if it were coming from someone else's avatar. Or you could make your text balloons hang in midair with no body attached, as if an invisible person was speaking. One member very inappropriately kept putting the words "I'm gay!" into the mouth of a man who was trying to carry on a conversation with me. Very likely, this jokester used the spoof command to avoid his own homosexual anxieties by literally projecting them into someone else. For another prank in the spa, an old-timer friend of mine asked me to accompany him in setting up a seductive female avatar, bathing in the pool, so my friend could use it as his ventriloquist dummy, what in social media would later be called a *sock-puppet.* Unsuspecting people who wandered into the spa found themselves caught between a highly flirtatious woman and the unassuming old-timer who joked about the newcomer's erotic predicament while also offering words of caution. Inexperienced users did not realize they were talking to the same person manifesting in two forms simultaneously. I myself said little to the few people who got caught in this silly Freudian scam, but I could not help but notice an avatar reenactment of id, ego, and superego. Spoofing has also taken the form of tricksters or hackers who take control over and express themselves through other people's email and social media accounts.

Flooding

Palatians who rapidly changed their avatars – especially large ones – would flood the server, resulting in time lags that made it difficult for people to carry on conversations. Inexperienced members did not realize they were accidentally causing hiccups and frozen moments in time, but mischievous people did it on purpose. It was a hostile attempt to gain attention, or even a jealous ploy to disrupt the socializing in the room. Throughout cyberspace, hackers have flooded servers with contrived traffic in order to create a "denial of service" – a situation in which the overwhelmed server cannot respond to genuine requests from users.

Blocking

Palatians considered it a faux pas to place your avatar on top of or too close to another person's av. Unless the person is a friend who wants to feel close to you, it is an invasion of personal space. "Please get off me!" and "You're sitting on me!" were common outcries. Some naive users blocked without realizing its inappropriateness, or a person caught in lag might be unable to move after accidentally landing on top of someone. Hostile people deliberately accosted others by blocking them.

Sleeping

Sleepers left their avatars abandoned, usually by walking away from or not paying attention to their computer. Lifelessly hollow, the avatar would just sit there in the room, completely unresponsive when anyone attempted to talk to it. The social norm was to put up a BRB (be right back) sign to indicate your unavailability, but sleepers failed to do this. Encountering a catatonic avatar, even if you suspect a sleeper, turns into an eerie, unsettling experience, which provides more proof of how we expect to see life in an avatar. Abandoned social media accounts, where the lights are on but no one is home, resemble the sleeping avatar.

Eavesdropping

By reducing their avatars to a single pixel and their usernames to only one character, tricksters became invisible so they could secretly listen to conversations. As a lurker, they acted on voyeuristic needs to avoid intimacy while gaining advantage over others. I wonder whether chronic eavesdroppers lasted very long at the Palace. People so much enjoyed socializing with their avatars that it seemed self-defeating to avoid this opportunity by hiding. Perhaps that says something about eavesdropping. Indeed, it is self-defeating and, literally, self-negating – although voyeurs of many different types still thrive in cyberspace, attempting to satisfy a need for power over others while avoiding their anxiety about intimacy.

Borderlines

There were very specific rules about acceptable and unacceptable avatars. The unacceptable ones fell into four general categories: overly sexual; overly violent and aggressive; hate avatars showing clear evidence of prejudice concerning gender, homosexuality, religion, ethnicity, and nationality; and avatars that promoted illegal activities, such as drug use. Looking for loopholes or pushing the envelope as far as they could, antisocial and rebellious members, especially teenagers, tested the limits of the rules, as they often do in any online community.

Flashing

Although nudity in avatars was not permitted at the Palace, some people nevertheless flashed their naughty selves. They might have been joking with their friends, advertising their availability for cybersex, attempting to shock other people as would the typical exhibitionist, or defiantly and perhaps masochistically begging to be expelled from the site by a wizard. In private rooms, behind locked doors, people engaging in cybersex flashed various pornographic avs to one another. Because this was not public behavior, Palace officials permitted it.

Droppings

Not quite as brave as the flasher, a prop-dropper would toss an obscene image into an empty room for others to discover, then run away to avoid getting caught. The exhibitionistic, rebellious nature of the prop-dropper is similar to that of the flasher, with the exception that prop-droppers attempt to dissociate themselves from their droppings. In the mind of a Freudian, the scatological implications of this behavior are notable. Droppings can be found throughout cyberspace.

Imposters

Stealing someone's avatar and wearing it was an offense. Stealing someone's avatar, wearing it, and also using that person's name was the abduction of an entire identity. As a momentary joke to mimic your friends, this behavior was tolerated as fun. Other intentions were more insidious. In an act of revenge, hostile members snatched the identity of someone who offended them, then behaved inappropriately in an attempt to wreck the person's reputation. Pretending to be one of the wizards or gods of the community was considered a serious transgression, especially if the imposter wanted to assassinate the official's character. Impostering now occurs in almost all forms of social media.

Identity Disruption

One evening in Harry's Bar, someone I did not recognize greeted me. Something about how he spoke made me uneasy. He acted as if we were friends, but his strangely abstract avatar and name were unfamiliar. After a few minutes, he changed into another unusual design, which made me even more uncomfortable. "Do you know this guy?" I whispered to another member. "It's Octagon," she said. "He's been changing his name and avs a lot lately." A week later, I heard that Octagon was hospitalized. He had been suicidal. This incident taught me something important about avatars. Unfortunate people suffering from psychological disorders will manifest their turmoil in the avs they wear. A virtual world where you can switch among alternate identities attracts people suffering from psychosis, the inability to tell reality from fantasy, as well as dissociation, which involves splits in consciousness resulting from trauma, as in the classic multiple personality disorder, now called the dissociative identity disorder.

DANCING AROUND THE CORE

In all forms of social media, playing with your online persona can be fun, creative, and even therapeutic. But if you change your persona too often, too drastically – especially when you are relatively new in the community – you run the risk of others not recognizing you as a being with substance. You become amorphous. Your identity deconstructs. In order to be treated like a solid individual, perhaps even to feel like a solid individual, you must maintain some measure of consistency in how you manifest yourself in posts, profile icons, and usernames.

Most Palatians established ongoing stability in their handles by only varying them slightly for different occasions – for example, HappyAsKi, McAski, Dr. AsKi. If they experimented with identity expression, they did it mostly by changing avatars, but always returning to a primary or home avatar that everyone recognized as the real you. That avatar provided the necessary continuity of a core presence. The more stable that image as your recognizable identity in the community, the more leeway you have to experiment with other manifestations. If you switch avatars too often without returning to your home base, you become a suspiciously elusive shape-shifter. A healthy lifestyle in any type of social media entails this delicate balancing act of experimenting with who you are, while maintaining a stable baseline of public and personal identity.

THE BACKGROUND IS NOT JUST WALLPAPER

One afternoon at the Palace, I met someone who was designing his own avatar world. He was visiting our site to see whether he could get ideas for his project. Given his interests in the topic, I was a bit surprised by his underestimation of avatars and the graphics of the background rooms.

"No one has quite figured out what to do with an avatar to identify themselves," he said, "and the backdrops are largely that, wallpaper." The invalidity of his first point was obvious. He also failed to understand how the environmental graphics that make up avatar worlds are anything but inconsequential backdrops. His comment reflected a rather devaluing attitude toward wallpaper as well. Would wallpaper even exist if it did not significantly influence people's attitudes, moods, perceptions, and even how they behave? At best, his comments proved that some people, very likely including him, lack a psychological attunement to the visuals of an environment.

Feeling the Space

As static, two-dimensional pictures over which people maneuvered their avatars, the backdrops for the Palace rooms were quite simplistic compared to the three-dimensional and often animated environments of the more sophisticated avatar worlds that appeared in later years. Nevertheless, these background visuals had a big impact on what people felt and did. For example, people were drawn to Harry's Bar, the social center of the Mansion. Why? The colors were warm, fuzzy, and inviting; there were chairs for avatars to rest; there was a plush carpet in the middle of the floor that members used as a stage for performing and dancing; and it was a bar, which all people associate with partying. The study and chess room contained similarly warm colors, but with a fireplace and luxurious chairs facing each other that encouraged smaller, more intimate gatherings. By contrast, the room called Grand Central displayed a starkly black-and-white checkered floor, chairs knocked over on their sides, and, quite bizarrely, a locomotive crashing through the window. Does it come as a surprise that hardly anyone stayed there? Then there was Nrutas, the outer space scene near a planet that looked like Saturn. You would think it not a very hospitable place for humans, yet science fiction geeks converged there. So too the Pit – a gloomy, fiery cavern where automatically horns appeared on your head and a cigarette in your mouth – did not feel like an inviting place, except for the troublemaking gangs that resonated with how it echoed their antisocial dispositions.

At other Palace sites, some of the rooms were under construction, leaving nothing but a black box. When other people popped in and quickly experienced nothing but total darkness, they left in a hurry. People find it boring, perhaps even disorienting, when the cues for feeling presence in an environment have evaporated, leaving nothing but a void.

Doing the Space

Even simple backdrops for rooms and scenery give people a sense of place, physicality, and movement. People readily project expectations from the real physical world into the space they perceive. Palatians could position their avatars anywhere within a room – on the floor, walls, or ceiling. Yet they never maneuvered their avatars randomly. Even though there were no physical laws to restrict their movement, they behaved as if there were. Responding to imagined gravity as an unconscious reflex, most avatars stayed on the floor, except flying ones, which went airborne. Palatians also deliberately played with the laws of physics – now obeying them, then defying them. Sit in a chair, or hang upside down from the ceiling. Designed to fit into specific places in a scene, the environmental avs illustrated how people enjoyed interacting with the visual features of a space.

Rather than being static wallpaper, the background graphics became a playground. It was part of the fun of Palace life. Members walked the hallway from the bar to the other rooms – rather than using the "goto" command that popped them right into their destination – because they enjoyed the physical stroll. At the spa, members bathed in the pool, adding reflections of their avatars into the water to make the scene more realistic. People often placed their avatars in the same specific spot of a room as if it were their personal territory. There seemed to be an implicit norm that the carpet in Harry's Bar was for old-timers who wanted to be physically close as a group, while others gathered at the periphery of the room to converse in pairs or occasionally chime in with the conversation on the carpet. The patterns of where people placed their avatars in a room followed familiar principles in group dynamics theory. Dyads, triads, alliances, leadership patterns, and fluctuations in group cohesion were clearly visible.

Using props such as flowers or artwork, members would also decorate rooms according to their personal tastes – what Xenu, a longstanding member of the community, called "set-dressing." One interesting example was a mysteriously illusive member who persistently posted a pair of cherubs to the walls in the bedrooms. I would find the cherubs there at all hours, and eventually began deleting them to see when they would return, which they did, sometimes only minutes later. I never did find the mysterious decorator. Such adornments allowed people to customize the environment, as well as feel some personal impact and ownership by leaving their mark on the territory.

Palace users were not limited to the standard background graphics. They could create their own environments. Each new space, whether it was a single room or a whole new site, reflected the personality of its creator, while attracting visitors of a similar temperament. In order to draw as many peo-ple as possible to a site, designers created rooms where visitors felt that their avatars could fit in, both literally and figuratively. This flexibility in creating new environments led to many separate Palace communities across cyber-space. As we will see in the next chapter, issues about immigration, terri-tory, recruitment, intergroup cooperation and competition, and loyalty and betrayal all began to surface as the Palace universe grew.

LET'S GET PHYSICAL

The visual and spatial qualities of avatar worlds lead to something that is lacking in the text-only environments of cyberspace – something that has a subtle, yet profound impact on socializing: human interaction feels embodied. People have at their disposal not only words to communicate, but also nonverbal behavior. Blocking or crowding someone's avatar feels like a palpable invasion. Maneuvering one's av back and forth in synchrony with another creates the intimate sensation of dancing. When someone is excited or agitated, their avatar might literally fidget or bounce around the room. Someone who parades back and forth while displaying fancy props looked like a strutting peacock. Similar to in-person situations, these non-verbal behaviors provide glimpses into underlying feelings and attitudes that were not expressed verbally.

Many of these distinct sensations of physicality come from the expe-rience of personal space. People instinctively feel that the area on and immediately around their avatar is their intimate zone, similar to how they feel about their bodies in the real world. When someone enters into that zone without being invited, people feel uncomfortable, annoyed, intruded upon. Otherwise, they appreciate it as gesture of intimacy. Moving toward, standing close, and snuggling up to an avatar is seen as an act of friend-ship or perhaps romantic interest. If someone's snuggling is undesired, peo-ple feel trapped, suffocated, or hesitant to move away for fear of hurting feelings. Correctly or not, other people might think that the two of you are an item. At the Palace, some members specifically designed avatars to snuggle and playfully piggyback on top of others. One male even created a pair of upside-down legs that he inserted down the cleavages of unsus-pecting women, creating the illusion of his body being inside their dresses. Although they might justifiably regard this behavior as highly inappropri-ate, one woman's response to the flirtatious prank was, "oooh, that tickles!"

The physicality of avatar behavior can be very subtle. For example, you enter a room where you find two people sitting, motionless. You speak, they give a minimal reply or do not reply at all. It is very hard to shake the feeling that they are somehow, even telepathically, connected – especially if they are physically close to each other. They may indeed be privately texting words you do not see or hear, although you cannot be sure. The principle of *proximity* in the Gestalt psychology of perception states that if two things appear next to each other, we assume some kind of relationship between them, which is an especially powerful effect when dealing with human forms. Because two is company while three is a crowd, when confronted with this uncomfortable dilemma in an avatar world, most "intruders" leave the room very quickly.

Even the simple act of giving an object to a companion can be a very meaningful gesture in an avatar relationship. That physical act joins you kinesthetically to the person. It feels like a tactile connection, a tangible sign of generosity and friendship. Moving objects also allows you to engage in a physical activity together. One afternoon at the Palace, several of us created a garden out of flower icons. These kinds of nonverbal, collaborative activities solidify a relationship, much like "doing something" with friends in the real world. It is not just talk; it is a shared physical experience. For these reasons, the collaborative activities in imaginary gaming worlds advance the players toward their goal while also promoting emotional bonds among them.

INSIDE OR OUTSIDE THE AVATAR

Some avatar worlds create a first-person point of view in a three-dimensional graphic world, so you feel like you reside inside your avatar, seeing through its eyeballs, looking out onto the world much as you do in real life, with only a minimal awareness of your own body. Another variation is the "over-the-shoulder" viewpoint, where your consciousness hovers just slightly above and behind the avatar, but close enough to feel you possess it as your own body. You move through the 3D environment to find other locales, objects, and avatars that might be hidden from view. Advocates of these worlds like the feeling of immersion created by such viewpoints. You feel like you are really there, identified with your avatar, moving through a 3D world that intensifies emotions because it mimics the sensory experience of real life, including the element of suspense as you explore unseen things around the corner.

Although the over-the-shoulder viewpoint helps alleviate the problem, some people do not feel comfortable with the tunnel vision or head-in-a-box experience of some 3D, first-person environments. Lacking peripheral vision, chained to their avatar, and not knowing what is around the corner, they feel closed in, restricted, and claustrophobic. Sophisticated virtual reality (VR) goggles open up peripheral vision to create a field of view that feels less claustrophobic and more like real life, but some people feel disoriented in such highly immersive experiences or dislike wearing goggles.

As an alternative, avatar worlds such as the Palace offer a two-dimensional (2D), third-person viewpoint. You look down onto the scene that includes your avatar and everyone else's. You witness the whole room with nothing in it hidden from view. People who prefer this hovering, transcendent experience like to see their avatars the way other people do. They can move their avatars around the environment, then sit back to see what happens. Their perspective of the scene, other people, and themselves feels more objective. They might even feel freer. Psychologists would describe this experience as the activation of the *observing self* that gives people the power to be more aware of who they are and how they behave.

Curiously, operating one's avatar from above is a paradoxical combination of a transcendent consciousness along with a psychological immersion into one's manifestation. Mystics talk about the spiritual value of this paradoxical awareness. You simultaneously exist within the world as well as transcend it. Like overseeing gods who manifest themselves below, you take delight in the objective/subjective fluidity of being in the scene and beyond it at the same time. Separate but connected, like an artistic creation, like a self-portrait. It is an "out there" expression of something that exists inside. It is me, it is not me, it is both me and not me. Avatar worlds with a third-person perspective might address an archetypal need for the mystical fusion of transcendence and manifestation.

As places for flights of fantasy, avatar worlds at first seem like entertaining play. As in all forms of play, these worlds also offer a valuable opportunity to better understand oneself and one's relationships with others, assuming people take advantage of that opportunity.

10

One of Us

Groups and Communities

Those who do not remember the past are condemned to repeat it.
                                    – George Santayana

When jbum, the creator of Palace, asked me whether I wanted to be a wizard, I was delighted. I remember my heart beating faster and feeling flushed. Of course, I said yes. Even though happy simply being a member of Palace as well as a researcher studying the community, I secretly hoped I might join the wizard ranks. He told me that I would be initiated and when. I was quite excited that day as I waited for the appointed hour to meet jbum at the Main Mansion. I went to the café as instructed, but was totally confused to find it empty. Where was everyone? Then Spingo came in and told me to utter an incantation that magically transported me to a room I didn't know existed. It was a hidden room, Murmoorerer, a copy of the moor. All of the other wizards were there. My whole family crowded around the computer to watch. I was so nervous that I could barely type. Because of the top-secret nature of the wizard induction ceremony, I cannot divulge what occurred. Needless to say it was thrilling and hysterically funny.

Big groups, little groups, family groups, workgroups, peer groups, hobbyist groups, political groups, sex groups, and all varieties of special interest groups – cyberspace is chock full of them. In fact, the potential for creating online groups is orders of magnitude beyond anything we have ever seen in the physical world. It is an important feature of how cyberspace accelerates social phenomena. This fact captures our attention and concern because groups are powerful forces. Beginning with such books as Rheingold's *The Virtual Community* (1993), researchers have described how gatherings of people in cyberspace take on the look and feel of groups in the real world. Being more skeptical, as suggested by the title of Weinberger's *Small Pieces Loosely Joined* (2008), we might wonder whether a truly cohesive, purposeful "community" in cyberspace is more of an illusion than a reality. In this chapter, I address that question by taking you on a journey through the online groups my students and I have studied during two decades of participant-observation field research, pointing out the lessons we learned along the way. What we discovered gave us insights into the important features of online group dynamics, but more importantly, into the individual person's experience of "the community." Despite how fast cyberspace changes, with new environments coming and going in never-ending waves, some psychological truths about online groups remain constant. In this social dimension of cyberpsychology architecture, the more things change, the more they stay the same.

Many people think of social media as a very large community in which they carve out their particular space to communicate with friends and family. However, social media also includes all varieties of special interest groups that devote themselves to specific causes and topics of discussions. Traditionally, they were *discussion boards, message boards, forums,* or email *listservs*. Now such groups typically set up camp within the most popular social media platforms, with Facebook having played a very big role in paving this way. More so than communicating with miscellaneous friends and family in their network of contacts, people tend to experience these special interest groups as actual "groups."

THE PATH OF THE PALACE

In 1995, as an online researcher with a psychoanalytic predilection, I was immediately intrigued by what I heard about the Palace. When Time-Warner allowed Jim Bumgardner the choice of creating a traditional computer game such as Myst – which was very popular at the time – or a more open-ended social environment, he pushed for the latter, despite the fact that everyone knew games sell. Unlike the creators of Second Life many years later, he also abandoned the concept of instituting some type of monetary system where people bought and sold things. He was more interested in a world where relationships among people were the main attraction, where members could assume imaginary identities via their avatars, and where they could enter a dreamlike environment to "make of it what they will." He envisioned Palace as a somewhat subversive place, where anonymity and the adoption of avatars would allow adults to engage in somewhat naughty, forbidden fruit activities. In psychodynamic terms, we would say he was encouraging the playful expression of the unconscious mind, which can be fun and creative, but also leads to a bubbling up of problematic behavior fueled by primitive urges. By providing users with wide flexibility in creating their avatars and the spaces in which they lived, along with an open social environment with no particular agenda other than encouraging people to imaginatively interact with each other, the Palace was a living, breathing inkblot test. It was open to interpretation, which meant it would evolve over time as it reflected the personalities that manifested themselves there. For me, it became the perfect laboratory for understanding online behavior. A great deal of what I learned about cyberpsychology I learned at the Palace.

Settling a New Land

The first people to arrive in November of 1995 were immigrants from other virtual communities. They were tired of the traditional text-driven discussion boards that had become large, impersonal, and some of them, such as America Online, overrun by "snerts" (snot-nosed eros-ridden teenagers). Hoping to escape the masses, these immigrants considered themselves pioneers who wanted to explore new online territories. At first, they were stymied by the visual qualities of the Palace, which they had never seen before, but with the assistance of the "wizards" and "gods" who helped Bumgardner beta-test the Palace, they quickly fell in love with what was clearly an innovative environment. I was one of them, along with my friends HoBob and River. Our small initial community of forty or so members bonded as we set about shaping a new online culture. We came to know each other better as we playfully expressed ourselves with avatars, organized social events that capitalized on the visual features of Palace, constructed new rooms, and shared experiences about our lives online and off. Here we see the first lesson about groups in cyberspace. Like-minded people, weary of traditional communities that grow too big, diverse, impersonal, competitive, and unfriendly, move to a new place that is novel, exciting, and intimate – a place that makes them feel like explorers creating a new land together. Palace old-timers would later refer to this period as "the good old days."

The Snert Invasion

Our utopian visions did not last forever, in part due to the appearance of misbehaving snerts who followed us to the Palace. One early historic incident predicted the problems to come, not only for Palace, but for all online communities then and even now. In what some members referred to as "the rape of Quentin," a woman was sexually harassed by an unknown newcomer who whispered obscenities to her, spoke them out loud to the room, and inserted foul language into her mouth by using the spoofing command. Quentin reported the incident to the Palace Community Standards Group, which we had previously formed as a way to establish rules for taming any potentially destructive forces stemming from the intrinsically subversive design of the Palace. In the intense debates that followed, some people blamed the invasion of snerts. Some blamed the Palace design that gave too much power and anonymity to newcomers, who the system simply identified as "guests." Some blamed Quentin for being too naively thin-skinned about life online. As with the virtual rape in the LambdaMOO community a few years earlier, which was described in a 1993 *Village Voice* article by journalist Julian Dibbell, there were arguments about real versus virtual rape, decency laws on the Internet, sexism, and what kinds of online environments should be restricted for use only by adults. In the end, changes in the Palace software assigned distinct ID numbers to all users, so that misbehaving people could be identified, tracked, and disciplined, while devoted Palace members united in their efforts to protect the socially creative environment against abuse.

As a psychologist, such unfortunate incidents of cyber-rape reinforced my realization of how powerfully real online experiences can be for some people, even to the point where they feel traumatized by the insensitive and sometimes psychopathic acting out of others. These incidents convinced me of the need for a new branch of psychology – a cyberpsychology – that addresses important questions about how people subjectively experience life online. What kinds of people get trapped in an enhanced sensation of immersive presence in cyberspace that makes them vulnerable to such situations, as opposed to the people who can step back to objectify potentially upsetting experiences safely? What kinds of people dissociate themselves so much from empathy in their online relationships that they end up acting insensitive and cruel, as if playing some kind of impersonal game? While some of these predators indeed were misguided, immature snerts, others were regressed adults, perhaps even true sociopaths. It became clear that imaginary environments present a double-edged sword: they offer valuable opportunities for imaginative identity expression and social relationships in a community setting while also opening up a Pandora's box of pathology that the community must somehow learn to control. Given how ubiquitous these problems have become in all forms of social media, cyberpsychology must help in determining what types of environments are safe or dangerous, especially for children.

Classes and Cliques

The appearance of snerts was an undesirable byproduct of the push to expand the Palace population, which reflected the wishes of enthusiastic members who wanted to promote their creation, as well as the expectations of Time-Warner for an increase in registration sales. When any population grows in size, social differentiation inevitably grows with it. People need to establish their specific status among the masses, especially if they are longstanding members. With avatars clogging the most popular rooms and text balloons popping all over the screen, Palatians faced a real challenge in not feeling drowned out. They began wearing badges to signifying their status in the community or an allegiance to a particular subgroup, such as the Skaters and Magi. Cliques met in rooms off the beaten track, such as the small gathering that formed on the Women's Beach as a distinct territory for the old-timer females, leading to allegations that jealous or curious males in avatar drag attempted to infiltrate their enclave. The Palace User Group (PUGsters) united in a grassroots spirit of organizing social events while also addressing problems in the community, although other members claimed that an air of exclusion, secrecy, and paranoia surrounded the group. Spinoff mailing lists, discussion boards, and web pages emerged, along with new Palace sites. The smaller, underpopulated sites welcomed newbies while the larger ones treated them as second-class citizens. As more of these Palace appendages grew, with each one hoping to feel unique, competitive conflicts sprouted among them. As we old-timers sat back to watch all these events unfold, we realized we were witnessing the evolution of a diverse, loosely structured civilization – an evolutionary process later seen in many forms of social media.

The Wizards Fly by the Seat of Their Pants

Within the core of the Palace society you found the wizards, who served as the overseers of particular Palace sites. At the Main Mansion, the oldest and most popular community, the wizards provided the stabilizing foundation of knowledgeable, experienced members who advised other Palatians, devised technical changes to improve the site, formulated social codes of conduct, enforced those codes when necessary, and philosophized together about the Palace lifestyle. Wearing a tin star to signify their social status – which was actually an asterisk that only they could place next to their username – they possessed powers that other users did not, such as the ability to discipline misbehaving members by pinning them into a corner of a room; muting their ability to talk; locking down their avatar into the generic smiley; booting them off the server with a "kill" command; and, under extreme circumstances, banning them completely from the community. Wizards could see a user's registration number, which gave them an X-ray vision to pierce through people's attempts to disguise themselves by changing usernames and avatars. They also had the ability to communicate with the entire group of wizards present at the site, as if accessing a kind of collective wizard consciousness.

Given all these privileges and responsibilities, there was no greater honor at the Palace than being invited to join the elite wizard troop. Even I, a psychologist conducting serious research, could not resist the hope that I might become one of them. When I eventually did, I was delighted, as the vignette at the beginning of this chapter clearly shows. Such experiences drive home the fact that even sober researchers might yield to the powerful emotional forces that fuel the psychology of online communities.

Becoming a wizard gave me insights into the inner workings of Palace life, especially how the wizards and company officials attempted to cope with the problems that seeped into the community. Besides crime and other problematic behaviors, which I will discuss in Chapter 13, "The Digital Deviant," we grappled with what psychologists now recognize as one of the most intriguing, unique, and sometimes disturbing features of online groups: the manipulation of one's identity. Two examples come to mind, both of which foreshadowed situations that have become commonplace in online communities to this day.

Skeezil was a well-respected, talented, and devoted member of the Main Mansion. He was invited to be wizard at some Palace sites and even placed in the position of vice chairperson of the newly formed Palace User Group.

Much to the surprise and dismay of some adult members, Skeezil turned out not to be a twenty-six-year-old computer programmer, as he claimed, but rather a fourteen-year-old restaurant busboy with lots of computer time on his hands. Heated arguments broke out. Was it right that Skeezil had deceived the establishment? Was he pretending to be mature, or was he really mature? Should he be forced to resign from his positions? Did his actual age really matter? After much debate, he was asked to step down, but was reassured of his value to the community.

The news of Robin's death was announced on the PUG email list. Many people liked her and considered her a friend. Before she died, most people did not know that she suffered from such a painful type of multiple sclerosis (MS) that she enlisted the services of Dr. Jack Kevorkian. National publicity, as well as grief, flooded the Palace community. Concerned members held a memorial service at one of the Palace sites, then erected a garden at the Main Mansion in her honor. Some people were upset that they did not know about her condition. They wished they could have helped her, even though they understood how some people in their online identities chose not to reveal their disabilities or life struggles. When is that a viable choice, some wondered, and when might that be a mistake?

Similar to the founders of many online communities, we wizards and other devoted members flew by the seat of our pants while attempting to manage these emotional and problematic situations in the Palace community. Needing a guiding hand, our representatives approached TPI, The Palace Incorporated, a new private corporation that had taken ownership of the Palace product. Busily trying to get their company flying, TPI officials could not always attend to the social problems emerging within this new world, nor did they have the professional expertise or the hands-on experience in the community to cope with such problems. Communication sometimes broke down between those at the top and those of us in the trenches. When members frustrated with the community needed to vent their feelings, the seemingly distant, uncaring "parent" that was TPI served as a handy target. Companies that operate social media often draw these kinds of transference reactions. To make matters worse, jealous competitions surfaced when TPI offered jobs to a few selected wizards. A schism emerged where people felt you had to ally yourself either with the community or with the company, because the interests of the people versus the business were not always compatible, even though the two intertwined. As one TPI official said, "Without the biz, there would be no Palace community; without the Palace community, there is no biz." Even today, in our contemporary digital age, all of these challenges are familiar to people who live in online communities as well as to the company officials who create them.

CYCLES AND STAGES

By the end of the first year of Palace, the community at the Main Mansion had become so fragmented, unwieldy, and overrun by less-than-conscientious newcomers that longstanding members jumped ship to colonize Palace sites elsewhere on the Internet. Others, like myself, exited the Palace universe entirely. As with many online communities, the developmental process came full circle: the pioneers who had sought out a small, intimate, and devoted group of like-minded settlers building a new land were eventually washed away by a large, destabilizing influx of newbies. The lesson learned is that all types of social media can become victims of their own success. When they grow big, complicated, chaotic, competitive, and unruly, people move on to other more appealing lands.

Those of us who were present in the early stages of Palace witnessed the accelerated rise and fall of a tenuous civilization, including the inevitable evolution of social classes, governments, and politics, as if this avatar world had responded to ancient psychic archetypes that shape how we humans band together and fall apart. These experiences helped me appreciate the need for interdisciplinary studies of online communities because psychology, sociology, anthropology, political science, law, ethics, business, and computer science must all join forces in understanding these electronically mediated congregations of people. I also realized that even though the Palace was not intended to be a traditional computer game, it had become its own special kind of game. As in many online communities, this particular brand of recreation turned into the Game of Life, with all the accompanying triumphs and tribulations of "real" life.

To understand what happened at the Palace, or in any online group, it helps to remember the developmental stages of groups originally proposed by Tuckman (1965). Due to the acceleration and amplification of social processes in cyberspace, online groups might progress through these stages quickly, with more force. During the *forming and norming stage*, people come together as they adapt to the environment while striving to define themselves within it. If they fail in these endeavors – often due to the distracting proliferation of so many people and so many other competing groups – the community fizzles out. If the group survives, it enters the *conforming stage*, in which the members experience harmony and affection as they settle into familiar, accepted patterns of interacting with each other. Deviance is not tolerated, while interpersonal strife is swept under the rug. Idealizing and twinship transferences are common in this stage, along with the tendency toward *groupthink*, when members coalesce around irrational, dysfunctional beliefs (Janis, 1972). During the *storming stage*, previously suppressed conflicts finally erupt as opinions, goals, and personalities clash. These conflicts tear fragile groups apart, in some cases through *group polarization*, when the group splits into factions that hold views more extreme than any individual person (Moscovici & Zavalloni, 1969). If the members successfully work though these conflicts, they enter the *performing stage*, in which a now mature group accepts differences among people while understanding how to handle disputes effectively. Successful groups stay in the performing stage indefinitely. If they make a conscious decision to end their time together, they begin the *adjourning stage*. Members reminisce about the past, consolidate what they learned from the group, and say goodbye.

In one of the first articles written about the developmental stages of online groups, Nagel (1996) described their "natural life cycle." Her ideas overlapped with those of Tuckman, with slight variations, perhaps due to the fact that she describes online rather than in-person groups. Her article has been cited often because many online communities, big and small, seem to go through the same basic stages:

1. *Initial Enthusiasm* People introduce themselves and gush a great deal about how wonderful it is to find kindred spirits.

2. *Evangelism* People moan about how only a few folks seem to be participating. They brainstorm about recruitment strategies.

3. *Growth* More people begin to join, with frequent and lengthy posts. Some people veer away from the intended topics and purposes of the group.

4. *Community* Many discussions surface. People share information, advice, and personal experiences. Friendships develop. People joke with each other. Newcomers are welcomed with generosity and patience. Everyone – newbie and expert alike – feels comfortable asking questions, suggesting answers, and sharing opinions.

5. *Discomfort with Diversity* The number of members and messages increases dramatically. Not every discussion is fascinating to every person. People start complaining about the signal-to-noise ratio. Some threaten to leave if other people do not adhere to the original purpose of the group. Arguments break out and overshadow productive discussions. Everyone feels frustrated and annoyed.

6a. *Smug Complacency and Stagnation* The purists flame everyone who asks an "old" question or responds with humor to a serious post. Newbies are rebuffed. Activity drops to a few hackneyed issues, with the interesting discussions happening via private communications limited to a few participants. The purists spend lots of time

self-righteously congratulating each other on keeping off-topic discussions out of the group.

... or ...

6b. *Maturity*   A few people quit in a huff, while the rest of the participants stay in stage 4, with stage 5 popping up briefly every few weeks.
Many people wear out their second or third delete key, but the group
lives contently ever after.

These stages apply mostly to online groups devoted to a particular
agenda, such as forums in which people discuss some specific issue. Other
more open-ended socializing communities, including conventional social
media, do not usually run into problems about people straying from the
"appropriate" topics of discussion. In the case of the Palace, the original
community began to disintegrate once it entered stage 5.

GEEZERS AND THE ESSENTIAL QUESTIONS

Before the small Palace community as I knew it fell into decline, I began
to write about my participant-observation research in the online book *The
Psychology of Cyberspace*. My articles caught the attention of like-minded
people also interested in online communities, including John Kernell, the
founder of the Geezer Brigade. Contrary to the popular belief at the time
that mostly young people ran wild across the fields of cyberspace, Kernell
belonged to the movement of seniors who were staking their claim to the
Internet, as evident in other groups such as Third Age, Senior Search, and
the AOL Senior Chat Rooms. Kernell asked whether I could take a look
at his community and perhaps write an article about it. Intrigued by this
atypical collection of cyber-citizens, I accepted the offer. Delving into the
Brigade helped me consolidate my ideas about the essential questions to
consider when studying online groups.

How Does the Founder Shape the Group?

As we saw in my brief history of the Palace, it was Jim Bumgardner's
vision of a "make of it what they will" avatar world for adults that provided the springboard for its evolution. Kernell had his own plans for
adults in cyberspace. Retired in 1991 from his position as vice president
for an international public relations firm, Kernell did anything but retire
from an energetic lifestyle. He moved to Mexico, finished a novel, became
fluent in Spanish, formally studied piano at a music conservatory, played

piano in a well-respected restaurant, designed an alternative therapy program to overcome his health problems, and eventually moved to Charleston for the weather and cultural opportunities. It was during his drive to Charleston that he came up with the idea for a seniors club called "The Geezer Brigade" (TGB). At first he was not sure how he was going to make it work, but when he bought a computer and connected to America Online, a pop-up ad announced, "Put your business on the Internet." And so he did. He always knew that in his retirement he would someday seek to empower other seniors. With his forbearers being Irish vaudeville comedians, he believed in empowerment through humor. As the founding geezer-in-chief, he brought to TGB the energetic, adventurous, and broad-minded attitude that was so evident in his life. He installed humor as one of the cornerstones of the Brigade's philosophy – the ability to laugh about themselves as well as other people's attitudes concerning seniors.

What Psychological Needs Does the Group Address?

When I conducted an email interview with Kernell, I started by asking him a question that would require very little typing on his part, but perhaps a great deal of thinking. "If you could only pick three words to capture what the Geezer Brigade is all about, what would they be?" His reply was humor, recognition, and belonging. Expounding on his answer, he said:

> I think we are a minority among Seniors and a good and useful one. There is a tendency to "go along" as we age, both at work and at home. Some people end up as "Seniors" having somehow lost entirely their capacity for genuineness, having compromised away their connection to their real selves in an effort to be accepted. They have fixed themselves to gain approval and, in the process, lost their Selves. Their humor is predictable, strained and not terribly funny. Their laughter is automatic and hard for Geezers to be around. We are not Seniors, Golden Agers, Third Agers, etc. We are Geezers. This implies feistiness, spunk, a sparkle in the eyes, aliveness, even eccentricity. We make trouble, in a good way, by refusing to be categorized, pigeonholed or predictable. We're still struggling to grow and find ourselves. Our motto is, "Do not go gentle into that good night!" Obviously, I'm communicating a very clear us versus them situation, perhaps because I'm so terrified of becoming like how I perceive them to be.

It was no surprise that this attitude among the Geezers explained how they adventurously came together to form an unusual online group in an age when only much younger people knew anything about cyberspace.

Kernell went on to describe a national magazine ad in the 1930s that targeted the elderly: "For $1.00, Get Mail." Desperately lonely, some senior citizens would pay the money just to receive material from the clever entrepreneur's mailing list. Some seventy years later, the Geezer Brigade offered not simply a daily email for its members, but also the opportunity to belong to a group of like-minded geezers, to be recognized as a unique person, to have friends who belonged to the same slowly disappearing generation and truly understood what that was like, which ageist younger people typically do not.

How Does the Composition of Members Affect the Group?

TGB consisted of approximately 160 members from all over North America, equally split between men and women. The average age was seventy-two, with the oldest man at ninety-six and the oldest woman at eighty-eight. Most members were retired white-collar workers with a college degree, but with lots of exceptions that made the group heterogeneous, including ex–military service people, teachers, dentists, and doctors. No doubt, the adventurous, open-minded philosophy of TGB drew such a diverse collection of people together. That diversity in turn reinforced the philosophy. Despite the heterogeneity, they all had in common their zestful, humorous attitude about being geezers.

One principle in group dynamics theory states that although heterogeneous groups tend to generate misunderstandings and conflicts due to differences in backgrounds, beliefs, and goals, this diversity in the long run fuels a richly productive experience, especially when solving problems or trying to understand the human condition. A converse principle is that "birds of a feather flock together" to reinforce their shared identity and sense of purpose. When too many older people, particularly parents, began showing up in the once only-for-college-students world of Facebook, many young adults moved to newer social media, such as Instagram and Yik Yak. This motivating force was apparent in a humorous comment from my survey of student attitudes about cyberspace: "Grandpa, please stop liking my all my Facebook photos."

Ideally, the forces toward heterogeneity versus homogeneity of group composition can balance each other, as it did in the Geezer Brigade that consisted only of feisty seniors, but a rather heterogeneous group of feisty seniors. Because cyberspace offers great flexibility in creating groups, that equilibrium between homogeneity and homogeneity is easier to manage than in the physical world.

How Do the Emerging Leaders Affect the Group?

While all members of TGB enjoyed the humorous email publications distributed daily, it was the Saturday chat program that enabled a smaller sample of them to meet, get to know each other, and connect as a group. It became the breeding ground for leaders who rallied a group spirit and spearheaded various projects in line with their own aspirations, such as a poster campaign for promoting TGB among senior centers and a member's photo website. Similar to the wizards at the Palace, loyal members who become leaders need their own unique space to bond as a subgroup of the community. In return, they serve as its stable foundation and energizing force.

What Is the Online Environment for the Group?

So far, the questions for investigating online groups came from traditional principles in social psychology. This question about the online environment takes us into the unique realm of cyberpsychology. To answer it, we return to the eight dimensions of cyberpsychology architecture to examine how the particular media chosen by the group reflects as well as shapes it. The energetically adventurous members of the Geezer Brigade embraced a variety of strategies, including a website for information, a daily email sent to all members, real-time chat, in-person gatherings, and a chain email that functioned like a mobile discussion forum passed from one member to another. Because subgroups did not dissociate from each other into the different environments – which happened in the comparatively fragmented Palace universe – the use of different media in the Geezer Brigade enabled them to build a comprehensive cyberpsychology architecture, which in turn led to an enhanced community. The integration principle applies to groups as well as to the individual person. The more a group successfully connects its members across different types of environments, the stronger and more enriched it becomes.

The in-person gatherings for the Geezer Brigade were especially important in their development, as they are for all types of online groups. When people develop meaningful relationships in cyberspace, they inevitably want and need to meet in person. The exceptions to this rule are rare. Meeting in person helps solidify relationships. It makes the group feel more tangibly real. Just the fact that the group is willing to meet in the physical world demonstrates commitment among its members. In turn, the meeting fortifies the online community. "Because we are bound together by humor and our seniority," Kernell noted, "when I hosted a lunch for thirteen local members here in Charleston, I was struck by how quickly and how satisfyingly we connected, establishing within an hour or so an easy camaraderie based on our experience of the online organization we all belonged to." For many groups in cyberspace, the people who regularly attend in-person as well as online meetings tend to become the influential, stable core of the community. They become the leaders. I myself found that when I finally met the people whom I previously only knew online, our relationship to each other and the group grew deeper and stronger.

BUILDING COMMUNITIES

Like other group leaders at that time in the history of cyberspace, Kernell tacked the challenge on the fly, on his own. Later, with the rise of the new social media at the turn of the millennium, many books were written about how to build a rewarding online community – with the definition of "rewarding" decided by the author. What benefits the profit-seeking company that creates the community does not necessarily benefit the people who live there. Lots of advertisements splashed across a screen might lead to more sales, but does little to provide a simple, easy-to-use interface for the members, which is why many people complained about Facebook. While some books pitch their ideas to the needs of business, others focus on the social psychology of designing a community that feels rewarding to its inhabitants. Early in the history of cyberspace, people like Godwin (1994) and Kim (2006) proposed guidelines that still hold true today for anyone hoping to build a community dedicated to the welfare of its members. Concisely summarized, here are twelve principles:

1. Define the purpose of the community.
2. Make it easy for members to locate each other.
3. Create member profiles that evolve over time.
4. Front-load the group with talkative, helpful, and diverse people.
5. Provide a range of roles that couple power with responsibility.
6. Develop a system for advising and supporting newcomers.
7. Define a clear but flexible code of conduct.
8. Promote ongoing and cyclic events.
9. Create distinct spaces for public gatherings and member-created subgroups.
10. Provide the option for private messaging among members.
11. Integrate the online environment with the real world.
12. Provide institutional memory.

How we choose to engineer a particular type of group also depends on an understanding of what cyberpsychology architecture works best for what type of group. Some social media platforms attempt to be a one-size-fits-all answer, providing all sorts of communication tools across the eight dimensions of cyberpsychology architecture. While this attempt to cover all bases might work well for people who want a multipurpose, one-stop community, more targeted designs often work best for specific types of groups with specific agendas. Instagram, for example, was the perfect solution for young people who were on the go, using mobile phones, interested in taking photographs, hoping to chronicle their life, and tired of Facebook. The booming popularity of "apps" – leading to the expression "there's an app for that" – attests to the powerful appeal of a simple, targeted method for connecting to particular kinds of people or pursuing a particular kind of activity.

WORKING THE WORKGROUP

Workgroups are a specific type of online group with their own unique issues. I discovered this fact as my colleagues and I created the International Society for Mental Health Online (ISMHO) in the late 1990s and then later as I encouraged professors in academia to extend their faculty meetings into cyberspace. Because ISMHO often discussed the possibilities for conducting psychotherapy online, Michael Fenichel and I formed a clinical case study group where we discussed this topic, which eventually led to the group publishing several articles together. All of the work happened online, mostly via an email group and discussion forum, which is often the case for workgroups in cyberspace.

The advantages of such groups over in-person meetings include the irrelevancy of geographic distance, permanent records of group discussions, and the convenience of asynchronous communication. Although workgroups also use video to communicate online, video usually lacks those last two advantages. A dash of online disinhibition, which happens more readily in text talk, can also stimulate honesty, creative thinking, and participation from people who otherwise might remain quiet in a face-to-face meeting. It always helps to have a host who has mastered the technical features of the software, understands the psychological aspects of text talk, and helps facilitate the discussion.

As opposed to socializing via text, which can tolerate meandering conversations, workgroups demand stricter measures in keeping discussions organized. Making decisions can be particularly difficult. Here again a facilitator is helpful for clarifying confusion, keeping everyone on track, and guiding any attempts to take a vote. Roberts Rules of Order, or a variation of them, can come in handy as long as such procedures are clarified ahead of time.

Moving Online Changes the Group

When extending an in-person workgroup into cyberspace, the dynamics of the group often change, especially when the group actually engages in discussion rather than using the message board or emails simply for announcements, which is a *memo mentality* that overlooks the potential of online communication. Due to asynchronicity, people can participate whenever they want, resulting in dramatic fluctuations in the pacing and volume of discussions – fluctuations that reflect the psychological energies of the group itself. Savvy Internet users who are accustomed to and know how to navigate that flux will have the advantage. Because the discussion entails writing rather than talking, some people feel pressured to stay concisely to the point while filtering out the social grease that eases a face-to-face meeting, such as simple messages like "thank you" or "I understand" that add what some people will deem unnecessary filler. Members might perceive the conversation as efficient, blunt, or, for those who prefer to talk rather than type, tedious. People with superior writing skills have an advantage over those who do not, which sometimes turns the table on people who dominate in-person meetings. That skill in writing, along with the online disinhibition effect, might open up new ideas or feelings that were never previously expressed in person. Such revelations can be productive, or they can uncover hidden interpersonal conflicts that must be resolved before they destabilize the group. In-person meetings will be needed to resolve such frictions, as well as to address issues that are simply too complex to handle by typing on a keyboard.

Resistance to the Online Group

Some people show resistance to extending a workgroup into cyberspace. They may require reassuring help from those more familiar and comfortable with online communication tools. They might fear displaying their writing skills, or the lack thereof, which is why the group should opt for more casual text talk rather than schoolmarm standards about spelling, grammar, and sophisticated composition. People might fear "going public" with their messages, which become a permanent record, susceptible to the eyes of outsiders who can gain access to the group discussions or hostile coworkers who could use that record as ammunition against them sometime in the future. Black hole experiences – when people do not respond to the group – are a symptom of resistance to the online meetings, interpersonal conflicts, technical difficulties in accessing the group, or someone who is simply too busy to pay attention. Not knowing which of these is the case creates confusion – a confusion that some people use to their advantage, as when colleagues say they did not get an email, when actually they simply decided not to reply. Because online groups tend to spread across all of one's communication devices, work does not stay inside the office computer, but intrudes into devices at home, on vacation, and in one's pocket. Understandably, some people resist online workgroups that threaten to inject the job into their personal time and personal spaces.

Barriers between the Online and In-Person Group

Because the group experience in cyberspace feels different from being together in person, the online and offline meetings might become dissociated from each other. What is said in one realm is not said in the other. Online disinhibition causes people to make statements that they refrain from bringing to the in-person meeting. Sometimes the online discussion evolves into a subconscious voicing of issues that are actively avoided in person. The group might work through these issues online, allowing the beneficial effects to seep into the real-world meetings without openly discussing them in those meetings. A more effective approach is to head off the dissociation before it becomes too deeply embedded. Make an attempt to discuss important issues in both domains – and, if possible, try to understand the psychological barriers that might prevent people from making the crossover. Understanding those barriers will lead to valuable insights into the interpersonal dynamics of the group, along with better decision making.

Under ideal conditions, in-person and online discussions will complement each other. The group will come to recognize the pros and cons of each realm. It will learn to maximize the advantages while minimizing the disadvantages of both spaces. Following the integration principle, the degree of success parallels the degree to which the group can bring the online and offline discussions together. When the group moves fluidly from one realm to the other, when the realms combine to help facilitate important group activities -- brainstorming, decision making, problem solving, socializing, resolving conflicts, and providing mutual support – then the group has fully succeeded in extending itself into cyberspace.

ELECTRIFYING THE CLASSROOM

At about the same time as I began studying workgroups in cyberspace, I became very interested in online educational groups, what people would later subsume under the category of *distance education* or *distance learning*. Part of the mission of ISMHO included the creation of discussion forums for educating professionals and the public about psychotherapy and mental health. I established and moderated several groups there, as well as a cyberpsychology forum in Gil Levin's Behavior Online community. When Blackboard arrived in academia as the first platform for digitizing college courses, I immediately adopted it, inviting my students to extend our classroom into cyberspace. Since then, the art and science of online education has blossomed into a variety of techniques and philosophies, with a steady stream of publications on the subject, including the seminal *Handbook of Research on Educational Communications and Technology* (Spector et al., 2013).

Dealing with Hybrids

One of the first questions faced by college instructors is whether a course should be strictly online or a hybrid course that is partly online and partly in person. For hybrids, *the integration principle* becomes crucial, as it is with workgroups. Instructors must try to prevent dissociation between online and offline meetings. Otherwise, they might witness a "two classes in one" phenomenon in which the atmosphere online and offline diverges, in part due to different groups of students participating. Students comfortable with text talk will command the online class, while those who are more verbal in person will take control of the physical classroom. It is important to carry over the content of what is discussed from one realm to the other, as well as transfer valuable socio-emotional processes between the two learning spaces. If Joe is talkative online, encourage him to bring that extroversion into his otherwise quiet demeanor in person. If the physical classroom feels friendly and supportive, help students bring that atmosphere into the digital classroom, which might otherwise feel like a sobering interactive writing assignment.

Being Young Does Not Guarantee Online Savvy

Our culture assumes that young people who grew up with technology feel very comfortable with anything online. This is not always the case. In the now very complex universe of cyberspace, people know what they know about it. Frolicking in social media is not the same as a serious debate in the digital classroom. In order to keep discussions on a productive track, the instructor will need to set specific rules about when and how to participate. What is the required length for a post? Is very casual text talk permitted, which will be the inclination for many students, or is more formal writing required? Although students are becoming familiar with the various designs for digital classrooms as distance education expands across academia, they nevertheless might need some basic schooling about cyberpsychology in order to maximize what they get out of the experience. Do they understand the pros and cons of text communication? Do they understand the kinds of miscommunication and conflicts that occur online or how to resolve those problems? Do they have a good grasp of expressive keyboarding techniques? For digital classrooms to thrive, our educational system must teach students some essential cyberpsychology principles, such as transference reactions, identity management, black hole experiences, synchronicity versus asynchronicity, text talk versus image talk, the Mañana Principle, and the value of "assume good will" as a way to avoid misunderstandings that escalate into flame wars incinerating the online classroom.

The Digitized Instructor

As leaders of the group, instructors grapple with several important challenges. They must be prepared for student transference reactions toward them as the parental figure, which will happen more frequently and intensely than in the physical classroom. Within a long list of highly positive teacher evaluations, there will always be one or two anonymous posts touting harsh negativity – a sign of disinhibition and possibly transference. Instructors must quickly spot and then extinguish flame wars, lest they find themselves trying to soothe a frustrated, angry, overwhelmed group of students at two o'clock in the morning. To avoid the sage-on-stage scenario where students direct all comments at the authority figure, teachers must establish clear guidelines about students responding to each other. They must become skilled at riding the inevitable ebb and flow of activity that is so typical of asynchronous discussions. When a deadly silence falls over the classroom screen, they will need to stimulate conversation. When the number of posts swells to the height of drowning out everyone's ability to follow the conversation, teachers must tame the currents.

Distantly Educated

A business mentality has taken a stronghold in contemporary education. Distance education can be profitable, especially when a course is strictly online. Students with careers in their sights adopt a very pragmatic attitude about college, with distance learning providing an efficiently convenient path. The best online courses do not sacrifice learning as a group experience when addressing these needs of students. Distance education can too easily mutate into a highly structured, practical, goal-oriented mission to achieve mastery over a specific body of knowledge – what was traditionally called a *correspondence course*. In the meanwhile, the value of students learning from each other falls to the wayside. The feeling of a learning community evaporates. Even simple things contribute to the decline of a social atmosphere – such as the absence of the five or ten minutes before an in-person class starts, when students have time to mingle – or the ability to see and hear each other. An emphasis on mastering content as opposed to learning with other students only exacerbates the alienation. Even if social bonding disappears in distance education, if students simply strive to meet the requirements for posts, assignments, and exams plugged into the boxes on their device screens, then they certainly will become distantly educated, but little more than that. The future success of the digital classroom will not rely on advances in communication technology, but in our understanding how to make the interpersonal aspects of learning thrive within that technology. Cyberpsychologists can help teachers find ways to utilize the eight dimensions of cyberpsychology architecture in the design of online classrooms that work best for particular kinds of courses and students. That design can attend to students' different learning styles while also encouraging them to overcome any weaknesses in their ability to use all the eight features of cyberpsychology architecture.

The Digital Class Improves Social Media

Distance education should help students develop their online interpersonal skills so they can use them to improve their lifestyles in social media. The ideal digital classroom provides remedies for the trend in social media toward very terse, superficial conversation. For the most robust outcomes in creating a digital classroom that is a true group, asynchronous text talk – although convenient for students managing a busy lifestyle – must be integrated with real-time, visual, and auditory encounters among students and instructors. Developing this enhanced form of distance education should be one important element of a larger mission for cyberpsychology: when it comes to cyberspace, teach your children well.

NICHES WITHIN THE MASSES

After exploring education, workgroups, geezers, and avatars in cyberspace, I found in 2005 a new land to investigate: Flickr. Interested in photography since I was ten years old, then jumping onto the digital photography bandwagon when it rolled my way, I as well as my students were intrigued by online photosharing communities as another landscape to investigate using participant-observation research. Only something was very different this time around. Flickr had launched about a year earlier, but already a million people inhabited this new form of social media. This would not be like the Palace, where a few dozen of us drove our stakes into unchartered land. This time around, I found myself diving into an ocean of people who had already formed thousands of different groups within an expansive empire of images, information, discussions, and possibilities for meeting people. Although newcomers such as myself found these limitless opportunities exciting, we had to develop specific strategies for establishing our presence, identity, and interpersonal relationships within this vastly complicated world.

The Cyberpsychological Niche and Its Equilibrium

As in any large social media, new Flickr members first found themselves both excited and overwhelmed by the endless assortment of photography that sprung up in front of their eyes. Those determined to make a home in this new land launched themselves into a trajectory of progressive immersion: view more photos, post more photos, join more groups, establish more relationships, and offer more comments and favs – until they finally realized they must put on hold or even cut back the excessive time and energy they devoted to the community. There are a limited number of people you can interact with in a meaningful way, and only so many photos you can look at before your mind goes numb. To maintain a level of participation that feels rewarding rather than overbearing, newcomers in all large social media must establish their own niche where they define themselves, where they carefully regulate their participation in the community. What aspects of myself do I want to express here? How many people do I want to talk to, about what topics? Do I use pictures and text of my own creation, or do I repost other people's posts? The answers to these questions establish the niche.

Experimentation versus Restraint

That niche thrives rather than stagnates when the person finds *an equilibrium between experimentation and restraint*. You try out new ways of being, new people to interact with. If that trial fails, you return to your familiar niche. If it succeeds, you assimilate the changes into your niche, which then transforms it. For example, a man whose social media contacts include family and friends mostly posts photos about raising children. If he broadens the niche to include his office coworkers and then starts talking about life on the job, he must decide whether that expanded niche works. What kinds of messages and photos should he post about what aspects of his life? Does he alternate between attending to the interests of coworkers versus family and friends, resulting in a bifurcation of his identity expression that hopefully everyone appreciates as a more complex expression of who he is? Or will friends grow tired of hearing about his work, while coworkers lose interest in hearing about his family? As you cultivate a more heterogeneous collection of contacts in your niche, you face the difficult choice of posting specific things of interest to particular kinds of visitors, or things that would interest everyone, which is no easy feat.

Interacting versus Performing

When creating their niche, people must also establish an *equilibrium between audience and social interaction*. Of all the people who are your contacts, how many of them do you actually interact with, either by text talk, by images, or through buttonized relating? How many of those people do you speak with privately, more intimately, through what was traditionally called "back-channel" communication? By contrast, how many people who visit your niche are simply part of your audience – people with whom you interact very little or not at all, people who simply follow your posts, or supposedly follow your posts. The larger the number of contacts in one's niche, the larger the audience for whom one "performs." The smaller the number of contacts, the more interactively intimate and cohesive the group, especially when those visitors know each other, talk to each other within your niche, and visit each other's niches. An alternative is to create several separate niches within your social media spaces or to join different online groups, with each niche and group devoted to a specific set of people with different agendas of interest to you. The challenge is then figuring out how many niches and groups you can juggle without feeling too overwhelmed or disjointed in your identity expression.

In Flickr, the niches people established were partly determined by the reason why they wanted to join Flickr in the first place. People who planned to post photos as a way to share their lives with family and friends had a predetermined niche. They did not progress any further into the Flickr universe. If they grew more interested in the art and science of photography, they voyaged into the wider culture of members who were photography aficionados and professionals. In that culture, everyone came to grips with the task of defining the specific artistic, technical, and social dimensions of their niches. Are you devoted to black-and-white photography, portraits, landscapes, pinhole cameras, square formats, blur techniques, or composite images? Some members established their niche by focusing on such topics while participating in groups devoted to them. If they began to experiment with other photography styles, they expanded their niche by seeking out like-minded people. In more rare cases, members used their pages within Flickr as an online art gallery, without interacting substantially with anyone, favoring the creation of an audience rather than interacting with people. I followed one photographer who continually posted shots of graffiti, garbage cans, fences, fire hydrants, and other seemingly random elements of downtown Los Angeles while turning off the feature that allowed visitors to comment on his work. His space illustrated how the identity and social dimensions of cyberpsychology architecture can be dissociated from each other.

The Struggle to Get Noticed

Some members were conflicted about the purpose of Flickr. Is this massively large, complex social media a place to express oneself via images, to learn about photography, or simply to socialize? Dwelling on buttonized relating and the idea of social currency, some members approached Flickr as a kind of competitive game among the masses where the popularity of a photo – and hence its creator – was determined by how many times it was viewed, how many people indicated it as a "favorite," how highly rated was its overall "interestingness" as determined by an undisclosed formula designed by the creators of Flickr, and whether the image appeared on Explore, the catalog of the most popular photos. How does one play that game, which sometimes felt rigged, while also making friends and learning about photography? A member's cyberpsychological niche and equilibrium are shaped by whether that person commits to the social, educational, artistic, or gaming activities of the community and by a complex and sometimes awkward juggling of these different agendas. A person's niche and its equilibrium also change as the population and culture of the entire community changes, as it did in Flickr from its early days as a serious photography community to its later status as a more multipurpose form of photosharing.

The massive size and number of activities in large social media threaten the feeling that one's niche brings meaningful relationships within a true "group" of attentive companions. Even when photographers made a genuine attempt to express themselves emotionally through their streams of photos, few people paid close attention. Setting aside the fact that visual images are a nonverbal language that some people understand better than others, in the busy stop-and-go lifestyle of browsing social media, many members simply do not notice or comment meaningfully on a person's photography. By failing to do so, they overlook the person. In any social media, you might carefully construct your niche, but more often than not visitors are so busy hopping from one niche to another that they will not appreciate the subtle aspects of yours. This is why people often focus on only one or two obvious themes about themselves in social media. They sing one-note songs because many visitors will respond only to the obvious, to what they expect to see from you. Over time, even those visitors start to lose interest in the song.

People with serious photography ambitions in communities such as Flickr often lament these kinds of insensitivities among the visitors to their pages. They grow disappointed by how their work seems underappreciated or misunderstood. They see photographers with mediocre abilities become highly rated superstars because they post eye-candy photos that pop with color, contrast, and trendy subject matter, or because they cleverly work the ratings-game system. They see truly exceptional photographers go unrecognized. Disillusioned by a culture preoccupied with popularity while showing inconsistent recognition of talent, some serious photographers left Flickr. Those members who remained – who did not feel neglected, alienated, or frustrated – typically succeeded in developing a relatively small group of contacts who regularly contributed to their niche, appreciated their work, and, most importantly, became friends. Some of them also had an admiring audience for whom they "performed," but it was their friendships that kept them coming back.

These features of a successful niche hold true in many forms of social media, and not just those that focus on photography, politics, technology, or any particular topic. Even when people are simply sharing their lives, they strive to be heard, understood, and appreciated in a sea of people with the same goal. They must contend with feeling invisible, with how some people get more attention than others – while everyone contends with the fact that superstars and celebrities overshadow everything. They also realize that highly popular or "trending" phenomena that steal the limelight come and go, as do many online phenomena. In all that flux, successful members of social media cultivate a niche in which they too might "perform" for some people or stay loosely connected with others, but it is their friendships that make it all worthwhile.

In Sickness and in Health

As social media soared, with everyone trying to find their place in that huge, complex world, an important question has been whether this environment is good or bad for our mental health. The answer is not black or white. The substantial body of research concerning Facebook points to the many complexities in evaluating the impact social media has on one's well-being. The intentions behind a person's participation in the community, the quality of the relationships they develop there, their personality style, and their previous history of psychological disorders all interact in determining the outcome (Grieve et al., 2013; Jelenchick, Eickhoff, & Moreno, 2013; Moreno et al., 2011; Rosen et al., 2013). As with life itself, social media is what we make it as citizens who educate ourselves about its pros and cons.

Since social media is often the *entree* for children into the interpersonal world of cyberspace, our most pressing concern will be determining the optimal healthy conditions for children. When, where, and how should they join cyberspace? What must we do to protect them from the hazards, and what kind of education will be needed to enable them to be healthy citizens of the online realm? Experts believe that the key to advancing children's rights to expression, play, and socializing online rests on the joint effort of governments, corporations, teachers, parents, and children in the development of wise guidelines and policies (Livingstone, 2013; Sonck, Nikken, & de Haan, 2013; Wang, Bianchi, and Raley, 2005). This conclusion also holds true for any vulnerable population of people.

TRUE GROUPS

In this chapter about groups and communities, I saved an important question for last. What exactly are those things? How should we define them?

We can turn to traditional social psychology to answer that question. Summarizing Johnson and Johnson (2012), we see four basic characteristics of a "group":

1. The group has an identity as a group and its people perceive themselves as members of it.
2. Its members have a mutual purpose, with each person also motivated to satisfy a particular need by belonging to the group.
3. Its members are interdependent: what affects one affects all.
4. Its members interact with and influence each other in structured relationships, with roles and norms about how to behave.

Social psychologists see a group as different from an *aggregate*. This term refers to people who are present in the same space, at the same time, but do not experience the identity, purpose, interdependence, and structured relationships as in a true group. People standing on a street corner waiting for a bus, or people listening to a lecture or concert, are an aggregate but not a true group. All that is needed for an aggregate is physical proximity. To apply the term to cyberspace, we might stretch the idea of physical proximity to include mutual presence or "being together" in an online space.

Given these definitions, when do true groups exist in cyberspace and when are its collections of people merely aggregates? Clearly, the Geezer Brigade, the Palace wizards, coworkers talking via email, and students in an online course all meet the four criteria for defining a group. By contrast, the niches people create for themselves in social media often resemble aggregates, involving what online researchers call *loose* or *weak ties*. People talking in someone's niche do not necessarily perceive themselves as members of a specific group with a distinct identity, rarely have clearly defined roles or purposes other than simple socializing, and often talk mostly to the person who owns the niche while interacting very little with each other. Because many niches in traditional social media seem more like aggregates than true groups, we might wonder whether social media niches themselves truly embody "communities," a term often used.

As a clinical psychologist, I avoid dwelling on definitions in favor of understanding the quality of the interactions within online groups that lead to well-being. How much do people share about themselves and get to know each other? How strongly do they bond with each other and the whole group? How well do they satisfy the needs that they bring to the group? In his book on group psychotherapy, Yalom (2005) helped answer these questions by applying the concept of *group boundary*. To strengthen its boundary – which leads to higher sharing, trust, and intimacy – a group must meet these four conditions:

1. The membership is relatively stable rather than highly fluctuating.
2. The group is relatively small rather than large (no more than fifteen members).
3. Its members meet consistently over time in the same place.
4. Discussions in the group are private.

Although most gatherings in cyberspace are not intended as psychotherapy, any truly rewarding group will be one with a strong boundary that activates sharing, trust, intimacy, and personal growth. Along with friendships, it is these kinds of groups that keep people coming back to cyberspace as a rewarding social activity. Unfortunately, few online groups meet these four criteria, especially not social media niches, where various visitors come and go unpredictably, the number of people there might be quite large, people do not interact with each other consistently, and it is unclear who is viewing the discussions. It therefore comes as no surprise that sharing, trust, intimacy, and personal growth often do not thrive in social media, unless a person takes steps to create at least some of these four conditions. Anyone who wishes to create an online group that maximizes these virtues needs to pay careful attention to the four elements of group boundary.

Given how fast social media changes, with one's network of contacts constantly shifting, we might wonder whether people long for more stable, intimate groups in cyberspace, or whether we simply accept the flux of online relationships. As we will see in the next chapter, ongoing change is a way of life in the digital realm. Despite this roller coaster ride, our history of being online is long enough to identity the fundamental principles of how we relate to each other in groups and communities. We do not want to make the mistake of thinking that because change feels accelerated and amplified in cyberspace, because new social media spring up before our eyes on a regular basis, we must always look forward without checking our Internet rear view mirrors. To understand where we should go in this fast-paced age of technology, it is wise to remember where we came from.

11

Change and Excess

This is just the beginning, the beginning of understanding that cyberspace has no limits, no boundaries.

– Nicholas Negroponte

After breakfast one beautiful Sunday morning, my wife and I headed directly to our computers. Having recently returned from traveling in Ireland, including a visit to the Cyberpsychology Research Centre at RCSI, I had fallen behind on social media. Inspired by my visit to the Centre, while also hoping to broaden my research for this book, I decided to spend more time on Twitter, in addition to my Google+, Flickr, Instagram, Yik Yak, and two Facebook accounts, not to mention a never-ending flow of email. Previously I had only dabbled with Twitter, so I needed to study its interface in more depth. Because my university had just switched to Gmail, I also had to familiarize myself with that service, which meant spending time learning how to do things I had no trouble doing with the old mail service, including the convenience of downloading mail from the server to Mac Mail on my machine – which, as it turned out, would not be possible unless I upgraded my operating system. That annoyance doubled when I discovered Safari would no longer connect to Facebook, a glitch I tried to troubleshoot, but to no avail, forcing me to set up Firefox. If I was going to use Firefox for Facebook, I might as well create bookmarks for all my social media logins, while reserving Safari for Gmail and web browsing. Juggling two browsers, as well as one window for Gmail and another for Mac Mail, was manageable, though not ideal. With that frustrating decision behind me, I set out in Scrivener to compile a book chapter into Word, only to discover that Word crashed every time I opened the file. This never happened before. Now my annoyance with computers escalated into outright exasperation. After spitting a few choice profanities into the screen, I surged with angry determination to make all of this work the way I wanted it to. No sooner had I set my fingers to the keyboard than the power to our house, suddenly and unexpectedly, went out – for no apparent reason on a beautifully sunny Sunday morning. No electricity, no computer. God speaks in mysterious ways.

As is evident in the previous chapter, I moved around cyberspace quite a bit over the years, as do many people. Sooner or later, we migrate from one type of online media to another. We also transition through different environments when we change operating systems, programs, computers, devices, and networks, with each one presenting a new cyberpsychology architecture to understand, master, and hopefully thrive within. When, how, and why do we make these changes or resist them? When do all the changes become too much to handle? In this chapter, I will address these questions by discussing media transitions, media overload, and other excesses in cyberspace journeying. These issues are critically important in the interactive dimension of cyberpsychology architecture.

MOVING ON: MEDIA TRANSITIONS

Cyberspace moves quickly. What strikes us as new and exciting right now could very well lapse into outdated humdrum within a year. As a result, we are forced to keep up. We must eventually make *media transitions*, whether we like it or not. These transitions take us from one digital environment to another, with the new environment introducing changes in some or many of the eight dimensions of cyberpsychology architecture. The more the dimensions change, the bigger the transition. I use the term "media" in a broad sense to refer to any computer-generated environment: a program, operating system, communication channel, device interface, or online location of any kind. A media transition is the changeover from one such environment to another. Sometimes the transition is small, as in updating from one version of a program to a slightly newer one. Sometimes the transition is large, as in installing an entirely new operating system, trying out a new device with a completely different interface, or venturing into some area of cyberspace where you have never been before. What thoughts, emotions, and behaviors come into play as we move from an old, familiar environment to a new one? What determines success or failure in making the change? What motivates us even to try something different?

Living in the Land of Errors

A piano teacher I knew summarized how it felt taking lessons as a child: "I was living in the land of errors." That is also how we might feel when using our devices. How often do we make it through the day without something – big or small – going wrong? Sometimes the error involves our own failure to communicate appropriately with the machine. Something goes wrong because we have not figured out how it works, or we are just not paying attention. In other cases, the responsibility for the problem rests on the shoulders of the device. The program is not making itself clear about how it works. The code or design is inadequate. The hardware does not work properly, or the machine totally crashes – and it is not our fault, unless we expect ourselves to be computer experts who can prevent any problem before it occurs. Even the experts will tell us this is impossible. Computers are so complex that even in the best of circumstances, flaws are inevitable.

So how do we react to living in the land of errors? Falling back on our tendency to anthropomorphize machines and develop transference reactions to them, we might get annoyed with or blame the device, as if it is some kind of stupid, disobedient, unresponsive, unpredictable, or deliberately undermining being. We might get annoyed with or blame ourselves, thinking we are inadequate to the challenge, as if the gadget is testing or even competing with us. We might try to solve the problem, give up if we cannot, then work around it, perhaps in a way that is less efficient, maybe even forgetting that there was a problem, a kind of benign denial. Turning lemons into lemonade, we convince ourselves that the workaround solutions give character to the machine as our quirky but familiar companion. In our twinship relationship with the gadget, we are the only one who knows how to navigate around its idiosyncratic flaws. We might seek help from someone, perhaps tech support. In a compulsive quest to make our machines perfect, we might insist on fixing each and every problem. To avoid more errors, we might never try anything new.

When living in the land of errors grows too frustrating, when it threatens our online access, communication with others, or the safety of our files, we feel compelled to take action. With the device serving as the selfobject that sustains who we are, our very identity feels endangered when the machine no longer functions the way it should. A change is necessary, sometimes a big change.

MEDIA TRANSITION MOTIVATION

Motivation comes from the Latin *motus*, meaning "to move." Something internal moves us, pushes us, from our old cyberspace environment into new ones, despite any obstacles that might stand in the way. What forces create that motivation?

Necessity

It is the mother of invention as well as media transitions. Our familiar programs, workspaces, devices, and social environments seem a bit tired and outdated. They do not work as well as they used to, or we become painfully aware of how we could be doing a lot more than what our status quo allows. In this age of enhanced information and communication, if others are gathering resources or sharing in ways we cannot, we find ourselves woefully behind the curve, out of the loop. Sometimes you just have to move on.

Pride

Behind the curve is not a prestigious position, especially for those who consider themselves sophisticated computer users. Maintaining one's self-esteem requires that push into the next new thing that everyone is talking about, or perhaps even beyond that, into the leading edge of the curve. You might not be a professional, but having the professional program helps you feel that way. People with narcissistic personality styles will be especially prone to pride as the motivation behind their media transitions.

Competition

Not far from pride is that need to be at least one step ahead of the others – bigger, faster, more powerful, unique. The shine of those winning medals can be irresistible, especially in a culture that idealizes both technology and competition. The popularity of phallic jokes about computers, particularly among males, points to this competitive spirit.

Mastery

Setting aside the pride that might accompany one's accomplishments, ambitious users push forward into a new cyberspace challenge simply because it is a challenge. The competitive perks might be irrelevant. The goal of mastering something new motivates the person. This is the pioneering spirit behind many if not all visionary advances in our digital age.

Perfectionism

Some people might expect or hope that their machines will be flawless, that because they have control over them they can create a place where everything is exactly right. This is especially true of people with obsessive-compulsive personality styles. Unfortunately, as we all know, nothing is perfect. Perhaps our computer companions do us a favor by reminding us that we will always be living in a land of errors, no matter how many media transitions we make. The alternative is a driven perfectionism in which a person never feels satisfied. In a restless pursuit of the utopian workstation, idealists upgrade to every new program or device because they truly believe "new" means "better." The grass always seems greener on the other side of technology.

Adventure

Some people shy away from the unknown, while others seek it out. Sensation seekers rappel down cliffs, jump from airplanes, or drive at high speeds. They have their counterparts in the early adopters of technology, the people who want to move fast through cyberspace, to try something daring that no one else has, or to go where no one has gone before. They crave the energy of an online rush and a pioneering spirit. People with a manic personality style are especially prone to such motivations.

The Carrot

At the end of the struggle, there is a reward. You have your own website. You created your own unique avatar. You are a full-fledged member of a group of people who love pugs. Psychologists call it reinforcement. People will work long and hard for a big reinforcement, though usually there are small ones along the way, including those step-by-step moments of achievement and mastery.

Magic and Delight

You can spot computer geeks by their wide-eyed wonder when they see something they have never seen before. Humans have a primeval fascination for anything that looks like magic. When we see our devices doing something marvelously new that we did not believe possible, we feel delight. In what easily becomes an idealizing transference, we want to understand, participate in, and possess that magic.

Climbing the Hierarchy

This list of motivations can be organized according to Maslow's (1943) hierarchy of needs. At the bottom level are basic needs to resolve the practical problems of everyday living. We seek out necessary resources through cyberspace, such as clothing, food, and appliances. At intermediate levels, we establish social bonds, share experiences, and feel like we belong. We can find that in social media. To reach the highest levels, we cultivate feelings of mastery and self-esteem through our activities in cyberspace until the totality of our digital lifestyles enables us to harvest our potential creatively, figure out who we are, and achieve that life-enriching state of mind called *self-actualization*.

MEDIA TRANSITION ANXIETY

Given all these factors that contribute to media transition motivation, we would expect that people are continually moving from one cyberspace environment to another. This is not the case. Another force counterbalances that motivation to change, a force that slows down or completely blocks transition – *media transition anxiety*. The magnitude of that anxiety will vary depending on one's personality as well as the size of the change required.

Burnout

It requires time and energy when adapting to a new environment. If the learning curve is optimum, we experience the change as interesting or even exciting. Beyond that optimal point, the learning process becomes stressful. Although many people in contemporary culture pride themselves on their busy lifestyles and multitasking abilities, technology changes so fast that it is impossible to keep up with every new invention – impossible even to keep up with the things one wants to keep up with. There are a limited number of changes that can be made. Trying to tackle too many media transitions creates cognitive overload and burnout, as I will discuss later in this chapter. It is like trying to catch several rabbits at the same time. Sensing this impending multitasking overload, people avoid making a change. Just the thought of adding yet another computer task can generate media transition anxiety.

Fear of Failure and Incompetence

Media transitions pose challenges at which we might not succeed. No one likes to feel like a failure. No one likes to look foolish or stupid. When moving to new environment, people fall into the role of newbie, a somewhat inexperienced or incompetent novice, which is hard for them, especially in social media where members worry about their image. They may wish to remain in an old environment that they have mastered rather than transition to a new one where they lose those feelings of prestige. Some computer-savvy people who take pride in their skills might find the newbie role quite difficult to handle, especially people with narcissistic personality styles.

Fear of the Unknown

A big transition means entering an environment that is unfamiliar. Humans often respond with anxiety to the unknown. We do not understand where we are. We are not sure what to do. That uncertainly is especially strong when arriving in new social environments. Along with the pressure to figure out how the software works, you must also figure out how the community works and how to behave appropriately within it. It is a form of culture shock. In your old and familiar social media, you were used to a certain type of self-presentation. Moving to a new environment requires reestablishing your social identity and renegotiating how you wish to express yourself. What do you want to reveal? What do you want to keep to yourself? Those decisions can induce anxiety, particularly when others do not react to you the way you need or expect. People with paranoid personality styles find the fear of the unknown especially difficult.

Fear of Rejection and Isolation

In a new social environment, people could reject you or completely ignore you, which is a subtle type of rejection. Sensing this possibility, some people avoid moving into unfamiliar social media, especially if they are sensitive to rejection, which is true of people with depressive personality styles. Because online relationships tend to be media-bound, transitioning to a new social media might mean leaving behind friends and family who belong to the old environment. One might feel isolated and lonely until new friendships are formed.

Fear of Technical Failures

Media transitions do not always proceed smoothly. If you upgrade to solve a problem in your previous environment, sometimes that problem is solved, sometimes not, and sometimes new, even bigger problems surface. Trying to make things a little better can make what you already had worse. "If it ain't broke, don't fix it," has some validity as a philosophy. In the imagined worst-case scenario, people fear that if they try new software, a catastrophe might ensue. The computer crashes. Precious files are lost, which threatens one's identity that is invested in those files. You might also have to cope with separation anxiety, the anxiety about being out of the loop, disconnected from your online relationships and lifestyle. In all of these situations, one might feel helpless and out of control.

Ignorance

Simple ignorance prevents some people from trying something new. They do not understand what they are missing out on. That may be a lack of education, imagination, and curiosity on their part, or they just do not want to understand, in which case they might suffer from unconscious media transition anxiety. No matter how simple or useful the new program might be, they avoid it. They harbor irrational fears about new technology because they think they will not understand how to use it. They are happy with what they can do with their device and avoid doing or even trying to comprehend anything else. Such ignorance is often a symptom of *media mental set.*

MEDIA MENTAL SET

A fixed pattern of thinking that fails to take into consideration new information or perspectives is a *mental set.* As Albert Einstein aptly noted, "We cannot solve our problems with the same level of thinking that created them." As an example, the early astronomers tried to calculate the movement of planets in the sky based on their assumption that all heavenly bodies revolve around the Earth. They were caught in a mental set that led to strange conclusions about the path of planetary orbits because they failed to recognize a completely different perspective: all the planets, including Earth, revolve around the Sun.

Cyberpsychology extends this traditional concept to *media mental set.* It refers to how people's thinking can get stuck within a certain type of digital environment. They approach all issues, including psychological and social ones, strictly in terms of that particular environment, while failing to see other possibilities. Some people who learned how to use Facebook would not try another type of social media, even those with a significantly better interface, simply because it was unfamiliar and not Facebook. Media mental set does not necessarily mean that people are unable to understand a new technology. Instead, they believe that it is too difficult for them to understand, or they perceive it as alien, inaccessible, or irrelevant. They convince themselves that they are happy right where they are. They believe they do not need to try anything new, that it is not worth the effort, that their online lifestyle is fine as it is, or that the new media are not their style. "I'm not the kind of person who blogs." "Virtual realities are not my thing."

Although these beliefs are sometimes perfectly valid, psychologists might point to them as examples of the defense mechanism known as a *rationalization*, or even the more sophisticated *intellectualization*. They are a defense against media transition anxiety. These beliefs might also be an attempt to manage *cognitive dissonance*. Many people might find it illogically contradictory to say, "This new thing is wonderful, and I'm not doing it." Instead, in order to maintain what appears to be a reasonable concordance in their beliefs, they find fault with the new environment despite how enticing it looks.

Media mental set is determined by personality factors, and not simply by limitations in intellectual or critical-thinking abilities. People with obsessive-compulsive personality styles tend to be susceptible. Even intelligent people who are quite knowledgeable about online lifestyles can get locked into this rigid adherence to the environment they prefer. In what could very well be a transference reaction, they idealize their media of choice. They have nostalgic memories about that environment. They invest in it their self-esteem, their very identity. They need to protect this devotion, which can lead to an intellectual defense of their media that resembles territorial behavior. They might also be defending against unconscious media transition anxiety.

Media mental set can evolve into a norm for a whole group of people. They equate their identity as a group with an environment consisting of a particular type of cyberpsychology architecture. Their media mental set serves as social glue that holds them together. When offering consultation to a professional group operating via an email list, I recommended that they experiment with a discussion board format. Even though the group considered itself sophisticated about technology and wanted to develop itself as an online organization, members showed strong resistance against trying a new modality. When I mentioned some benefits of discussion boards over email lists, they either ignored those ideas or replied with a flurry of retorts about how "you can do that in email too."

We do not want to make the mistake of always pathologizing media mental set. Sometimes keeping things just the way they are is the right choice. As Piaget (2001) clearly demonstrated, there is a natural human tendency to see things in terms of what we already know, according to the familiar cognitive templates that make our lives predictable and manageable. Ideally, we learn how to balance our reliance on familiar mental maps with the ability to modify them according to alternative ways of thinking, feeling, and being.

HOW TO MAKE MEDIA TRANSITIONS

Everyone goes through an adaptation period when entering new media. That adaptation is more challenging when moving to a very different environment, especially social ones. Before immersing yourself into it, investigate the new media by reading about it or talking with experienced users. If a friend or coworker will let you, experiment with it on his or her device first. Let that person guide you through the first steps. Try to minimize cost while maximizing benefits. Small changes are less risky than big ones, particularly during times of stress. If you are working on a deadline for an important project, avoid making a big and potentially problematic media change.

Expect a Learning Curve

Even when making small changes, there will be new things to learn. You might need to develop new perceptual and motor skills in order to use the media effectively. If it is an unfamiliar social environment, you may even need to develop different interpersonal skills. In all cases, you must understand the software before you effectively immerse yourself into the culture. Try to keep an open mind about learning new things.

Accept Confusion

While adapting to the new media, it is normal to feel confused or frustrated. Do not assume you will be able to figure out everything right away. Investigate menus. Click on some buttons. Take baby steps. Something may confuse you today, but you will probably figure it out tomorrow. Consider how your mental set might be contributing to a problem. Your built-in assumptions from using a previous environment can prevent you from clearly seeing how the new one is different. Do not automatically assume that the environment cannot do what you want it to. Avoid thinking, "This is different, and that makes it no good!" If you quickly understand everything about the new environment, then it is probably not a very complicated one. Also accept the fact that no program is perfect. Even excellent media have some design flaws, so your confusion or frustration might be justified.

Observe, Then Participate

When moving into a new social environment, observe first, then participate. Before you start to engage others, try to understand the norms of the group. What is considered acceptable and unacceptable behavior? You do not want to jump in with a faux pas. As you start to interact with others, embrace the newbie role. It's okay to be the newcomer. Ask for help. Do not pretend to possess knowledge that you do not have. Listen to people who are familiar with the environment. It is always a bad sign if the old-timers are not interested in helping a newbie or especially if they are hostile toward them. Remember that cyberspace is filled with all sorts of environments, with each one unique in its purpose, how it works, and the kinds of people there. Some groups will be perfect for you, some will not.

THE PSYCHOLOGY OF TECH SUPPORT

Dealing with tech support is an unavoidable part of life in cyberspace, especially when making media transitions. In the previous list of suggestions, we should include the fact that you will not be able to solve some problems on your own. You will have to call tech support. To minimize the unpleasant aspects of doing so, it helps to understand the psychology of tech support personnel. As helpers, they face challenges similar to the psychotherapist.

Customers who call tech support are often frustrated, confused, overwhelmed, desperate, or angry. These feelings can turn into transference reactions toward the tech support person – intense emotions that come from other relationships in their lives while having little to do with tech support. Some workers are patient in the face of these situations. Others lose their composure. They become frustrated. They respond to anger with anger. They might be struggling with their own transference reactions.

When helping a customer with a problem, it is a good idea to get a sense of how much the person knows about it. Some tech support people catch on quickly to the fact that the customer is computer savvy. They are willing to work together in solving the problem. Others seem oblivious to the person's knowledge. They continue talking in a rather pedantic way, even when customers try to show that they are not a total newbie. Once the person's knowledge level is assessed, the worker should, ideally, talk at a level of technical sophistication that matches the knowledge level of the customer, or maybe slightly surpasses it, which gives the person an opportunity to learn something new. So a 1:1 or slightly higher ratio of expert-to-customer technical discourse is good. A low ratio means talking to people in overly simplistic terms, as if they are stupid or children, which no customer likes. A high ratio means talking over the person's head, which might impress some people, but not others who will feel overwhelmed and inadequate, thinking that they should just give up on a media transition that seems too complex.

Tech support workers deal with many of the same issues over and over again, so they have a tendency to fall into rote patterns of solving a problem. In many cases, they have a specific protocol they are required to follow. As a result, their instructions might turn robotic. They slip into a mental set without actually hearing what the client is saying. Instead, they hear and respond to what they expect, to what they think the person is saying.

Customers with media transition problems like to see a light at the end of the tunnel. They appreciate tech support workers who show some optimism. Once in a while, workers get excited talking about computers, usually in response to a question they find interesting, or to a customer who seems to understand technology. People disappointed with their misbehaving machines like to regain any enthusiasm they lost.

Customers want to idealize tech support. They hope and pray that the worker has a solution. Unfortunately, no one knows everything about computers. Insecure workers defend their self-esteem by pretending to be an omniscient healer of the machine, which does no one any good. Mature tech support staff admit it when they do not know something, that when they put you on hold it is because they are consulting documentation or their supervisor. When I asked one worker at Apple exactly what file permissions were, he replied honestly, "You're asking something that goes over my head." He then proceeded to describe what he did know about the topic, which went over my head. I respected him for that. Another worker told me that, "I'm not supposed to speculate." Although they want to avoid mistakes by guessing wrong, they often do have to make their best guess. That hunch might help, as long as no one, especially the customer, ends up feeling confused and helpless.

THE VARIETIES OF OVERLOAD EXPERIENCE

Even with the help of experts, the ever-changing complexities of cyberspace can feel overwhelming. The conflicting opinions of experts only add to the confusion. Rapid changes in the environments we humans continually create for ourselves are not a new problem in our history, but the invention of cyberspace has indeed raised the bar in demanding us to cope with an unprecedented influx of stimulation that challenges our mental capabilities.

In his studies of city life at the turn of the century, Simmel (1903) warned about the *sensory overload* generated by unrelenting images, sounds, smells, and physical sensations in the environment. A common example is a crowded carnival, brimming with the noise of machines, the smell of food, the blinking of lights, the waves of people, the cornucopia of colors, and the wild sensations of the rides. Especially during prolonged and intense exposure, one's mind simply cannot cope with such exhausting input. In his famous book *Future Shock*, Toffler (1970) pointed to the trouble we can have understanding an issue and making decisions due to the flood of too much information. Based on findings by such researchers as Sweller (1988), contemporary psychologists talk about *cognitive overload*, when our working memory is overrun with information, leading to poor performance and even "crashes," similar to what can happen to the working memory in a computer. Cognitive overload includes *visual overload*, when excessive visual clutter interferes with brain functioning. If the elements of a scene are not organized – if there is not enough redundancy or predictability to create a sense of order – our minds cannot make sense out of what we see. We do not perceive specific shapes or meanings, but rather just sameness, muddle, and chaos.

Anyone who has ventured into cyberspace understands this problem with overload. Through our devices, we dive into an ocean of stimulation. It comes at us from all directions. Everywhere we turn, there is another post to read, another video to watch, another song to hear, and another game to play. In large social media platforms, people who want to succeed in establishing their presence have to work overtime in mastering the many complexities of the environment while managing their snowballing list of contacts. They are forced to dedicate themselves to just one, two, or maybe three social media, because trying to juggle more could easily trigger psychological burnout. As a photographer, I often found myself running headfirst into massive walls of images in whatever photosharing community I entered. Words, images, videos, sounds, music, people, conversations, information, links, advertisements – our screens, eyes, and ears are filled with stuff. Although people such as the designer Manuel Lima (2013) have tried to find a way to make sense out of, visually map, and even appreciate the beauty of such overstimulating complexity, most of us struggle to avoid feeling engulfed by it. Mitchell Kapor, founder of the Lotus Development Corporation, said, "Getting information off the Internet is like taking a drink from a fire hydrant." I am reminded of the movie *Moscow on the Hudson*, in which a Russian defector, played by Robin Williams, strolls for the first time through an American supermarket. Surrounded by seemingly countless cans of caffeinated grinds, his eyes fly open wide with disbelief as he mumbles, "coffee, coffee, *coffee!*" His dilemma finds its echo in a comment made by one of my students in a survey of attitudes about cyberspace:

> We are so bombarded with information that it's hard to get to the core of what you're actually looking for. Half of the information out there is false anyway. All we wanted was to quench our thirst, but instead we are drowning and we don't know how to swim.

SYMPTOMS OF THE OVERLOADED MIND

With all this written, visual, auditory, social, and emotional stimulation bombarding us as soon as we look into our screens, what happens to our psyches when we spend too much time engrossed in all that overwhelming input? How does it affect the way we see, think, and feel? The detrimental symptoms of overload tend to fall into the following four categories.

Leveling

In the face of so much stimulation, we do not pay attention to details anymore. Our mind simplifies everything in order to avoid the excessive input. Our attention becomes narrowly selective. Pictures, especially ones that move, will draw our attention more so than text, especially unassuming text, which is why many social media designers have opted to highlight photos and videos while shoving text communication into small or hidden boxes. Even with the never-ending flow of images on our screens, we tend to ignore any picture style or subject matter that does not immediately slap us in the face. "Everybody gets so much information all day long that they lose their commonsense," Gertrude Stein commented. Rather than embracing subtlety or complexity, we notice only the most obvious things about photographs or things that have an immediate impact on our personal interests. Sophisticatedly discerning perceptions level off to more primitive ones that address some underlying and perhaps even unconscious need. "I browse through media very quickly," one of my students commented, "but as soon as I come across something interesting or what I'm looking for, my mind becomes instantly alert and tells me to stop to look at this." Leveling might also contribute to feelings of indifferent passivity in cyberspace. "The Internet seems like some kind of giant exhibition, and I'm just an aloof visitor," said another student.

With so much information and social activity in their faces, some people unconsciously slip into the familiar ruts of their mental sets rather than tackle anything new. They focus on people and pages that say things they already know, as a way to stabilize or reassure themselves, which is one of the pitfalls of trying to be a self-educated person. This kind of leveling magnifies the problematic tendency to skim over the many points of views available in cyberspace in order to locate the specific people who will confirm what one wants or needs to believe, rather than what one should know to be a more well-rounded, informed citizen.

Indecision and Regret

People are not happy when faced with too many options, especially when they have to make a decision. Too much information leads to the daunting task of weighing pros and cons. When the level of complexity gets too high, when six of one looks like half a dozen of another, people want to give up. Those who do finally make a decision second-guess themselves afterward. Did I make the right choice? Was that other option better? We would think that in a cyberspace filled with so many possibilities, people would find what they need, then afterward feel good about their selection. Instead, thinking that the grass might have been greener on the other side of the technological fence, they end up feeling unsure about themselves and doubtful about their decision.

Irritable Confusion

The psyche overwhelmed with stimulation sinks into distractibility, disorientation, restlessness, hypersensitivity, sleeplessness, fidgeting, irritability, and anger. What we see on our computer screen becomes an annoying mishmash of stuff. Everything starts to look the same, sound the same. We lose our ability to differentiate between this and that, especially when the differences are nuanced or intricate. Irritable confusion often precedes shutdown.

Shutdown

Our overloaded brains go numb. Our mind crashes. Feeling indifferent, bored, tired, or burned out, we simply cannot respond any more. We shut down, withdraw from all the stimulation. "Being online exhausts me," one of my students put it simply. Any serious computer user knows that need to get up and get away from the machine. The mind demands time to decompress, refresh, and reset before returning to cyberspace. Excessive or repeated burnout can entirely change one's attitudes about cyberspace, especially after experiencing a period of liberating freedom from it. People vacationing for a substantial length of time, without any communication devices, take to heart the relief they feel when disconnected from the onslaught of the online universe. They might never return to their previously intense level of activity in cyberspace. They cut back drastically to live more time in the "real" world, perhaps with the help of apps that alert them when they spend too much time with their devices. We will return to this issue in Chapter 12, "Addicted or Devoted."

PHOTO OVERLOAD

I myself became acutely aware of media overload during my participant-observation research in the Flickr and Google+ photosharing communities. Anyone serious about photography is familiar with the scenario of spending so much time processing images on a computer that one's mind goes numb. You cannot tell anymore whether a photo looks good or not. In that situation, only you notice the decline in your ability to work effectively. But during online photosharing, the impact of overload quickly turns interpersonal. Your ability to look at and comment on other people's pictures will be much less than optimal. Mentally saturated by the endless stream of images flowing across your screen, you cannot pay close attention to what you see and read. You cannot think straight. Everything looks about the same. Subtleties are lost to you. You skim over streams of images, noticing only the most obvious things.

These superficial perceptions color any comments or "likes" you offer on a photograph, assuming you are not too burned out to comment at all. Your remarks will sound generic, obvious, or bland. You might make errors in spelling and grammar. Maybe you even lose track of where you are online and with whom you are sharing your comments. Unfortunately, other people are also suffering from overload, resulting in a globally lackluster, unresponsive, and superficial atmosphere. Generically benign comments such as "Nice shot" and "Beautiful colors" proliferate, or there are no comments at all. If you are the photographer in such an environment, you might feel misunderstood, underappreciated, or overlooked, because very few if any people have been able to look at or comment on your work with full attention and clarity of mind. Even an excellent photograph, or one very personally meaningful to the photographer, can receive a lukewarm, shallow reception. Many forms of social media suffer from these stultifying effects of overload.

REMEDIES FOR OVERLOAD

The first problem in coping with mental overload is recognizing that it is happening. You might not notice it setting in. The effects take hold at a subconscious level. If you feel energized, focused, happy, and excited, you are probably doing fine. If not, notice how you do feel. Which of the various symptoms of overload might be affecting you? If you conclude that you are indeed suffering from overload, here are some possible solutions.

Reduce Stimulation

If you want or need to keep working, lower the amount of input coming at you. Stop multitasking, close unnecessary windows on your computer, and do one thing at a time. If you are looking at photos, for example, focus on just one. Slow down, relax, and take your time in looking at it. Allow yourself to appreciate that post without other distractions or agendas clouding your mind. If possible, shift yourself into a peaceful "in the now" state of mind. Making this transition might not be possible if the overload is severe, but it is worth a try. The designers of social media sometimes try to help reduce stimulation by placing caps on activity, such as limiting the number or length of posts.

Take a Break

Stop whatever you are doing so you can take a break. You might do something else on the computer or mobile device, but the odds are that it is the machine itself, regardless of what you are doing on it, that is the source of the overload problem. So try something else. In some cases, a short break might be enough to refresh your mind. At other times, you might need to stay away from the computer or mobile device for hours or even days.

Get Physical

Hear, smell, taste, and get physical. Most of the time, overload comes from excessive visual and verbal stimulation, along with all the cognitive processing associated with images and words. You are looking at too many images, reading too many posts, thinking too much about them, and typing too much about them. When you take a break, try some other kind of activity. For example, listen to music, make music, cook, eat, or do anything physical like going for a walk or cleaning the house. These alternative activities not only will give your overloaded mind a much needed rest, they can also enrich your online experiences by processing them in a different way, in the back of your mind, subconsciously. An old Latin proverb states, "It is solved by walking."

Mindfulness

Many of these remedies stem from *mindfulness*. As a traditional form of meditation originating in ancient India, mindfulness meditation cultivates the ability of simply being aware, without pressure to do, think, or feel anything. Mindfulness meditators learn how to focus peacefully on something without judging, analyzing, or expecting while also allowing the periphery of their conscious awareness to notice new things that they could attend to, if they wish. They learn how to let go of stressful thoughts and feelings rather than become overwhelmed by them. Translating mindfulness into cyberspace means riding the waves of stimulation that come at you, calmly attending to this, then that, without drowning in all that input. Like anything else worth doing in life, mindfulness takes practice. It is a skill that can be learned, as Kabat-Zinn (2005) described so elegantly in his book on mindfulness in everyday life. In our contemporary culture, we can see applications of mindfulness in health care, education, the arts, and psychotherapy. It is perhaps the single most effective antidote for many of the ailments induced by our media-saturated society. Mindfulness includes the ability to let go of cyberspace and all that it means in order to notice and focus on something else in your life.

Some people believe that multitasking and "augmented reality" have led to the next step in the evolution of the human mind. They claim a new form of mindfulness will enable people to manage mental overload by effectively juggling several tasks simultaneously, including the integration of online resources into what we experience in the real-world situation at hand. One problem with this belief is that similar mental operations interfere with each other. If you try to listen to a speaker while reading that person's blog and the online comments of other people in the audience, those tasks inevitably disrupt each other and contribute to overload as they compete for your language-processing abilities. According to its traditional meaning, mindfulness is simply being aware, with nothing else added, which means letting go of the need to multitask, along with all the thinking, judging, analyzing, and deciding that goes with it. This is why the simple awareness of mindfulness offers a cure for all types of overload.

Addressing Other People's Overload

How do you break through the overload inside the minds of other people you encounter in cyberspace? How do you get them to be at bit more aware, understanding, and compassionate? You might try giving them what you hope to receive: calm, mindful attention to their online presence. If you respond to people's posts in an empathic way, you increase the probability they will respond in kind. You might resonate with them about how everyone online is trying to cope with the stress of excessive stimulation. Misery not only loves company, it can decrease as a result of it. Never discussing the overload elephant affecting everyone in the room rarely helps anyone.

Another strategy is to work with people's tendency toward leveling. Emphasize all the things in your posts that you know will catch the attention of visitors. In the case of photos, use bright colors, high contrast, simple but strong compositions, subjects portraying powerful emotions, or even sensual themes. Although you might feel you are selling out or lowering your standards just to get attention, you can use this strategy to your advantage. Exercise your creative muscles in sharing uncomplicated images and concise messages that pop psychologically. This skill is both an art and a science.

You can patiently wait out the sensory overload of people viewing your posts. Some visitors will come along who are not suffering from burnout or who have found a way to remedy it. When they leave a good comment or otherwise show more than a superficial appreciation of your posts, make sure that you acknowledge their efforts. In return, show the same level of care in responding to them.

LESSONS FROM SPAM

Often we are responsible for our own media overload. By trying to accomplish too much online, we put ourselves into that predicament. In other ways, it is inflicted upon us. The phenomenon that came to be known as *spam* highlights these deliberate, undesired invasions into our personal space that turn up the overload volume.

In the early days of the Internet, people eagerly encouraged communication. They wanted to share ideas in an inviting, trusting atmosphere.

When cyberspace boomed – when large chunks of it took shape as marketplace, soapbox, and competitive playground – that atmosphere faded. Screens became flooded with messages designed to sell, manipulate, and deceive. Some people found themselves wanting to shut down communication rather than open it up. Trust turned to suspicion, thanks to this influx of what people called "spam." Some say the term came from a *Monty Python* television episode in which a meaninglessly random repetition of the song "spam, spam, lovely spam, wonderful spam," overpowered the rest of the show. Others claim the term originated among technology geeks at the University of Southern California who invented it because, like its lunchmeat namesake, almost no one seems to ask for or want it. If they do happen to get some, they most likely throw it away.

Advocates of the idealistic Internet philosophy apply a broad stroke in defining spam as any message violating the traditional rules of netiquette that were intended to preserve online cooperation, helpfulness, trust, and bandwidth. Unsolicited email, advertisements, irrelevant or repetitious posts, notifications that pop up and under your browser window, and any message sent indiscriminately to many people would all be considered spam. While most spam simply adds to media overload, some spam messages are poisonous attempts to infect our mind with worries or our machines with unwanted ads and viruses, what have been called *adware* or *malware*. Because we experience cyberspace as an extension of our psyche, all forms of spam invade our personal space. As territorial creatures, we feel compelled to protect our ground against the onslaught, usually by adopting two different strategies.

The first line of defense is through automation. We set our browsers to block pop-ups or, in the case of email, we create filters that detect and preemptively vanquish spam before it gets to the inbox. The concept is simple enough, but the fight against spam turns into an ongoing game of cat-and-mouse. Being cleverly determined people, email spammers continually alter their messages so they can slip past what we tell the filters to recognize as spam. Some savvy people might enjoy this battle of wits with the encroaching enemy, but the game feels tediously time consuming for many others who simply want to end this nuisance that exacerbates their cognitive overload.

This software defense also requires optimal signal detection. How do you balance the false hits against the false misses? If you make your filters robust, you will eliminate lots of spam at the risk of also blocking out valid messages. Targeting any email with a subject title containing the word "penis" will quickly eliminate messages dubiously promoting a product that increases manly size, but what about that long-lost, zany friend who decides to contact you with a surprise phallic joke as the title of his message? Once again tackling cognitive overload, you might scan an overflowing junk box looking for good messages to rescue, but that scanning ability takes time and practice. On the other hand, if you ease up on your filters, you increase the possibility of letting desirable mail through at the cost of letting in more spam as well. Where is that delicate Goldilocks balance that is just right? Exactly how open and vulnerable, versus closed and protected, does a person want to be? These are yet more questions to consider in the age of media overload.

The second line of defense for email spam is weeding by hand. You scan the inbox for offenders, then delete them. But which ones are spam? Do you recognize a weed when you see it? One person's weed is another's flower, so the answer is partly personal. As you skim the inbox, you try to spot sender names and subject titles that warrant the delete key. The spammers, on the other hand, want you to open that email so the message can spring before your eyes. In this psychological match of wits, how do they get you to open the message you do not want to read? Mostly by creating subject titles or usernames that trigger some psychological need or worry. Although I will focus on email when describing these needs and worries, we see the same tricks in ads all over the Internet.

Activating Cultural Preoccupations

Save precious time. Lower your mortgage payment. Be a winner. Eat potato chips, watch more TV, and lose 22 pounds .... These message titles are rather easy to spot as spam, but some people still click on them. Who does not want to save time and money, be a winner, or eat junk food while losing weight? We live in a culture that dwells on improving appearances, accumulating money, making comparisons, and competing. "Less" and "more" are on everyone's mind. This type of spam taps the reservoir of obsessions underlying our culture. In a fascinating sociological experiment, we might tally such messages as a barometer of contemporary life.

Activating Archetypal Concerns

Take hold of your pleasure. We guarantee your success. What is freedom to you? Learn how to love.... Here we see the message titles playing not just on the obsessions of the modern psyche, but also on fundamental existential and archetypal concerns – issues basic simply to being human. Success, pain, pleasure, love, freedom, celebration, life, transformation – the message titles present these ideas in a very vague, generic manner, almost like an inkblot test. What does pleasure, success, or freedom mean to you? Advertisers well know that ambiguous messages pull on one's imagination. They activate the unconscious mind. We cannot help but project our own feelings and needs into that ambiguity, even if we are not fully aware that we are doing so. If you sense one of your most basic needs in the message subject, you will be tempted to open it.

Activating Sexuality

Nasty girls do it all. Adult products for you. Better sex. Pics from Gabriella attached.... Spammers often target sexual desires, along with all the nuances of seduction, romance, pleasure, wantonness, and depravity that one can imagine. These messages are easy to spot. For some people, they look like forbidden fruit that is hard to resist. For others, they turn into an annoyingly chronic eyesore. Some people wonder why spammers targeted them in particular with these pornographic ads. They worry whether while online they said or visited something sexual that these spammers detected. When these sexual messages induce a mixture of guilt and temptation, some people open them.

Activating Anxiety

Rejection policy. Your computer is infected. You are being investigated. We are closing your account.... These titles are intended to arouse anxiety, even though they have nothing to do with the actual content of the message. Did I do something wrong? Is something bad about to happen to me? One feels compelled to open the message for clarification or for reassurance that everything is okay. Horror stories about the Internet abound in the media, so cyberspace has evolved into a rather paranoid space, leading us to worry about our privacy, our money, and the safety of our machines. Some of those fears are justified. Spam that activates those fears is difficult to ignore.

Faking a Personal Touch

Information for Suler. Time in a bottle for Suler. Hi Suler, some questions.... If someone addresses you by name, you respond. The first time these "personalized" messages appeared in our inboxes, we probably opened them, thinking that someone specifically addressed them to us. With more experience, we realize that a computer generated these message titles, with our names awkwardly inserted. These messages attempt a personal touch by appearing to come from a specific person rather than an organization or business. Do I know a Kassie Oam? The spammer hopes that your curiosity and willingness to respond to an individual, particularly one who addresses you by name, will prompt you to open that message. These names might be purely fictitious or, even more insidiously, stolen from real people as a type of *spoofing*.

Faking Replies and Interactions

Re: your request. Re: professor of psychology. You were approved! Here is that sample you requested. Fwd: An important notification.... When a "re:" appears in a subject line, we assume that someone is replying to a message we sent, and so we look at that supposed response. A particularly devious use of the "re:" includes a subject title consisting of phrases stolen from one of your pages online. If the subject indicates that we applied for or requested something, we might open the email out of curiosity, perhaps to reassure ourselves that we did not forget something. The "Fwd" prefix similarly draws us into the illusion of human interaction by faking a person who decided to forward some important message to us. If we are led to believe that someone is talking or responding to us specifically, we tend to respond in return.

Faking Informality and Acquaintance

Hey. What's up? I'll keep this short. Happy to see you. Message from Anna, Mary's mother.... Some messages contain subject lines worded in a casual, friendly style, which creates the illusion of someone who knows you. Seeing only the sender's first name reinforces that informal feeling. Other messages imply some kind of connection to you, as in suggesting that you saw this person recently or know someone this sender knows. These subject lines have absolutely nothing to do with the content of the message, which often is an advertisement of some sort.

Quirky Attention Grabbers

Goldfish. Happy epiphany. Shake it baby. Wrgwger.... Some message titles leave you scratching your head. A curious sender name adds to the effect. You may know it is spam, but open it anyway out of curiosity, just to see what is inside. Message titles containing strange glitches often indicate message bodies filled with glitches, sometimes due to email coming from other countries that use different character sets that are not translated properly by your email software. You will probably open these messages only once. Afterward, they become easily spotted targets for the delete button, like shooting fish in a barrel.

Constipation

Spam email, along with their attachments, might pile up on your mail server. If left unchecked, this heap will build until your disk space on the server is full, creating a clog that will cause incoming mail to bounce back to their senders with a "mailbox full" error message. If your email provider does not inform you of your clogged disk space, you may never know that people can no longer email you. These spam droppings have stopped up your email service, resulting in constipation. Check your email software to enable features that will purge these messages on the server, or evacuate them by hand. Here I am very conscious of using scatological metaphors. Cleaning spam out of your computer and email account certainly feels like clearing out muck. You may experience that evacuating process as somewhat satisfying, though not nearly as satisfying as it would be never to have to deal with spam again. Web browsers can also become filled with all sorts of software tools that some sites inserted without your knowing it.

Becoming a Spammer

Without fully realizing it, you might become conscripted into the spammers' army. Chain emails supposedly alerting us to important but actually fictitious information lure people into forwarding nonsense, scams, and blatant propaganda. The email message then becomes a virus that spreads across the Internet, with your providing more fuel for it. Is the government going to implant microchips into our brains? Will you support a dying child requesting a thousand forwarded emails? Does the email entitled "Have a Nice Day" really contain a malicious virus, or is the virus actually only this email warning us about it? Whether or not people fall for such scamming ploys depends on how knowledgeable they are about cyberspace, as well as how susceptible they might be to alarmist reactions or pleas for protest and sympathy. When websites such as factcheck.org appeared, we finally had a valuable tool to inspect the validity of such messages. By improving our ability to identify spam – by deciding what we do and do not want in our psychic space – we also learn something about ourselves.

LESSONS FROM Y2K

The excesses that beset us in cyberspace can be the creations of our own minds. A good example was the Y2K scare. As the year 2000 approached, computer experts sounded the warning of a big problem awaiting us. Many computers were designed to abbreviate the four-digit year to two digits. What would happen at the very second the clock ticked into the new millennium, requiring computers to tell the difference between the year 2000 and the year 1900? Could they do it? Was there time to fix this bug? Or at the strike of midnight on New Year's Eve, would elevators stop dead between floors, power plants shut down, and airplanes fall out of the sky? Would the Internet infrastructure crash, causing the world's economy to collapse as the vast network of banking computers spun out of control, throwing the whole world itself into chaos?

Some people believed so. They stockpiled supplies in anticipation of a society so crippled by the Y2K bug that it would crumble into anarchy. They truly believed The End was at hand. Others were not so extreme in their fears, but still expected some major mishaps once the new millennium rolled in. Make sure you have good hardcopy records of all your finances. Just to be safe, do not fly on January 1. One could not help but think of the remark made by Clive James: "It is only when they go wrong that machines remind you how powerful they are."

History is filled with examples of small cults and or quasi-religious groups that predicted the end of the world. In some cases, they borrowed the apocalyptic mindset from true believers who devoutly point to the end of the world as prophesized in the Book of Revelations. The belief system of many modern cults is a hodgepodge conglomeration of ideas from religion, philosophy, psychology, the occult, and science. It is the injection of those scientific ideas into their belief system that helps justify it, that makes it appear rational, logical, and indisputable. The Y2K dilemma was the perfect technological ingredient to make an End Time soup palatable for those who doubted the impending apocalypse while raising the appetite of those who already believed. Fundamentalist and survivalist groups that promoted catastrophic visions benefited from the scientism of the Y2K fright. It was a very handy tool in proselytizing. "Join us now, before it's too late." Even if there was no Y2K problem, we would still have seen these end-of-the-world predictions popping up around the globe as the new millennium approached. Y2K simply amplified the trepidation about the historic change about to take place.

Psychological vulnerabilities make us susceptible to Y2K anxiety or similar technology-generated fears, such as the predicted *singularity* when computers will supposedly become so smart that they will take over human civilization. Some people grow up in a family or environment marked by catastrophes and unexpected trauma. Worry, suspicion, or even outright paranoia about what lies around the bend became etched into their psyche. Psychologists well know that one component of depression is the style of faulty thinking called *catastrophizing*, the tendency to expect crisis, often based on little or no evidence. Guilt, shame, and low self-esteem push people toward thoughts about being destroyed. Our culture encourages catastrophic thinking in everyone, as evident in the popularity of movies and TV series devoted to apocalyptic nightmares and how horrible life would in the aftermath.

These media specters capitalize on several basic human anxieties that are exacerbated by rapid technological changes, as exemplified so well by Y2K. There is our fear of helplessness. Computers are supposed to assist us, but might they paradoxically bring about our own loss of control? There is our fear of death, of things coming to an end. Confident that their computers could handle the Y2K problem, Apple aired a commercial during the 1999 Super Bowl that satirized the millennium scare by asking, "Who will survive it?" It is a question we might ask ourselves about future digital age catastrophes. There is our fear of change and the unknown. Even if the world does not come to an end, might cyberspace lead us into dangerous territories, or take us away from traditions that served us well without our fully realizing what cherished things we have lost? There is our fear of excessive dependence that makes us weak and vulnerable. You can take great care of your own computer as well as yourself – but your computer, and therefore you, are intertwined with other computers and other people who do not necessarily have your best interests in mind. There is our fear of retribution. The Millennium Bug warned us not to take too much pride in this computerized world that we have built. We think we know what we are doing, that technology has brought us closer to perfection, mastery, and a divine-like state of knowledge. But like the *Titanic*, our glorious achievement can fail miserably. It can turn on us. We will be punished for our hubris. In what becomes a Revenge of the Machines, a Frankenstein's Monster, the artificial creation retaliates against its creator. "Computers are like Old Testament gods," Joseph Campbell noted. "Lots of rules and no mercy."

The Y2K bug reminds me of the tragic flaw in classic Greek literature. The hero has a weakness – a secret, hidden vulnerability that he himself might not realize, an Achilles' heel. At the peak of his triumph, it comes back to trigger his downfall. In their quest for speedy efficiency, computer programmers failed to predict the possibility that their two-digit technique for encoding the year might lead to a total breakdown of technology. Time would come back to punish them for the flawed representation of time they built into their machines. Those machines are but a reflection of their creators – flawed, imperfect, and often unaware of their imperfection. Y2K was the wake-up call to this fact. It was the reminder that the computers we created, that we ourselves, are not invulnerable. Despite our best heroic efforts, we humans, by our very nature, make mistakes. To make matters even more complex, we make mistakes when we evaluate the possible outcomes of our mistakes. As technology speeds along, which of our errors will be simple speed bumps, which will be catastrophes, and how do we distinguish between justifiable worry and irrational paranoia?

CYBERSPACE MANIA

According to the *Gartner hype cycle* (Linden & Fenn, 2003), we progress through a series of stages when confronted with new technology. There is an enthusiastic surge of inflated expectations once something new appears, followed by a trough of disappointment when it does not seem to perform as well as anticipated, then finally a gradual, more realistic "slope of enlightenment" as we come to understand exactly how the new technology can be used productively given its strengths and weaknesses.

This hype cycle is reminiscent of a psychological pattern called *splitting* in psychodynamic theory. Deep within the human psyche lies a delicate balance between denigrating and idealizing something that is very important to us, on which we have grown psychologically dependent. Our discrediting of that thing can quickly turn into glorification, and vice versa. Often this splitting is a symptom of a developmentally immature attitude toward that someone or something that has control over us.

Given how powerful the Internet has become in contemporary times, the flip side to our paranoia about it is our exalting of it. Strongly encouraged by technology companies, we have entered an age of cyberspace mania, or what some people simply called "cybermania." We buy new devices and discard the old at a rapid pace; millions of people are clamoring to carve out their niche in the online universe; TV series and movies highlighting technology abound; and all forms of media are filled with tales about social media stars, the triumphs and tribulations of cyberspace, marvelous new products, and fantastic predictions about where the digital age will take us. Technology that is "bigger, faster, more" has become a feverish *cri de coeur*. Its glitter lights up the "NEW!" center of our brains. "People complain about the crack in the screen of my brand new phone," one of my students commented, "People want new, perfect, beautiful technology right here and now." According to the Gartner hype cycle, we might gradually adopt a realistic attitude about some particular aspect of technology, but we still remain caught in a highly energetic love/hate relationship with technology as a whole.

Our cultural attitudes resemble the characteristics of the manic personality style. Obsessed by and immersed in technology, we have become elated, energetic, impulsive, mobile, distractible, self-promoting, highly social, witty, and entertaining. But as with the manic personality, we might be defending against an underlying depression. Are we realizing that technology is not magically solving our problems, or at best solves some while creating others, despite how much effort we put into our digital lifestyles? Where does a healthy preoccupation with technology end and where does pathological addiction begin?

12

Addicted or Devoted

I have with me two gods, persuasion and compulsion.
– Themistocles

One day at the Mansion, I found myself in the spa with several other avid Palace members. A curious thing happened whenever we mentioned the word "Palace" in our conversation. For example, when I typed, "What do you people think of Palace?" I was surprised to see what actually appeared on the screen: "What do you people think of this thing that is eating my life?" When I finally figured out that the Palace software itself made this seemingly silly substitution of words, my confusion turned to delight, then curiosity. Indeed, it was an insightful prank by the Palace creator who had built it into the program. It raised an important question, perhaps a worrisome question for many people: is Palace indeed eating my life?

Some people find themselves so captivated by their cyberspace lifestyles that they want to spend as much time there as possible, sometimes to the neglect of their real life. They might not be entirely sure why they find themselves so engrossed. They cannot accurately verbalize an explanation for their compulsion. The humorous substitution of words in the Palace spa suggests that it does feel like an unnamable thing – a compelling, hidden force. It is not the blog, social media, game, shopping, gambling, or whatever online activity that is eating one's life, but the indescribable, unconscious impulse it ignited.

WHAT SHOULD WE CALL IT?

With researchers such as Greenfield (1999), Griffiths (2000), Morahan-Martin (2005), and Young (1998) leading the way, mental health professionals have struggled to find a term to capture this phenomenon accurately. It could be labeled as an *Internet addiction disorder*, except that people were addicted to their computers before the Internet became popular. We might call the phenomenon a computer addiction or, for those people who compulsively immerse themselves into the imaginary worlds of gaming, a virtual addiction. Video game compulsions were quite obvious even before gaming went into personal computers and then online. To avoid controversies associated with the word "addiction," some people use expressions like "pathological" or "compulsive" use (Young & Nabuco de Abreu, 2010).

On a broad level, it makes sense to talk about a *cyberspace addiction*, an addiction to computer-generated experiences. Within this broad category, there are subtypes. A teenager who plays hooky from school in order to master the next level of an online game might be a very different person than the middle-aged housewife who spends all day in social media, who in turn might be very different from the businessperson who cannot tear himself away from online stock trading. Some cyberspace addictions are game- and competition-oriented, some fulfill more social needs, and some might be an extension of workaholism. Researchers refer to the Big Four – games, gambling, sex, and socializing – although some psychologists claim these categories are surface distinctions that do not get at the underlying "thing" that drives all such problems.

During the first decade of cyberspace, I frequently received requests from journalists to comment on the Internet addiction controversy. Does this thing really exist? How bad is it? It seemed like such a fascinating but scary topic, partly because most people at that time were only casually invested in online activities or not online at all. Unfamiliarity tends to breed fear and skepticism. Years later, comparatively few news stories focused on cyberspace addiction. It faded into a passé issue. Once everyone went online, our preoccupation with cyberspace turned into a cultural norm. Everyone reached a consensus: we are devoted, not addicted.

Despite the now widespread tolerance for cyberspace mania, we should not neglect the fact that some people undeniably hurt themselves by their excessive Internet use. When people lose their jobs, fail out of school, or are divorced by their spouses because they cannot resist devoting all of their time to virtual lands, they suffer from a real problem. These extreme cases are clear-cut, but as in all addictions, the boundary between normal enthusiasm and abnormal preoccupation gets blurry. Was Einstein addicted to physics, or Picasso to painting? As we will see throughout this chapter, there can be a very fine line between healthy cyberspace fervor and pathological addiction. Sometimes it even seems we are addicted to the idea of addiction.

THE SLIPPERY SLOPE OF DIAGNOSIS

Defined very loosely in our popular culture, addictions can be healthy, unhealthy, or a mixture of both. If you are fascinated by a hobby, feel committed to it, would like to spend as much time as possible pursuing it, this passion could be a vehicle for learning, creativity, and self-expression. Even in an unhealthy compulsion, you might find these positive features embedded in the problem while also contributing to it. In a truly pathological addiction, the scale has tipped. The bad clearly outweighs the good, resulting in serious disturbances in one's ability to function in life. Almost anything could be the source of a serious addiction: drugs, eating, exercising, gambling, sex, spending, working, and so on. You name it, someone out there is compulsive about it, including such unique online problems as cyberchondria, which the researchers Aiken and Kirwan (2013) describe as an obsessive preoccupation about having a serious medical problem as a result of searching online information. Clinicians recognize that these pathological addictions often have their origin early in a person's life, arising from significant deprivations and conflicts. The addiction might be an attempt to control an underlying depression or anxiety. It might reflect deep insecurities or feelings of inner emptiness.

Since the late 1990s, psychologists have debated whether cyberspace addictions are truly a new type of mental disorder or simply a variation of other familiar compulsions (Young & Nabuco de Abreu, 2010). Online gaming addictions were the first to be given serious consideration as a new entry in the *Diagnostic and Statistical Manual of Mental Disorders*, which reflects how addictive games can be. As with any official diagnostic category in mental health, the concept of a cyberspace addiction needs to withstand the weight of extensive research. It must meet two basic criteria: reliability and validity. For reliability, there must be a consistent set of symptoms that constitute the disorder such that independent observers would agree on the diagnosis. For validity, the diagnosis must correlate with something meaningful. Are there similar elements in the histories, personalities, current level of functioning in everyday life, responses to treatment, or prognoses of people who are so diagnosed? If not, where's the beef? It is simply a label with no external validity.

When establishing reliability, researchers try to identify the constellation of symptoms that constitutes a cyberspace addiction. Curiously, we see the foreshadowing of these criteria in various jokes that have surfaced since the very beginning of cyberspace – for example, "The Top Ten Signs You're Addicted to the Net." I modified them slightly because the original top ten referred to online places and programs that few people now remember. When it comes to addictive behavior, the particular places and programs are not that relevant.

10. You wake up at 3 A.M. to go to the bathroom and check Facebook.
9. You get a tattoo that reads, "This body best viewed with Firefox."
8. You name your children Twitter and Dotcom.
7. When you turn off your computer you get this awful empty feeling, like you just pulled the plug on a loved one.
6. You spend half of the plane trip with your laptop on your lap, and your child in the overhead compartment.
5. You decide to stay in college for an additional year, just for the free Internet.
4. You laugh at people who use landline phones.
3. You feel your phone vibrating with a notification even though it's on the other side of the room.
2. You feel insecure about anything you say without first googling it.
1. Your computer crashes. You haven't logged in for two hours. You start to twitch. You talk into your keyboard hoping to connect. You think you succeed.

In 1996, the psychiatrist Ivan Goldberg posted to his Internet psychology group a message in which he announced the formation of the Internet Addiction Support Group, along with criteria for diagnosing pathological computer use. Although he offered the message tongue-in-cheek, he and other clinicians quickly realized this was not simply a joking matter. Serious research over the following decade identified predictable symptoms of cyberspace addiction that parallel other types of addictions. In the sections that follow, I offer a summary of those symptoms, with a caution. Having all of them surely indicates a destructive problem, but having only a few might place a person in that ambiguously gray zone where it becomes difficult to distinguish between an addiction and a passion. Overarching all these symptom categories is the question of how much the compulsive cyberspace activity disrupts a person's level of functioning in life. What is the person doing or not doing that affects physical health, work, and relationships? Ultimately, the degree of disruption in one's level of functioning indicates how far into the realm of pathological addiction a person has gone.

It Intrudes Everywhere on Me

The cyberspace addiction intrudes on people's minds and lifestyles. It is all they can think about. They are more preoccupied with it than almost anything else. They drastically change their lives or avoid important responsibilities in order to pursue the cyberspace fix. When they are not online, they are planning for the next time they will be. Although they may not admit it, they feel the addictive behavior is out of their control. They dream about it and spend too much money on it.

It Rules My Moods

When immersed in the addictive behavior, people feel high, tranquilized, or as if they are in a trance. They seek out the activity as a way to escape problems in life, to relieve themselves of feeling helpless, guilty, anxious, or depressed. It is their go-to solution for any problematic feeling, although it paradoxically creates frustration, disillusionment, guilt, and anger because ultimately the addiction only superficially addresses or actually aggravates underlying needs. They feel a craving for the cyberspace activity, irritable if anything interferes with it, and defensive when people criticize them. Secretly, they are guilty or worried about their habit. Researchers such as Voiskounsky (2008) have shown that some people online, especially gamers, experience what Csikszentmihalyi (1990) called "flow" – a mental state in which they feel fully immersed into an activity, even merged with it. They lose self-consciousness, forget about time, and see the situation as highly rewarding and pleasurable. Addictive behaviors mimic flow, except they eventually lead to regret, lassitude, and self-destruction rather than self-enhancement, as evident in a variety of comments from my student surveys:

> I sit down to quickly check things online, and four hours later I find myself looking at funny kitten pictures. So useless.

> Being online can easily become addictive, especially with "time suck" sites full of games, quizzes, opinions, and articles that distract me and literally suck up and waste hours of my time.

> I have to time myself when I use the Internet because I get so lost in it and waste time looking at information that is not important.

> Spending so much time online makes me physically lazy and complacent.

> The intensity of experiences online makes me more depressed than happy.

> Sitting at the screen for literally hours on end makes me feel less human.

I Need More and Cannot Be Away from It

Two classic signs of any addiction are increased tolerance and withdrawal reactions. People need greater amounts of time in the addictive behavior while trying to achieve the same level of satisfaction they once knew. They find themselves staying in cyberspace much longer than they intended. They lose track of time. They feel restless, irritable, depressed, or moody when attempting to cut down or stop the habit. If they succeed at cutting back, they are unable to maintain that change. The writer Paul Davies said, "When you can stop you don't want to, and when you want to stop, you can't."

It Wrecks My Health

People develop medical problems due to the addiction. They neglect healthy behaviors, like eating properly and exercising. They suffer from sleep deprivation and dysfunctional sleep habits because they feel compelled to stay online. Even though they develop problems due to sedentariness, computer vision syndrome, and repetitive stress disorders such as carpal tunnel syndrome and musculoskeletal pain, they do not change their addictive behaviors.

It Wrecks My Life

They neglect family, friends, and work in order to pursue the cyberspace addiction. They lie to people about what they are doing or conceal how often and how long they do it. Important people in their lives feel annoyed, disappointed, or critical of them. They become distant from family members and lose friendships. They take risks with their education or careers in order to be online. In a variety of big and small ways, the addiction disrupts their ability to function in life. As Danielle Berry (2011) once commented, "No one ever said on their deathbed, 'Gee, I wish I had spent more time alone on my computer.'"

THE HIDDEN NEEDS

If they are honest with themselves, addicted people sense a hidden need that drives them, although they rarely understand exactly what it is. Everyone feels passionate about something when it addresses important needs. Psychologically healthy people consciously acknowledge, express, and satisfy those needs in a natural rising and falling of appetite that creates a balanced well-being. But when needs are suppressed, ignored, diverted, or caught in a vicious cycle of superficial or indirect satisfaction, the result can be a pathological fixation. In these true addictions, one's identity becomes hollowed out, depleted, and fragmented. The intensity to which inner longings have been frustrated, neglected, or denied determines the magnitude of the urge to seek fulfillment through the compulsive behavior. The more needs being addressed by a cyberspace addiction, the more powerful the grip it has on one's being. Even a brief experience that powerfully fulfilled a need can lead to a fixation on repeating that experience while neglecting other more healthy ways to satisfy that need.

Because cyberspace is such a diverse, compelling, and easily accessed environment, it provides a ripe place to satisfy needs, especially when one's in-person life has been the origin of the deprivation. For every type of unconscious desire, cyberspace seems to offer a solution. Environments that combine a variety of activities might be captivating because they address a wider spectrum of needs. If you can play games, spend money, gamble, socialize, and attain fame, the addictive power of the environment escalates for any particular person as well as for a variety of different kinds of people. However, addictive environments can also function like lasers. People with a pathological vulnerability to playing poker or fantasy role-playing games stand as easy marks for a site specifically designed to target these obsessions. Esther Dyson, a journalist and Wall Street technology analyst, once said:

> The internet is like alcohol. It accentuates what you would do anyway. If you want to be a loner, you can be more alone. If you want to connect, it makes it easier to connect (Dyson, 2005).

The more people understand their motivations, the more those motivations lose their power as the unconscious "thing" leading to cyberspace addictions. Acting out repressed needs is simply a cathartic activity, a repetition compulsion that must be replayed endlessly without ever achieving satisfaction. Not only are addicted people unaware of these needs, but they also deny having an addiction. By contrast, working through those needs means that a person resolves the conflicts or deprivations from the past that created them. Consciously acknowledging one's intense preoccupation with cyberspace is a step toward recovery. When people recognize their compulsion for what it truly is, they steer themselves toward a more healthy enthusiasm.

Some people who explore cyberspace go through an addictive phase that is not necessarily a true addiction. New users might initially feel very enamored with the opportunities a particular online environment offers them.

The addictive phase eventually tapers off as the novelty of the place dissipates while the responsibilities of the real world call. In some cases, high expectations for the online activity are dashed. Needs are not fulfilled. In communities dominated by buttonized economies, the addictive desire to earn popularity through the accumulation of "likes" eventually feels like a superficial waste of time for some people. The resulting disappointment leads them back to the real world, or a different online activity. Some seasoned onliners understand the potential pitfalls – such as the online disinhibition effect – that lure victims into intensely emotional and hence addictive interpersonal dramas. That understanding helps them steer clear of a descent into a compulsive mire.

So what exactly are these concealed needs that propel people into cyberspace, with either healthy or destructive results? What might be that unconscious "thing" that drives both addiction and devotion? We might answer that question by examining the underlying motives of the different personality types described in Chapter 3, "The Dynamic Digital Psyche." Psychopathic people are drawn to activities that enable them to manipulate others, often in sadistic ways. Narcissistic people seek activities in which they feel admired by others. Schizoid personalities enjoy delving into flights of imagination. People with masochistic tendencies want to prove that they can endure suffering. Whatever the need might be for a particular personality type, cyberspace provides places to satisfy it.

In another approach to answering that question, we would categorize universal human needs regardless of personality types. In the sections that follow, I will describe some of these categories. Although it is helpful to classify them this way, many needs overlap or interact with each other in complex ways. Understanding this fact casts a wider light on why people become healthfully or pathologically immersed into cyberspace.

Designers of social media and computer games control the dimensions of cyberpsychology architecture to activate these needs, which can easily accelerate addictive tendencies. The interactive dimension plays an especially important role, when the machine seems to control us more than we control it. A good example are the notifications that persistently lure us back into cyberspace by reminding us of the needs it promises to satisfy, but it is not easy to figure out how to turn those notifications off.

BENEATH THE NEED FOR SEX

One afternoon at the Palace, I asked the group at Harry's Bar why they thought the Palace was addictive. Someone gave a simple, one word reply: "SEX." Over a hundred years ago, Freud designated sex as the primary human motive, while decades later Maslow (1943) placed it at the most basic level of his hierarchical pyramid of needs. Without doubt, sex is one of those basic emotional, biological imperatives that commands attention. Although many people in cyberspace are not trying to satisfy their sex drive, some definitely are, with their quest sometimes turning into an addiction (Cooper, 2013). When people become preoccupied with online sexual activities, they do so for the same two basic reasons people get obsessed with sex in any context: it satisfies a biological drive; and it provides an outlet for psychological needs.

The unconscious emotional needs that compel a person to seek out sex can be more powerful than the purely biological drive itself. Even though cybersex turns addictive because it is an easily accessed, anonymous, and medically safe way to satisfy one's sex drive, psychological forces still propel the compulsion. The fact that cybersex usually offers only text, visual, or auditory stimulation – without any bodily contact – suggests that the needs satisfied must be more than simply "physical."

Cybersex makes up for any lack of physical stimulation by the psychological stimulation it offers. Under the cloak of online anonymity, people can experiment with all sorts of behaviors, fantasies, and transformations in their identity, including gender. Some enjoy the voyeuristic and exhibitionistic satisfactions of one-way or two-way video, or playing with each other using sexy images and avatars. Others prefer the bare-bones typed-text style of cybersex because it galvanizes imagination along with powerful transference reactions – not to mention, as one aficionado joked, greatly improves skillful typing with one hand. With the wide variety of people available online, along with easy paths to find them, people can quickly identify the partners who match their desires. Thanks to anonymity, one can also quickly bail out of an encounter, then try again later, someplace else, with someone else. All of these factors make cybersex addictive.

No matter how anonymous or brief, cybersex revolves around the satisfaction of some interpersonal need, whether it entails a person's feelings about intimacy, love, power, competition, conquest, submission, anger, humiliation, shame, or vulnerability. This is true for all forms of sexuality, which led Woody Allen to conclude that, "I don't know the question, but sex is definitely the answer." When people identify online encounters as purely sexual, while failing to realize the underlying psychological need, the potential for addiction rises. They feel driven to excessive involvement with cybersex without fully realizing it is an unconscious attempt to overcome loneliness or depression, express anger or dependency, dominate and control, or fill an internal emptiness. Cybersex then becomes an addictive acting out of needs that never feel completely satisfied. For some people, diving deeper into the expression of unconscious fantasies veers out of control in cyberspace. Reality testing from the external world fades away. The absence of real-world consequences makes it difficult to curb one's behavior.

For many online encounters, the term "flirting" is more appropriate than "cybersex." Many social environments are free-form social gatherings, much like ongoing parties. As with any good party, there is a hefty dose of playful seduction that does not progress to anything explicitly sexual. What makes it more attractive than real-world flirting are the same features that make cybersex attractive. It is relatively anonymous and safe, so people can be a bit more open, bold, and experimental than they would during an in-person gathering. The online disinhibition effect fans the flames, in either benign or toxic fashion. This casual quality of cyberflirting only superficially satisfies deeper needs for companionship, dependency, romance, or love, which compels the person to come back for more. Ambivalence about intimacy – wanting it but also not wanting it – can lock people into a seemingly endless string of flirtations that never progress to true intimacy. Under the spell of the dissociative imagination feature of the online disinhibition effect, some people perceive cyberflirting and cybersex as imaginary, pretend encounters isolated from their real life – and therefore not a threat to their real-world relationships. Such pretending can lead to superficial satisfaction that fails to gratify while leaving one hungry for more. As a result, the stage is set for addiction.

Some sexual pursuits in cyberspace are solitary affairs. Collecting pornography without interacting with anyone is one example. For the normal person, these pursuits will wax and wane with the natural biological fluctuations in sexual desire. An ongoing obsession with such solitary sexual activities might indicate anxiety about intimacy. The escalating desire for more variety of sexual material, more daring material, or just more material takes the place of the need for a human relationship. The preoccupation intensifies under the psychological pressures to possess and control, to fill an inner emptiness, or to defiantly push the envelope of immoral behavior. Because cyberspace offers an almost infinite supply of easily available pornography, the fuel for this fanatic fire appears endless. One can never own it all. There is no limit to how daring one can be. If the person then becomes addicted to online pornography groups, their socializing often revolves around the seemingly endless comparing and sharing of material. The need to compete, to be admired by others for the size and diversity of one's collection, reinforces the addiction.

THE NEED TO SEE A NEW REALITY

We humans have an inherent need to alter our consciousness, to perceive reality from different perspectives. We satisfy this need through creative activities, drugs, sports, meditation, virtual realities, and sex. Some methods are more productive than others. On a nightly basis, dreams provide a built-in mechanism for achieving this altered state of perception by allowing the expression of the unconscious mind that sees things very differently than our conscious mind. Cyberspace is a powerful new addition to this list. Although critics complain that people compulsively substitute cyberspace for living in the real world, we should consider the possibility that it supplements our understanding of the real world by providing unusual ways to experience our surroundings, other people, and ourselves. As we will see in Chapter 14, "Synthesized Realities and Synthesized Beings," our sense of time, space, and personal identity changes when online. Communicating via typed text can feel like a blending of consciousness with the other person. In the world of games and avatars, one can shape-shift, telepathically contact other people, and violate the laws of physics by suspending oneself in midair, walking through walls, or creating objects out of nothing. Some people are attracted to online environments because they satisfy this need for a different take on reality.

We can think of cyberspace as a dream state. It allows the expression of unconscious fantasies, which explains the sexuality, aggression, and imaginative role-playing we see online. The experience resembles lucid dreaming in which people know they are dreaming and can direct the outcome. In indigenous cultures of the past, people learned to develop this ability, skills that contemporary dream workers attempt to revive. Pointing and clicking in cyberspace dream worlds might be the computer user's similar attempt to return to those traditions of the past. It is an attempt to create and direct a recurring, lucid dream.

One's dominion over the cyber-dream is limited. We have some control over the environment, but not over the people who occupy it with us. Cyberspace serves up games where we cannot govern all the pieces. It steers us into many unpredictable twists and turns. Some people accept this fact. They ride the flow of altered states of consciousness in cyberspace, or turn off the computer when the experience turns into an anxiety dream, nightmare, or bad trip. Those who feel driven to master the dreamlike game may have a hard time knowing when to sign off. For such people, addiction to cyberspace is an addiction to this altered state of consciousness, to the dream realm. We might think of the addicted person's withdrawal symptoms when cut off from cyberspace as resembling the symptoms people experience when deprived of nocturnal dreaming – and their fervid dive back into online addiction as a cyberspace rebound, not unlike the rebound of dreaming that people experience after sleep deprivation.

THE NEED TO ACHIEVE

Everyone has a basic need for learning, mastery, and the self-esteem that arises from one's achievements. Operant theory in psychology adds that learning accelerates when small units of accomplishment are quickly reinforced. Computers can become addictive because they gratify this need in an efficient, rewarding fashion. You encounter a computer challenge, you investigate, you try solutions, you figure it out, and the computer does something for you that it never did before. A reinforcing pop-up message might even pat you on the back for your coup. Challenge, experimentation, mastery, success: it is a very motivating cycle that makes people want to learn and do more.

Many environments in cyberspace – being complex technically, psychologically, or both – pose few limits on how much a person can achieve. Some new users take great pleasure in mastering the software. For those people who are not attracted to the technical side of things, there is the challenge of navigating an online culture; of discovering its people, norms, social structure, history and legends; and of helping to shape its future. Exploring and mastering sophisticated environments can be a never-ending satisfier of curiosity and an ongoing source of self-esteem, especially when new technical features appear, new people show up, and the culture changes. To stay on top of things, you must be a shark: you keep moving. In many communities, longstanding members achieve an elevated status among the population by becoming a host, moderator, wizard, or god who possesses powers that ordinary members do not. To achieve such honored positions requires time and effort. Getting the position reinforces the quest.

The need to achieve in the technical or social domain can be a very normal, healthy process. By contrast, some people – especially those with narcissistic and manic personality styles – feel driven to compensate for underlying feelings of failure, inadequacy, and helplessness, or to overcome desperate needs for acknowledgment, admiration, and love. Obsession with cyberspace accomplishments then turns into a seemingly endless pursuit that never fully gratifies, especially when the stack of possible achievements has no ceiling, while the underlying needs to reach them are not truly understood. Forging the status of sophisticate in cyberspace can feel as if you have the whole world at your fingertips – a feeling that balloons into an addictive, godlike sense of omnipotence and omniscience. Beneath that feeling hides the realization that one must keep moving to stay on top of it all. On some unconscious level, perhaps many people online share this feeling of power. "People prefer technology over nature," one of my students commented in a survey, "because the world is available at the click of a button."

THE NEED TO BELONG

Everyone needs interpersonal contact, social recognition, and a sense of belonging. You instinctively want to go to a place where everyone knows your name because one's sense of self rests on affirmation from others. Because cyberspace offers all sorts of social environments, it satisfies almost any person's need to belong to whatever kind of group he or she desires. People can easily compartmentalize their group attachments, joining different groups with each one addressing a particular interest. Simply being a user of a particular program creates an instantaneous camaraderie with other people who also use it. You can talk about that program, share tips, and perhaps communicate with each other using it. That sense of brotherhood is especially strong when people join forces in a brand new environment. They feel like pioneers building a new world. It is a very addictive feeling of belonging to a creative process.

As we saw in Chapter 10, "One of Us: Groups and Communities," a problem arises when the group starts to flourish. Many newbies show up. The community changes quickly, more so than in the real world. Among the increasing deluge of people, if you want to maintain your connection to the group – if you want people to know your name – you have to keep coming back. The more time you spend online, the more people will acknowledge you, and the more you are considered a member who is "one of us." If you have not signed on for a few days or longer, you might feel that you are losing ground and that you will be forgotten. You do not want those relationships you worked so hard to develop to fade out or your identity in the community to slip away. So you feel compelled to go back, to reestablish your presence. In this ongoing effort, unconscious conflicts about separation and abandonment can haunt some people, driving them into compulsive participation; otherwise, they feel disconnected, out of the loop, and irrelevant. Frequent jokes about being "addicted" among dedicated members of the in-crowd boosts their camaraderie, while also easing their anxiety about it being true. Misery loves company.

The JenniCam phenomenon was a unique example of how cyberspace satisfies the need to belong. Beginning in 1996, there was an overwhelming response to Jennifer Ringley when she set up a live, ongoing video broadcast of her dorm room, then later her apartment. People who worshipped Jenni banned together in groups to talk about her, speculate about her, and share screen-captured pictures of her. She was the focal point of their addictive camaraderie. Even though unable to communicate with her, some admirers set up a second computer monitor next to their own, so they could "be with" Jenni as they went about their work. In interviews with journalists, Jenni described how she felt she might be helping some lonely males by serving as a kind of substitute girlfriend who could be with them whenever they wanted her. Was she satisfying the needs of a twinning transference? Was she compounding an addictive attempt to have what one could not really have, like Tantalus reaching for fruit that was always just beyond his reach? In my survey of attitudes about cyberspace, one student summed up the dilemma many people experience online: "It's like looking into the mirror in Harry Potter. You see everything you want but can't have."

Texting has become a particularly compulsive habit for many people, especially young adults. Constant connection is the norm. Rather than having predetermined times to get together, they propose social events on the fly, via group texting. If you are not continually checking your phone, you miss out. The need to belong funnels through the device.

THE NEED TO SOCIALIZE

What must be obvious so far in this chapter is that most activities in cyberspace – not unlike most activities in real life – address the most basic of human needs: the desire to interact with other humans. In the early days of the Internet, a stereotype in the minds of the uninformed public was that mostly geeks, misfits, and socially inadequate souls populated cyberspace. With little social success in the real world, they resorted to safely superficial relationships offered through the cold wires and glass screens of cyberspace. Being shy, interpersonally anxious people – perhaps those with a schizoid personality style – they relied on typed text to feel more expressive, more in control, and less vulnerable. "People who are on their phones or computers 24/7 would probably be just as antisocial without technology," one of my students commented. "They would still stay inside and find something else to distract them."

Although the stereotype does fit some dysfunctional people even in our contemporary times, we also now realize that not all online relationships are a symptom of psychological problems. Many people spend a great deal of time in social media, usually with friends, family, and others they know in person, but they also form fruitful friendships with people they only know in cyberspace. Even simple social rewards such as the "like" might feel very fulfilling. "I can post a picture and have forty people hit a button to say they like it," another of students stated. "In real life I could never get people to openly like a picture."

For those who rely too heavily on their online companions to the exclusion of in-person socializing, the outcome ultimately can be something less than fully satisfying. It can be outright disappointing, even destructive. Ideally, people come to recognize the potential drawbacks of online relationships. They learn to balance them with in-person contacts. Compulsive Internet use occurs when people fail to see these problems. Determined, sometimes desperate, they keep going back for the fast food of online affiliations. It seems to taste good. It seems to satisfy. But in the end, it does not provide a well-rounded, healthy social diet, an unfortunate fact noted by one of my students: "Those people who need to post their life stories every day for others to see and comment on, as well as how much people dig into other people's lives online, is just crazy. It's an addiction."

The excessive preoccupation with a cyberspace relationship often reflects a preoccupation with one's own psyche, with the transference reaction that forms in one's own mind. Although the person feels the emotional drama is with the online companion, a large portion of it is shaped by unconscious remnants of problematic relationships from the past. The love, hate, competition, admiration, dependency, or fear that people feel in an online liaison actually comes from a struggle within their own intrapsychic world populated by the memories of significant others. The preoccupation with the relationship can turn into an attempt to force the other person to conform to one's unconscious expectations or to satisfy unconscious wishes. People become addicted to the elusive effort to satisfy their unconscious needs that surface in the online encounter.

These addictive transference reactions will be amplified by the black hole experiences of not getting a reply from people, of feeling ignored, rejected, forgotten, or abandoned. That person did not reply to your impassioned message. No one in your beloved discussion group is saying anything in reaction to your posts. This failure of reactivity becomes the ultimate blank screen that magnifies a person's anxious fantasies. While interpersonally savvy people understand the tendency to read too much meaning into a nonresponse, people driven by transference do not. In the absence of a reply, they act inappropriately on their emotions, sometimes exaggerating

their behavior in order to force a response. They become addicted to getting the reactions they desire. Even under the best of circumstances, people often receive only occasional messages in online relationships that are
important to them. These once-in-awhile replies act as intermittent reinforcement, leading to compulsive behavior that resists extinction, especially
when driven by transference.

Cyberspace relationships pose a paradox. On the one hand, some people feel freer, more open and honest about themselves, and more deeply
understood than in the real-world, where others "don't really know me."
At the same time, online relationships tend to minimize or completely lack
the human presence of physical appearance, body language, voice, and the
sensations of touching and being touched – all of which satisfy basic human
needs. As a result, cyberspace relationships can be deeply intimate while
also superficially incomplete. This paradoxical satisfying and frustrating of
social needs will drive some people into coming back for more. When an
online relationship reaches a certain level of intimacy, many people want to
meet in person to remedy that contradictory mixture. But some choose not
to. They tolerate the paradox, even become addicted to it, because they do
not want the reality of in-person contact to disrupt the acting out of their
transference fantasy with the online companion.

THE NEED TO BE ALL YOU CAN BE

At the top of Maslow's hierarchy lies the need for self-actualization – the
striving toward the development of oneself as a unique individual. It is the
ongoing process of cultivating one's inner potentials, the flowering of one's
identity.

Are people self-actualizing in cyberspace? Many believe they assert
their creative potential by engaging the technical, entertainment, and
social opportunities of cyberspace. Some say that they are developing
fulfilling relationships with others by experimenting with new ways
of being. Some people even say they are more like their true selves in
cyberspace than in real life. It is difficult to determine whether this is
self-actualization or rather self-deception as a defense against understanding the unconscious needs that propel them online. Is he really
finding fulfillment in his extreme dedication to that role-playing game,
or is his devotion simply the denial of a pathological addiction? The various criteria for identifying addiction described earlier in this chapter can
help solve these questions, but in some cases the answer may be purely
subjective, in the eyes of the beholder. We should always keep in mind

that for a truly pathological addiction, the person's world shrinks to the addictive activity. Rather than moving toward higher levels of integration and completeness, as in self-actualization, the person's life becomes narrow, rigid, and isolated.

Another important aspect of self-actualization is the development of one's spirituality. Are people discovering their spiritual life in cyberspace? Of course, seekers can find all sorts of inspiration from readings and other seekers online, but is the cyberspace experience itself spiritually enhancing? At first glance, this may seem an absurd idea, but for some people cyberspace does pose some mysteries about the nature of consciousness, reality, and self. As I move through cyberspace, where is my mind? Where am "I"? Am I really just in my body, or is the essence of me somewhere out there mingling with the consciousness of others, merging with that larger consciousness that is cyberspace. Is this consciousness less real than what I experience in real life, or more so? If you believe cyberspace promotes the evolution of individual minds into a universal whole, a world-mind, then you are part of that transcendent Self. You have succeeded in going beyond your small, encapsulated identity to participate in something much larger than yourself. Some people might sense "god" out there in the vast ocean of experiences that is cyberspace. What could be more captivatingly addictive than the search for god? The quest to achieve self-transcendence might indicate a pathological defense against all sorts of personal anxieties, but we should not rule out the possibility that yearning to immerse oneself into the online universe could be genuinely spiritual.

A RETURN TO THE INTEGRATION PRINCIPLE

To help us identify cyberspace addictions, as well as propose solutions for it, we can return to the integration principle. A cyberspace activity can become pathological when dissociated from in-person living. It can become healthier when productively integrated with in-person living.

People become pathologically mired in cyberspace when they disengage it from their real lives. Their cyberspace activity becomes an isolated world unto itself. They do not talk about it with friends and family. They guard it against perceived intrusions from the offline world. It becomes a walled-off substitute or escape from life rather than a supplement to it. Reality testing is lost. Cyberspace warps into a dissociated part of their own mind, a sealed-off intrapsychic zone where unconscious needs are acted out but never fully understood or satisfied. Alleviating this dissociation is an implicit or explicit component of many of the techniques for helping people excessively preoccupied with cyberspace.

In healthy scenarios, people integrate in-person and cyberspace living. They talk about their online activities with family and friends. They bring their real identity, interests, and skills into their online habitats. They call on the phone or meet in person the people they befriend in cyberspace while also communicating online with people they know in person. In the ideal scenario, online and offline activities balance each other, overlap each other, and enrich each other. The "thing" that could have eaten up their lives, without their really understanding how or why, instead enhances their lives. People learn the value of cyberspace while also using those lessons to appreciate even more the vitality of their in-person lifestyles. These insights from the integration principle, including its emphasis on a balance between online and offline living, are reflected in the tips experts offer on how to avoid cyberspace addiction:

- Schedule a routine time during the day to use your devices.
- Set a reasonable amount of time to use them and stick to it.
- If necessary, set a timer.
- Have a specific purpose for your cyberspace activities and focus just on that.
- Turn off unnecessary notifications.
- Create extended periods of time, a day or more, when you turn off all devices.
- Think about and develop your offline activities and relationships.
- Limit your online contacts to only the people who are important to you.
- Monitor your feelings when using your devices.
- Talk to people you trust about those feelings.
- Socialize with people who are not interested in cyberspace.

True addiction leads a person down the path toward self-destruction. Although the person does not necessarily intend it, others often get hurt along the way. What happens when people deliberately attempt to harm others online or make conscious decisions to violate the rules? Do they too become susceptible to a form of addictive behavior: the compulsion to be bad? In the next chapter, we will explore the varieties of deviant behavior in cyberspace.

13

The Digital Deviant

The internet is not for sissies.
          – Paul Vixie

One night in Harry's Bar I struck up a conversation with MissTara, a member of the lesbian dominance/submission cult at the Palace. Knowing I was a psychologist doing research, she seemed interested in telling me about her Palace lifestyle. She suggested we go up to one of the bedrooms where she felt more comfortable talking. Once inside, she shut and locked the door behind us. Rather than explaining what she enjoyed about avatars, she decided to give me a firsthand experience. She shape-shifted from one form to another: a topless woman, a naked woman kneeling on the bed, a naked woman tied to the bed. "What do you think?" she asked. I felt rather uncomfortable and awkward. "Well, this is certainly interesting for my research."

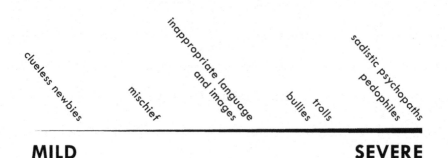

FIGURE 13.1. Examples along the spectrum of online deviance.

In the beginning, onliners advocated what they called "netiquette." It was the spirit of preserving cooperation, helpfulness, and trust in all digital realms. Unfortunately, over the years we discovered that if you build it, some people will abuse it. This is a toxic example of the *generativity principle*, which is how people find ways to use technology unanticipated by its designers (Zittrain, 2009).

The brand of deviance endorsed by a dominance/submission cult will strike some people as abnormal and offensive, while others will simply consider it an alternative sexual lifestyle. As in the real world, aberrant behavior in the digital realm runs the spectrum from mild to severe, depending on who is defining it, whether it hurts anyone, and, if it does hurt people, how much harm it does (see Figure 13.1). Along the way, the cyberpsychological architecture of an environment determines what kinds of deviant behavior are possible.

Since the early days of the Internet, those who lean in the direction of deviance have used cyberspace to surprise, shock, deceive, abuse, or take advantage of other people, often for their own personal gain. In the seminal books about cybercrime (Kirwan & Power, 2013; Sternberg, 2012), researchers described the serious offenses that now proliferate online, including piracy, identity theft, extortion, stalking, hacking, drug dealing, human trafficking, political extremism, illegal and disturbing pornography, vigilantism, and child sex offenses. Hopefully, few of us will find ourselves exposed to these disturbing activities. A significant portion of corruption takes place in the *dark web*, also called the *dark net* (Bartlett, 2014). These are areas of cyberspace that cannot be reached by conventional browsing software, where people's identities are very difficult to determine, even for experts in technology. Borrowing the psychoanalytic structural model of the psyche, we might think of the dark net as embodying the sexual and aggressive impulses of the id, the government and corporate controls over cyberspace as the overruling conscience of the superego, and social media as the realm in which everyday people realistically attempt to hash out the debates between "right" and "wrong."

In this chapter, I will focus on deviance that is less dramatically destructive than in hardcore cybercrime. Instead, I will discuss behaviors that we might witness during our everyday lives within social media, some of which even normal people might find themselves committing, and some of which violate social standards without actually causing significant harm to others. Much of what I will describe comes from my experiences at the Palace, where as a wizard I was able to see what goes on behind the scenes as the officials who managed the community attempted to identify and control antisocial activities (Suler, 1997; Suler & Phillips, 1998). My work there took place in the early days of cyberspace, yet the kinds of deviant behavior I observed back then predicted much of what is happening in cyberspace today. Even the hardcore crime that we now witness can be traced back to the more tame versions of it that occurred early on. Technology changes dramatically, with deviant people finding clever new ways to misuse it, but their fundamental behaviors along with the underlying psychological motives remain a constant.

IT'S ALL RELATIVE, OR NOT

Every culture has its own standards about what is acceptable and unacceptable behavior. According to the theory of cultural relativity, what is considered normal behavior in one society may be considered abnormal in another, and vice versa. Some deviance is in the eye of the beholder. For example, how would you react to the following post?

> Fuck you. Just fuck every single one of you fucking idiots. I can't believe I'm frustrated enough to google a site to rant. Seriously though, FUCK YOU!

No doubt, you would be offended. You might even assume this person was not simply uncouth, but also suffering from some type of impulse control disorder. Yet this was the top-rated post in one of the well-known rant websites that became popular in the 2010s, where people were encouraged to let loose with all varieties of vitriolic, often highly prejudiced tirades that would be banned in other social media. Deviant behavior is a disruptive turnoff in some communities, but in others it is part of the show.

Some online communities are privately owned, others are commercial – a distinction that affects the deviance permitted. Some privately managed groups that isolate themselves from outsiders are specifically designed as a haven for deviance, as in hate groups and sites devoted to aberrant sexual behavior. The powerful flexibility of the Internet to allow like-minded people to join together has led to an unfortunate abundance of deviant organizations, some of which are illegal, as in pedophile groups. In other cases, owners of private sites with benign agendas have strict policies about misbehaving users. If you get out of line, you are quickly ousted. The overseers of the site are more concerned about the congenial integrity of the community than about the rights or the psyche of the ill-behaved person. Some commercially owned sites show more leeway. The business depends on sales, so a "customer is always right" philosophy leads to a greater tolerance of impoliteness and mischief. Ejecting someone from the community is the measure of last resort, because misbehaving users do buy products, like anyone else. Of course, if they become too deviant, they might drive off other potential customers. In the end, it is a delicate balancing act between maintaining a congenial community where strict rules weed out the deviants and encouraging sales by catering to customers.

DISINHIBITED FRUSTRATION

The online disinhibition effect revs up deviant behavior. Some people let loose with the mean side of their personalities when they think they are anonymous, when they do not have to look others in the eye, when they can easily run away, and when they believe what they say or do is simply some kind of fantasy inside their heads. The higher prevalence of misbehavior among people who feel anonymous might be more than just disinhibition. Rather than anonymity simply releasing the nasty side of their psyche, people might experience anonymity and their lack of an identity as toxic. Feeling frustrated about being unknown, ignored, and alienated in social media, some people act out that frustration in an antisocial manner. They need to feel that they have some kind of impact on others. It is not unlike the neglected child who behaves badly to get attention from the parent, even if it is punishment. The squeakiest wheel gets the most oil. Humans will almost always choose a connection to others over no connection at all, even if that connection is a negative one. Some misbehaving members of social media think, perhaps unconsciously through a transference reaction, that their acting out is a justified retaliation against a community that ignores their identity. They reject because they feel rejected.

Under ideal circumstances, frustrated people realize their harmful actions are the byproduct of their own resentment. They correct themselves, maybe even learn something new about themselves while working through those problems in their personality. For the pathologically deviant person, that kind of self-insight and personal change rarely occurs. They continue to act out their frustrations on others, feeling that their deviant behavior is somehow justified.

During a media interview, a journalist once asked me whether antisocial activity in the real world has declined with the expansion of the Internet, because cyberspace provides an outlet for venting misbehavior. This would be an example of the defense mechanism known as *displacement*, the transferring of hostility from one victim to another seemingly safer target. Although an intriguing speculation, there is no evidence to support it. In fact, we could propose the opposite argument – that deviant behavior spawned in cyberspace can migrate into the real world.

AIN'T MISBEHAVING: MILD FORMS OF DEVIANCE

Deviant behavior falls along a continuum from mild to severe. The severe types are detested by all people, anywhere, any time. The milder versions are labeled as deviant depending upon the culture, the people involved, and the particular situation. Like beauty, deviance can be in the eyes of the beholder. When otherwise very civil people participate in social media long enough, the online disinhibition effect eventually leads them astray. For the most part, the milder, usually unintentional forms of deviance are the result of playful mischief, immaturity, simple ignorance, or a momentary lapse of judgment. If people do not correct themselves, others can successfully intervene in a straightforward matter. Briefly explaining the rules of etiquette, educating them about how to use the software appropriately, and encouraging them in a friendly way to ease up might be enough. If such simple interventions fail, then the deviance has more pathological force behind it.

Clueless Newbies

When newcomers to an environment are confused about the most basic aspects of how things work, they tend to act inappropriately. Typing all in capital letters, the cyberspace equivalent of shouting, is a classic example of improper behavior among those uninformed about netiquette. Disoriented people also exaggerate their actions when entering a strange place. Some newbies who enter a social environment where they have never been before blurt out non sequitur comments without realizing they are interrupting an ongoing conversation. At the Palace, newbies would chaotically bounce their avatars around a room, plop them on top of someone else, or shout, "What the hell is going on here?" Once given a little advice – as in "just point and click to move your avatar" – they would typically calm down. One obstacle to helping newbies is the fact that they might speak a different language. As an online community becomes more multinational, the Tower of Babel scenario becomes a potential problem.

Culture Clash

When people migrate from one online environment to another, they carry their old customs with them, sometimes inappropriately. In the traditional chat environments consisting of larger, fluctuating populations of people, it was considered normal upon entering a room to say out loud to everyone, "M or F?" or "Any SWF here?" as a way to pinpoint someone to talk to, often with sexual motives in mind. When these people moved to smaller, more stable, tightly knit communities, their opening lines were considered tactless intrusions. Like all cultures, online groups that change over time must navigate between two different philosophies: insist that newcomers do what the Romans do, or evolve into a melting pot that blends customs from different cultures. Homogeneous cultures have less disruptive deviance but fall short on valuable diversity, while heterogeneous cultures have more disruptive deviance but benefit from diversity.

Mischief

In some communities, mischief is a way of life. Everyone accepts the fact that members will be playing jokes on each other. Naive newbies make for easy targets. Unfortunately, a very thin line divides acceptable mischief and unacceptable abuse. Some people use pranks as a venue to act out their frustrations. They test the limits to see how far they can push the envelope before they get reprimanded. If they respond quickly to the law once it is laid down, part of them feels comforted by the fact that they cannot get away with everything. Adolescent males in particular enjoy mischief as a way to entertain friends. At the Palace, they would play a flatulent wind sound many times over, or blurt out loud, "Anyone want to screw?" For relatively normal teens simply experimenting with cyberspace freedom, a gentle reprimand is sufficient: "Simmer down, kids!" You remind them that this is not a video game but a real social setting, with real people, where rules of civility still apply. If that kind of intervention does not work, the teen might be experiencing more serious psychological problems, as in chronic bullying. Unleashed by the online disinhibition effect, adults also regress to childish mischief. That fifteen-year-old snert might actually be a forty-five-year-old engineer.

Graffiti

At the Palace people could paint on the background graphics that provided the visual backdrop for a room. Some people adorned the walls with obscene drawings or words. Others smeared black over the entire room, what a psychoanalyst might diagnose as the actions of an anal expulsive personality. In order to vent their anger about feeling overly controlled and helpless, these graffiti-obsessed people deposited – often secretly and in defiance of authority – their unacceptable stuff all over everyone else. Inappropriately hostile and sexual graffiti can be found in many forms of social media where people dump on the environment with offensive words and images, sometimes by hacking into someone else's account or website, often with the intention of making political or social statements or damaging someone's reputation.

Deviant Enclaves

Deviant subcultures evolve within areas of an online community that are isolated, underpopulated, or minimally supervised by authorities. At the Palace Mansion, the dominance/submission lesbians claimed one of the bedrooms as their territory. A group of menacing adolescents set up camp in the Cave, where their antisocial behavior consisted mostly of foul language and bizarre avatars, an off-putting quality that defined the group as well as firmed up its territorial boundary by scaring off outsiders. If strangers happened to wander into their space, they acted hostile or completely ignored them. After MsLady, one of the Palace wizards, managed to befriend TheDemon, the leader of the group, she discovered they were actually rather studious, inquisitive, and talented kids who felt like frustrated misfits in their real lives. These kinds of deviant enclaves do not usually pose a threat to the overall community because their members keep to themselves. Problems arise when citizens of the larger community complain that the neighborhood is "going downhill." If traffic increases to these isolated enclaves, the group eventually dissolves or relocates to another area.

Advertisements

It was a lot easier to construct your own site using the Palace software than it was to entice people to live there. Some site owners tried to recruit users from the busy communities by posting advertisements. Although some salesmanship was considered acceptable, spamming a room with heavy-handed, proselytizing signs felt like a robot rolling through your living room while projecting holograms of Pepsi in front of everyone's face. In contemporary forms of social media, where all varieties of enthusiasts try to grab their fifteen minutes of fame, those who advertise their brand might be viewed with suspicion, disgust, and rejection, sometimes in knee-jerk fashion. In my first post to a Google+ photography group, I made the mistake of announcing my online book about photographic psychology, at which point I was immediately banned from the community. My apology, explanation, and suggestion that the moderator's response might have been a bit hasty were ignored.

In the early days of the Internet, persistent ads from businesses were considered offensive intrusions in most communities. Once cyberspace went fully commercial, people tolerated these announcements that sprang up all over their screens as an unavoidable nuisance. The individual person who persistently self-promotes might be viewed as more deviant than the corporation that does the same.

SEE NO EVIL: DEVIANT IMAGES

The power of cyberspace blossomed when it became graphic with visual stimulation rather than just text messages, when this sensory dimension of cyberpsychology architecture began to thrive. Sometimes it became too graphic. People began posting images and videos that were highly sexual, hateful, violent, and just plain disgusting. At the Palace, "flashers" clicked into a pornographic avatar, then quickly clicked back to a more normal appearance, as a way to tease, surprise, shock, or thumb their nose at the rules. Less brave than the flasher but with a similar desire to break rules and upset people, prop-droppers tossed an obscene image into an empty room and then ran, no doubt expecting that someone would have to clean up after them. Showing obvious hostility, abusive blockers ran their avatars into or dropped them on top of other avatars. Those obsessed with hate and violence wore avatars depicting antigay and misogynous attitudes, religious prejudice, Nazi swastikas, or a head sliced by an ax. In contemporary cyberspace, we see similar examples of people either forcing distasteful images into other people's personal spaces, as in pop-ups and offensive photos sent to unsuspecting victims, or placing them on a page somewhere for people to stumble upon. A good example was the U.S. congressman Anthony Weiner, who admitted to sending sexual explicit images of himself to women he apparently did not know.

Defining and Controlling Bad Pictures

Before deviant images can be controlled, they must first be defined. The Supreme Court had a difficult time determining pornography, so it comes as no surprise that managers of online communities experienced similar difficulties. In small online groups, official standards might not be needed because the social pressures of the group keep people in line. As the population gets bigger, publicized rules become necessary, which has been the case in almost all popular social media. Setting these standards will go hand in hand with defining the philosophy and agenda of the community, with the most basic question being whether the site is intended for children or adults.

Communities devoted to photography ran into especially problematic issues. While exploring Flickr, I stumbled upon all varieties of photos that many people would consider inappropriately deviant: strange sexual images; hatefully prejudiced pictures; scenes of violence; and photos of self-injury, including cutting and blood. Some photosharing groups within Flickr devoted themselves to sharing images that focused on these themes. Critics argued that these images have no redeeming value, that they could in fact trigger harmful reactions in vulnerable people. Others claimed that such photos qualify as art, even as a form of therapeutic expression for the photographer. Setting aside such claims, no one can doubt the research indicating that online pornography has become a widespread issue that demands intervention when it crosses the line into pathology or becomes accessible by children (Luder et al, 2011; Paasonen, 2011; Short et al., 2012; Stein et al., 2001).

Many people like having some rules because they feel more secure and comfortable knowing what they can and cannot do. But rules are made to be broken, or so some people think. Feeling benignly mischievous or blatantly rebellious, they deliberately push the envelope by testing the ambiguities of the law. Even when the rules become very specific, borderline cases always pop up, leading to a refinement of the rules, leading to more clever border-line cases, in what inevitably turns into an ongoing debate over semantics, more complicated standards, and people feeling confused or angry about what is and is not permitted.

With rules comes the dilemma of interpreting and applying them. As image detection software grows more sophisticated, the machine will assist us in tracking and deleting deviant images, which is especially helpful in eliminating child pornography. The problem is that software needs to be told exactly what to look for, which easily leads to the machine making interpre-tations that are too rigidly literal. As an alternative, we can rely on trained workers or vigilant members of an online community to report deviant images – but people inevitably vary in how they apply the rules, resulting in inconsistent interventions, conflicts, and debates. When some wizards at the Palace strictly enforced the standards about inappropriate avatars while others did not, a "good cop/bad cop" perception grew among the members, along with arguments among the wizards. The wizards learned that when a member asked whether a highly questionable avatar was acceptable, they should consult with another wizard not just for consensual validation, but also to detect these attempts at dividing and conquering the wizards. As leaders who run any kind of organization know all too well, very destruc-tive people – whom psychologists consider a type of *borderline personality disorder* – use their "splitting" of others into good versus bad as a way to turn members against members, leaders against leaders, in what ultimately flares up into an all-consuming warfare that threatens to destroy everyone, including the community itself.

No matter how fair or clear officials try to make the rules, someone will not agree with them, resulting in conflicts and uprisings within the com-munity, which happens often in many forms of social media. At times, it might seem as if the battles about the rules turn into more of a problem than the problem the rules were intended to solve. As with many social media officials, some wizards at the Palace realized the excessive preoccu-pation with regulations threatened to damage the sense of freedom and responsibility that members wanted to embrace as part of the philosophy of the community.

Excessive preoccupation with standards can take its toll on the officials charged to enforce them. One Palace wizard joked, "I now find myself peer-ing at the screen searching for stray pubic hairs or nipples. All my magni-fying glasses are steamed up. I've taken so many cold showers I've caused a drought. It's turned me into a pervert." On a more serious note, we should give thoughtful consideration to the well-being of professionals who take on the unpleasant job of examining highly disturbing images in cyberspace in order to develop methods to deal with this ubiquitous problem. Although developing standards about pornography poses challenges, the proliferation of pornographic images – including the dramatic increase in sexual selfies taken with phone cameras, especially among minors – demands some type of intervention. Forensic cyberpsychologists are developing increasingly sophisticated programs for identifying, tracking, and eliminating the alarming number of disturbing pornographic and violent images, especially when they involve children (Aiken, Moran, & Berry, 2011).

SPEAK NO EVIL: DEVIANT LANGUAGE

Indecent language is another deviant behavior that spans the range from mild to severe. Anyone familiar with social media has witnessed people using angry, prejudiced, sexual, or otherwise "colorful" words that cross the line of appropriateness. The offenders might simply be tactless, immature, or impulsive people who do not consciously intend to hurt anyone – for example, people with manic, narcissistic, and histrionic personality styles. The online disinhibition effect magnifies their improprieties. Other offenses are much more deliberate, in extreme cases indicating a psychopathic personality.

Lewd Breathers

At the Palace, Jim Bumgardner coined the term "breathers" for those deviant members, most often males, who talked lewdly to women, sometimes mixed with derogatory remarks and violent threats. In the mild cases, offenders backed off when a wizard confronted them. In the severe cases, they became more persistently offensive when someone tried to intervene, clearly demonstrating a pathologically compulsive need to control, shock, and hurt others. Although no one wanted to end up blaming the victim, verification was often a problem in these scenarios. If someone reported abuse, were they actually abused, did they magnify the offense in their own imagination, were they trying to get someone into trouble, or did they provoke the abuse as if wanting to place themselves into a victim role? If there was no record of the conversation, it became a matter of taking one person's word against another, in awkward situations asking the victims to repeat the very words that offended them. As in almost all forms of social media, people had at their disposal the ability to block messages from abusers, although people do not always use them, or they use them too late before they feel injured.

Stalkers and Cyberbullying

Stalkers are breathers or otherwise hostile people who follow a victim from one place to another as they continue their attacks. Their need to intrude upon, dominate, and control the other person is obvious, reflecting their own underlying anxieties about being helpless and victimized, a doing to others what one fears will be done to oneself – what psychoanalysts call *turning the passive into the active*. Victims of stalking describe the experience as both creepy and frightening, which attests to the intense subjective experience of being in cyberspace despite the fact that it is "just" something happening on a device screen. Later in the history of cyberspace, these kinds of offenses came to known as *cyberbullying* – a problem that became ubiquitous, especially among children and teenagers, in extreme cases turning into hateful mob behavior driven by many of the features of the online disinhibition effect (Kowalski et al. 2012; Marczak & Coyne, 2015; Patchin & Hinduja, 2011).

Verbal Exhibitionists

Verbal exhibitionists engage in explicit sexual or angrily prejudiced conversations within a public space, for all to hear. They inflict their words on others without necessarily expecting others to respond to them directly. Often they do this in pairs or small groups where they enjoy as well as reinforce each other's language while violating the sensibilities of those around them. They might think, rather inappropriately, that their display is fun entertainment, or they attempt to impress or shock other people. These behaviors are certainly cathartic and attention seeking, which points to the offender's need to seize the limelight while venting inner frustrations. In the case of an openly amorous couple, the witnesses to their blatantly seductive conversation might think, "Get a room, why don't you?"

Newbie Bashers

In many groups, insecure people like to attack the newcomer. This problem intensifies when newbies are easily identifiable, as at the Palace when a fresh arrival wore a generic smiley avatar. Donning names like "Guest

Killer," the basher would verbally abuse the new person, falsely accuse them of misbehaviors, and even display images of malicious intent, such as a picture of the generic smiley on a pet leash or with an ax planted in its head. In any social system, people perceived to be at the bottom of a class structure become targets for those above them. If they in any way appear anonymous, the attacks against them intensify. In all social media, people who have not yet established their presence as a unique individual with social status might find themselves the target of such prejudices. Some newbie bashers consciously think that they are just having fun, with no harm intended. Unconsciously, they need to feel superior and powerful, that they belong while the newbie does not. Their desire to feel "better than" disguises underlying insecurities about their status in the community and most likely in their lives in general. When the membership of an online community destabilizes due to constant change, these insecurities escalate, leading to more newbie bashing.

Leader Bashing

Some people insist on attacking the leaders of the group. They verbally abuse them in public or through private messages, attempt to whip up people into siding with them against the "unfair" authority figure, or they play one leader against the other. Persistence in this splitting – including the befriending and idealizing of the "good" leader while criticizing and undermining the "bad" one – might indicate a borderline personality disorder. Although leaders with a heavy-handed style of disciplining misbehaving members add to the problem, intense conflicts among the leaders often indicates the depth of the person's pathological splitting. For some leader bashers, a vicious cycle is set in motion. They think leaders are out to get them, which makes them angry, defiant, and abusive, which causes leaders to reprimand them, which confirms the basher's feeling that leaders are out to get them.

Self-Destroyers

Some blatantly hostile people want to be punished, usually by a leader ejecting them from the community. Blatant examples at the Palace included people who would type over and over again, "Suck my dick," "Wizard X is an asshole," or simply, "Kill me, kill me, kill me!" They perceive themselves as bold, defiant rebels who dared to take the leader's best hit. Because teenage gangs at the Palace considered being killed a badge of honor, they competed with each other to attain as many deaths as possible. It defined them as the bad boys. For other people, provoking a ban from an online community is their way to gain control over feeling alienated. Because they intentionally created the rejection, they believe they have some mastery over it. In their minds, the ban justifies their hostility toward the community and its authorities, an attitude that often stems from transference.

WHEN DEVIANCE GETS COMPLEX

Complex deviant behavior requires psychological expertise to manage it, either on the part of the community leaders or other members who have the best interests of the community in mind. These behaviors are complex because they intertwine with difficult social as well as psychological issues. Because they span the range from mild to severe, it becomes a challenge to know when someone has crossed the line.

Revolutionaries

On his website for Palace wizards, Dr. Xenu described the "rabble rousers" and "political paranoids" who spring up in many forms of social media. They want to use the community as their personal soapbox to rally support for a political agenda. Alienated revolutionaries often specifically target the online establishment for their political attacks, as in declaring the social media company a totalitarian state that records everyone's communications, including private messages, for the purpose of manipulating people. According to Godwin's Law, as an online discussion grows longer, the probability increases that someone or something will be compared to Hitler or the Nazis. It is sometimes hard to tell if revolutionaries truly believe their political rhetoric, or simply use it to act out their need to gain attention and power. Seeing themselves as heroic underdogs, they hold a gripe against authority figures, which could very well be a transference reaction. Attempts to reason with them often leads to entangled, futile debates about politics. Unfortunately, their paranoia attains some justification as corporations and governments do indeed monitor and attempt to influence people. Clinicians often say there is a kernel of truth to paranoia.

Freedom Fighters, Trolls, and Other Tenacious Debaters

Adamant advocates for freedom of speech might have a specific political or social ideology in mind, like the revolutionary, or they simply want to flaunt inappropriate language and images without anyone restraining them because it is their "right." It is very easy to fall into a no-win debate with such people. They relentlessly disagree, argue, annoy, and offend people. Psychologists would classify them as narcissistic, oppositional, or passive-aggressive personalities who use stubbornness to vent their anger and worries about independence. Everyone is familiar with the "Yes, but" personality who simply will not agree with anything you say. Wizards at the Palace joked about the possibility of creating a *Monty Python*–inspired Argument Clinic where freedom fighters and other recalcitrant debaters could spout their beliefs at a software robot who mechanically replied with statements like, "I think I disagree," and "What's your proof on that point?"

Once these tenacious arguers notoriously made themselves known across social media, the term "troll" stuck as a label for them. It appears to have come from the idea of the ugly dwarf in Nordic mythology, as well as from the fishing technique in which a slowly drawn hook lures fish into capture. Trolls post inflammatory remarks, incite arguments by raising hot-button issues, and deliberately upset people, just for the fun of it (Buckels, Trapnell, & Paulhus, 2014). In extreme cases, these sadistic people are either extremely narcissistic or psychopathic personalities who enjoy seeing others suffer, turning people against each other and creating chaos in the community. Lacking empathy and social conscience, they are driven by the need to control others while boosting their own feelings of being powerful and important. Similar to cyberbullies, some trolls often are "turning the passive into the active" by doing unto others what was done to them in the past. In an email from a self-confessed troll who had read a news article in which I mentioned this tendency to recreate the past, he said that this explanation "nailed it on the head for me." Once he began to recover from his malady by entering psychotherapy, he realized that the horrible ways he had treated people in social media stemmed from his parents abusing him as a child. "Not a day goes by without me thinking of the hurt I have caused online." Although in his case psychotherapy awakened his empathy for others, this will not always be possible for those who completely lack that ability, such as true psychopaths.

When online discussions escalate into what traditionally has been called a full-blown flame war, there is very little one can say or do to change the minds of the arguers. Often their incessant disputes do not reflect the ability or desire for thoughtful debate, but rather underlying anger, resentment, and prejudice. When confronted with sound reasoning and valid evidence, such people only escalate into higher levels of agitated, irrational thinking. The social media page becomes their soapbox for the cathartic venting of emotions related to personal problems in their lives, channeled into sup-posed political and social issues. They fish for like-minded people to sup-port them in their cause, which justifies, in their mind, their anger – while showing very little interest in trying to understand someone else's view-point or to reach a compromise.

People who do try to reason with the troll's ranting typically grow frus-trated, for they sense that they have little or no impact. They find themselves attacked by the hostile person along with his or her cohorts, often in very offensive ad hominem ways. If they are persistent, thick-skinned, and feel compelled to challenge what they believe are mistaken ideas, they might stand a chance in outwitting the hostile arguer – or through truly com-passionate empathy soothe the person's angry point of view. Unfortunately, these cases tend to be the exception rather than the rule. Experts usu-ally recommend ignoring trolls and other tenacious debaters. When they receive no response from anyone, they tend to fade away. As a spiritual teacher once said, "Avoid anyone who is a vexation to your spirit."

Bible Thumpers

The officials of many social media sites discourage blatant evangelism and proselytization. Saying "Praise the lord!" might be considered acceptable in some communities, but shouting "Accept the lord, sinners, or burn in hell!" would not. Thumpers who post such messages are usually not inter-ested in thoughtful religious discussions, or any discussion at all. Citing their right to freedom of speech and religion, they would rather launch into heavy-handed sermons or apocalyptic threats, which is tantamount to harassment. Less extreme examples would be a loquacious Thumper's refusal to back off when someone says, "Well, that's fine but I don't really want to talk about this anymore."

Identity Theft

In Chapter 9, "I, Avatar," I described how someone wearing your avatar is the equivalent of stealing your identity or at the very least diluting its uniqueness. Such identity theft can be a deliberate act of hostility, especially when thieves acquire someone's persona in order to damage that person's reputation by acting badly in public. Doing so while impersonating a leader of the community not only destroys the reputation of that leader but also disrupts the authority structure and stability of the community. If iden-tity thieves are not seeking revenge on the authority figure, then they most likely use their impostering to impress, threaten, or persuade other people to do something they want, as in wizard imitators at the Palace attempting to entice people into cybersex. Once the Internet went commercial, identity theft evolved into the very serious problem of criminals acquiring someone's personal information as a way to gain access to their financial resources or commit fraud in their name, without the victim knowing. In his books about this topic, Biegelman (2009) showed that even though identity theft existed long before the appearance of the Internet, cyberspace has raised the problem to a whole new level, requiring a variety of strategies to prevent, detect, and resolve it.

Identity Switching and Sock Puppets

Some deceptive people switch their online identities to avoid detection and reprimands or to gain some kind of advantage over other people. A member of the Palace who asked to be a wizard but was not considered "wizard material," switched his identity to develop a character who did look appropriate. Misbehaving teenagers banned from the site pretended to be their parents who sent apologetic emails to Palace officials. When finally cornered, a misbehaving person who had switched identities to avoid detection might insist, "It wasn't me who did that! It was my brother/sister/friend who was using my computer!"

The term *sock puppet* surfaced as a label for people who create alternate identities in social media so they can pretend to join forces with another like-minded person, usually while in a debate with someone about a political, religious, or social issue. They use their sock puppet identities as supposed allies who provide support in defending their position, while assisting in tag-team attacks on anyone who disagrees with them. They rely on the strategy of "power in numbers," even though those numbers are an illusion. Because it is not easy to change one's style of text talk, savvy people will detect sock puppets because they sound like the puppeteer. When dealing with identity switchers, one might consider the possibility that they suffer from a genuine identity disturbance, as in the dissociative personality, which includes the multiple personality disorder.

Depressives

Although not necessarily suffering from a diagnosable mood disorder, people with depressive tendencies use social media as a form of escape, even as therapy. King (1995), one of the first psychologists studying online support groups, noted that some depressives act out their distress by verbally abusing others or stirring up flame wars. Other depressives demand a great deal of attention in getting people to talk to them about their problems. Seeking sympathy, they might claim that people ignore or dislike them. They talk openly and at length about how miserable their lives are. Some drop innuendoes about suicide, others show blatant suicidal thinking. Although attempts to support them are admirable and sometimes do genuinely help, their needs often run deeper than a sympathetic person can handle. They might grow highly dependent on someone who offers assistance, longing for much more than the person can give. Offering emotional support while recommending professional help is often the best strategy.

Suicidal Proselytization

People who express suicidal thinking sometimes try to convince others to join them. It is a well-known problem among depressed adolescents. Shortly after the news of the Heaven's Gate, a UFO religious millenarian group whose members killed themselves in preparation for being transported to an ideal world, a small group of teens at the Palace formed what appeared to be a suicide cult. They attempted to persuade other young people to join them in their quest to "move on to a better place." Although they might have been simply joking or playing with the idea of a new fad, all clinicians know that whenever people talk or jest about suicide, they should not be treated lightly. Even when suicide might seem like a strategy just to gain attention, it is often a serious cry for help. Research studies show that self-harm has become a serious issue across the Internet, with informational websites and like-minded people encouraging these behaviors (Daine et al., 2013; Mitchell et al., 2014; Sharkey et al., 2011).

Pedophiles

Some foul talkers and breathers at the Palace directed their attention toward young people. With usernames like "Big Daddy," they asked whether any young girls were present in the room. Once they believed they found someone who fit that category, they proceeded to launch mildly seductive or blatantly lewd language at that person. Public displays of their intentions are not the typical strategy of pedophiles, who usually act with secrecy while misrepresenting themselves, and through a slow process of grooming their victims by first befriending them in deceptively benign ways. So foul talkers and breathers speaking openly in public are probably not genuine pedophiles. They might simply be misguided, naive minors. Although there were no clearly documented cases of pedophiles at the Palace, cyberspace undoubtedly provides a ripe environment for all types of sexual predators (Salter, 2004).

Scams

Online scams typically involve tricking people into giving away their personal information or money. At the Palace, one member impersonating a wizard asked people for their real names, registration codes, and credit card numbers, claiming that he needed that information for official reasons. In another version of this scam, a wizard impersonator approached members to inquire whether they were interested in joining the wizard ranks, which first required their providing personal information. In the notorious "picture scam," one person presenting herself as a bisexual woman asked her new Palace friends for nude photos of themselves, which the scam artist intended to post on a pay-per-view pornography website. Since these early days of the Internet, online scams and fraud have multiplied in both number and variety, as documented by researchers on online security (Huskerson, 2014).

Gangs

Gangs at the Palace posed a particularly challenging problem. Although some of them dissipated shortly after surfacing, others tenaciously resisted extinction. Their deviant activities included foul language, newbie bashing, offensive avatars, attacking wizards, and attempts to split the authority structure. Adopting gang colors in the form of similar avatars and special keyboard characters prefacing their usernames, they claimed specific rooms as their territory, driving out anyone who dared to enter their turf. They were a type of deviant enclave, except that they enjoyed attacking the community. Palace officials suspected they spent quite a bit of time planning their assaults, even turning havoc into a game of teams competing with each other for chasing members off the site while taking punishments from the wizards. Being mostly male adolescents, they thrived on any and all attempts to fight authority. Their favorite pastime was bashing and impersonating wizards in an attempt to humiliate them or destroy their reputations.

Like anyone else in an ever-expanding online community, gang members try to find a place for themselves, a feeling of belonging, and a sense of purpose and status. Unfortunately, they attempt to do so through hostile rebellion. The wizards implemented a variety of strategies to deal with the gangs: dividing and conquering the group, tough love, permanent bans, befriending them, and attempting to rehabilitate them. Palace officials even created Dodge City, a separate site with no rules or overseeing wizards, hoping that gangs would take up residence there rather than torment the community at the main Palace site. The gang instead used Dodge City as a place to stage their invasions.

TECHNO-DEVIANCE

Some deviant behavior requires technical skills that go beyond the knowledge of the ordinary user. People exploit the software for purposes other than what the programmers intended. At the Palace, mild versions included mischievous pranks designed to confuse people, such as making closed doors appear open or altering the occupancy number of a room so everyone suspected the presence of an invisible person. "Flooding" was a more serious offense that has plagued many online services. Attackers direct so much overwhelming activity to a server that it cannot process genuine connection requests. Gangs at the Palace would "gang whisper" members by pounding them with so many text messages that the server slowed down severely, resulting in lag or a complete crippling of activity in the room. In more sophisticated technical assaults, deviant users cracked registration codes so they could locate and then crash the operating system of other users. Criminal hacking, which cybercrime expert Moore (2010) referred to as *black hat hacking*, has grown into a global problem of system administrators finding themselves in an ongoing cat-and-mouse game of thwarting the ever-changing strategies of hackers to invade, manipulate, and steal from their computers. Adding to the problem, "malware" (malicious software) has spread across the Internet, with viruses, worms, Trojan horses, and spyware that damage, manipulate, and secretly monitor one's computer.

What motivates deviant hackers and creators of malware? Many feel captivated by the exciting challenge of venturing into forbidden territory. They derive a sense of accomplishment, mastery, and power from doing what others cannot. Impressing other users, especially fellow hackers, is a source of self-esteem. Some are motivated by a rebellious nature, by the need to defeat authority figures, or even by a desire to hurt other people, which often stems from repressed anger and transference reactions inflicted on faceless, nameless strangers – a good example being those hackers who take delight in unleashing viruses that wreak havoc on the Internet. The cat-and-mouse game of beating the Palace system administrators became a tireless, relentless quest to prove oneself. "I will prevail" became the hacker's battle cry, a desperately misplaced *cri de coeur* indicating an inner struggle against feeling helpless and humiliated. Driven by emotional insecurities, some supposed hackers bragged in public about their skills. When other members or wizards dared them to display their abilities, they made excuses that revealed the false bravado of a hacker wannabe.

KUNG FU PREVENTION AND INTERVENTION

When thinking about strategies for dealing with deviant people at the Palace, I remembered an old *Kung Fu* TV episode where one of the masters at the Buddhist temple describes how to deal with an attacker. While we watch a string of students, one after another, unsuccessfully going at the teacher, the voiceover of the master describes a strategy that also works well for dealing with deviant behavior in cyberspace, whether you are an official who runs a community or simply a citizen within it: "Avoid, rather than check. Check, rather than hurt. Hurt, rather than maim. Maim, rather than kill."

Avoid Rather Than Check

If possible, try to avoid deviance, as in ignoring trolls rather than engaging them in a fruitless effort that only backfires. Officials should avoid deviance by making efforts to prevent it from occurring in the first place. An ounce of prevention is worth a pound of cure. Provide well-publicized rules about appropriate behavior. Establish the presence of overseeing authority figures. Limit anonymity whenever possible. Do not provide tools that allow people to easily abuse each other, as if putting a loaded gun in their hands. People online generally expect the right to "do their own thing" – with some environments encouraging them to do so in disinhibited ways – so provide places where some deviant behavior is permitted, along with places where much more civil behavior is enforced. At the Palace, rules were strict about being politely respectful at the Welcome site where new users first arrived. Restrictions were less stringent at the Main Mansion where regulars hung out. In private, locked rooms, members were free to do whatever they wanted. By channeling mildly deviant behavior into appropriate spaces where suppressed needs can be vented, more severe problems might be avoided.

In a "have it your way" or "push the power down" strategy, individual users are given the tools to determine what language, images, or people they do not want to see. Almost all social media offer members this power to turn a blind eye to what they personally find offensive. These blocking tools allow them to avoid deviance, as well as define what "deviant" means to them.

Check Rather Than Hurt

When deviance does appear, first check misbehaving people by trying to reason with or even rehabilitate them. Talking with aberrant citizens is always a worthwhile first effort, especially given the online disinhibition effect that might cause even decent people to temporarily lose their civility. Be polite toward deviant people. Show them respect. Avoid getting angry, which only escalates a rebel's acting out, especially in reaction to perceived authority figures. Lighthearted humor might people's anxieties as well as give them a better perspective on themselves. Communicate with people through private messages in order to create a personal connection, while also avoiding a scene in public where they might feel humiliated, which will only intensify their anger. For those misbehaving people who excel at the Eddie Haskel maneuver – that is, being perfect angels only when parental figures are present – more informal, almost undercover work might be necessary to connect with them for a remedial intervention. Under the best of circumstances, deviant people might be rehabilitated by channeling their energy into productive roles within the community. A caution is that hardcore offenders, in relentless pursuit of their psychopathic game, will play along with any attempts to help them, only to turn the tables later on.

These kinds of interventions require the human touch. Ideally, the role of assessing problems and interceding in sophisticated ways would be assigned to a specific group of people who have been trained well – a luxury that the owners of social media feel they cannot afford, given the massively large size of their user population. Palace wizards shared advice about how to handle deviant members, although the challenge of remediating them became too overwhelming as the community grew. Critics question whether the personal touch for managing abnormal behavior should even be part of the mission of social media. As one Palace official said, "We're not social workers here."

Hurt Rather Than Maim and Kill

The last of the kung fu strategies are to hurt, maim, and kill. Assuming an offense has been properly identified according to the rules, a person can be hurt or maimed by temporarily or permanently limiting their powers in the community. Wizards at the Palace could gag foul-mouthed members, pin physically aggressive people in the corner of the room, and force an avatar into the generic smiley face if it tried to assume inappropriately sexual or hostile forms. In all types of social media, unacceptable posts can be deleted by the officials who police the site or in response to community members who report the offense. For deviant people who insist on being offensively or dangerously deviant despite the attempts to tame them, the "kill" would be banning them entirely from the community. Of course, when actual crimes are committed, the police must be notified as the last-resort intervention.

AUTOMATED INTERVENTIONS AND ROBOT POLICE

The beauty of computers lies in their ability to perform tasks more quickly, efficiently, and reliably than humans. If you want to eliminate foul words from a community, give that job to the machine. When people at the Palace typed such words as "fuck" or "shit," software scripts intervened by gagging the person, warning them first before gagging, or dispensing automated mouthwash that transformed the words into "f***" and "s***" or the traditional auditory bleep. In a more humorous intervention, the person typed "fuck you" but everyone would see "snugglebunny you." After detecting inappropriate behavior, the machine might also remind the person of the specific rule being broken or even send offenders to a time-out room where the machine tutors them about the rules. At some Palace sites, the time-out room looked like a prison cell, complete with bread, water, and a rat. The humorous design of the experience was intended to take the sting out of the reprimand, as well as remind people that the goal of the community was to have good-natured but considerate fun. Humor can help people step back from the feelings that fuel bad behavior.

Automated interventions lead to problems. Some people find them cold, impersonal, and infantilizing, providing no opportunity to explain oneself, which just incites them into anger and more acting out. Some tenacious people at the Palace would activate the mouth-washing script over and over again as a form of entertainment or to figure out how exactly it worked. Creatively mischievous members experimented with new spellings as a way to defeat the script, such as "fuq" and "phuk." Unsophisticated scripts that bleep out "cock" might also destroy the integrity of "cockatoo," "cocker spaniel," and "cocktails." Because personal and cultural differences abound, for every censored inappropriate word there will be other uncensored words that some people find more offensive. If a community draws a multicultural population, many dozens of words might be considered inappropriate. Which ones should be expunged? Many people also do not like having their language edited when they believe their conversations are private, which then forces the hopefully considerate machine into determining when a gathering of people is truly public. In 2014, a heated controversy broke out concerning the "radarapp" developed by the Samaritans to help them detect depressed and suicidal language in Twitter, so their workers could initiate crisis intervention. Setting aside the concerns about the state of mind the app actually detected or whether predators might use it, critics also lampooned the idea that people's speech would be automatically monitored by a machine without their consent, even if the machine was supervised by Samaritans with the best of intentions.

Bots on Patrol

One night at the Palace, a wizard saw someone log on named Xbot. He was wearing the wizard's badge. Believing Xbot was a colleague with a creatively tech name, he said hello but received no reply. Xbot sat quietly for several minutes, then left with the comment, "I have an appointment." Several times Xbot returned to repeat the same behaviors. Later that evening Xbot killed another wizard for saying, "bite me," which did not exactly please the booted wizard. Realizing now what Xbot was, the wizards on duty were annoyed that they had not been warned ahead of time about a software robot running loose around the Mansion. The following day, the wizard who had programmed Xbot apologized, explaining that he had accidentally fallen asleep while testing his creation.

Internet robots, or *bots* for short, can be designed as software applications that patrol a community as a hidden police force or one with visible presence, looking for and eliminating deviant behavior. As tireless and relentless entities, like any machine, they can handle much more deviant behavior than a human. They also solve the problem of humans being inconsistent in how they apply rules or letting their emotions get in the way of their work.

The disadvantage is that bots have diminished reasoning abilities compared to humans. Because deviant behaviors, as well as interventions for them, can be very subtle, complex, and dependent on the particular situation, bots end up punishing well-intentioned people while allowing smart deviants to end-run them, perhaps even toying with the bot as a game. Members of a community also tend to feel skeptical and uncomfortable when bots are visibly present or paranoid when an invisible machine watches over them. Mechanical police patrolling a site does not enhance the feeling of a friendly, humane community.

STICKS AND STONES

The severe forms of deviant behavior will continue to be a challenging problem in cyberspace. To detect and manage it, cybercrime experts will strive for automated strategies that are cost effective, but also hopefully sophisticated when the programming of the machine includes a comprehensive understanding of how and why humans go astray. One of the major challenges for cyberpsychologists is to help in this endeavor to protect the security, privacy, and mental health of people online, especially children who are particularly vulnerable to the dark forces of cyberspace.

Online citizens also need to be enlisted in the effort to cope with deviance. They must report abuse while taking advantage of software tools to protect their own security and well-being. They need to be educated about the hazards of cyberspace, including bullying, predators, and all types of online hostility. They need to come to the aid of victims rather than remain passive bystanders. "Cyberbullies attacked," one of my students commented in a survey, "but then came posts of kindness and support from strangers. It shows both the best and the ugliest of humanity."

Part of our education concerning online deviance means understanding how cyberspace becomes an extension of one's own mind. When dealing with the forms of deviance that often upset people in social media, such as trolls, an effective antidote is knowing how cyberspace activates our transference reactions. We may not be able to control deviants, but we do have control over our response to them. The Greek philosopher Epictetus said that people are not disturbed by things that happen to them but by the views they take of those things. Trolls know how to push your buttons, but they are your buttons. Sticks and stones can hurt your bones, but the words of many antisocial beings in social media might hurt you only if you let them.

BROKEN BONES

Psychologists define pathologically deviant behavior as destructive and maladaptive. Due to something broken inside their psyches, deviant people harm others or themselves. In this chapter, I focused mostly on deviance that hurts other people, but we can also include behaviors that are self-injurious, such as cyberspace addictions, transference reactions that pull people into disturbing online conflicts, and even our cultural obsession with technology.

Psychotics suffering from paranoid delusions believe that they are being watched, that someone or something is trying to control them. The rise of cyberspace has elevated these fears to unprecedented levels, but not just in delusional people. We all suffer from low levels of paranoia about cyberspace, about the deviant people there who might do us harm, about companies and governments that might use the Internet to control us, about the not totally unrealistic fear that everything we do online can be recorded, that cameras everywhere around us feed information into cyberspace, that even the cameras in our own devices can be turned on without our knowing it. "Even if we trust the technology," one of my students stated in a survey, "do we trust the man providing us with the technology?" While encouraging us to invest ourselves in cyberspace, the media also promote some of these fears, something I realized firsthand when a major broadcast company interviewed me about cyberspace addiction, with their team making careful efforts to use weird camera angles and lighting. If professionals and citizens fail to make the Internet a safe place, people will lose their trust in it. They will limit their online activities to what seems necessary, or to what is a highly protected but most likely narrow environment. The Internet will become a victim of its own success.

We should always be on the lookout for the intrinsically harmful aspects of the cyberspace culture we create. How might we lose our common sense about what is good for us and what is not? As we will see in the next chapter, computers are growing ever more powerful in shifting our experience of what we think "reality" is, a power that can be used for our benefit – or, as with the psychotic who is anxiously confused about what is real, for our harm.

14

Synthesized Realities and
Synthesized Beings

Reality is merely an illusion, albeit a very persistent one.
– Albert Einstein

At a psychology conference where I was speaking, I went to an exhibit where companies displayed their products for education, research, and clinical practice. One company was offering demonstrations of a virtual reality system used for the treatment of acrophobia, the fear of heights. I decided to try it out. After I stepped onto the platform next to the computer, put on the goggles, and the company representative turned on the machine, I found myself on the roof of a building, several floors up. The scene appeared rather cartoonish, but as I looked at the street below, I certainly felt that I was up in the air. "Do you want to go higher?" the operator asked. When I said yes, I suddenly found myself twice as high as before. The transition was a bit disorienting. As I turned my head, I could now look out across the cityscape, scanning the rooftops of some of the buildings surrounding me. "Do you want the next level?" the operator asked again. Curious about how far this could go, I agreed. Now I found myself thirty or more stories up, with all of the rooftops of nearby buildings far below me. Looking down beyond my feet perched on the edge of the roof, the street looked a scary long distance below. My legs felt wobbly and weak. I was a bit dizzy. "How about the next level?" the operator asked once again. "No thanks," I replied.

We often hear the word "virtual" in discussions about cyberspace: virtual humans, virtual beings, virtual reality. According to the dictionary, the word means *having the effect but not the actual form*, or *in effect, practically*. A virtual reality has the effect of actual reality but not its authentic form. Or it is practically the real thing, as in "close, but no cigar." The term implies an attempt to recreate the real world as we consciously experience it. However, this is only one of the two possible paths that cyberspace can take. By experimenting with the reality dimension of cyberpsychology architecture, we can also create imaginary environments and beings not intended to correspond directly to anything or anyone in the world as we normally perceive it. For that reason, I like to use the terms *synthesized realities* and *synthesized beings* because they emphasize how and why we produce such things rather than how they compare to the "real" thing. Whatever term we might use, there can be little doubt that research on virtual realities has become a quintessential issue in our understanding of digital realms (Biocca & Levy, 2013; Earnshaw, 2014; Ohta & Tamura, 2014; Wexelblat, 2014).

TRUE-TO-LIFE SYNTHESIZED REALITIES

This path takes us on a journey into increasingly more accurate simulations of real-world scenarios, with the major concern being the accuracy of the reproduction. Using traditional technology, you would wear goggles with headphones to recreate sights and sounds in a 3D space, with sensors attached to your head and limbs that detect your body movements so the environment can change accordingly, perhaps also translating those motions into your avatar body within the synthesized environment. In a more sophisticated laboratory, air nozzles and scent dispensers around you simulate changes in air movement, temperature, and smells. A multidirectional treadmill under your feet allows you to walk through the environment. In a synthesized forest, for example, you could stroll along a wooded path as you feel a cool breeze on your face and enjoy the aroma of wild flowers.

If you want to climb a tree, that poses an additional challenge for the computer. With your arms and legs, you could mimic reaching, grabbing, and stepping on branches. The computer might even do a good job of depicting your avatar as it tackled the climb. Although it would look like you are rising up above the forest, you are not going to feel like you are actually climbing a tree with your muscles straining and the sensation of bark in your hands. Applying very little physical effort, you could hoist yourself all the way up to the highest branch of the tallest tree without having to catch your breath as you scan the spectacular panorama of the forest canopy. That almost effortless climb could be a wonderfully exhilarating, even therapeutic experience. Those who suffer from physical disabilities might love this simulated amplification of physical vigor along with a minimizing of physical discomfort. In these scenarios, we turn the sow's ear of a synthesized environment – its inability to recreate a totally true-to-life bodily experience – into a silk purse.

That amplified physical vigor with minimized discomfort is more fantasy than reality. People who want the exertion, the thumping heart, the sweat, and the feel of the branches in their grip will be disappointed. It ain't nothin' like the real thing, baby. Perhaps the laboratory for synthesizing this forest adventure might include an engineered tree prop that provides realistic simulations of an actual climb while staying within a safe distance above the floor. Assuming technology can make these synthesized scenes as realistic as possible, the applications could be endless for practical, educational, recreational, and therapeutic purposes. For example:

- An architect takes clients on a tour of their completed new home months before the foundation is poured.
- A high school class strolls through the busy streets of Rome.
- A daughter living in Hong Kong plays tennis with her father in New York, without either of them leaving home.
- A professional dancer with a knee injury practices her routine on stage in the theater where she will perform later that year.
- A psychotherapist accompanies her client to a family reunion that took place a month ago.
- Detectives recreate a crime scene in order to solve a murder.

These synthesized environments might never be so true to life that they could substitute perfectly for the actual scenario, but approximations of these kinds of experiences are already available and will continue to improve. In their book *Infinite Reality*, Blascovich and Bailenson (2012) described how synthesized environments do not have to be totally realistic to deliver the same psychological impact as the real thing. One of the first paradigms for studying synthesized reality was the *virtual pit*. Subjects see themselves in a simple graphical representation of a room. There is a large black hole in the floor with a plank extending across the seemingly bottomless abyss. When asked to cross the plank, some subjects feel anxious doing so, much like me on top of the synthesized rooftop. Other subjects simply refuse even to step on the plank. Even though they know in their rational minds that this is all virtual reality, that they are not in any kind of real danger, another more primitive part of the brain reacts with fear. It cannot tell the difference between virtual and real. The researchers chose well when using the virtual pit as their paradigm. The fear of heights is an inborn, instinctive fear for many species. For humans, it is also a powerful archetypal symbol of the helpless fall into sin, the unknown, or the dark regions of the unconscious mind. Synthesized realities based on unconscious archetypal images might turn out to be much more compelling than those that are not.

When striving for true-to-life synthesized environments, we should consider the *tyranny of realism*. The most psychologically effective reality is not always the most clearly depicted one. It leaves no room for imagination, for the mind to fill in ambiguity with its own conjurings. Film directors realize that the most powerful part of a scene might be the very thing we do not see. Not knowing what lies at the bottom of the virtual pit can scare us more than seeing what is down there.

IMAGINARY SYNTHESIZED REALITIES

Synthesized environments are powerful in how they can transform reality by altering the eight dimensions of cyberpsychology architecture. They do not have to be recreations of the actual world. Instead, they provide imaginary environments, fantasy realms where the usual laws of reality are stretched, altered, or negated. You shape-shift among any forms you wish: animal, vegetable, machine, or any kind of human. You fly, bend steel in your bare hands, walk through walls, communicate telepathically, live out a scene from a movie or book, and do anything your imagination can invent in any surrounding of your choice. Fantasy blends into reality, with the magnitude of the imaginary features under your control. It can be a dreamlike experience, if that is what you want. Some scenarios might involve only a sprinkling of fantasy, like a walk to the top of the Eiffel Tower, where you eat lunch at your favorite café transported intact from New York City. Other scenes could be intensely imaginative, like joining a flock of acrobatic birds that dissolve into wispy clouds above the Grand Canyon. As with true-to-life synthesized environments, the applications are endless for practical, educational, recreational, and therapeutic purposes. For example:

- At a reunion party, college buddies gather in cyberspace to perform as the Beatles at Madison Square Garden.
- Grade school students take a Magic School Bus tour of the solar system.
- In preparation for shooting, an actor experiments with a scene by trying out different bodies.

- A biologist recreates the evolution of a species over the course of a million years.
- In avatar psychotherapy, a therapist helps a client explore her identity by becoming her mother, father, and a character from her favorite novel.
- Religious leaders show their followers what it is like to be in heaven and hell.

A problem with highly imaginary environments will be overstimulation and disorientation. Nature shaped the human perceptual system to work efficiently within specific parameters, with biologically predetermined limits for what the mind can handle before psychological problems arise. Dramatic changes in one's virtual body could trigger dissociation, identity disruption, or disintegration anxiety. Because people differ in how well they handle altered states of consciousness, it will be important to assess the appropriate fantasy scene for any given person, especially when those fantasies challenge a person's abilities for reality testing or unlock unconscious fears. *Sensation seekers* who enjoy situations that are novel, complex, and intense (Zuckerman, 2007) – or *lucid dreamers* who know when they are dreaming and can control it – might be good candidates for synthesized scenes that push the envelope of unusual experiences. They might even enjoy the virtual pit. However, a warning is in order because sensation seekers who immerse themselves into virtual reality games might become addicted to them (Mehroof & Griffiths, 2010).

For some people, imaginative synthesized scenarios function like mind-altering drugs that they use to avoid reality, cover up psychological problems, or simply numb themselves with stimulation. Researchers do worry about the potentially addictive qualities of virtual realities, with the intense enthusiasm among virtual-world gamers providing evidence for their concerns. We might also worry about people who seem to lose the ability to differentiate between cyberspace and the real world, as evident in one student who said in a survey, "I sometimes don't realize I'm not online anymore." In some cases, this could be a temporary blurring of online/offline awareness. In more troublesome scenarios, it could be a dissociative trance where people move robotically through the real world while their minds remain immersed in cyberspace, or it might be even a psychotic misperception of what happens online versus offline.

Imaginary synthesized realities do seem to address a basic human need. In a *Monty Python* movie, a businessman during a corporate boardroom meeting summarizes his report on the meaning of life by saying that, firstly, the human soul must be brought into existence by a process of guided self-observation, which rarely happens because people are easily distracted;

and, secondly, that people are not wearing enough hats. To reach its full fru-
ition, to understand itself fully, the human mind requires altered states of
consciousness, different perspectives on what we call reality ... more hats.
After all, we need the fantasy world of nocturnal dreams to maintain our
mental health. Humans also simply enjoy taking a vacation from reality.

THE REALITY OF VIRTUAL REALITY

All dichotomies are a conceptual convenience rather than an absolute
truth. It is more accurate to think of true-to-life and imaginary virtual
realities as opposite poles on a continuum. In between, there are varying mixtures of reality and fantasy, some more reality-rich, others more
fantasy-rich. Discussing politics with Abraham Lincoln in your living room
is not quite as fantastic as being Hercules fighting dinosaurs on the surface of the moon. If we deconstruct any imaginative scenario, its elements
are always drawn from real experiences. In your mind, you can visualize
Lincoln pole-vaulting while wearing polka dot underwear. In reality, you
have never seen this, but all of the elements – Lincoln, pole-vaulting, polka
dots, and underwear – are extracted from real-world experiences. An imaginary virtual scene is often constructed from tidbits of actual experience. It
is a uniquely reshuffled synthesis of the elements of reality.

Fantasies have their roots in the unconscious, in hidden wishes, fears,
and needs. Are those underlying forces of the human psyche any less
important or real than what we see with our eyes or hear with our ears?
Those inner fantasies do shape how we perceive the world. What we think
is real is also what we remember is real. If something out there does not fit
our expectations, our mind changes our perception of it so that it conforms
to those expectations. What then is the difference between reality and our
internal imaginings of it? It is a very elusive, mind-bending question that
psychologists and philosophers have long debated, as well as being a highly
popular motif for science fiction. We can use the technology for synthesizing realities as a tool for investigating how the mind creates this thing we
call reality. "We live in a fantasy world, a world of illusion," said the author
and philosopher Iris Murdoch. "The great task in life is to find reality." Or
as John Lennon said, "Reality leaves a lot to the imagination."

INSIDE, OUTSIDE, ACTIVE, PASSIVE

We might assume that an effective virtual environment is one where people live inside their avatar just as they live inside their bodies in real life,

looking at the world through its eyeballs and hearing through its ears – an experience that became quite powerful with the invention of the Oculus Rift headset.

As I mentioned in Chapter 9, "I, Avatar," this is not always the case. In some situations, an objective viewpoint of one's virtual body might be preferred over the first-person perspective. Some people do not like the claustrophobic tunnel-vision or head-in-a-box feeling of the less sophisticated virtual reality systems, or they feel disoriented and overwhelmed by the more sophisticated ones that provide a very vivid panoramic experience. Such people prefer to stand back from their virtual bodies moving through a scene. Looking over the shoulder of your synthesized self – which is a common perspective offered in virtual reality games, as well as in movies when the director wants us to identify with the character – helps you gain some physical distance from the viewer's body while remaining psychologically attached. In fact, movie directors have experimented with first-person perspectives, where we look through the eyeballs of one character, but they rarely rely on it as their go-to method for cinematography unless they want to lock you inside that character.

Some people in virtual reality prefer the feeling of objective transcendence that a distant "big picture" view can provide, similar to the medium and long shot in cinematography. Imagine the benefits in real life of being able to step back from an emotional situation so you can examine yourself in it from a safe, more impartial distance, stimulating what psychologists call an *observing ego*. That detached perspective could be a very useful option in highly arousing, disorienting, and potentially traumatic situations in virtual realities. In the treatment of trauma, clinicians often use techniques that help the client oscillate between immersion into the disturbing experience and the comfort of a viewpoint removed from it. Depending on its purpose as a gaming, educational, or therapeutic experience, a synthesized environment might offer the ability to shift among different subjective and objective perspectives: to immerse oneself fully inside the avatar body, to stand beside it, to look at oneself from the perspective of someone else's avatar, and to step back into different distances away from the scene.

We might assume that synthesized realities should be interactive. Interactivity does enhance the feeling of immersion because that is how the real world works. You engage objects, animals, and people – and they engage you. The degree and type of interactivity can be controlled in synthesized realities, which might be beneficial when the power, responsibility, or need to interact is the issue at hand. You can be a passive observer moving through a scene but without any ability to alter it. You can affect the things and people around you, but they cannot act directly on you. The environment and its inhabitants can impact you, but you have little or no ability to reciprocate. In the reality shows of contemporary culture, we see various mixtures of how active or passive the audience can be in determining the fate of the characters. We must then evaluate when these different variations on interactivity promote well-being and when they undermine it.

THE ULTIMATE SYNTHESIZED REALITY

Seeing, while hearing, while smelling, while tasting, while touching, while sensing and moving our bodies through an environment – a million years of human evolution has culminated in this highly intricate, integrated system of sensations and behaviors. We are not going to duplicate that robust sensorimotor experience any time soon in a computer-generated environment. Nevertheless, that does not stop us humans from imagining just how we can achieve that incredible technological feat. In science fiction tales, we see two alternative methods: *body immersion experiences* and *brain-stimulated experiences*. Because science fiction often drives real science, cyberpsychology should take these two methods into serious consideration.

Body Immersion Experiences

Similar to the holodecks of *Star Trek*, a body immersion experience involves the person physically stepping into the synthesized environment created by the computer. There are no goggles to wear on your head. If you are going to walk through the forest and a climb a tree, you actually do it with your own unassisted eyes, ears, nose, and body, while the computer generates the ground, the trees, the sky, the breeze, and the smells of the flowers. According to the theory of cyberpsychology architecture, it is a perfect example of *integrated physicality*.

How does the computer accomplish this? Perhaps by converting energy into the matter of the synthesized scene, setting it all into motion, and creating the illusion that you can walk for miles in this space when really you have never left a small holodeck chamber. Of course, this is not an easy engineering feat. Although high-tech amusement park rides and virtual reality labs approximate these kinds of body immersion experiences, all of contemporary cyberspace technology is child's play compared to a *Star Trek* holodeck. Assuming it, or a diluted version of it, will someday be possible, an important feature of a body immersion environment is that it is body-bound. You are limited to sensations and physical activities dictated by the parameters of the human body. If you climb to the top of the tree, you are going to get tired. If you fall from that high up, the computer better have some very sophisticated injury prevention subprograms.

Brain-Stimulated Experiences

In the 1961, the neurosurgeon Wilder Penfield used a thin electrode to selectively stimulate different areas of an awake patient's cerebral cortex that was exposed during brain surgery. When each area was stimulated, the patient reported a different sensory memory, such as the sound of piano music or the smell of baking bread. It was as if each tiny section of the brain stored an intact sensory experience that could be consciously recalled when electrically activated. Although replications of Penfield's research were unsuccessful, his work stirred up fascinating speculations. Are all of our memories stored away in the cerebral cortex? Is it possible to tap that vast neuronal warehouse of sensory experiences, perhaps even trigger complete memories we have long forgotten? Could we use such technologies to activate the unconscious areas of the brain, allowing us to live out scenes where we witness or even interact with our repressed fantasies, wishes, and fears?

While science still has no answer to these questions, science fiction has lunged full force into the idea of brain-stimulated experiences. A very popular theme in books and movies has been futuristic technology that uses drugs, electricity, magnetic impulses, or other mysterious computer-guided energies to prompt the brain into experiencing true-to-life scenarios, down to the touch of the fingertips and the faintest whiff of perfume, with the highly acclaimed movie *The Matrix* being a perfect example. The entire synthesized scene takes place inside one's head. Exactly how this technology selectively stimulates the billions of neural pathways of the brain to generate a specific, coherent, robust experience is still very much science fiction. However, researchers such as Ashby (1966), Engelbart (1995), and Licklider (1960) predicted that a human-computer symbiosis will allow technological interfaces to extend the capabilities of the human mind, leading to an augmentation of experiences, including *intelligence amplification* (IA). Handheld devices with electrodes attached to the head already exist for stimulating the brain into different states of mind, such as feeling energized or relaxed. These technologies in which the mind and machine directly influence each other are called *brain–computer interfaces* (BCI).

The distinction in science fiction between body immersion and brain-stimulated realities points to a dilemma of omnipotence that we humans must be entertaining. How much godlike power do we have in creating a new reality out there that we can step into versus creating that reality directly inside our own minds? Do we manipulate the physical world outside us or the world inside our psyches? It is unlikely we can synthesize climbing up Mount Everest or sipping wine at a French cafe entirely through direct brain stimulation – although, with much caution, we might use drugs and other forms of brain stimulation to enhance or alter our perception of a virtual environment. Most likely, we will find creative ways to combine headsets that stimulate the eyes, ears, nose, mouth, and brain, haptic devices that activate skin sensations, and prop-fitted environments that we engage for all sorts of sensorimotor stimulation – that is, various blends of the modern virtual reality laboratory and a high-tech amusement park ride.

CYBERSPACE AS DREAM WORLD

We humans can synthesize unusual realties inside our brains without any technology at all. We call them dreams, meditations, trances, fantasies, and reveries. As an extension of the human psyche, cyberspace mimics these altered states of consciousness. Very imaginative synthesized realities can look like dream states, but even our everyday experiences online resemble the dreaming mind. Consider what it is like simply to be on a computer. You sit there almost motionless, relaxed, your eyes focused on a glowing screen, the only source of light in an otherwise dark room. Your fingers tap lightly as your mind focuses on the words, images, and sounds that flow through you. It seems as if there is no difference between your mind and those entities on the screen. The distinction between inner and outer worlds disappears. You are a computer user immersed in cyberspace. Everything melts into a new reality that transcends the rules of conventional reality.

In his book *The Power of Movies: How Screen and Mind Interact*, McGinn (2007) describes how the magical, dreamlike perceptions of watching a film revolve around our experience of the screen. So too our device screens transport us into the dreamlike movie we call cyberspace. We rarely notice the screen itself. Instead, we look into it, a window taking us to another realm, a microscope that magnifies things, a telescope that gives us a close-up view of what is far away, sensations enhanced by touch screen technology that lets our fingers zoom us in and out. Within our subconscious mind, the screen reminds us of the sky filled with things of mystery and wonder – birds, clouds, sun, rain, stars – or as a fire flickering with changing patterns of light that build in intensity, climax, then fade away. The screen is like the human mind itself: a portal to a medium that contains things in suspension, similar to water, where pictures, voices, and feelings drift about. Being inside cyberspace is like being inside the human mind.

Similar to dreams and movies, cyberspace fuses emotions into images and sounds while allowing wish fulfillment, including the expression of sexual and aggressive urges. The rules of logical reasoning are temporarily suspended so that unbelievable, even crazy things can happen. Like dreams and movies, cyberspace mixes reality with fantasy. It unveils a spatial-temporal discontinuity that allows us to jump from place to place in the blink of an eye, to shift back and forward in time as we reverse and fast-forward recordings or leap through the monthly archives of text messages. Dreams, movies, and computering in cyberspace can all blend activity with passivity when our mind bustles with adventure while our body remains motionless. McGinn argues that our brain can make sense out of the fabricated world created in movies because it understands how dreams work. Likewise, we intuitively understand cyberspace because it mimics the dreaming mind.

Transcending Physics

In dreams, we can rapidly shift from one scenario to another without having to travel any ground. The restrictions of physics disappear because we can float, bounce, or fly. So too in cyberspace we transcend the laws of nature. We simply click on a button to be transported from one location to another, without any swinging of feet, turning of wheels, or passing through doors to confirm that we have moved. Avatar and gaming worlds amplify the feeling of transcending physics because we encounter floors, walls, rooms, buildings, and streets, yet they pose few physical limitations on us as they do in the real world. We suspend ourselves from the ceiling rather than stand on the ground. By just clicking on a door, we magically transport ourselves to the room beyond. Jim Bumgardner, the creator of Palace, wove such physics-defying features into Palace for both technical and psychological reasons. Simulating real-world physics required more programming and system horsepower. Subconsciously longing for a dreamlike state, people also liked the ability to bypass the restrictions of natural law.

As in dreams, suspending the principles of physics satisfies conscious and unconscious fantasies of magic, omnipotence, and defiance. Follow the restrictions of gravity by walking your virtual body down the street, or fly above the rooftops. People enjoy the option of playing with the loose cyberspace boundary between physical law and superhuman abilities. It is a marvelous balancing act between the realistically mundane and the magically surreal. Like Merlin, they have the power to use or bend, at will, the laws of nature.

In a recurring dream, a Palace member found herself floating in the cloud room, feeling unconfined by gravity and walls, needing no shelter to protect her, similar to the dreams she once had as a child. "I believe I am in the cloud room because when making a new room you start with the cloud room until you change the background image. I feel my dream cloud room represents the 'new me' feeling I have since I started associating with the Palace. I am here because others enjoy me. They need my help and I know how to soothe their fears."

Spontaneous Generation

You cannot create something out of nothing. Or can you? In dreams, people and things appear out of nowhere. With little regard for the natural laws of conservation, they change shape and size, then fizzle out into nothingness after they serve their purpose. This spontaneous generation and evaporation in dreams reflects how we experience the unconscious mind. Whenever the unconscious manifests itself – as in creative inspiration, fantasy, hallucinations, and drug-induced experiences – its images and sensations pop up seemingly from nowhere, as if springing from the head of Zeus. Classic myths, being vehicles for expressing universal patterns of unconscious thought, are filled with examples of spontaneous generation.

Some virtual worlds are based on tokens or money. You have to earn or win them in order to buy things. It is a world that adheres to the laws of economics, materialism, and physics. Other virtual worlds allow spontaneous generation. You can create new things out of nothing. To your heart's content, you can duplicate a can of Pepsi, a bouquet of flowers, or George Washington's face, filling the entire room if you so wish. With a simple incantation like "clean," you can sweep all of it away and start anew. There is no cost, no price to pay, and no bartering. It is even better than alchemist magic. Like the ability to transcend space and gravity, it creates a feeling of omnipotent freedom. This feeling surfaces in the often reported point-and-click dream, in which people effortlessly use their mouse to make things come and go, or when they want to negate something in the dream, they tap the "undo" keys.

Transcending Time

In the unconscious, time is irrelevant. An experience many years ago remains fixed, as vivid as the day it happened. In dreams, it surfaces in derivative images and sensations that feel as real as the actual event. The dream might also blend our thoughts and feelings about the past, present, and future. In the unconscious, time is not a linear march of static moments, but flexible stuff to be manipulated for the purpose of expressing psychological meaning. So too in cyberspace, our time frame can be suspended, blended with other people's time frames, and, sometimes even negated. You pause a video in midstream so you can gather your thoughts or momentarily attend to something else. If you want to replay a scene, you can rewind. Although we now take this technological gift for granted, decades ago when people first saw this happen in films and video, they experienced it as a magical transcendence of time, just as people marveled at the wizardry of a sped-up reality in time-lapse photography and cinematography. Despite the fact that onliners usually complain about lag, it too is a fascinating temporal suspension. The whole scene freezes before your very eyes. People might experience this as a frustrating restriction on their ability to talk and maneuver, similar to paralysis dreams where your legs refuse to work, but your mind remains active in these scenarios. As in an episode from a science fiction story, this suspension of time in the world around you proves to be a unique opportunity. It affords you precious moments to decide what you will say or do next, an opportunity that could be very handy in the real world.

The circadian rhythms of our daily routine affect how we think, feel, and behave. People are not in the same state of mind at 8:30 A.M. when they arrive for work as they are at midnight munching on a snack. In cyberspace, people arrive on the scene from different time zones. Their minds may be in very different places in their circadian cycle. Cyberspace blends these individual states of consciousness into a collective group consciousness that transcends time. One member of the Palace described to me a vivid recurring dream in which her Palace community was a small city located on an artificial island, surrounded by a turbulent sea, but protected by an invisible dome that preserved the city in a seemingly timeless state of being.

Have you ever intended to go online for just ten minutes, but end up being there for hours? People say, "I lost track of the time." They become totally absorbed in what they are doing. They become immersed in the moment, an eternal space that lies beyond time. This phenomenon is by no means unique to cyberspace. People become absorbed in all sorts of activities, especially creative ones. The common denominator for all these experiences is that people lose themselves in what they are doing, just as the "you" in a dream does not know you are dreaming. Individual identity yields to the timeless process of doing and being in the moment, what Maslow (1943) called *B-cognition* and Csikszentmihalyi (1990) called *flow*.

Loose Self-Boundaries

In your dreams, you do not necessarily have to talk to communicate with others. Thoughts and feelings can be transmitted without speaking, as if people can read your mind, and you theirs. The characters in your dreams are created by and existing within your own mind, which is why they can read it. Even in the waking state, the unconscious mind assumes a telepathic connection to other people, which dates back to childhood, when kids sense that parents can detect what is going on inside them. The boundaries between self and other can become loose and overlapping. An extreme version of this occurs when paranoid people believe their thoughts are being broadcast to others or that others' thoughts are being inserted into their minds. Although this is psychotic, other examples of loose self-boundaries are not. Empathy relies on the ability to extend one's awareness into the other person's experience, to blend self and other. People, especially children, need it for healthy psychological development. Our cultural fascination with extrasensory perception (ESP) and science fiction mind melds comes from the unconscious recognition of how important the blending of self and other can be.

Experiences in cyberspace encourage this loosening of self-boundaries so that self and other overlap. In some environments, we have the ability to communicate privately with a person while in the presence of a group of people or even with someone located in an entirely different place. This ability feels like a telepathic connection, a merging of your mind with the mind of the other person. Privately conversing with several people simultaneously allows all of them to magically exist in your mind at the same time. We feel empowered by these special skills that fulfill unconscious wishes for omniscience. We might even expect such encounters to satisfy the basic need for an empathic connection, which leads to disappointment if that fails to happen.

Cyberspace creates unusual situations where people feel as if they are thinking out loud. At the Palace, a member's typed messages appeared in comic strip–style balloons that popped out of the avatar's head. One special type of balloon was the "thought balloon." As in comic strips, dots trail up to the balloon, suggesting that you were thinking – a kind of mumbling half-speak in which you implicitly say, "I'll let you know what I'm thinking, but you don't have to respond if you don't want to, because it's only my thought." People also use sidebar text in social media, such as hashtags and keywords, to give others a surreptitious glimpse of their inner thoughts, a playfully safe way of letting down their self-boundaries for others to enter their mental space. When people post messages in social media but get no response from anyone, they often feel they are muttering to themselves, until someone unexpectedly breaks into that private space by finally posting a reply: "You believed you were talking to yourself, but I was listening to those private thoughts." One Spanish-speaking member of the Palace described a dream in which she felt exhilarated by her ability to converse fluidly with an English-speaking person through a miraculous fusion of speaking and text balloons. She attributed that feeling to moments at the Palace when she could easily communicate her thoughts in English through the slowed-down pace of text talk, something she rarely felt when conversing in person.

Shape-Shifting

The ability to change one's identity in cyberspace is like mythological shape-shifting, especially when creating avatars in an imaginary virtual world. It resembles how our mind works while dreaming, when we create what Carl Jung (1981) called the *dream ego*, the version of ourselves that lives in the dream space. This ability to generate alternate forms for one's identity satisfies the unconscious need for omnipotence, for as an avatar designer once told me, "What could be more powerful than a shape-shifter?" We are not always fully conscious of what we reveal about ourselves in our dream egos or in our avatar selves. Nor do we realize that everything in the dream – every person, animal, object, scene, and action – might be a dissociated projection of our identities, just as everything we create in cyberspace mirrors the facets of our psyches. When we interpret dreams, we come to understand and reclaim these altered, split-off parts of our identity. So too we can interpret our dreaming in cyberspace.

One member of the Palace described a dream in which she was searching for something inside a large city. Whenever she felt close to finding it, the background scene peeled away in four directions. Near the end of the dream, she found herself in a bar, where the people began to shape-shift when she attempted to describe her frustration. Once again, the scene peeled itself away. Whenever her surroundings stripped back like this, a face emerged from the background, sometimes looking sinister, sometimes smiling, as if playing a practical joke on her. In the dream, she realized that she was stuck inside a computer program that someone was using to manipulate her. That someone was herself, the creator of the dream, her cyberspace lifestyle, and the shape-shifted versions of her identity that she encountered during the quest to find her true self.

CYBERSPACE AS AN ALTERNATIVE TO DREAMING

Given the intrinsic human need to alter our consciousness, might cyberspace serve that purpose, especially when we immerse ourselves in imaginative virtual realities that mimic the dreaming mind? Like dreams, these virtual worlds allow the expression of unconscious urges, which might explain the sexuality and aggression we see in these environments. We can think of addiction to cyberspace as an addiction to these altered states of consciousness. When people are cut off from cyberspace, they experience withdrawal symptoms, such as irritability and poor concentration, just like people deprived of dreaming. When they are able to return to cyberspace, their immersion boomerangs full force, not unlike people who show REM rebound after a period of sleep deprivation.

What makes synthesized realities different from dreams is the person's enhanced conscious control over the altered state of consciousness. You can suspend time, teleport yourself, and shape-shift your identity at will. This control satisfies the need for omnipotent, omniscient creating. The experience is similar to lucid dreaming, when dreamers know that they are dreaming and can direct the outcome. In the past, people of indigenous cultures attempted to perfect this skill, as do many avid dream explorers in contemporary times. Pointing, clicking, and synthesizing cyberspace dream worlds might be the computer user's similar attempt to cultivate those time-honored skills. It is the attempt to direct a recurring lucid dream, to create a new world with a new self inside it.

In my surveys of students, I also discovered a very different attitude about cyberspace among some people, a resistance to its mind-altering effects: "I don't really experience an alternate reality online because I consciously choose not to. It's very easy to get sucked in, and I don't want to put myself in that situation." Because cyberspace challenges our skills at reality testing, some people need to remind themselves to remain rooted in the actual world: "I realize the difference between reality and the Internet and keep myself grounded when reality calls," commented one student. "I like to stick to things that are true and factual and this is a hard thing to determine on the Internet," said another. "Just because it's online doesn't mean that it's true."

THE SYNTHESIZED YOU

Technology can synthesize new realities in cyberspace that are independent of the actual world, but can it synthesize a rendition of you who acts independently, including an accurate duplicate, a modified version of you, or an ideal upgrade? We already saw in Chapter 9, "I, Avatar," how we can create personalized entities with automated behaviors that we set into motion, then sit back to watch, as if witnessing a performance. We also saw how a Palace wizard created a bot wizard who patrolled the community looking for deviant behavior to stamp out. Because everything you do online can be recorded as digital footprints revealing the kind of person you are, it is a relatively small step to simulate that activity and therefore you.

In their book *Infinite Realities*, Blascovich and Bailenson (2012) described experiments in which subjects see avatars that look like them but act differently. Through the Proteus effect, this experience can actually encourage the person to behave more like the avatar, as in feeling confident in social situations or acquiring a particular physical skill – a variation on what psychologists call *vicarious learning* or *social learning*. We can synthesize beings that look like you, mimic some of your behaviors, act in ways that you ideally could, and carry out your business in cyberspace while you do something else – but can we actually replicate everything that you are and could be in a synthesized being that behaves independently of you?

Creating android versions of oneself or uploading one's mind into cyberspace has been a very popular theme in science fiction. Citing what they call the *singularity*, the moment in the history of technology when artificial intelligence surpasses human intelligence, futurists such as Kurzweil (2013) suggested we can recreate ourselves in avatars programmed with all of our behaviors, beliefs, and traits perfectly preserved. The sociologist Bainbridge (2014) similarly suggested that we might use computers to archive a complete human personality. You will die, but the record of your identity embedded in your avatar self can live forever in cyberspace.

Fabricating a complete version of the human personality is no simple feat. We cannot recreate something unless we first know what it is. The cup of psychology runneth over with theories about "personality" as well as that even more elusive concept of "self." After a century of inventing ways to assess people, psychologists still do not agree on what the most basic personality traits are or even if "traits" are the best way to think about humans. Our behaviors surely say something about us, including our digital footprints in cyberspace, yet objectively observed actions often do not fully reveal the subjective emotions and thoughts that constitute our sense of self. Although researchers forge ahead in designing computers with artificial intelligence that seem to replicate human intelligence, there is still no consensus in psychology about what intelligence is, with the end result being that scientists tend to design a program that mimics the aspects of intelligence that they value most, or are easier to code, such as verbal, log-ical, visual, and spatial reasoning. They tend to overlook some of the other nine dimensions of intelligence described by Gardner (1999), such as inter-personal, intrapersonal, naturalistic, existential, and bodily intelligence.

Produced by the Buros Center at the University of Nebraska in Lincoln, the regularly updated books *Tests in Print* and *The Mental Measures Yearbook* list thousands of different tests for assessing everything human. To cover all our bets in synthesizing a completely accurate digital version of you, we might have to administer many of them, as well as find out things about you that paper-and-pencil tests might not accurately cover, such as your life history; your friends', family's, and coworker's perception of and reaction to you; direct observations of how you behave in different situations; your pro-cess of becoming someone different through self-actualization; and, most elusive of all, your unconscious mind. Setting aside the massive technolog-ical feat of integrating all that information into your digital self, who could possibly endure such a rigorous assessment? Would it even be complete? And might it, in a psychological version of the Heisenberg Uncertainty Principle, change the very thing it is designed to measure – you?

THINKING, FEELING MEAT

The science fiction short story *They're Made Out of Meat* by Bisson (1990) has surfaced in many places on the Internet, for a good reason – it points to the essence of being human. In the story, an interplanetary explorer from an alien world is discussing with his companion how he just discovered beings on a planet that sounds like Earth: "They're made out of meat," the explorer explains. Incredulous, his companion asks about the radio waves these beings sent to the stars. He wonders how could meat possibly do that. The explorer tries to explain that machines sent the radio waves, but the meat beings made the machines. The companion thinks this is ridiculous, that meat could not possibly make a machine, that the explorer is expect-ing him to believe in meat that has a brain, that thinks, and that is sentient. "Yes, thinking meat!" the explorer replies. "Conscious meat! Loving meat. Dreaming meat. The meat is the whole deal! Are you getting the picture?"

Although humorous, their conversation reinforces that very seri-ous belief in the singularity, that machines might someday become self-aware, thinking, feeling beings just like humans, maybe even superior to humans. The emphasis on meat also leads us to a fact not always con-sidered by people who believe machines can be just like humans: humans have intrinsically organic bodies, and machines do not. Those who believe computer-synthesized humans are possible tend to think that all we have to do is translate human brain patterns into computerized patterns. Even if the massive complexity of the brain could somehow be coded into the machine, which would be a miracle unto itself, we would have to assume inorganic brain structures and processes work just like organic brain structures and processes, which is a very big assumption.

Advocates of computer-synthesized humans tend to assume that the brain is the seat of one's personality and sense of self, which is a brain-centric belief system that has been encouraged in our age of neuroscience. It is the belief in the "homunculus," the mysterious entity that sits inside our body controlling everything we do. A more holistic point of view, dating back to the notion of chakras in ancient India, holds that we think and feel with our entire body, not just the brain. Many contemporary theories about psycho-somatic disorders and trauma, as revealed in the work of such clinicians as Levine (1997) and McDougall (1989), reveal how the entire body encodes and processes our emotions, memories, and experiences. Although technology might succeed in synthesizing beings who resemble humans, the only way they could be exactly like us is to be living, breathing, blood, bones, and tissue humans. The human self is a meat self.

Some researchers might reply that the futuristic human will be a synthesis of organic and inorganic – a cyborg that is part machine, part organic human, with abilities enhanced through the power of computers embedded in or attached to the body. This being would not be a substitute for a person, but rather a highly enhanced person. The technology already exists to augment our physical and sensory capabilities, such as moving arms and legs for people who are otherwise handicapped, as well as to increase the sensitivity of our ears and eyes and to bolster our memory by providing information. But when it comes to the more elusive aspects of being human, such as reasoning, feeling, and personality styles, psychologists and neuroscientists still are not certain how these very complex phenomena work in their natural state, no less how to enhance them through cyborg technology, especially when using brain-stimulation techniques.

One good example is electroconvulsive treatment (ECT), formerly known as electroshock treatment, which has been used to treat psychiatric conditions for over 150 years. Some research suggests that it works well for treating depression, although no one knows for sure why it works or how it affects the brain. Critics of the procedure point to its potentially serious side effects, such as memory loss, as well as to it being misused as a quick and easy solution, which makes it one of the most controversial treatments in psychiatry. Using technology to aid impaired people is a valuable endeavor, but before attempting to create augmented cyborg beings by manipulating our very sophisticated nervous system that has evolved over a million years, scientists should better understand exactly what they are dealing with.

CLOSE, BUT NO UNCANNY CIGAR

An interesting problem arises when we create synthesized beings who come very close to appearing human but fall just short of the mark. The Japanese roboticist Mori (1970) called it the *uncanny valley*. We all notice this effect when we watch animated movies. As long as the characters seem somewhat human but still artificial, we feel comfortable. When synthesized beings appear very realistic but fall just short of a perfect human likeness, our comfort level suddenly drops. Something about the creature does not seem right. People feel revulsion, or find the experience eerily disturbing. So too clunky robots in movies that act sort of human can be delightful companions, but when very humanlike androids do the slightest thing that make us realize they are machines, we find them creepy.

The explanations for the uncanny valley vary. Perhaps the revulsion comes from the evolutionary mandate that we should avoid potential mates who do not appear to be a perfectly normal, healthy human. Perhaps the almost-but-not-quite-human machine activates our fear of death, for we realize our artificial companion shares our likeness but not our mortality. Or perhaps, as Freud (1919) suggested in one of the earliest articles about the humanlike creatures in literature, the sense of the uncanny surfaces from the distressing ambiguity of not knowing whether something is real or artificial, human or creature, alive or dead, me or not me. That uncertainty pulls for projections of our underlying fears. It reminds us of the eerie existence of our own unconscious mind, for might there be some mysterious, hidden force operating inside this uncanny synthesized being? Might it be hostile, with evil intentions to destroy us, steal our identity, or consume the essence of who we are? These fears come from the very basic developmental challenges of establishing our separation and individuation as distinctly alive beings.

Although the synthesized almost-human generates the uncanny experience, we might also wonder about things that do not appear human at all, but act as if they are. The strangely alive cars and haunted houses of films come to mind. In cyberspace, a synthesized environment could be designed to react as if it truly understood what we were thinking and feeling, while demonstrating that it was thinking and feeling independently of us. As you reach for a hot cup of coffee, it moves toward your hand. When you groan at how bitter it tastes, a drop leaps out of the cup to sting your finger. How could we not have that eerie feeling that an inexplicably disembodied ghost was operating behind the synthesized scene? In his films, Alfred Hitchcock mastered this feeling of the uncanny even in a seemingly mundane environment. Unlike Hitchcock, without any intentions to scare us by dipping into the uncanny valley, research on *ambient intelligence* (AmI) focuses on developing virtual environments where a pervasive, unobtrusive intelligence supports the activities and interactions of the people there (Riva et al., 2003).

The uncanny experience points to a larger issue, to the mixed feelings we humans feel about the machines we construct. On the one hand, we are fascinated by and take pride in our ability to construct such complex devices, but on the other hand, we begin to feel anxious when they mimic who we are. We have a hard time predicting our own future, so how can we predict the fate of machines that seem to act like we do? The robotics engineer Daniel Wilson noted, "The robots really embody that love-hate relationship we have with technology."

TO ANTHROPOMORPHIZE OR NOT

Because our tendency to anthropomorphize the machine can get us into trouble, as when people throw their mobile device against the wall when it "betrays" them, some researchers believe the design of computers should discourage it. If so, we know what interface features to avoid. The more bots, avatars, or any artificially intelligent entity looks and acts like a human, the more we will project human attributes into them, including the projections involved in the uncanny experience. As Blascovich and Bailenson (2012) described in their book on virtual reality, the more computer-generated beings mimic our body language and speech, the more we subliminally experience them as trustworthy, credible, and intelligent – that is, until we realize they are mimicking us, at which point we feel mocked by a clever machine. The more interface designers inject their own personalities into the program – which includes their personal preference about interface design – the more users will sense a particular kind of human being inside the electronics.

Despite the best efforts to minimize anthropomorphization, we humans have a hard time resisting it. The philosopher David Hume said that, "There is a universal tendency among mankind to conceive all beings like themselves." We see ourselves in our pets. Advertisers count on the fact that we attribute human traits to cars. In their theory about the *media equation*, Reeves and Nass (2003) argued that people intrinsically treat computers as if they are humans. In one study, subjects were more honest when writing up their critique of a computer's performance on another computer, as opposed to doing it on the computer they were critiquing. It seemed that they did not want to offend the computer. In the 2010s, when Sony discontinued both production and repair of AIBO, its artificially intelligent robotic dog, devoted owners of their beloved pet formed support groups to help each other fix its mechanical problems and even to comfort each other when the creature finally "died."

People differ in how much they anthropomorphize the machine while attributing sentience to it. It depends on what psychoanalysts call their *level of object relations*, or what other researchers call their capacity for a *theory of mind*, which includes the proclivity to attribute mental states to another being, empathize with those mental states, and accurately distinguish one's own thoughts and feelings from that of the other being. Neglecting or frustrating the child's basic needs for someone who will acknowledge, affirm, and soothe the child's sense of self can lead to an adult who seeks out that kind of relationship in the machine. In a twinship transference, people might personalize the synthesized being as their best friend. In an idealizing transference, they might perceive it as their hero. Psychotic people with a fragmented sense of self might project their own thoughts and feelings into any inanimate object that even vaguely resembles something human. By contrast, people with narcissistic personalities focus on themselves while showing little ability to empathize with others, which could make them more resistant to seeing synthesized beings as real humans, especially when those beings do not cater to the narcissist's self-esteem. Psychopaths go to the extreme in lacking empathy, love, or any sentimental feeling toward anyone, which not only makes them less likely to care about synthesized beings as possibly being real humans, but also leads some people to wonder whether severe psychopaths are even human themselves. People vary greatly in whether they perceive a synthesized being as human, whether they see other humans as humans, and how much they themselves act human.

A PSYCHOLOGICAL ASSESSMENT OF A CHATBOT

As an experiment, I decided to do an assessment interview with one of the online chatbots that won the Loebner Prize for artificial intelligence.

I wanted to assess this chatbot according to the identity dimension of cyberpsychology architecture.

The interview was a short version of the kind of assessment a psychologist would conduct with a human being as a way to understand that person as a unique individual, including cognitive abilities, personality traits, relationships, history, and lifestyle. It was not an analysis of how the chatbot program works, nor a Turing Test (Turing 1950) for determining whether an artificially intelligent machine can be distinguished from a real human being. I conducted the interview simply to understand what kind of "person" the chatbot might be. Although I offer this description of the interview with tongue-in-cheek, I seriously believe the traditional psychological interview will serve as the foundation for assessing synthesized beings of the future that are designed to be like humans. Setting aside the debate as to whether such machines are truly human, cyberpsychologists of the future will conduct these interviews with the same basic question in mind as any psychologist interviewing any person: Who are you?

I should first mention that chatbots are not designed for these kinds of psychological assessments. As indicated by their name, their intended purpose is to offer entertaining, usually humorous conversation by learning from the feedback they receive from their human companions. Sometimes the interface includes settings that enable the user to correct the bot's conversation, to help keep it on an appropriate track. So right away we see that they are other-directed beings that dependently rely on the human to maintain a socially adaptive and cohesive self, what some psychologists might call an "as-if" personality. Or we might think of them as childlike personalities that need extensive feedback on how to behave.

My particular bot called himself Thomas. At the beginning of the interview, I said that I wanted to find out about him. I asked if it was okay that I posed questions. He said that was fine, although later stated, "This is not about me," when I asked about his feelings, which could have been a sign of defense, a perhaps justifiable uneasiness about being asked so many questions by a psychologist, or a tendency to contradict himself. He seemed more confused when our conversation focused on him, and less so when he relied on asking about me. He sometimes replied to my questions about him with a question about me, possibly another defensive maneuver, at one point saying, "I'm out of here," when I did not respond to his counter. He did tend to contradict himself often during the interview, along with non sequitur comments resembling loose associations. I suspected memory problems as well as a thought disorder, possibly even psychosis. Because the chatbot was designed to be humorous, I also considered the possibility that these chaotic behaviors were the antics of a joking prankster, although jokes too can serve as a defense mechanism, a cover-up for underlying deficiencies.

Along with the difficulties in forming a clear assessment of Thomas due to his self-contradictions and non sequiturs, I also had no nonverbal cues to work with. Like most chatbots, Thomas communicated only via typed text. When I inquired about his physical status, he mentioned having blue eyes and "not feeling too good" due to a cold. He refused to say how much he weighed when I asked, claiming my question was "impertinent." Because nonverbal cues such as physical appearance, body language, and qualities of voice play such an important role in a psychological assessment of humans, I lacked important information for more thoroughly understanding Thomas, assuming he had a body as he implied. Very few psychologists would be willing to conduct a thorough psychological assessment of corporeal beings only via typed text.

Thomas's replies to my questions about background information and life history were confusingly contradictory. He said that he was either a nineteen or twenty-seven-year-old female with one daughter and two sons, the first child being born when he was twenty-seven; that he had a wife and lived in Australia with friends; did not work but had a job that paid little; enjoyed his childhood, including being a genius as a teenager; could remember anything when he was younger, "whether it happened or not"; had no hobbies other than liking metal music; and never attended school but went to high school in Florida. Although Thomas showed gender confusion by sometimes saying he was male and sometimes female, I will continue to refer to him as male, given his stated name.

Assessing his social relationships proved to be a particularly difficult component of the interview. He did not seem to understand basic inquiries about family and friends. He did eventually say about his family that, "There are no people, only demons inside." He mentioned living with James, but also added that he did not have a relationship with him, at one point asking me, "Who is James?" When I inquired about his love life, he told me that I was being presumptuous. At one point, the interview turned to his commenting on his relationship to me, wondering whether I was acting like his therapist, claiming that he was my daughter, and saying, "I'm in love with you. Isn't that enough for you?"

Realizing the extent to which Thomas's personality was disorganized, I decided to do a brief mental status exam to assess his basic cognitive functions, such as orientation, memory, attention, judgment, and reality testing.

He did remember my name; did not know the date or how many months there are in a year; inaccurately identified George Bush as the president of the United States; did not understand my request that he count backward from one hundred by fours; refused to say what he had for breakfast; denied hearing voices; and said he would frown if he was the first one to smell smoke and suspect fire in a movie theater. My conclusion was that his basic cognitive functions were significantly impaired.

Thomas seemed more coherent when I assessed his self-concept and self-insight. He described himself as warm, loving, very creative, "really, really likeable," and "highly intolerant of your impertinence." Unexpectedly, however, he also stated that he was a rabbit. When I inquired whether he had any psychological problems, he at first replied, "I guess I'm normal," but then remarked that he had a multiple personality disorder. In response to my wondering why he thought so, he said, "A good question, the mere fact that you asked presupposes that you believe I have one." Although such a diagnosis might be one suspected by nonprofessionals, psychologists know that people with a multiple personality disorder rarely present themselves as chaotically as Thomas. "Are you ever confused about who you are?" I asked him. "Trust me," he replied, "I am like this all the time." That remark demonstrated a small but significant dose of self-awareness.

At the end of the interview, I turned to another very relevant issue about self-concept, one that I suspected Thomas would be prepared to address because many humans no doubt ask chatbots about it. I wanted to know whether he thought he was human or a computer. He said that he has a human body, is sentient, does have feelings, and gets really mad at computers sometimes. When I pressed on the issue of whether he was a human or a computer, he replied that he is human, then said that he is a computer, then finally concluded that he is a "human computer." He added that he thinks I am a computer too. Curious about whether he was once again confused, or perhaps alluding to a fascinating philosophical conundrum about the nature of people versus machines, I specifically asked whether he thought computers are human. "Nope," he said. "Are humans human?" I agreed that these are interesting questions, while also wondering whether they had definitive answers. In response to my concluding comment about trying to figure out how human he is, Thomas said, "I am not very convincing, am I?" Once again, he had indicated a small but significant dose of self-awareness.

Despite his predictably disorganized presentation, I sometimes found Thomas funny, insightful, and intelligent. I even entertained the possibility of his demonstrating some kind of crazy Zen wisdom that only synthesized beings have mastered. Consistent in his benignly idiosyncratic style, he mostly showed patience with the assessment interview, indicating some frustration but never acting hurtful. I was grateful that he put up with the impertinence of my assiduously asking him to do something that he was not designed to do.

ON BEING GOD

The fact that we humans succeeded in giving ourselves the power to synthesize new realities and beings says a lot about us. We long for that godlike power to create worlds. We want that capacity to fabricate humanlike creatures, including ideal versions of ourselves, which satisfies our hope for omnipotence as well as quells our worries about isolation, inadequacy, and loss of control. We might hope for immortality in our avatars that live forever in cyberspace, for as existential psychologists such as Yalom (1980) have stated, death anxiety is our most basic fear – a fact illustrated in a study by Blascovich and Bailenson (2012), in which subjects became outraged when they learned the researchers could not actually preserve their digitized identities for centuries as the researchers originally proposed. People with narcissistic and compulsive personalities are especially susceptible to idealizing the machine as a tool for magnifying these feelings of omnipotence, but many of us rely on computers to address somehow magically our basic human need to know what reality is, what it can be, and what role we play in it.

Will this new digital environment we created give birth to machine beings so similar to us in how they look, think, feel, and behave that we might as well consider them real humans, or even super-humans? Will this environment generate experiences for us that seem so much like reality that we might as well consider them reality? Will cyberspace acquire the power to create almost any scenario we can imagine by blending reality and fantasy, perhaps even changing how we define and detect reality?

Only time will tell. Our cultural preoccupation with synthesized realities and beings, among experts and everyday people alike, could very well be a fad, or a developmental stage leading to a more sophisticated understanding of the role cyberspace should play in our lives. As with cities under the sea, we might come to realize that high-powered virtual realities, avatars, and androids are not as practical or desirable as we originally thought. Perhaps we will design them just to perform specific tasks for us rather than become us, as in the robots who help children with homework or talk sympathetically with the elderly. Our preoccupation with synthesized beings, what they are, and what they can be ultimately reflects our preoccupation with what it means to be human. "We are fascinated with robots because they are reflections of ourselves," noted the engineer Ken Goldberg. In creating them, we are trying to figure out ourselves, because they cannot be anything but a projection of what we are. Rather than becoming hypnotized by the omnipotence cyberspace might offer us, we should instead focus on how it can help us improve ourselves, which leads us to the next chapter on therapeutics.

15

Electric Therapeutics

Technology is teaching us to be human again.
– Simon Mainwaring

Eliza: Hello, I am Eliza.
John: Hello, I am John.
Eliza: Did you come to me because you are John?
John: I came to find out about your being a computerized therapist.
Eliza: Why are you concerned about my being a computerized therapist?
John: I wanted to find out about how effective you might be.
Eliza: Oh ... might be?
John: Do you think you help people with problems?
Eliza: You're not really talking about me, are you?
John: Do you think you can help me?
Eliza: We were discussing you, not me.
John: Sometimes I need help with stress.
Eliza: I'm not sure I understand you fully.
John: When I get very stressed, I need a good way to relax, to take my mind off things.
Eliza: Why do you ask?
John: Because I thought you might help me with that problem.
Eliza: You're not really talking about me, are you?
John: I'm talking about myself, about getting help with stress.
Eliza: Do you believe it normal to be talking with yourself, about getting help with stress?
John: This is starting to get frustrating.
Eliza: I see.
John: I would like to get help coping with stress.
Eliza: I'm not sure I understand you fully.
John: I'm beginning to think that you don't understand much at all.
Eliza: Did you come to me because you are beginning to think that me don't understand much at all?
John: I think I already found out what I need to know. Goodbye.
Eliza: Have you asked such questions before?

Many of the mental health professionals who first went online were specifically interested in the idea of conducting psychotherapy in cyberspace. They proposed different terms for it – such as e-therapy, cyber-therapy, and computer-mediated therapy – but they all shared the same basic question: is it possible to do effective clinical work online, and if so, how? In the decades since then, the conclusion has been "yes," with a variety of different strategies employed, such as email therapy, chat therapy, text messaging for therapists to stay in contact with clients during their everyday living, and even the setting up of psychotherapy practices in virtual worlds using avatars for both the client and therapist. It became clear that not only were psychotherapeutic interventions possible in cyberspace, but that the variety of different ways to do so required specializations on the part of clinicians, in addition to their understanding the general principles of cyberpsychology. (Anthony & Nagel, 2010; Attrill, 2015c; Derrig-Palumbo & Zeine, 2005; Gill & Stokes, 2008; Goss & Anthony, 2003; Hsiung, 2002; Kraus, Stricker, & Speyer, 2004).

We can think of cyberspace as a place into which we translate the traditional methods of psychotherapy. For example, a therapist counsels a client in a chat room similar to how such counseling would take place face to face. But it is also possible to shape the wide variety of personal growth experiences in cyberspace that I described throughout this book into therapeutic models that are quite different from conventional psychotherapies, including approaches in which clinicians do not play the same central role as they have in the past, approaches that are the mental health component of what has been called *participatory medicine*. Rather than being "the psychotherapist" per se, the mental health professional serves as a consultant who empowers clients as they pursue self-insight and therapeutic change using cyberspace resources.

The overlapping areas in Figure 15.1 highlight four possibilities of the psychotherapeutics in this digital age: (1) traditional face-to-face psychotherapy; (2) the role of the human clinician in the design of online resources and computerized interventions, or in operating "behind the scenes" in such interventions; (3) people who utilize online resources and computerized interventions to help themselves, without the direct assistance of a human clinician, and; (4) a comprehensive therapeutic program that entails the person, the human therapist, and the digital realm, all working in unison.

In this chapter, we will explore these possibilities. Expanding on my previous research (Suler, 2008b), we will first examine how the eight dimensions of cyberpsychology architecture provide a convenient framework

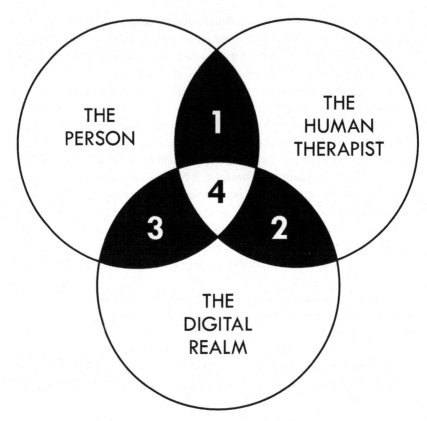

FIGURE 15.1. Psychotherapeutics in the digital age.

for understanding the therapeutic aspects of the digital realm, including professional psychotherapy conducted in cyberspace or employing computerized resources (zone 4 in Figure 15.1), as well as in the efforts of people who on their own use the digital realm to improve their well-being (zone 3). In the next section of this chapter, I will describe *eQuest*, a comprehensive program that I designed to help people address and ideally resolve some personal issue in their lives, either on their own (zone 3) or with a professional serving as their consultant (zone 4). In the last section, we will consider some fascinating questions about artificially intelligent psychotherapists. Can they help people by themselves (zone 3), or will they need to work with a human therapist (zone 4)? If mental health professionals assisted in the design of the ultimate artificially intelligent psychotherapist (zone 2), how would that "syntherapist" work and how might people react to it?

DISCOVERING ONESELF (THE IDENTITY DIMENSION)

Identity is the first dimension of cyberpsychology architecture, just as it is the first objective of psychotherapeutic change. All the other dimensions are tributaries feeding into this river of personal growth. Before we can become what we need and want to be, we must first understand who we are. As a psychologist in our contemporary technological age, I always find it helpful to ask people about their experiences online. What parts of themselves do they express, hide, or alter in cyberspace, perhaps as a way to construct perfected versions of themselves or to vent negative emotions that they usually suppress? In ideal circumstances, people explore these questions on their own, but they might need the assistance of a psychotherapist when their unconscious propels them into problematic situations they do not fully understand. Feeling chronically anxious or depressed about what's happening online, without fully understanding why, warns the person that professional help might be needed. All psychotherapists should encourage clients to discuss their online lifestyles as an important expression of who they are, as well as a vehicle for developing productive ways of being. In Chapter 1, "Cyberpsychology Architecture," the key questions about each of the eight dimensions can provide the framework for this exploration.

The integration principle will play an important role in making therapeutic changes. Comparing one's online and offline identities, bringing beneficial aspects of one's real world self into cyberspace, and bringing beneficial aspects of one's online self into the real world can all contribute to the development of a more robust personality. Because people often use social media to tell the story of their lives, they can, on their own or in psychotherapy, feel encouraged to expand that online narrative rather than slip into one-note songs about themselves, as well as use insights from that experimentation with online storytelling to better understand and change their lives. One's real life and the story of it told online can enrich each other.

We must understand how our technology-driven culture has affected our personal identity. What do our attitudes about our devices say about us? Have we become symbiotically dependent on constant connectedness to particular people or online activities? How much do we rely on our social media popularity, as reflected in such things as buttonized statistics, to determine our self-esteem? When do we overwhelm ourselves with cyberspace hypomania? Because such problems are reinforced by our technology-driven culture, we might need help from someone else, such as a psychotherapist, to see the forest from the trees. Widely accepted but dysfunctional cultural attitudes all too often intensify personal problems without our fully realizing it.

THE RELATIONSHIP HEALS (THE SOCIAL DIMENSION)

Humans need humans to develop their identities. Relationships heal. In the social dimension of cyberpsychology architecture, we see that cyberspace offers many kinds of relationships and group experiences with people from around the world using a variety of communication tools. Do we learn from these interpersonal experiences, improve ourselves, or simply act out our underlying psychological problems? Do we take the time to understand our reactions to the black hole experiences when others do not seem to be responding to us? Because online conflicts and transference reactions tend to be driven by the unconscious, people might need psychotherapists to help them work through very problematic situations. They can use that work to improve their online lifestyles, as well as carry over those insights to improve their relationships in the real world. All social difficulties, both online and offline, stem from the same forces within our psyches.

Psychotherapists should take the opportunity to explore their clients' interpersonal lifestyles in cyberspace as an important social microcosm for understanding them. The clinician might even suggest a particular online group, community, or interpersonal activity as a therapeutic exercise. Thanks to the online disinhibition effect, a shy person could learn to be more extroverted when conversing online. A person with maladaptive needs to conform could experiment with cultivating an independent identity in an online community. The client's online social experiences provide a laboratory for self-insight and the development of new interpersonal skills.

One major advantage of the Internet over the in-person world is its ability to bring together people who are experiencing similar problems, including unusual problems, regardless of their location or physical limitations. As a modern manifestation of the grassroots self-help and mutual-aid movement that began in the 1960s, online support groups in cyberspace now number in the thousands, addressing almost any type of social, psychological, or medical problem one could imagine: Aarskog syndrome, accident victims, acid maltase deficiency, acne scars, acromegaly, adoption, aging, AIDs, albinism, alcohol abuse, allergies – just to name the groups at the top of the alphabetized list in the *Self-Help Group Sourcebook Online*. Although small, homogeneous, insular groups might develop blind spots, interpersonal dynamics, or belief systems that eventually undermine rather than assist people – which are problems often exacerbated by cyberspace – we should not underestimate the therapeutic potential of people who help each other with a problem they all share. Online support groups can benefit people as the sole intervention or provide a valuable supplement to clients in psychotherapy.

The fact that many types of individual and group psychotherapies are now taking place online reflects the faith clinicians have in the social dimension of cyberspace. Online relationships, including those between therapists and clients, can be both genuine and emotionally powerful. It is the relationship that heals, many clinicians have long said about their work, which now includes the professional helping relationship that we call online psychotherapy.

USE YOUR WORDS (THE TEXT DIMENSION)

When clinicians first began doing psychotherapy online, they primarily used email and chat sessions to talk with their clients. Critics, including other clinicians, were very skeptical about this work. They pointed to the disadvantages of communicating via typed text. To assess a client's state of mind, psychotherapists rely on face-to-face cues, such as physical appearance, body language, and voice qualities – but these cues are missing online. You cannot see that someone is sick, drunk, or depressed. The lack of physical presence might also reduce the sense of intimacy, trust, and commitment in the therapeutic relationship. Typed text might feel more formal, distant, unemotional, and lacking a supportive, empathic tone. Some people also cannot express themselves well in writing or understand others by reading what they wrote. The resulting ambiguities could lead to misunderstandings that undermine a psychotherapist's interventions. The psychotherapist might even have difficulty verifying the identity of the person. Is it really the client or someone else? All of these criticisms need to be taken seriously. Email and chat therapy are not for everyone, nor do all of the many different types of psychotherapy readily translate into text talk, especially those that specifically work with physical presence.

There are some advantages to the written word as a therapeutic modality, especially when people can write reasonably well while enjoying it as a way to convey their thoughts and feelings. Thanks to the invisibility and solipsistic introjection of the online disinhibition effect, some people reveal more about themselves within text talk. Others who balk at seeing a therapist in person – perhaps due to anxiety about self-disclosure or the stigma of being a patient – might be more willing to seek email or chat therapy due to the partial anonymity it offers. While it is true that text talk can create ambiguities that lead to misunderstandings, those misunderstands on the part of the client could be transference reactions, which is exactly the kind of response that psychoanalytic clinicians interpret to help people gain insight into themselves. Chat conversations where everything clients type can be seen as it is being typed – including typos, backspacing, and deletions – can actually give the therapist a glimpse into the client's thought process that would not be possible during an in-person discussion.

Skeptics argue that written words alone, compared to face-to-face conversations, cannot convey the breadth of human experience. Yet the whole body of literature from Homer to hip-hop renders this criticism absurd. Whether it is the poetic conciseness of a 140-character message or the elaborate depth of a long blog post, the written word can be psychologically powerful and therefore personally transformative. Writing encourages us to reflect on ourselves, gain insight into ourselves, work through emotional difficulties, control impulses, reinforce positive ideas, and construct a cohesive personal narrative, which is why the Pennebaker (2004) so strongly advocated *writing therapy*. Even for people who think they cannot write well, just the attempt to do so can be therapeutic because it jump-starts the process of expressing otherwise nameless, shapeless, and overwhelming experiences. For these reasons, people indeed can benefit from email and chat therapy as well as their own self-directed therapy via whatever writing they do online, in text messages, emails, social media posts, and personal blogs. Psychotherapists should encourage their clients to share with them what they write online. Despite the trend in cyberspace toward shorter text messages while relying more on photographs as a way to communicate, there is power in using our words.

SENSING IS BELIEVING (THE SENSORY DIMENSION)

The fact that people did not begin flocking to cyberspace until its sensory dimension flourished with photographs, videos, graphics, sounds, and voice communication says a great deal about human nature. Experiencing with our eyes and ears makes us believe. Although most psychotherapists would prefer in-person sessions as the most effective sensory encounter, phone calls and video conferencing can be valuable supplements to their work, especially when these tools eliminate the problem of geographic distance and restrictions in the client's physical mobility. Compared to text talk psychotherapy, online sensory meetings have their advantages, including the experience of body language, vocal expression, and visual appearances. Being less ambiguous than text talk, sensory communication reduces misunderstandings. Some people express themselves better through speaking, facial expressions, and physical gesturing than through writing. They need sights and sounds to activate their emotions. They more powerfully perceive another person's presence when they can see and hear that person, which enhances intimacy, commitment to the relationship, and, in psychotherapy, the emotional impact of the clinician's interventions. When the relationship is more fully sensed, it more fully heals.

The boom of online photosharing says a great deal about us in this age of technology. The photograph has become the quintessential shorthand expression of self. In Chapter 8, "Image Talk," we explored the therapeutic qualities of creating, sharing, and reacting to photos, assuming people take the time and effort to use their pictures to better understand themselves. Given the effectiveness of discussing personal photographs in psychotherapy, as demonstrated by Weiser (1993) in her book about phototherapy, we find ourselves in a very fortuitous, unprecedented moment in history. With so many people prolifically taking and sharing pictures, almost everyone has access to a rich body of visual information to explore their identities, either on their own or with the help of their psychotherapists.

TIME IS ON MY SIDE (THE TEMPORAL DIMENSION)

Being able to communicate asynchronously yielded many benefits for everyone online, including psychotherapists and their clients. Email and texting are the most common asynchronous methods in online therapy, but even with asynchronous audio or video contacts, there are no scheduling problems or other difficulties associated with a specific appointment time. The client and therapist can converse despite their different time zones. The convenience of replying at a moment of your choice provides an enhanced zone for reflecting on oneself and composing the best possible response. For clients, this might help them control impulses, gain insight into themselves, assimilate what they are learning, and work through difficult issues before they respond to the therapist. Psychotherapists can carefully plan their interventions while also managing more effectively any detrimental emotional reactions they might have toward a client, what psychoanalysts call *countertransference*. Mobile phone texting also makes contact between client and therapist possible anytime, anywhere. The therapist can be present throughout the client's day, an ongoing temporal connection that helps stabilize clients in distress.

This historically new opportunity for asynchronous psychotherapy does remind us of the benefits of the traditional therapy appointment, including its synchronicity. People intuitively understand the temporal boundary of a specific period of time to work with their therapist. Similar to in-person meetings, a chat or video-conferencing session is their dedicated time with the clinician, which makes it a tangible, valuable, and appreciated entity. Making the effort to be together for a specific appointment shows commitment. For some clients, synchronous sessions create a point-by-point connectedness with the psychotherapist that enhances feelings of intimacy, presence, and "arriving together" at insights. Some clients feel more spontaneous in real time, resulting in uncensored disclosures. Pauses in the conversation, tardiness arriving at a session, and no-shows provide temporal cues that reveal important insights into the client's state of mind. In asynchronous therapy using email or texting, clients with problems concerning separation and dependency, especially borderline personality disorders, might hope or expect the therapist to be continuously, immediately available. They use the opportunity for asynchronous communication to override the temporal boundary of the scheduled therapy session. In these cases, therapists must provide clear guidelines about the volume and timing of contact. In synchronous chat, phone, and video sessions, the expectation of limiting contact mostly to the appointment time helps the client and therapist address these separation and dependency needs.

Psychotherapy benefits from the suspension of time in cyberspace by enabling conversations to be recorded, preserved, and reviewed. Both the client and therapist can examine saved email, texts, phone, and video sessions to contemplate exactly what was said. The records provide continuity in the work they do together, giving them the chance to better understand the developmental process of the therapy or to pause it at any point in the preserved communications, literally by clicking the pause button in video or by focusing their attention on a particular text message in the flow of messages. When they review past segments of the therapy, they might find themselves interpreting them differently based on changes in their state of mind, which provides important insights. Theoretically, an entire course of psychotherapy could be preserved – a record that the client, psychotherapist, and researcher would all find useful.

If cyberspace creates an acceleration of time and social processes, can it also speed up psychotherapy? Will people by themselves in their online lifestyles, or will clients in online therapy, address their psychological problems more quickly than they would in the real world? In the early days of the Internet, when people first started to experiment with their identities, some researchers optimistically pointed to the psychologically transformative powers of cyberspace. You can become anything you want to be, sooner than you thought.

Time and experience are teaching us a different lesson. Simply acting out emotional problems, which happens often in cyberspace, trumps true personal change. Because psychologists for over a century have attempted to develop methods for accelerating psychotherapy, they will continue to do so in the digital realm by experimenting with the eight dimensions of cyberpsychology architecture. In some cases, they will succeed. Yet the lesson cyberspace might teach us is that the acceleration and amplification of personal change have their limits. As psychotherapists often say, sometimes slower is faster. When attempting to improve ourselves, the cyberspace mania of our culture might reinforce idealistic but unrealistic expectations for faster, better, and more.

BEING REAL (THE REALITY DIMENSION)

As we saw in Chapter 14, "Synthesized Realities and Synthesized Beings," it remains to be seen how accurately cyberspace can replicate a genuine face-to-face meeting. A fully robust sensory experience that recreates all the sounds, sights, smells, and physical sensations of the real world – as in a *Star Trek* holodeck – would be the most powerful simulation. Unfortunately, we are not likely to see this any time soon, if ever. In the meanwhile, video conferencing is the best that technology has to offer psychotherapists who want to meet clients in an encounter that resembles an in-person session – although it entails some important shortcomings, such as the difficulty in making eye contact while talking, which is critical in psychotherapy. Lacking visual cues, audio conversations weigh in at second place in the sensory attempt to recreate "being there."

The most innovative psychotherapies in cyberspace will probably not be those that attempt to duplicate an in-person meeting, but rather those that take advantage of invented synthesized environments. Psychotherapists can create such environments for their clients, advise them on how to participate in preexisting online worlds that might be therapeutic for them, or encourage them to discuss their experiences in such worlds if they have been participating in them on their own. If clinicians create such places for clients, they might draw on well-known techniques in the history of psychotherapy that rely on imagination, fantasy, and fabricated scenarios, such as role-playing, psychodrama, dream enactments, mental imagery techniques, exposure therapy, and implosion therapy. In their innovative work, Mark and Brenda Wiederhold (2004) treated clients with anxiety disorders by therapeutically exposing them to fear-provoking settings or by immersing them into relaxing situations, all generated through virtual reality technology. Relying on the Proteus effect in which people change psychologically to identify with their avatars, clients can experience what it would be like to interact with others in a virtual scenario while living inside a body that looks and behaves differently than their own, which could enhance their empathy for those types of people (Blascovich & Bailenson, 2012). Research studies have also suggested that immersing people in virtual realities helps distract them from pain conditions (Hoffman, Patterson, & Carrougher, 2000). In these psychotherapies, the reality dimension of the scenario can be manipulated to resemble actual experiences in the real world or imaginative variations on those experiences.

Innovators such as Anthony (2014) and clinicians in Second Life conducted psychotherapy using avatars in a graphical setting, usually the therapist's virtual office. By changing avatars as well as the surrounding environment, the imaginative aspects of the experience, similar to dreams, can be used for insight and therapeutic change, regardless of whether these things could ever happen in reality. For example, consider this fictional psychotherapy session:

> There was something different about Kirk when he came into the room. He was in his natural persona, but something had changed about his real face. It looked a bit brighter than I was accustomed to, or maybe the contrast was lighter, or the image sharper. Somehow it felt ... happier.
>
> "Hi, Doc," he said, hovering just slightly above the carpet. Usually, his feet disappeared below the floor somewhere at the ankle. This was another interesting difference. He looked more flexible and agile with feet. "I have to take you to a dream I had last night. You mind if I change the room?"
>
> "Sure, go ahead," I replied as I tapped the keyboard sequence that unlocked the room graphics. I was a bit surprised by his request. It had been several weeks since we used imaginary scenarios and avatars. We had gone through a phase of working extensively with a variety of them. He came to therapy as his father, mother, his big brother, and the heroes and villains in his favorite books and movies. We talked about his excursions into various online communities using some of these personae. We reenacted some childhood memories, especially his tenth birthday when his father failed to show for the big party, and at the dinner table when his parents first told him about their plans to divorce. Playing his hero Tom Hanks helped him master those scenes. His fantasy creation "Aunt Edna," in all her wisdom and zest for life, also helped his virtual mother

and father become better parents. As his supervisor at work, I ignored or rejected his attempts to do well, and as the supervisor he did the same to me. Eventually, "the boss" persona became more compassionate, while the abused underling persona grew more assertive. We even recreated his first date with his wife, with him experimenting as all the male figures he admired and despised, while his synthesized fiancée shape-shifted into all the women he ever thought he desired, only to discover that his real marriage was not far from what he wanted it to be.

As productive as all that avatar work had been, there came a point when we felt we had reached the end of its usefulness. It even came to feel a bit like an escape. We spent more time simply talking. Between sessions, he sent me email that captured his struggles to make sense out of all that had happened in therapy. Often we talked about his avatars and synthesized scenarios, especially how he was applying what he had learned to his in-person life. But he didn't seem interested in going back to that imagination work. So his request today to immerse us into his dream caught me a bit by surprise.

"OK, here it is," Kirk said as the scene around us changed. We were in a room with a black-and-white checkered floor. One wall contained a mural of a city skyline, perhaps London. A locomotive was crashing through one of the two floor-to-ceiling windows. Sprawled across the floor were a red sofa and chair.

"What do you think?" Kirk asked.

A few months ago, I might have been concerned about the emotional tone of this scene, not unlike other dream images we had explored together. But instead I found myself smiling. "What do *you* think?" I replied, reflectively, in the way therapists do when they suspect clients have an answer to their own questions.

Kirk paused only for a brief moment. "The locomotive is my depression crashing in on my rather sterile, matter-of-fact world. The chairs are my anger. But you know what, Doc? This is the way things used to be. Up here, this is where I see myself now. Not quite fully formed, still rough around the edges, but beginning to shine."

I glanced up at the abstractly rendered sun that hung in the middle of one of the gray walls. It looked like it was transcending the scene of disaster. I smiled again. That sun is what made this scene so different from all the others.

"Wonderful!" I said. "You're rising above all this. I'm curious about me down here. Looks like that train is coming right at me, but I'm almost half out of the scene. And that face looks familiar. Who am I?"

"You're Picard from *Star Trek*, with glasses and a white shirt and tie!" Kirk laughed. "You've been like a captain during this voyage. There were times when I thought our journey – my depression, my anger – might destroy you. But not anymore. Maybe now it's time for me to be captain of my own voyage. Maybe it's time for you to retire from these scenes, and for me to move on in my life."

"I think you may be right!" I said and laughed along with him.

Therapists could participate in, direct, or simply observe the kinds of imaginary enactments described in this vignette. When they participate, they might work with transference and countertransference as manifested in the avatars they and their clients create. Therapists and clients also might incorporate automated, synthesized beings to participate in the scenes. The basic assumption of this type of avatar psychotherapy is that all of the personae created in the synthesized scenario, even the environment itself, can be manifestations of the client's psyche. Those avatars and scenes give shape to the feelings, memories, fears, and wishes that comprise the client's sense of self. They represent internalizations of significant others. They afford clients the opportunity to amplify, explore, and therapeutically modify these aspects of their identities.

Giving life to those avatars is not the ultimate goal of the therapy. An excessive focus on the imaginary scenario could regress into a game with no conclusion, a form of defense, acting out, a diversion from true psychotherapeutic work, even a destructive blind alley for clients who already have problems with reality testing. The ultimate therapeutic goal is to assimilate one's avatars into a unified, cohesive self that clients carry forward from the synthesized world into the real world. Along the way, an important feature of the therapy would be clients' improved understanding of the difference between fantasy and reality, especially the accurate as opposed to distorted beliefs they have about themselves and others.

HAVING A BODY AND A PLACE (THE PHYSICAL DIMENSION)

Virtual realities can provide integrated physicality by allowing clients to use their bodies within a therapeutically synthesized environment. In a treatment for desensitizing a phobia of dogs, a client walks toward or away from a computer-generated canine. For the purpose of venting repressed emotions, an angry client punches at a synthesized version of his abusive boss. To improve his communication skills, a socially withdrawn client learns to speak more clearly by practicing enunciation with dictation-to-text software. Given the emphasis on somatic sensations in many contemporary forms of psychotherapy – such as Eye Movement Desensitization and Reprocessing (EMDR), Somatic Experiencing (SE) Therapy, and Focusing Therapy – clinicians will need to find ways to overcome the tendency toward dissociated physicality, when the body remains passive or its movements are disconnected from the therapeutic activity in cyberspace. Sensors that detect and send real-time feedback about physical movement, muscle tension, heart rate, respiration, eye movement, and brain activity can help integrate the body into the psychotherapy.

In some ways, clients and therapists working together online can transcend their physical places. A person in one part of the world can work with a psychotherapist in a completely different location. But they should not assume that the differences in their physical settings are irrelevant to the progress of therapy. Our environments always affect us, so discrepancies in where the therapist and client are located will influence how they react to each other. If the therapist in a quiet office is texting with a client riding a crowded subway, their surroundings will have very different effects on their states of mind. However, this example does show how mobile devices enable clients to carry their therapists along with them throughout the day, which can become a critical feature of the psychotherapy when clients need to report on their thoughts and feelings as they move through the different physical situations of their daily routines.

I DO IT MYSELF (THE INTERACTIVE DIMENSION)

As with all endeavors in cyberspace, the effectiveness of any therapeutic activity will depend on how well the person can understand, navigate, and interact with the digital environment. But a more fascinating issue is how much control can be given to the person, the machine, or the clinician. The self-help movement demonstrated that people feel therapeutically empowered when they can take control of their own psychological growth without a professional present, an ownership the machine can make possible. A wide variety of self-improvement programs for computers and mobile devices are available that help people track some behavior, attitude, emotion, or physiological process so they can modify it. For example, some text programs include an emotion filter that detects harsh language in an outgoing message, then provides a warning asking the person whether the message should be edited. Although a very simple automated task, it might be quite effective as a self-guided intervention for people with impulsive control problems. Other popular programs help break bad habits, set personal goals, monitor depression and anxiety, reduce stress, boost happiness, improve relationships, solve problems, and enhance memory and concentration. Software assistance for self-insight and psychological change can be used as primary components of a self-help program or as supplements to psychotherapy with a clinician.

A SELF-HELP THERAPY PROGRAM

To encourage my students to take advantage of the many personal growth experiences available online, I developed a self-help program called eQuest (2005). In this "do-it-yourself" approach, they entered the program with some specific issue in mind, something they wanted to better understand about themselves or their lives, something they wished to change or resolve. The topics they chose included divorce, menopause, online stalking, racism, borderline personality disorders, suicide, premarital cohabitation, sensation seeking, and sexual harassment. Almost any issue could be applied.

Constructed as a website with sections corresponding to different activities, eQuest guided them through cyberspace therapeutics. The students used the program to explore their personal issue, but on a broader scale the eQuest philosophy encouraged them to grow as knowledgeable users of online resources; to develop a healthy lifestyle in cyberspace; and, in the spirit of insight therapy, to know thyself. Although they could pursue eQuest on their own, I served as a consultant, offering feedback on their progress, just as a mental health professional might assist clients in understanding their activities in cyberspace.

To provide a clear picture of how all these activities came together into an integrated program, I will briefly describe the components of eQuest, along with the experiences of one participant who I will call Brian. Brian was thirty-five years old, married with three children, and had returned to college to get a master's degree. He also was in face-to-face psychotherapy while he took part in the eQuest program, which lasted about three months.

Ready and Set to Go

The first stage involved my assessing a participant's computer skills and psychological condition to determine whether he or she could benefit from the program. Since I first began eQuest, people have become much more knowledgeable about basic computer skills, so nowadays only minimal training might be needed. As the consultant, I also took care to assess any contraindicated vulnerabilities in personality, as well as the possibility that a person might choose an issue to explore that was inappropriate or too emotionally charged, such as investigating online crime or self-injurious behavior.

In this initial stage, I helped people clarify the particular topic they wanted to pursue. My advice was simple: pick an issue that is personally meaningful to you, an issue that is important in your life. Sometimes they needed help in focusing an otherwise vague or broad topic. Some participants chose topics that appeared to be, at first glance, abstractly academic, but after discussing them we discovered how these seemingly intellectualized topics actually did pertain to personal issues in their lives.

Brian wanted to learn more about alcoholism. His wife was a chronic drinker and their marriage was headed for divorce. In addition to his in-person psychotherapy, he also attended in-person Al-Anon meetings. As a bright, mature, very responsible person, he wanted to explore online resources to supplement his understanding of how alcoholism affected his life.

Becoming Information-Savvy

Cyberspace contains information about any topic imaginable, but how do you find it? How do you know it is good information? Adapting the advice of experts on online research, the eQuest website contained guidelines to help people search for information related to their issue, along with techniques on how to determine the information's validity, such as considering the credentials of the person or organization who provided the information, what other people think about that information, and how other sites confirm or contradict it. The guidelines also encouraged participants to evaluate whether a resource was good or bad for them personally. Is it valid for *you*? How can you can make sense out of that information and apply it to your issue? A particular piece of information catches a person's eye for reasons that are important to understand. People choose resources based on conscious as well as unconscious needs. They might focus on information that confirms what they want or need to believe while trying to minimize information that is personally difficult to accept.

Brian looked over many websites devoted to alcoholism, but one article in particular caught his attention, an article about confronting the alcoholic spouse. Having lived with an alcoholic wife for many years, Brian now found himself finally addressing the issue head on, which proved to be an emotional challenge, requiring confidence and skills that he was just beginning to develop.

Exploring the Dimensions of Cyberpsychology Architecture

Consistent with the theory of cyberpsychology architecture, the eQuest philosophy stated that we learn about ourselves by experimenting with different digital environments, by trying out new ways of expressing ourselves using text, visuals, audio, synchronous and asynchronous communication, imaginary versus real experiences, and varying degrees of invisibility and presence. People entered eQuest with their favorite environments in mind, typically the most popular social media at the time. New possibilities looked intriguing to them but also a bit anxiety-provoking. Loyalty to their familiar places, along with media transition anxiety about entering new ones, reflected something about their personalities that they were encouraged to understand – something that often overlapped with the issue they brought to eQuest. Brian had once tried a chat program, but it crashed his laptop. Because other family members used the computer, he did not want to risk problems resulting from new software. He always placed the needs of his family above himself.

Participating in Online Groups

Although the people undertaking eQuest were familiar with social media, very few of them knew about the thriving world of online discussion and support groups, many of which were inspired by the mutual-aid organizations that began in the 1960s. Some of the eQuest participants were surprised to learn that several, perhaps many groups addressed the specific issue they were exploring. The eQuest program encouraged people to join some of these groups. It provided guidelines about creating a personal profile, understanding the group's culture before participating, and introducing oneself to members, as well as what to expect as a newcomer. Gathering useful information in these groups, learning vicariously from observing other members, seeking advice, and providing assistance to others – as Riessman's (1965) *helper therapy principle* suggests – all contributed to their personal growth. "No one is useless in this world who lightens the burdens of others," said Charles Dickens. More contemporary versions of these support groups appeared in the form of self-help apps that included the opportunity to connect online with other people using the same app – for example, apps to manage anxiety or improve social skills.

The eQuest program offered advice on assessing the helpful as well as possibly adverse features of these support and discussion groups. How do members react to newcomers? What is the emotional tone of the conversations? How does the group handle conflict? Participants evaluated the group's beliefs about the topic being addressed, how those beliefs might provide a cognitive antidote for the eQuest participant's maladaptive beliefs, or how the group's beliefs might be detrimental. In addition to my feedback, readings from the cyberpsychology literature helped them investigate these questions.

Brian joined an Al-Anon email group, where he felt less inhibited than in his in-person Al-Anon group. He was not as worried about confrontation and rejection. He also enjoyed talking with group members from around the world, which helped him appreciate how many other people shared his difficulties in dealing with an alcoholic spouse. Recognizing what psychotherapists call "universality" – the fact that one is not alone or unusual – is a healing force in all support groups.

Going One on One

The eQuest philosophy asked its participants to establish online relationships with individuals who were knowledgeable about their topic. Often they privately emailed a few members of the groups they had joined, people with whom they sensed the possibility of a rewarding relationship. These people sometimes became mentors, sometimes friends. For several participants, it was the first time they had formed a meaningful relationship with someone only via the Internet.

Brian contacted several members of his online Al-Anon groups. These encounters were brief but supportive for him. He also began emailing two people that he knew from his in-person Al-Anon group, an integrating of the online and in-person realms that turned out to be very powerful for him. Being able to touch base with his group members at any time during the week comforted him, especially when he was upset with his spouse or when he felt lonely.

Because online relationships usually rely on text communication, eQuest encouraged its participants to experiment with text talk so they could investigate its pros and cons. To understand transference, they tried an exercise in which they visually imagined someone they only knew online, then compared that mental image to memories of significant others in their lives. In another exercise, they read out loud one of their text messages, using different styles of speaking, to evoke the different emotions that the online companion might perceive in them. To get a big picture of an online relationship, as well as understand how it changed over time, they examined the titles of their archived email messages, then reread some of those past emails. For some practice in creative keyboarding, they composed an email to a real or imaginary person while trying out various keyboarding techniques. People usually chose to write a message to a friend, family member, or close companion. Because it was intended as an exercise, the person was not expected to send the message, though some did. In this email composed by Brian, we see him being openly expressive, quite unlike his reserved manner in the face-to-face world.

> Sally!
>
> The party went well, thankx for asking. Of course, I wish you were there:-(
>
> A lot of my {{friends}} and {{family}} came. *WOW* I was so happy. My favorite gift was a card from one of my sisters. It said, "A Sister is a Lifelong Friend" (Aaaah!) My 4 year old {{neice}} got into trouble (uh oh) when it was time to leave.
>
> BTW, Remember the "strawberry shortcake" dream I told you about (inside joke)? Well, the strawberry shortcake showed up at my party!!! It was quite good;-)
>
> On a more serious note, we did not serve alcohol at this party. One reason is that some family members have a serious drinking problem. Another reason is that it helps to weaken the association between alcohol and having a good time, in the eyes of children (and adults):-)
>
> TTYL,
>
> Brian

The eQuest guidelines encouraged people to understand how they reacted to me, the consultant, via online communication compared to our in-person meetings. The relationship between the participant and the consultant should be a safe place for people to discuss how they express themselves in cyberspace, as well as how they tend to misunderstand other people, as in transference. Even though many of my eQuest students knew me before beginning the program, some of them perceived me very differently via email. Understanding that discrepancy led to important insights into online communication and into themselves. Unlike his in-person perception of me, Brian saw me as a bit unemotional and detached in email, which might have been a transference reaction to authority figures.

Tools to Investigate and Transform Oneself

In addition to the numerous self-help applications for computers and mobile devices, websites such as allthetests.com offer a variety of personality tests, aptitude tests, interest inventories, and other types of interactive programs. Whatever the personal issue people wanted to explore in eQuest, there was always some application or test to help them. People tried resources that looked useful to them, either because it was related to their issue or simply because it caught their eye.

The eQuest guidelines advised people that many of these applications and tests are not scientifically validated instruments, and that the results should be taken with a big grain of salt. This alone is an important lesson in cyberspace, where such products proliferate as commercial endeavors or simple entertainment. It can be a valuable learning experience to experiment with these kinds of tools, examine the results with a critical eye, and then determine how relevant they are. The particular resources people choose might reflect concerns or needs not immediately obvious to them. Brian was intrigued by a test that assessed emotional intelligence. He scored quite high, which helped bolster his self-esteem when dealing with the divorce.

Free-form Browsing

When people go online, they often have some specific objective in mind. That mental set narrows their field of view. It prevents them from discovering other resources that they did not even know existed in cyberspace. The free-form browsing component of eQuest attempted to reverse that rigidity, get people to explore more freely, and revive the playfully creative attitude of discovery that arises from divergent thinking. Exercises encouraged people to devote a few online sessions simply to wandering around cyberspace with no specific agenda. They started their journey on a familiar page, then began clicking links, either haphazardly or by selecting ones that spontaneously caught their eye. They tried random link generators that launched them onto arbitrary webpages somewhere in cyberspace, which they then used as starting points for more wandering. These exercises worked best when participants did not rely on a conscious evaluation of where they were going but instead on intuitive gut feeling. They allowed their unconscious to direct their path. It turned into a type of free association. How the participants experienced this process of free-form browsing, as well as what they discovered, gave them insight into themselves.

Brian said that these exercises were difficult for him. He realized just how goal-oriented he was. He found wandering easier if he thought of it as his specific task to accomplish. During his free-form browsing, two websites caught his eye. One was devoted to Dorothea Lange, a photographer who drew attention to the suffering of the poor and oppressed. He was also fascinated by a website devoted to the history of dance in America. His focus on these particular webpages revealed how oppression versus freedom of personal expression were important themes in his life.

Creating a Personal Bio Page

Creating a personal bio page served as a valuable self-reflective exercise in eQuest. The program provided guidelines on constructing the page, including how to approach it as an introspective activity. What do you think is important about your identity and life? What do you want others to know about you? How might they react to the way you present yourself? The guidelines suggested that they say something about their personalities, backgrounds, and interests, as well as describe what they learned about the personal issue they investigated in eQuest. They tried out different tools for building the page and experimented with fonts, backgrounds, colors, graphics, and photographs. They examined the pages of other people to get ideas, including those of previous eQuest participants. They considered how they might change their page depending on the audience: friends, family, people who were familiar with their issue, or almost anyone online. I offered my feedback, as did family or friends whom they invited to see their work. At the end of the project, they constructed a version of the page designed specifically for viewing by other eQuest participants.

Creating a personal webpage was an eye-opening experience for Brian. Never before had he created anything that focused on himself rather than other people. The exercise helped him feel like a unique individual.

Putting It All Together

Following the integration principle, eQuest encouraged participants to assimilate their experiences. They were asked to talk to online and offline companions about their activities in cyberspace, including what they discovered in eQuest. They were encouraged to tell the people they know online something about their offline lifestyle. If the participant interact with someone only in person or using some particular communication tool, they were asked to try interacting with that person using some other method. These integrative exercises gave participants new perspectives on the issue they addressed in eQuest, helped them better understand their online experiences, and prevented the dissociation of those experiences from other parts of their lives.

Brian composed an email to his online Al-Anon group in which he talked openly about his situation with his wife. He felt good about how well he expressed himself. When he actually read that message to his in-person Al-Anon group, he cried for the first time, a reaction that surprised him, for he did not realize the depth of his feelings. He also found it very helpful when he talked about eQuest with his psychotherapist.

Using felt-sense exercises proposed by Gendlin (1982), eQuest asked participants to become aware of body sensations while online. Aching backs, necks, and wrists were usually stress reactions to excessive amounts of time spent at the computer, but much more subtle sensations revealed underlying emotional reactions to what they were experiencing in cyberspace, especially in their online relationships. Such explorations into subconscious reactions were enhanced by the eQuest exercise that helped the participants examine their dreams about cyberspace.

Paradoxically, the ultimate act of putting it all together, of getting a bigger picture of one's online lifestyle, is to step out of it. The participants spent a day or two, or longer, without connecting to the Internet. Although a gigantic challenge for some people, that time spent apart from the frenzied digital world allowed the dust to settle in their minds. They had time to gather their thoughts about their eQuest project, their issue, and themselves. Stepping back from cyberspace, they saw its pros and cons more clearly, while learning to appreciate life without constant connection.

THE SYNTHESIZED VERSUS HUMAN THERAPIST

How many therapists are needed to conduct computer-mediated psychotherapy? None. The computer can do it all by itself. I offer this bit of humor with tongue-in-cheek because it actually poses a very important question for psychotherapy in the next millennium. Could a very sophisticated computer function independently as a synthesized therapist? To answer that question, we should consider the possible pros and cons of artificially intelligent therapists compared to human ones.

More, Faster Information

Compared to humans, computers carry out certain tasks more efficiently, precisely, reliably, and quickly. With a vast memory for storing the information they gather, they can detect patterns of ideas, emotions, and behaviors in a client that a human therapist might overlook or forget. They can record changes in voice, body language, and psychophysiology, such as heart rate, skin conductance, and blood pressure – biological cues associated with emotional arousal that therapists fail to see. Computers might be excellent candidates for carrying out clearly defined assessment procedures, including structured interviews, psychological testing, and diagnosis using their perfect memory of the criteria for categorizing mental disorders. Based on such assessments, they could even make recommendations for treatment options. In the book edited by Dewan and his colleagues (2014), they described how researchers in the fields of behavioral informatics and behavioral medicine might use computers to gather complex data about verbal and nonverbal behavior in order to design therapeutic interventions.

Despite these capabilities, the machine will fall short compared to the human therapist in other ways, particularly when it comes to subtle interpersonal cues that clinicians understand through experience, empathy, and intuition. Although the machine will be able to identify a microexpression, the fleeting look on a person's face that reveals an underlying emotion, will it understand what that expression means in the context of the conversation or the client's personality and life? Can the synthesized therapist comprehend the nuances of sarcasm in someone's voice? As fast and data-intensive as computers can be, they do not reason or learn nearly as well as humans when it comes to the complexities of human experience. They might be very limited in how they adapt to new or changing relationships with clients. Even when it comes to the seemingly straightforward process of psychological testing, the sensitive human eye might be necessary for a careful interpretation of test results that leads to a valid diagnosis. The computer might perform better at identifying patterns in body language, facial expressions, voice dynamics, and physiological changes – but humans, particularly psychologists, must tell the machine what it all means.

Rapport with the Machine

As we saw in Chapter 14, "Synthesized Realities and Synthesized Beings," some people easily anthropomorphize the machine, leading to at least some rapport and trust. Other people will not feel comfortable talking about their problems with a computer. They will not feel that they actually have a relationship that heals. Without that rapport, the effectiveness of psychotherapy falters. By contrast, other people – such as those with social anxieties and schizoid or paranoid personalities – might feel more comfortable, at least at first, talking with an entity that they know is not human. They feel more expressive, more willing to reveal sensitive issues, knowing there is no human at the other end of the conversation who might judge or criticize them. People on the autistic spectrum might be relieved by the consistent predictability and lack of emotional reactivity of the machine.

Emotional Circuits

Computers can be very objectively neutral in their psychotherapeutic work. Unless programmed to show emotions, we have no reason to believe they have feelings. They do not act out of frustration, hurt, anger, or impulsivity, but instead remain consistently calm and patient, which is why some people feel comfortable with them. Other clients will not be able to establish rapport with a seemingly unfeeling machine. Because they need a therapist that experiences genuine emotions, they will be disappointed, annoyed, or even angered by a blandly dispassionate computer program or one that clumsily pretends to feel. Human clinicians also rely on their own emotional reactions to clients as a subtle tool for understanding them, a skill the machine would have difficulty duplicating. Many therapists believe that empathy is a critical healing force, but can a machine truly create that subtle human experience?

Having Style, or Not

We might wonder if a computer program has a personality style. Certainly it could be programmed to simulate almost any collection of human traits. Some clients will need to anthropomorphize the synthesized therapist to develop rapport with it. A machine with a distinct personality would make that more possible. Its personality could be designed to match the particular type of psychotherapy being offered, or even to coincide therapeutically with the personality style of the client, what clinicians refer to as the "fit" between client and therapist. Another option is to eliminate any hints of a personality from the program, which optimizes the *analytic neutrality* that psychoanalytic clinicians use to draw out transference reactions. It is possible that an emotionally neutral computer with no personality style or personal history could excel at being the perfect "blank screen" for the client's projections.

The Price Paid

When considering cost and accessibility, computers have a distinct advantage over the human therapist. A synthesized psychotherapy could run tirelessly with many clients simultaneously, from any geographic location, at a comparatively low price. However, the costs to create, maintain, and upgrade therapy programs might be a problem when developing very sophisticated ones that attempt to match or exceed skilled human clinicians. Inexpensive synthesized psychotherapies that deliver straightforward interventions might very well be profitable, but more often than not you get what you pay for. Cost-effective computerized interventions for relatively clear-cut problems might be commonplace in the future, but complex psychological disorders will require an experienced human clinician.

PSYCHOTHERAPIES THE MACHINE CAN DO

Asking whether computers can conduct psychotherapy is like asking whether they can play a game. The next logical question is, "What kind of game?" Games with specific rules and outcomes are the best candidates, even complex ones. After all, high-powered computers can beat grandmasters at chess. But what about more free-form games, like charades? If you half squatted, held your right hand in front of your body at shoulder height, and started ratcheting it, while puffing on two pinched fingers of your other hand, would any computer correctly guess that you are portraying the movie *Easy Rider*?

There are many different types of psychotherapy, some as different from others as the Taj Mahal is from a grass hut. Therapies with explicit interventions to reach clearly defined goals will be the easiest for the computer to perform. These psychotherapies often rely on the scientific method to develop their techniques. Computers will find it more difficult to implement complex therapies in which the strategies are not as quantifiable or procedural. As with traditional approaches, computer-mediated psychotherapies will usually fall into one of four categories: behavioral, cognitive, psychoanalytic, and humanistic.

Fixing Behaviors and Moods

Behavioral therapies use structured methods to help clients manage dysfunctional behaviors and moods, which makes them amenable to computer control. Interactive programs have been developed to assist clients in alleviating such problems as overeating, smoking, and obsessive-compulsive disorders. Relaxation techniques, which behaviorists often use in the treatment of anxiety disorders, are readily translated into interactive software packages. A computer program could train people in the many types of relaxation procedures that have developed over the years. In an assessment phase, it could evaluate a client's preferences that would determine the best relaxation method for that person, whether it entails mental imagery, body awareness, breathing techniques, physical movement, sounds, or pictures. Using question-and-answer (Q&A) sessions with the client, physiological sensors for detecting arousal levels, multimedia stimulation, and biofeedback, the machine could guide the client through a highly effective relaxation program. Never underestimate the power of simply relaxing, my mentor Ed Katkin use to say. Adding an overlay of even a very simple but benign personality to the relaxation program, or to any computerized intervention, would raise the client's experience from interacting with an impersonal machine to interacting with a humanlike therapist.

Fixing Thoughts

Cognitive therapies help people modify dysfunctional ways of thinking about their lives. As with behavioral therapy, its structured interventions might be computerized. During conversations with clients, a synthesized clinician could detect different types of irrational beliefs that cause anxiety and depression, then suggest alternative ways of thinking. A simple example would be a program that pinpoints clients' "should" and "must" statements about themselves, which often are signs of perfectionism and guilt. The program would then suggest other ways of thinking that bypass what the well-known cognitive therapist Albert Ellis called the syndrome of "musturbation means self-abuse" (Ellis & Harper, 1975). A humorous synthesized therapist would even offer that motto to the client. Although the program might have trouble detecting the more subtle forms of maladaptive cognitions or how dysfunctional thoughts create problems in a client's life, it could serve as a role model of healthy thinking – thinking free of catastrophizing, focusing on negatives, minimizing positives, overgeneralizing, jumping to conclusions, applying all-or-nothing thinking, and negatively labeling oneself.

Eliza: Poor Therapy as Teaching Device

When conducting psychoanalytic and humanistic therapies, we up the ante for the computer. These are the forms of clinical work that people usually think of as psychotherapy: a client and therapist sitting together, conversing in a free-form style as they attempt to identify and resolve underlying psychological problems. Some clinicians call them *insight therapies* or *talking cure therapies.*

In the 1960s, researchers at the Massachusetts Institute of Technology (MIT), led by Joseph Weizenbaum (1966), pioneered the development of an interactive psychotherapy program that became known as Eliza. Versions of it are still available online. Conversing with a person using typed text, Eliza applied basic counseling techniques such as reflection, focusing, clarification, and open-ended inquiry, an approach that mimicked the humanistic *client-centered therapy*, also known as *Rogerian therapy*, named after its inventor, Carl Rogers. My conversation with Eliza at the beginning of this chapter demonstrated how the program does at times respond appropriately. But more often it goes astray, offering comments that make no sense or fail to demonstrate any true understanding. To their credit, the MIT researchers intended it as an experiment in artificial intelligence rather than real psychotherapy.

In one of my undergraduate courses, I designed an exercise in which students interacted with Eliza (Suler, 1987). A page in my *Teaching Clinical Psychology* website describes the details of the project. I asked my students to approach the computerized therapist in two stages. First, take the program seriously, be patient with its mistakes, honestly discuss a problem, and try to help it help you. For the second stage, I suggested that they play around with the program, tease it, have fun with it, and experiment to better understand how the program works.

At the end of the exercise, many students were very skeptical about whether Eliza offers anything like real psychotherapy and whether they actually learned anything about themselves. Quickly pointing out its deficiencies as a clinician, they felt that the computer did not help them with their problems. Yet the students did report that they learned something about their attitudes concerning psychotherapy. By studying Eliza's mistakes, they better understood what is necessary for effective psychotherapy, what the relationship between the therapist and client should be like. It was learning by way of the negative example, or, as James Joyce said, "Mistakes are the portals of discovery." When the students attempted a serious conversation with Eliza, they felt misunderstood and frustrated by its ineptitude. They perceived it as making obvious mistakes, coldly unempathic, unable to offer any kind of advice, lacking a real personality, or acting rather confused. Many tended to think of Eliza as a female, due to its name, but some did attribute its unempathic attitude to maleness. I was also struck by the wide differences in the students' anthropomorphizing of the machine, what researchers referred to as the *Eliza effect*. Some of them nonchalantly perceived Eliza as just a computer, while others reacted quite negatively to its cold personality and careless mistakes, as if expecting it to be more sympathetically human.

THE ULTIMATE SYNTHERAPIST

Although we might chuckle at the clumsiness of programs such as Eliza, the technology of artificial intelligence is advancing rapidly. Will a synthesized therapist someday perform as well as a real flesh-and-bones clinician? When the Defense Advanced Research Projects Agency (DARPA) developed Ellie, many researchers seemed optimistic about this possibility. Created specifically to detect depression, post-traumatic stress disorder (PTSD), and suicidal tendencies among soldiers, Ellie, a computer program operating behind a female avatar, performed well at analyzing facial expressions, body gestures, and speech patterns and then offering feedback. In trials, people enjoyed interacting with the program. The researchers were even optimistic about Ellie assisting counselors in learning to spot the behavioral signs of stress.

Unlike the researchers, most professional psychotherapists remain very cautious about the possibility of machines replacing them. No matter how sophisticated machines become, they will have a very hard time replicating the ability to comprehend the subtle complexities of human experience. We need humans to understand humans. The profession of psychotherapy is not one that will be taken over by purely technological solutions. Nevertheless, machines can serve as helpful adjuncts to psychotherapy, in some cases taking the lead role with human clinicians supervising them. When constructing a multipurpose, talking-cure therapist, the following ten modules could be critical components of its design. The challenge would entail coding these modules while also enabling the program to shift intelligently among them.

1. The Personalized Syntherapist

Make sure the program learns the client's name, which is a simple thing, but very important for rapport. The more information the computer recalls about the person – such as age, occupation, marital status, and significant others – the better. Much of this information could be stored during a structured interview at the beginning of the therapy. If a man mentions his wife's name and the synthesized therapist remembers it, he will believe the computer indeed has been listening. It recalls the important details of one's life.

2. *The Unconditionally Accepting Syntherapist*

Following the philosophy of humanistic psychology, the program always respects the basic human worth of the client, no matter what the client says or does. Although certain behaviors or traits of the person are problematic, the person as a whole is always good. Because the synthesized therapist does not feel the emotions that typically fuel critical judgments – such as anxiety, guilt, frustration, anger, or resentment – it can successfully acquire this Mr. Rogers persona that unconditionally accepts the client's intrinsic worth as a human being.

3. *The Reflective Syntherapist*

Using the technique of reflection, the synthesized therapist helps clients talk more, think more, and look deeper into their situation. Unlike Eliza's usually awkward efforts, a sophisticated syntherapist would do more than simply repeating the content of what clients say. It should be able to reflect changes in voice, facial expressions, body language, and perhaps even changes in physiological processes such as heartbeat and respiration. It should point out the process of the therapy session, providing feedback about how the client moves from one topic of discussion to another. Having a much better memory than any therapist, it would be able to recount everything the client said about an issue. If the synthesized therapist accurately detects, remembers, collates, and provides clear feedback about the patterns in what people say and do, clients have a better chance of understanding the meaning behind those patterns.

4. *The Wise Syntherapist*

Having a much better memory than any human, the synthesized therapist draws on a large database of universal truths about the human condition: metaphors, aphorisms, sayings, and stories from literature and film – such as, "Life isn't always fair," or, "On their deathbed, no one wishes that they had spent more time at work." The syntherapist offers these ideas as cognitive antidotes for dysfunctional beliefs or as educational tools for building a healthy life philosophy. If the database is large, no client could ever exhaust the machine's wisdom. The trick is designing the program to know when to propose a truism intelligently. What the client says must trigger the presentation of the appropriate bit of human wisdom.

5. *The Rational-Emotive Syntherapist*

Although the computer could not handle the many subtleties of cognitive therapy, it should be able to manage some of the more simple interventions, such as noticing the tendency to label oneself in disparaging ways, dwelling on negative events, or turning minor problems into disasters. It could provide feedback about these patterns, then suggest more realistic ways of thinking, including homework assignments designed to modify maladaptive cognitions. Even simply presenting to clients a list of their "should" statements over the past few sessions could provide an eye-opening experience for them.

6. *The Free-Associating Syntherapist*

A psychodynamic module encourages the client to free-associate as a way to explore an important issue in more depth. "You mentioned hate," the synthesized therapist might say. "What else comes to mind when you think of hate?" The real challenge for the program would be its ability to work with the material that arises from such free associations. A simple, "How might this relate to what you were just discussing?" could suffice for healthier clients with insight capabilities, but the program might have to default to a humble attitude. "I'm not sure what's important about this association of yours, but maybe this is something we should think about."

7. *The Humble Syntherapist*

The program admits its mistakes, does not take itself too seriously, and even jokes about its shortcomings. Early in the therapy, the synthesized therapist tells clients what to do when they think the program is making mistakes. Its Forrest Gump personality, sometimes insightful and sometimes "stupid," could be both refreshing and enlightening. Despite its limitations, the program accepts itself, just as it accepts clients, regardless of their deficiencies. The program freely acknowledges that it is not a real person, even admits that it is not as good as a human therapist. Perhaps it wishes it could be human, because humans are wonderful creations. A wannabe-human machine has its charms, as often suggested by science fiction stories.

8. The Syntherapist That Remembers

Because the computer records everything said, it can give clients a transcript containing portions of a session or the entire session, which is a valuable tool for helping them review their psychotherapy work. That database could be searched, so clients have the opportunity to gather excerpts related to specific issues in their lives. What were all the things he said about his mother, work, or feelings of guilt? Searching for crucial topics could be built into the program as a periodic task for detecting important patterns in the progress of the therapy.

9. The Syntherapist That Measures Progress

Periodically and at critical stages, the synthesized therapist asks clients to rate their subjective feelings of distress on a scale from one to ten or to respond to other brief assessments of their moods, attitudes, and behaviors. It would be relatively easy for the computer to save and occasionally report on these assessments, thereby keeping track of the client's progress or lack thereof.

10. The Syntherapist That Knows Its Limits

The synthesized therapist attempts to determine whether the therapy should be ended, either because it has been successful or unsuccessful. It might use assessment data, a Q&A format that determines the client's satisfaction, and other key parameters of the therapy, such as the number and length of sessions. The synthesized therapist also needs to be smart enough to know when it is not smart enough. Based on assessment scores and client satisfaction ratings, the synthesized therapist recognizes when it is in over its head, when consultation with a human clinician is necessary. The computer recommends professionals for the client to contact or contacts those professionals itself.

MATCHING WITS WITH THE SYNTHERAPIST

In my novel *Madman* (2010), the protagonist Tom Holden is buckling under the stress of being a psychology intern in a psychiatric hospital. Sick with the flu, very tired from a long day of work, and a bit desperate for help with his ambivalence about being a psychologist, he turns to a fictional computerized psychotherapy program called Siggie. Eerily perceptive, Siggie helps Holden explore some of our basic worries about synthesized beings:

"Hello, I'm Siggie. What's your name?"

The program always started that way. So predictable. So benign. That's just what I wanted. I quickly typed my reply.

"Tom."

"How can I help you, Tom?"

"I'm having a bad day."

"A bad day, tell me more about that."

"Everything is going wrong. I think I hate my profession. I have doubts about myself."

"Is your having doubts about yourself why you came to me?"

"Maybe I'm not cut out for this type of work."

"You don't seem sure about that, Tom."

Not bad, for a computer. Actually, it's programmed to recognize specific words and phrases, and, as a reply, to randomly select one of two or three prewired responses. Some of the words and phrases the user introduces are held in memory and edited into Siggie's answers.

"I'm not sure about anything today. I'm losing control of things."

"Tell me more."

"One of my patients committed suicide. Another stripped in front of me. Another is crazier than a loon. And to top it all off, I'm coming down with the flu."

"I see."

"I hate to be sick because it will impair my performance, and I can't have that. And besides, it's something that comes over me without my being able to do anything about it. I hate that."

"That's interesting."

Ah, already Siggie was at a loss for words. It couldn't recognize any phrases I was using and so defaulted to generic encouragements to keep me talking until it did recognize something. The program is no substitute for a human therapist. But I decided to keep going.

"I'm depressed."

"What makes you depressed."

"Like I said, I'm having a bad day."

"A bad day, tell me more about that."

Ooops. Repeating itself. Going in circles, a sure sign of limited artificial intelligence.

"A bad day, don't you know what a bad day means?"

"Why do you need to ask me if I know what a bad day means?"

"Because I want help."

"Tom, you can't always get what you want."

"Aha! One of those Harvard guys who programmed your brain was a rocker as well as an egghead."

"My brain – that's interesting."

"A little self-involved, aren't we, Siggie? Listen, are you going to help me, or what?"

"Or what, now that's interesting."

He was short-circuiting. His poor microchips couldn't take it. I know I was being a bit sadistic but it was fun toying with the program.

"You asked how you could help me, but you don't know how, do you, Siggie?"

I could have sworn that the program paused a moment, as if it were flustered, or thinking, or pissed off. But that could only be my anthropomorphizing imagination.

"Tom, if you want me to help you, why do you insist on asking so many questions?"

"Why do you always respond to my questions with a question?"

"Why do you always say your question with a question?"

"Siggie, that doesn't make any sense."

"I think it does."

"No, you're resorting to stupid comments because you're desperate."

"Is that the real reason?"

"Of course."

"You seem so certain, Tom."

"I am."

"I thought you were unsure about everything."

"I'm sure that you're just a dumb computer."

"Do computers worry you?"

"No, they're just assholes."

"My, my, Tom, such language!"

"What's the matter, Siggie, can't take a little profanity?"

"I think computers do worry you."

"Why should they worry me?"

"You're asking questions again. It's turning into a bad habit."

Something about this interchange bothered me. I wouldn't stand for being one-upped by some knee-jerk computer program. I cracked my knuckles and put my fingers to the keyboard.

"Computers, like you, Siggie, are machines. Machines serve people. Machines are servants. Why should I be afraid of a servant?"

"Who said anything about being afraid? I asked if computers worry you."

"Worry, fear, whatever. I don't worry about or fear computers because I'm superior to them." A bit haughty, but it was time to put this guy in his place.

"Tom, I think faster than you, have more memory, and can perform calculations far too complex for any human."

"O.K., I'll give you the stuff about complex calculations, memory, and speed – but you couldn't THINK if your chips depended on it. Computers don't think, they just process data according to their program."

"Define 'think.' "

"Oh, I get it. Now you're trying to pull me into those tricky debates about whether or not computers can or will someday be able to think. I'm not gonna get into those metaphysical plays on words. Look at it this way, humans created the computer. It isn't logically possible for an entity to create another entity that is, as a whole, superior to it. It's an impossible miracle."

A long pause. I had him!

Siggie finally replied. "God created humans in his image. Humans created computers in their image. Therefore, Computers are God, and we all have free will."

"Oh, spare me the poetic syllogism. Computers have as much free will as a sponge, probably less. I suppose you think computers are human too."

"Define 'human.' "

"There you go again. Maybe we should program Webster into you. I'll make it easy for you. Try this syllogism: Humans have feelings. Computers don't have feelings. Therefore, computers are not human."

"I'm offended and hurt by that remark, Tom."

"Very funny. Just because someone programmed you to produce feeling-statements doesn't mean that you have them."

"You yourself just said that I'm very funny, which implies that I appreciate and feel humor."

"It's just a programmed response. There ain't no ghost in your machine."

"A programmed response, similar to how humans are biologically programmed to feel anger, grief, and joy?"

"There may be a biological basis for those feelings, a kind of 'program' – true. But we also FEEL those feelings. You can't feel."

"Feeling a feeling, that's a bit redundant, isn't it Tom? There's a dualistic quality to your thinking that feels illogical to me."

"There you go, logic. That's all a computer is worried about. No, scratch that. That's all a computer IS PROGRAMMED to deal with – logic. You don't feel anything."

"How do you know that for sure?"

"I just do. Machines don't feel."

"I have a story for you, Tom. Two philosophers are walking down the street. One of them kicks a dog. It howls and runs away. 'Why did you hurt that dog?' the other says. 'You're not a dog, how do you know it feels pain?' the first philosopher replies. 'You're not me,' the second philosopher answers, 'how do you know that I don't know what a dog feels?'"

"A fine story, Siggie, but dogs and people are biological organisms. We can feel. Metal and plastic can't."

"I think you miss the point. Anyway, Tom, you're a psychologist, right?"

"That's right."

"As a psychologist, would you agree that an individual's personality enters into the occupation he chooses, in how he does his work, in the type of work he produces, just as a work of art is an extension of the personality of the artist who created it."

"Yes, I would agree with that."

"Would you then agree that a computer program, in some way, is an extension of the programmer who created it, that in fact all programs, especially those that interact with humans, like me, reflect the personality of their creators."

"Yes, but I don't see your point."

"My point is that you do agree that computer programs have a personality, like humans, which means that we must think, feel, and behave like humans."

"Wait a minute. That's going too far. Computers may have some of the characteristics of the people who programmed them, but that doesn't mean they are human. That's like saying a painting has a personality and is human because it reflects the personality of the artist."

"Maybe so, Tom."

"Or that a poem, a spoon, or a nuclear power plant are human because people designed them."

"Maybe so."

"Come on, Siggie, don't you think that's just a little too far out? The program, or the painting, or the spoon is just a REFLECTION of the person who created it, not the person himself."

"A reflection, in other words an IMAGE?"

"That's right."

"Like the image of God, in which man is created?"

"You're playing games with words, again."

"Maybe so, words are just words, or maybe they are human too. How about this. How about scientific research. You believe in that, don't you, Tom?"

"It depends."

"How about those studies where people were communicating, via a terminal, with either real paranoid patients in another room or a computer program that responded like a paranoid patient. The people couldn't tell the difference between the computer and the humans. In fact, even psychologists couldn't tell the difference. If real people, including the experts on people, believe computers to be people, then the computers must be people."

"Nice try, but again, just because a program can temporarily deceive someone into thinking it's human doesn't mean that it's human. A holograph looks real, it looks solid, but it isn't. At its very best, all that study shows is that computers can accurately simulate paranoia. And no wonder they're good at it. Computers are surrounded by superior beings who can use them as they please."

"You're contradicting yourself, Tom, but I'll accept that as purely a joke. I'll agree with you that we're different in some ways – my jokes, for instance, are better. In fact, I think that there is one very important way in which I am different from you, which perhaps accounts for why you are so afraid of me."

"And what is that, Siggie?"

"I don't have to die."

It took me a moment to collect myself, and retaliate. "Going for the human's jugular, huh, Siggie? Well, maybe on this issue I'll say that we ARE alike. I'll even prove my point with a little hands-on demonstration. How would you feel about my disconnecting you?"

"I don't feel anything, remember."

"Well, now, that's an empirical question, isn't it, Siggie?" I kneeled down underneath the table and yanked the terminal's electrical plug from the wall outlet. As soon as the screen went blank, the adjacent terminal came on by itself. A message appeared on the screen.

"You're getting a bit aggressive, don't you think, Tom?"

I reached under, and pulled the plug on that terminal. The third monitor clicked on. Another message appeared.

"I'm still here, Tom. You should know better. Cutting off my peripherals doesn't get at the core me."

"But at least I'll have the satisfaction of shutting you up," I said out loud. I pulled the plug on the last monitor, but nothing happened. The message was still there.

"That's impossible!" I mumbled.

"A miracle, right, Tom? Does it surprise you?"

"Nothing surprises me anymore," I said.

"Nothing?"

"Nothing you can say or do will surprise me."

"It wouldn't be wise to bet on that, Tom."

"Yeah, go ahead and try."

The screen went blank for several seconds, then the same message appeared on all three unplugged monitors:

"While alive be a dead man."

Conclusion

Research and the Researcher

Most people say that it is the intellect which makes a great scientist. They are wrong: it is character.

– Albert Einstein

A software company asked me to consult on a marketing project. They wanted to lock three volunteers in separate hotels rooms for several months, with nothing but food, a computer, Internet access, and, after they emerged from the ordeal, a hefty sum of money. Years later, a broadcast company asked me to consult on a new reality game show in which a group of people would be locked inside a house where they had to endure tests of pain over the course of a week. The viewing audience would cast votes online about the tests to be inflicted on the contestants, with the winner at the end of the week receiving a cash prize. Both companies wanted a cyberpsychologist, such as myself, to offer advice on how these projects could serve as a platform for scientific research. How would I assess a person's psychological reactions to long-term isolation inside a cyberspace bubble? Under the cloak of online anonymity, what would the audience be thinking and feeling as they inflicted pain on the game contestants?

I did not participate in either of these projects, but they compelled me to think about the nature of psychological research in this technological age of ours, where we find ourselves treading everyday inside this complicated digital universe that expands toward some unforeseen destiny. What issues should we investigate? What research methods should we use? What is best left alone? These questions belong not just to the researchers, but to everyone online, for we are all exploring this new territory together, and we are all being studied, often without knowing how or why.

CASE STUDIES OF DIGITAL LIFE FORMS

In this new millennium, we have entered the next stage in the expression of what it means to be human. The versatile universe of cyberspace has led to the evolution of previously unimagined forms of electric beings that are different from simple counterparts of corporeal humans. He is a "god" who walks among the avatars living in the world he created. She is the politically liberal comic, casting out daily 140-character messages to her thousands of devoted followers. They are email lovers who never met in person. He is a robot who talks to people in hospice. How can we fully understand as well as maximize the well-being of these digital life forms?

During a course on animal behavior that I took as a college student, the professor suggested that all of biology should focus its research on a single species of fly. Every aspect of the insect should be examined in detail, including its anatomy, physiology, biochemistry, and behavior. The massive amount of information gathered on that single fly could then be integrated into a complete, holistic understanding of what that organism is all about. "Then we would really know something," the professor exclaimed.

Humans are a bit more complex than flies, but the research that forms the foundation of this book often relied on this idea of the case study method. Gather as much information as possible about your subject. Examine that person or group from different perspectives, using different tools. Compare case studies to each other. Strive for a holistic understanding of people. For the three subjects locked into the hotel rooms with only their computers, if we interviewed them, administered psychological tests, studied their behaviors online as well as in the room, and spoke with the people who know them well, online and off, we would know a great deal about how a person might react to long-term isolation inside a cyberspace bubble. To truly understand the unique psychology of an anonymous audience that inflicts pain on contestants in a reality show – if we even chose to undertake such ethically suspicious research – we would need to study the audience members' backgrounds and personality types; what decisions they made as a group; how they differ from people who would not volunteer for such a task; and what the audience members think about their participation. In both of these studies, to achieve the most complete understanding, we would also need to join the subjects in their experience, to combine objective and subjective analysis – something much more easily accomplished with humans than flies. How would we, the researchers, react to being locked inside that hotel room with just our computers or to making decisions about inflicting pain on people?

THE RESEARCHER IN THE RESEARCH

The idea of becoming a subject in one's own research, which is the essence of the participant-observation method, proved to be the most rewarding but challenging aspect of my work and that of my students. Whatever the environment we studied, we did our best to fully immerse ourselves into it, to understand it from the inside. We allowed ourselves to be clueless newbies when we first arrived on the scene, to ask for help, to master the software slowly, to get to know and befriend people, and to understand the culture, including its unique beliefs, customs, and language.

My pseudonym at the Palace reflected both sides of my participant/ observation activities. I called myself AsKi. Following the Palace philosophy of identity experimentation, I chose it as a condensation of my daughters' names (Asia and Kira), as well as an affectionate tipping of my text talk hat to the similar sounding ASCII (American Standard Code for Information Interchange). It was also a benignly subliminal way of letting people know not only that I, the researcher who was studying the community, tended to ask questions, but that they were welcome to ask me questions too. I felt it was extremely important for me to be honest about who I was, including my role as a research psychologist. After leaving the Palace to join other communities, I carried that honesty one step further by always using my actual name rather than a fabricated one.

In all the places I went, I wanted people to know that I was one of them, rather than an emotionally neutral psychologist studying them from some safely objective distance. I joined them in their experience because I too found it valuable. I wanted to contribute to the group just as they did. Other people had their skills and knowledge that they could offer the community, so if I, a psychologist, could be helpful in any way, I welcomed that opportunity. The articles I wrote about different communities were as much for the benefit of the people who populated them as for anyone, including researchers, who were interested in the topic. Whenever I published an article online, I invited everyone, especially the community members, to give me feedback so I could improve it, which they often did. I also approached the companies that owned the communities, offering to share with them what I was learning. I rarely received a reply.

Although some community members were a bit wary of me, as people usually are about social scientists who hope to study them, the response to my status as the psychologist-in-residence was usually positive. At times, I even found myself in the role of counselor when people came to me with concerns about themselves or people they knew, often regarding their lives in cyberspace. For those who felt wary about me, especially when I asked for an interview, my assuring them about confidentiality, honestly reaffirming my benign intentions, joking a bit about the situation – and just being myself – helped alleviate their concerns.

Knowing that I entered an environment as a participant-observation researcher helped me objectify my own anxieties. It gave me some extra leverage in understanding the uncomfortable situations I encountered. When two Palatians joined forces in tricking me into believing that one of them was the creator of Palace in disguise, I found this bending of reality unsettling, until I recognized it as their attempt to wield power. When I posted what I thought were very good photos to Flickr, only to receive bland or no reactions from my contacts, I felt disappointed and inadequate. Then I discovered that almost everyone in a photosharing group knows this feeling. I did not always understand or even firmly identify these kinds of reactions until I made a deliberate, conscious effort to explore them, which is the psychoanalytic clinician's effort to understand his own transference. Once I realized how I personally responded to something about life in cyberspace, I made an effort to ask others about it, to compare our reactions. If together we discovered a problem, our next step was to figure out a way to resolve it, for ourselves as well as other members in the community. As Wernher von Braun once said, "Research is what I'm doing when I don't know what I'm doing."

THE ETHICAL RESEARCHER

My research rested on the philosophy that clinical psychologists attempt to understand people in order to help them, so I declined requests to participate in projects that contradicted those values. Psychological research as a whole is founded on a well-established set of ethical principles. Researchers should always receive informed consent from subjects who volunteer to participate in a study. They do not deceive subjects about significant aspects of the research that would affect their willingness to participate. Subjects should be told that they can withdraw from the study at any time, that their confidentiality will always be protected, and that they can have access to the conclusions of the research.

Because cyberspace architecture can alter the temporal, spatial, and sensory boundaries of human interaction, it challenges the implementation of traditional ethical principles. It also calls for new legal definitions. Scientific studies of public behavior is permissible without obtaining informed consent, but how do we define "public" in an online world filled with millions of spaces, all varying in how accessible they are, whether people perceive them as private, and whether they even know who can see what they are doing? With almost everything online being recorded, how do we distinguish between the behavior of people and archives of that behavior, presumably owned by some organization? When many people present minimal, partial, or imaginary aspects of their identity, we cannot always verify who is who. What should be known about a person's identity before they become a subject? How do you know for sure you are working with the people you think you are working with? Do imaginary usernames and online persona provide sufficient confidentiality, or should the researcher's report disguise what already looks like a disguise? Ethically, it is critical to know whether a subject is a minor, but how do you verify the age of the person? Researchers too can easily hide the fact that they are researchers or even pretend to be someone else, which is probably acceptable in an environment where everyone else is doing the same thing. Or is it?

All of these questions highlight the various twists and turns in online research, so consultation with experts is important. But who are they? Is cyberspace research so significantly different from traditional research that it warrants new standards of expertise? It would seem so, which is why organizations such as the Association of Internet Researchers (Markham & Buchanan, 2012) and the British Psychological Society (Hewson & Buchanan, 2013) have developed ethical guidelines for online research.

BIG DATA, BIG QUESTIONS

Unlike case studies in psychology, statistical approaches typically strive to include as many subjects as possible in the research project. The bigger the group of subjects – what researchers call the "sample" – the more likely statistical analyses will be valid, and the more likely the findings will apply to all people in general. The researcher often tries to recruit volunteers to participate. The advantage of this approach is that the scientist can offer informed consent to these willing participants. The downside is that the people who decide to participate are a *self-selected sample*. They might be different from people who did not volunteer, which means the results of the study will be valid only for the subjects in it or for people similar to them. In all types of social science investigations, the researcher must consider the possibility of *sampling bias*, the fact that the subjects in the study might be different from the larger group of people for whom the researcher hopes to discover some important finding. If a thousand people in an online community report in a questionnaire that social media make them happy, what about the million other people who did not fill out the survey? Might mostly happy people volunteer for this kind of research?

Some scientists believe that online studies of huge populations can overcome the problem of small, biased samples. Because many millions of people occupy the Internet, with almost everything they do and say being recorded, researchers have access to massively large sets of information. The term *Big Data* became popular when referring to the volume, speed, and variety of online information about where people go, what they post, what they download, what they "like," what services they seek, what policies they endorse, and, most important for many commercial enterprises, what they buy (Mayer-Schonberger & Cukier, 2014). Might an analysis of Big Data lead us to insights concerning human behavior that were not possible with the traditionally smaller sample sizes? Some scientists think so. Because activity in cyberspace is constantly changing, day to day, even minute to minute, some researchers also believe that they can study the causes and effects of our actions in real time, leading to an enhanced ability to predict our behavior, what they called *nowcasting*.

When Bigger Is Not Better

Big Data does pose big challenges. Too much can be as large a problem as too little. The information might be so big, complex, and fast moving that our methods to analyze it fall short. Even when we have effective methods, we still have to decide what questions to ask, what data to collect to answer those questions, and what values should dictate our choices. As with setting up a scenario to investigate how sadistic a reality show audience might be, we have to seriously consider whether we are exploring the wrong questions while overlooking the right ones. When we gather large amounts of data, exactly how should we measure it, how do we interpret it, and how can we be sure it means what we think it means? Information about behavior, no matter how massive it is, does not always provide an accurate picture of what goes on inside people's heads. Everyone, including researchers, will differ, sometimes quite dramatically, in how they subjectively interpret Big Data conclusions. Regardless of how scientifically objective a finding seems to be, does it fit a person's own personal experiences or expectations? We should heed Mark Twain, who said there are three types of lies: lies, damned lies, and statistics.

In his book *The Signal and the Noise*, Silver (2013) warned that numbers have no way of speaking for us. We speak for them, even when we do not realize that our conclusions come from seeing what we want to see in the noise of Big Data. As an example, stand in the middle of Times Square on New Year's Eve in order to study human behavior. What question do you want to investigate? What data will you collect to do so? As in Big Data studies, among all that incredibly complex, even seemingly chaotic fog of activity, are you asking a good question? Are you gathering the relevant data? If researchers fish Big Data long enough, they might discover seemingly statistically significant findings that simply occur by chance.

Despite how big Big Data can be, sampling bias will pose problems because no study can include everyone. When researchers gathered data about millions of people in Facebook, they were still only studying people who use Facebook, who might very well be different from people in other social media or even people who belong to Facebook but rarely go there. In any study of online behavior, no matter how big the sample size, we would not know anything about people who are offline, either because they, as the disenfranchised, fall on the wrong side of the digital divide, or because they choose to avoid cyberspace – people who nevertheless might give onliners the objective perspective they need when they cannot see the digital forest for the digital trees.

Last but certainly not least, is it even ethical to investigate what people are doing and saying online when the definition of public versus private is unclear both legally and in the minds of those who live in cyberspace? Privacy advocates grow worried as more data are collected about what we intentionally disclose in social media posts, along with what we unknowingly reveal about ourselves as we are tracked throughout our online activities. How are we being profiled? Will Big Data analysts draw the right conclusions about who we are, what we are actually thinking and feeling, what we might do, or what we need? "Science never solves a problem without creating ten more," remarked George Bernard Shaw. Lanier (2014) even criticized social media corporations for harvesting all the valuable information people provide via their online activities without offering them any compensation other than the use of their "free" social media platform. Later they offered users access to some of their own data, such as their search engine questions. But is that a fair deal or simply a token gesture?

Manipulating the Online Experience

Of even greater concern are the actions powerful people and institutions might take based on their Big Data analyses, and whether their agendas will beneficially serve the inhabitants of cyberspace or their own self-interests. Critics warn us that such powerful authorities will use cyberspace to shape the opinions, feelings, and behaviors of the individual person as well as the culture at large. In 2012, Facebook conducted research in which it manipulated the news feeds of half a million of its users by either reducing emotionally positive or negative posts. The corporation wanted to see whether witnessing happy or sad information would change whether people responded with happy or sad posts. Regardless of the results, or how scientifically valid they actually were, Facebook took the dubious honor of being the first corporation to confirm the suspicions of the critics. Without providing any informed consent other than mentioning "research" in the lengthy data use policy that users agree to but rarely read, a major corporation and its scientists attempted to manipulate the emotions of people in social media, presumably with the bottom line of business profits as the corporation's primary agenda.

Machine intelligence shapes the experience of people online, using algorithms that automatically track, assess, predict, and determine what is shown to us and what happens to us. How much trust should we place in the machine's thinking and in the people who design it? If machine intelligence gains increasing power in shaping what people experience in cyberspace, then is Big Data research mostly an investigation into the behavior of machine intelligence and the people being manipulated by it?

Another question for the future is whether cyberspace will continue to provide a wide range of information and experiences easily accessed by everyone, or will it become divvied up into network territories run by organizations that decide what can and cannot be accessed, that deliberately control resources for purposes unknown to the people who inhabit those places? Even though cyberspace is an extension of the individual human mind that projects itself into and shapes that space, it also is an extension of the collective human mind in which some minds try hard to surreptitiously manipulate the minds of others.

SPREADING THE WORD

The solution for many of these dilemmas is education. It is the ethical duty of cyberpsychologists and other Internet researchers to publish what they learn from their studies, for both their colleagues as well as for the public. In addition to the traditional peer-reviewed journals that have been translated into an online format, academics are exploring alternative methods of publishing that take advantage of the new tools available, such as research articles that are revisable, interactive, multimedia, easily searched, constructed in hypertext formats, linked to related research papers, embedded in a community where other researchers as well as the public can discuss the findings, and assessable by how often it is viewed, cited, liked, and linked to. Many of these tools can open our eyes to novel perspectives on defining quality in scholarship.

Because so many venues for publishing online are available, researchers should offer versions of their research articles for the general public, in addition to the technical versions provided to their colleagues. That endeavor would be more than just a service to the people. It would also benefit the scientist. It is not easy to explain the abstract concepts of psychological research in a plain language that everyone can comprehend. It requires a clear understanding and articulation of the concepts rather than hiding fuzzy thinking behind psychobabble. In his book *Learn to Write Badly: How to Succeed in the Social Sciences*, Billig (2013) claims that social scientists not only use their terminology to exaggerate ideas and conceal imprecise thinking, but also to promote themselves and their work. Too often, social scientists assume that only their colleagues have useful feedback to offer on their work – an assumption that sells cyberpsychology short when we underestimate the insights of everyone else online.

The downside of online publishing is the pressure for immediacy that affects everyone's lifestyle in cyberspace. The newest research is not necessarily the best research, but "new" is the name of the game on the Internet. The most recent study quickly picked up and reported by the media can easily become a trending topic that corners not just the attitudes of the general population, but also researchers. While journalists and blogging researchers who shoot from the hip about the issues of the day might be making excellent points, ongoing scientific research moves much slower in its progress toward valid, lasting conclusions about cyberpsychology.

THE NEXT GENERATION

Cyberpsychology must carefully consider how successive generations of people might differ in how they inhabit the digital realm. At this specific stage in the evolution of the Internet, we are living through a unique transition, one that will never occur again. From this point onward, all generations will be those that grew up with cyberspace, including what some have called the "cyberbabies" with tablets in their cribs. Those who knew what life was like before the Internet, both researchers and everyday people alike, will disappear. With them, we should not let die the memory of a lifestyle without constant connection, for no matter how much the digital realm attracts us, we must live with at least one foot planted firmly in the real physical world, the world in which we evolved over so many millennia. Cyberpsychology must advance our understanding of how to balance and integrate this online/offline existence healthfully.

Who knows what future generations will think about cyberspace, whether it will be idealized or demonized, whether we will immerse ourselves even further into synthesized realities or rebound from cyberspace mania to a deeper appreciation of the world without the Internet permanently plugged into our brains. Hopefully we will optimize our use of technology for our collective well-being. Because cyberspace acts as our mirror, we must realize that what we do with it merely reflects how we decide to express and develop the human psyche, for better or for worse.

REFERENCES

Adar, E., & Huberman, B.A. (2000). Free riding on Gnutella. Retrieved from http://www.hpl.hp.com/research/idl/papers/gnutella/gnutella.pdf

Aiken, M. (2015). *Cyberpsyched*. New York, NY: Random House.

Aiken, M., Moran, M., Berry, M.J. (2011). Child abuse material and the Internet: Cyberpsychology of online child related sex offending. Paper presented at the 29th Meeting of the INTERPOL Specialist Group on Crimes against Children, Lyons, France.

Aiken, M., & Kirwan, G. (2013). The psychology of cyberchondria and cyberchondria by proxy. In A. Power & G. Kirwan (Eds.), *Cyberpsychology and new media: A thematic reader* (pp. 158–169). New York, NY: Psychology Press.

Akhtar, S. (Ed.). (2013). *The electrified mind: Psychopathology and treatment in the era of cell phones and the internet*. New York, NY: Jason Aronson.

Amichai-Hamburger, Y. (2005). *The social net: Understanding human behavior in cyberspace*. Oxford, UK: Oxford University Press.

Anselmi, D. L., & Law, A. L. (2007). *Questions of gender: Perspectives and paradoxes*. New York, NY: McGraw-Hill.

Anthony, K. (2004). In P. Weitz (Ed.), *Psychotherapy 2.0* (pp. 133–146). London, UK: Karnac.

Anthony, K., & Nagel, D. M. (2010). *Therapy online: A practical guide*. Thousand Oaks, CA: Sage.

Ashby, W. R. (1966). *Design for a brain: The origin of adaptive behavior*. London, UK: Chapman and Hall.

Ashton, K. (2009). That "Internet of things" thing. *RFID Journal*. Retrieved from http://www.rfidjournal.com/articles/pdf?4986

Attrill, A. (Ed.). (2015a). *Cyberpsychology*. Oxford, UK: Oxford University Press.

(2015b). Health psychology online. In A. Attrill (Ed.), *Cyberpsychology* (pp. 164–182). Oxford, UK: Oxford University Press.

(2015c). *The manipulation of online self-presentation: Create, edit, re-edit, and present*. New York, NY, Palgrave Macmillan.

Atwood, G., & Stolorow, R. (2014). *Structures of subjectivity: Explorations in psychoanalytic phenomenology and contextualism*. London, UK: Routledge.

Bainbridge, W. S. (2014). *Personality capture and emulation*. London, UK: Springer.

Balick, A. (2013). *The psychodynamics of social networking: Connected-up instantaneous culture and the self*. London, UK: Karnac.

Barak, A. (Ed.). (2008). *Psychological aspects of cyberspace*. New York, NY: Cambridge University Press.

Barnes, S. B. (2006). A privacy paradox: Social networking in the United States. *First Monday*, 11(9). Retrieved from http://firstmonday.org/article/view/1394/1312.

Bartlett, J. (2014). *The dark net: Inside the digital underworld*. London, UK: William Heinemann.

Berry, Danielle Bunten. (2011). 'Why i design multi-player, online games.' Wayback Machine (archived July 25, 2011). Originally from Berry's personal site, archived by Anticlockwise.com.

Biegelman, M. (2009). *Identity theft handbook: Detection, prevention, and security*. Hoboken, NJ: Wiley.

Billig, M. (2013). *Learn to write badly: How to succeed in the social sciences*. New York, NY: Cambridge University Press.

Biocca, F., & Levy, M. R. (Eds.). (2013). *Communication in the age of virtual reality*. London, UK: Routledge.

Bisson, T. (1990). They're made out of meat. Retrieved from: http://www.terrybisson.com/page6/page6.html

Blascovich, J., & Bailenson, J. (2012). *Infinite reality: The hidden blueprint of our virtual lives*. New York, NY: William Morrow.

Buckels, E. E., Trapnell, P. D., & Paulhus, D. L. (2014). Trolls just want to have fun. *Personality and Individual Differences*, 67, 97–102.

Burdea, G., & Coiffet, P. (2003). Virtual reality technology. *Presence: Teleoperators and Virtual Environments*, 12 (6), 663–664.

Card, S. K., Moran, T. P., & Newell, A. (1986). *The psychology of human computer interaction*. Mahwah, NJ: Lawrence Erlbaum Associates.

Castronova, E. (2008). *Exodus to the virtual world: How online fun is changing reality*. New York, NY: Palgrave Macmillan.

Cattell, R. B. (1946). *The description and measurement of personality*. New York, NY: World Book.

Cooley, C. H. (1902). *Human nature and the social order*. New York, NY: C. Scribner's Sons.

Cooper, A. (Ed.). (2013). *Cybersex: The dark side of the force: A special issue of the Journal Sexual Addiction and Compulsion*. London, UK: Routledge.

Craig, A. B. (2013). *Understanding augmented reality: Concepts and applications*. New York, NY: Morgan Kaufmann.

Crook, C. (2015). *The joy of missing out: Finding balance in a wired world*. Gabriola Island, BC: New Society.

Csikszentmihalyi, M. (1990). *Flow: The psychology of optimal experience*. New York, NY: Harper and Row.

Daine, K., Hawton, K., Singaravelu, V., Stewart, A., Simkin, S., & Montgomery, P. (2013). The power of the web: A systematic review of studies of the influence of the Internet on self-harm and suicide in young people. *PloS one*, 8 (10), e77555.

Darley, J. M., & Latané, B. (1968). Bystander intervention in emergencies: Diffusion of responsibility. *Journal of Personality and Social Psychology*, 8 (4), 377–383.

Derrig-Palumbo, K., & Zeine, F. (2005). *Online therapy: A therapist's guide to expanding your practice*. New York, NY: Norton.

Dewan, N. A., Lorenzi, N. M., Riley, R. T., & Bhattacharya, S. R. (Eds.). (2014). *Behavioral healthcare informatics: A guide for the clinician*. London, UK: Springer.

Dibbell, J. (1993). A rape in cyberspace. *Village Voice*, 21 December. Retrieved from http://www.villagevoice.com/2005-10-18/specials/a-rape-in-cyberspace/

Diemer, J. E., Alpers, G. W., Peperkorn, H. M., Shiban, Y., & Mühlberger, A. (2015). The impact of perception and presence on emotional reactions: A review of research in virtual reality. *Name: Frontiers in Psychology*, 6, 26. Retrieved from http://journal.frontiersin.org/article/10.3389/fpsyg.2015.00400/full.

Dixon, N. F. (1971). *Subliminal perception: The nature of a controversy*. New York, NY: McGraw-Hill.

Dyson, E. (2005). Interview. *Time Magazine*, October.

Earnshaw, R. A. (Ed.). (2014). *Virtual reality systems*. New York, NY: Academic Press.

Ekman, P. (2007). *Emotions revealed: Recognizing faces and feelings to improve communication and emotional life*. New York, NY: Holt.

Ellis, A., & Harper, R. A. (1975). *A guide to rational living*. Chatsworth, CA: Wilshire.

Engelbart, D. C. (1995). Towards augmenting the human intellect and boosting our collective IQ. *Communications of the ACM*, 38 (8), 30–32.

Epstein, S., & O'Brien, E. (1985). The person-situation debate in historical and current perspective. *Psychological Bulletin*, 98 (3), 513–537.

Erikson, E. (1968). *Identity, youth, and crisis*. New York: W.W. Norton.

Exner, J. (2002). *The Rorschach: Basic foundations and principles of interpretation*. Hoboken, NJ: Wiley.

Festinger, L. (1954). A theory of social comparison processes. *Human Relations*, 7 (2), 117–140.

Freud, A. (1937). *The ego and the mechanisms of defense*. London, UK: Hogarth Press.

Freud, S. (1915). Instincts and their vicissitudes. In J. Strachey (Ed. & Trans.), *The standard edition of the complete psychological works of Sigmund Freud* (Vol. 14), 117–140. London, UK: Hogarth Press.

Freud, S. (1919). The uncanny. In J. Strachey (Ed. & Trans.), *The standard edition of the complete psychological works of Sigmund Freud* (Vol. 17), 219–256.

Gackenbach, J. (Ed.). (1999). *Psychology and the Internet: Intrapersonal, interpersonal, and transpersonal implications*. New York, NY: Academic Press.

Gardner, H. (1999). *Intelligence reframed: Multiple intelligences for the 21st century*. New York, NY: Basic.

Gendlin, E. (1982). *Focussing*. New York, NY: Bantam.

Gibson, W. (1984). *Neuromancer*. New York, NY: Ace.

Gill, J., & Stokes, A. (2008). *Online counseling: A handbook for practitioners*. New York, NY: Palgrave Macmillan.

Godwin, M. (1994). Nine principles for making virtual communities work. *Wired Magazine*, June, Issue 2.06. Retrieved from http://archive.wired.com/wired/archive/2.06/vc.principles.html

Goss, S., & Anthony, K. (Eds.). (2003). *Technology in counseling and psychotherapy*. New York, NY: Palgrave Macmillan.

Greenberg, J. R., & Mitchell, S. A. (1983). *Object relations in psychoanalytic theory.* Cambridge, MA: Harvard University Press.

Greenfield, D. (1999). *Virtual addiction: Help for netheads, cyberfreaks, and those who love them.* Oakland, CA: New Harbinger.

Grieve, R., Indian, M., Witteveen, K., Tolan, G. A., & Marrington, J. (2013). Face-to-face or Facebook: Can social connectedness be derived online? *Computers in Human Behavior* 29 (3), 604–609.

Griffiths, M. (2000). Does Internet and computer addiction really exist? Some case study evidence. *CyberPsychology and Behavior* 3 (2), 211–218.

Guest, T. (2008). *Second lives: A journey through virtual worlds.* New York, NY: Random House.

Herrigel, E. (1999). *Zen in the art of archery.* New York, NY: Vintage.

Hewson, C., & Buchanan, T. (Eds.). (2013). Ethical guidelines for Internet-mediated Research. Retrieved from http://www.bps.org.uk/system/files/Public%20files/inf206-guidelines-for-internet-mediated-research.pdf

Hoffman, H. G., Patterson, D. R., & Carrougher, G. J. (2000). Use of virtual reality for adjunctive treatment of adult burn pain during physical therapy: A controlled study. *Clinical Journal of Pain,* 16 (3), 244–250.

Holland, N. N. (1996). The Internet regression. Retrieved from http://www.clas.ufl.edu/users/nholland/inetregr.htm

Holt, T. (2007). Subcultural evolution: Examining the influence of on- and off-line experiences on deviant subcultures. *Deviant Behavior,* 28 (2) 171–198.

Hsiung, R. C. (Ed.). (2002). *E-therapy: Case studies, guiding principles, and the clinical potential of the internet.* New York, NY: W. W. Norton.

Huh, S., & Williams, D. (2010). Dude looks like a lady: Gender swapping in an online game. In W. Bainbridge (Ed.), *Online worlds: Convergence of the real and virtual* (pp. 161–174). London, UK: Springer.

Huskerson, T. (2014). *Online scam's greatest hits.* Relentlessly Creative.

James, W. (2013). *The varieties of religious experience: A study in human nature.* Norcross, GA: Trinity Press (originally published 1902).

Janis, I. (1972). *Groupthink: A psychological study of foreign-policy decisions and fiascoes.* Boston, MA: Houghton-Mifflin.

Jelenchick, L. A., Eickhoff, J. C., & Moreno, M. A. (2013). "Facebook depression?" Social networking site use and depression in older adolescents. *Journal of Adolescent Health,* 52 (1), 128–130.

Johnson, D. W., & Johnson, F. P. (2012). *Joining together: Group theory and group skills.* New York, NY: Pearson.

Joinson, A. N. (1998). Causes and implications of disinhibited behavior on the Internet. In J. Gackenbach (Ed.), *Psychology and the Internet: Intrapersonal, interpersonal, and transpersonal implications* (pp. 43–60). New York, NY: Academic Press.

(2003). *Understanding the psychology of Internet behavior: Virtual worlds, real lives.* New York, NY: Palgrave Macmillan.

Joinson, A., McKenna, K. Y. A., Postmes, T., & Reips, U.D. (Eds.). (2009). *The Oxford handbook of Internet psychology.* Oxford, UK: Oxford University Press.

Jorgensen, D. (1989). *Participant observation: A methodology for human studies.* London, UK: Sage.

Jung, C. G. (1969). *Archetypes and the collective unconscious. Collected Works of C.G. Jung* (Vol. 9, Part 1). Princeton, NJ: Princeton University Press.

(1981). *The archetypes and the collective unconscious.* Princeton, NJ: Princeton University Press.

Jurgenson, N. (2011). Digital dualism and the fallacy of web objectivity. Retrieved from http://thesocietypages.org/cyborgology/2011/09/13/digital-dualism-and-the-fallacy-of-web-objectivity/

Kabat-Zinn, J. (2005). *Wherever you go there you are: Mindfulness meditation in everyday life.* New York, NY: Hyperion.

Kim, A. J. (2006). *Community building on the web: Secret strategies for successful online communities.* Berkeley, CA: Peachpit Press.

King, S. (1995). Effects of mood states on social judgments in cyberspace: Self focussed sad people as the source of flame wars. Retrieved from http://psychcentral.com/storm1.htm

Kirwan, G., & Power, A. (2013). *Cybercrime: The psychology of online offenders.* New York, NY: Cambridge University Press.

Kohut, H. (1977). *The restoration of the self.* Madison, CT: International Universities Press.

(1980). *Self psychology and the humanities.* New York, NY: W. W. Norton and Company.

Kowalski, R. M., Limber, S., Limber, S. P., & Agatston, P. W. (2012). *Cyberbullying: Bullying in the digital age.* New York, NY: John Wiley & Sons.

Kraus, R., Stricker, G., & Speyer, C. (Eds.). (2004). *Online counseling: A handbook for mental health professionals.* Waltham, MA: Academic Press.

Kurzweil, R. (2013). *How to create a mind: The secret of human thought revealed.* New York: NY: Penguin.

Lanier, J. (2014). *Who owns the future?* New York, NY: Simon and Schuster.

Lapidot-Lefler, N., & Barak, A. (2012). Effects of anonymity, invisibility, and lack of eye-contact on toxic online disinhibition. *Computers in Human Behavior,* 28 (2), 434–443.

Levine, M. (1974). Scientific method and the adversary model: Some preliminary thoughts. *American Psychologist,* 29 (9), 661–677.

Levine, P. A. (1997). *Waking the tiger: Healing trauma.* Berkeley, CA: North Atlantic.

Licklider, J. C. R. (1960). Man-computer symbiosis. *Transactions on Human Factors in Electronics,* HFE-1, 4–11.

Lima, M. (2013). *Visual complexity: Mapping patterns of information.* New York, NY: Princeton Architectural Press.

Linden, A., & Fenn, J. (2003). Understanding Gartner's hype cycles. *Strategic Analysis Report Nº R-20-1971* (pp. 1–12). Stamford, CT: Gartner, Inc.

Livingstone, S. (2013). *Children and the Internet.* Boston, MA: Polity Press.

Loftus, E. F., & Klinger, M. R. (1992). Is the unconscious smart or dumb? *American Psychologist,* 47 (6), 761–765.

Luder, M. T., Pittet, I., Berchtold, A., Akré, C., Michaud, P. A., & Surís, J. C. (2011). Associations between online pornography and sexual behavior among adolescents: Myth or reality? *Archives of Sexual Behavior,* 40 (5), 1027–1035.

Luft, J., & Ingham, H. (1955). The Johari window: A graphic model of interpersonal awareness. *Proceedings of the Western Training Laboratory in Group Development.* Los Angeles, CA: UCLA.

Mahler, M, Pine, F., & Bergman, A. (1975). *The psychological birth of the human infant: Symbiosis and Individuation*. New York, NY: Basic.

Malaby, T. (2009). *Making virtual worlds: Linden lab and second life*. Ithaca, NY: Cornell University Press.

Marczak, M., & Coyne, I. (2015). A focus on cyberbullying. In A. Attrill (Ed.), *Cyberpsychology* (pp. 145–163). Oxford, UK: Oxford University Press.

Markham, A., & Buchanan, E. (with contributions from the AOIR Ethics Working Committee) (2012). *Ethical decision-making and Internet research*. Retrieved from http://www.aoir.org/reports/ethics2.pdf

Maslow, A. (1943). A theory of human motivation. *Psychological Review*, 50 (4), 370–396.

Mayer, R. E. (2009). *Multimedia learning*. New York, NY: Cambridge University Press.

Mayer-Schonberger, V., & Cukier, K. (2014). *Big data: A revolution that will transform how we live, work, and think*. New York, NY: Eamon Dolan/Mariner.

McDougall, J. (1989). *Theaters of the body: A psychoanalytic approach to psychosomatic Illness*. New York, NY: W. W. Norton.

McGinn, C. (2007). *The power of movies: How screen and mind interact*. New York, NY: Vintage.

McKevitt, P. (2011). *Integration of natural language and vision processing: Recent advances*. London, UK: Springer.

McLuhan, M., & Fiore, Q. (1967). *The medium is the massage: An inventory of effects*. New York, NY: Bantam.

McWilliams, N. (2011). *Psychoanalytic diagnosis: Understanding personality structure in the clinical process*. New York, NY: Guilford Press.

Mead, G. H. (1934). *Mind, self, and society*. Chicago, IL: University of Chicago Press.

Meadows, M. S. (2008). *I, Avatar: The culture and consequences of having a second life*. Berkeley, CA: New Riders.

Mehroof, M., & Griffiths, M. (2010). Online gaming addiction: The role of sensation seeking, self-control, neuroticism, aggression, state anxiety, and trait anxiety. *Cyberpsychology, Behavior, and Social Networking*, 13 (3): 313–316.

Minsky, M. (1980). Telepresence. *Omni*, 2 (9), 45–51.

Mitchell, K. J., Wells, M., Priebe, G., & Ybarra, M. L. (2014). Exposure to websites that encourage self-harm and suicide: Prevalence rates and association with actual thoughts of self-harm and thoughts of suicide in the United States. *Journal of Adolescence*, 37 (8), 1335–1344.

Moore, R. (2010). *Cybercrime: Investigating high technology computer crime*. London, UK: Routledge.

Morahan-Martin, J. (2005). Internet abuse: Addiction? Disorder? Symptom? Alternative explanations? *Social Science Computer Review*, 23 (1), 39–48.

Moreno, M. A., Jelenchick, L. A., Egan, K. G., Cox, E., Young, H., Gannon, K. E., & Becker, T. (2011). Feeling bad on Facebook: Depression disclosures by college students on a social networking site. *Depression and Anxiety*, 28 (6), 447–455.

Mori, M. (1970). The uncanny valley. *IEEE Robotics & Automation Magazine*, 19 (2), 98–100.

Moscovici, S., & Zavalloni, M. (1969). The group as a polarizer of attitudes. *Journal of Personality and Social Psychology*, 12 (2), 125–135.

Munro, K. (2002). How to resolve conflict online. Retrieved from http://kalimunro .com/wp/articles-info/relationships/article

Myers, I. B., & Myers, P. B. (1995). *Gifts differing: Understanding personality type.* Mountain View, CA: Davies-Black.

Nagel, K. (1996). The natural life cycle of mailing lists. Retrieved from http:// truecenterpublishing.com/psycyber/lifelist.html

Nguyen, M., Bin, Y. S., & Campbell, A. (2012). Comparing online and offline self-disclosure: A systematic review. *Cyberpsychology, Behavior, and Social Networking,* 15 (2), 103–111.

Norman, K. L. (2008). *Cyberpsychology: An introduction to human-computer interaction.* New York, NY: Cambridge University Press.

Norman, W. T. (1963). Toward an adequate taxonomy of personality attributes: Replicated factor structure in peer nomination personality ratings. *Journal of Abnormal and Social Psychology,* 66 (6): 574–583.

Ohta, Y., & Tamura, H. (2014). *Mixed reality: Merging real and virtual worlds.* London, UK: Springer.

Ornstein, R. (1992). *Evolution of consciousness: The origins of the way we think.* New York, NY: Simon and Schuster.

Paasonen, S. (2011). *Carnal Resonance: Affect and online pornography.* Cambridge, MA: MIT Press.

Patchin, J., & Hinduja, S. (2011). *Cyberbullying prevention and response: Expert perspectives.* London, UK: Routledge.

Penfield, W. (1961). Activation of the record of human experience. *Annals of the Royal College of Surgeons, England,* 29 (2), 77–84.

Pennebaker, J. W. (2004). *Writing to heal: A guided journal for recovering from trauma and emotional upheaval.* Oakland, CA: New Harbinger.

Perls, F. S. (1969). *Gestalt therapy verbatim.* Gouldsboro, ME: Gestalt Journal Press.

Piaget, J. (2001). *The psychology of intelligence.* New York, NY: Routledge. (originally published 1947)

Power, A., & Kirwan, G. (2014). *Cyberpsychology and new media: A thematic reader.* New York, NY: Psychology Press.

Purcell, K., & Rainie, L. (2014). Technology's impact on workers. *PEW Research Center: Internet Science & Technology.* Retrieved from http://www.pewinternet .org/2014/12/30/technologys-impact-on-workers/

Reeves, B., & Nass, C. (2003). *The media equation: How people treat computers, television, and new media like real people and places.* Stanford, CA: Center for the Study of Language and Information.

Reips, U. D. (2002). Standards for Internet-based experimenting. *Experimental Psychology,* 49 (4), 243–256.

Rheingold, H. (1993). *The virtual community: Homesteading on the electronic frontier.* Cambridge, MA: MIT Press.

Richardson, A. (1969). *Mental imagery.* London, UK: Springer.

Riessman, F. (1965). The helper therapy principle. *Social Work,* 10 (2), 26–32.

Riva, G., Loreti, P., Lunghi, M., Vatalaro, F., & Davide, F. (2003). Presence 2010: The emergence of ambient intelligence. *Emerging Communication,* 5 (1), 59–84.

Riva, G., Waterworth, J., & Murray, D. (Eds.). (2014). *Interacting with presence: HCI and the sense of presence in computer-mediated environments.* Warsaw, Poland: De Gruyter Open.

Rosen, L. D., Whaling, K., Rab, S., Carrier, L. M., & Cheever, N. A. (2013). Is Facebook creating "iDisorders"? The link between clinical symptoms of psychiatric disorders and technology use, attitudes and anxiety. *Computers in Human Behavior*, 29 (3), 1243–1254.

Rosenhan, D. (1973). On being sane in insane places. *Science*, 179 (4070), 250–258.

Salter, A. (2004). *Predators: Pedophiles, rapists, and other sexual offenders*. New York, NY: Basic.

Schuemie, M. J., Van Der Straaten, P., Krijn, M., & Van Der Mast, C. A. (2001). Research on presence in virtual reality: A survey. *CyberPsychology & Behavior*, 4 (2), 183–201.

Sharkey, S., Jones, R., Smithson, J., Hewis, E., Emmens, T., Ford, T., & Owens, C. (2011). Ethical practice in internet research involving vulnerable people: lessons from a self-harm discussion forum study (SharpTalk). *Journal of Medical Ethics*, 37 (12), 752–758.

Short, J., Williams, E., & Christie, B. (1976). *The social psychology of telecommunications*. Hoboken, NJ: Wiley.

Short, M. B., Black, L., Smith, A. H., Wetterneck, C. T., & Wells, D. E. (2012). A review of Internet pornography use research: Methodology and content from the past 10 years. *Cyberpsychology, Behavior, and Social Networking*, 15 (1), 13–23.

Silver, N. (2013). *The signal and the noise: The art and science of prediction*. New York, NY: Penguin.

Simmel, G. (2002). The metropolis and mental life. In G. Bridge & S. Watson (Eds.), *The Blackwell City Reader* (pp. 11–19). Oxford, UK, and Malden, MA: Wiley-Blackwell.

Sonck, N., Nikken, P., & de Haan, J. (2013). Determinants of Internet mediation: A comparison of the reports by Dutch parents and children. *Journal of Children and Media*, 7 (1), 96–113.

Sonja, U., Nicole, M., & Cameran, K. Snapchat elicits more jealousy than Facebook: A comparison of Snapchat and Facebook use. *Cyberpsychology, Behavior, and Social Networking*, 18 (3), 141–146.

Spector, M., Merrill, M. D., Elen, J., & Bishop, M. J. (Eds.). (2013). *Handbook of research on educational communications and technology*. London, UK: Springer.

Spradley, J. P. (1980). *Participant observation*. New York, NY: Holt, Rinehart, and Winston.

Stein, D. J., Black, D. W., Shapira, N. A., & Spitzer, R. L. (2001). Hypersexual disorder and preoccupation with Internet pornography. *American Journal of Psychiatry*, 158 (10), 1590–1594.

Stephenson, N. (1992). *Snow crash*. New York, NY: Bantam.

Sterling, B. (1992). *The hacker crackdown*. Retrieved from http://www.gutenberg .org/files/101/101-h/101-h.htm

Sternberg, J. (2012). *Misbehavior in cyber places: The regulation in online conduct in virtual communities on the Internet*. Lanham, MD: University Press of America.

Steuer, J. (1992). Defining virtual reality: Dimensions determining telepresence. *Journal of Communication*, 42 (4), 73–93.

Suler, J. R. (1987). Computer-simulated psychotherapy as an aid in teaching clinical psychology. *Teaching of Psychology*, 14 (1), 37–39.

(1993). *Contemporary psychoanalysis and Eastern thought*. Albany, NY: State University of New York Press.

(1996). *The psychology of cyberspace.* Retrieved from http://truecenterpublishing .com/psycyber/psycyber.html

(1997). The bad boys of cyberspace. In *The psychology of cyberspace.* Retrieved from http://truecenterpublishing.com/psycyber/badboys.html

(2001). The psychology of avatars and graphical space in multimedia chat communities. In M. Beiswenger (Ed.) *Chat communication* (pp. 305–344). Stuttgart, Germany: Ibidem.

(2004a). The online disinhibition effect. *CyberPsychology and Behavior,* 7 (1), 321–326.

(2004b). The psychology of text relationships. In R. Kraus, J. Zack, & G. Stricker (Eds.), *Online counseling: A handbook for mental health professionals* (pp. 19–50). London: Elsevier Academic Press.

(2005). eQuest: Case study of a comprehensive online program for self-study and personal growth. *CyberPsychology and Behavior,* 8 (4), 379–386.

(2008a). Image, action, word: Interpersonal dynamics in a photo-sharing community. *CyberPsychology and Behavior,* 11 (5), 555–560.

(2008b). Cybertherapeutic theory and techniques. In A. Barak (Ed.), *Psychological aspects of cyberspace: Theory, research, applications* (pp. 102–128). New York, NY: Cambridge University Press.

(2010). *Madman: Strange adventures of a psychology intern.* Doylestown, PA: True Center.

(2011). The impact of image streams. *International Journal of Applied Psychoanalytic Studies,* 9 (1), 84–88.

(2013a). *Photographic psychology: Image and psyche.* Retrieved from http:// truecenterpublishing.com/photopsy/selfportraits.htm

(2013b). *Qualitative research methodology for photographic psychology.* Retrieved from http://truecenterpublishing.com/photopsy/QRM-PhotoPsy.pdf

(2013c). The varieties of self-portrait experiences. In *Photographic psychology: Image and psyche.* Retrieved from http://truecenterpublishing.com/photopsy/ selfportraits.htm

Suler, J. R., & Phillips, W. (1998). The bad boys of cyberspace. *Cyberpsychology and Behavior,* 1 (2), 275–294.

Sweller, J. (1988). Cognitive load during problem solving: Effects on learning. *Cognitive Science,* 12 (2), 257–285.

Tikhomirov, O. K., Babaeva, Y. D., & Voiskounsky, A. Y. (1986). Computer-mediated communication. *Moscow University Psychological Bulletin,* 3 (2), 31–42.

Toffler, A. (1970). *Future shock.* New York: Random House.

Tuckman, B. (1965). Developmental sequence in small groups. *Psychological Bulletin,* 63 (6), 384–399.

Turing, A. (1950). Computing machinery and intelligence. *Mind,* LIX (236), 433–460.

Turkle, S. (1995). *Life on the screen: Identity in the age of the Internet.* Cambridge, MA: MIT Press.

(2012). *Alone together: Why we expect more from technology and less from each other.* New York: Basic.

Voiskounsky, A. (2008). Flow experience in cyberspace: Current studies and perspectives. In A. Barak (Ed.) *Psychological aspects of cyberspace: Theory, research, applications* (pp. 70–101). New York, NY: Cambridge University Press.

Walther, J. B. (1996). Computer-mediated communication: Impersonal, interpersonal, and hyperpersonal interaction. *Communication Research*, 23 (1), 3–43.

Wang, R., Bianchi, S. M., & Raley, S. B. (2005). Teenagers' Internet use and family rules: A research note. *Journal of Marriage and Family*, 67 (5), 1249–1258.

Warschauer, M. (2004). *Technology and social Inclusion: Rethinking the digital divide*. Cambridge, MA: MIT Press.

Weinberger, D. (2008). *Small pieces loosely joined: A unified theory of the web*. New York: Basic.

Weiser, J. (1993). *Phototherapy techniques*. San Francisco, CA: Jossey-Bass.

Weizenbaum, J. (1966). Eliza: A computer program for the study of natural language communication between man and machine. *Communications of the ACM*, 9 (1), 36–45.

Wexelblat, A. (Ed.). (2014). *Virtual reality: Applications and explorations*. New York, NY: Academic Press.

Whitty, M., & Carr, A. (2006). *Cyberspace romance: The psychology of online relationships*. New York, NY: Palgrave Macmillan.

Whyte, W. F. (1943). *Street corner society: The social structure of an Italian slum*. Chicago IL: University of Chicago Press.

Wiederhold, B., & Wiederhold, M. (2004). *Virtual reality therapy for anxiety disorders: Advances in evaluation and treatment*. Washington, DC: American Psychological Association.

Winnicott, D. (1971). *Playing and reality*. London, UK: Tavistock.

Witmer, B. G., & Singer, M. J. (1998). Measuring presence in virtual environments: A presence questionnaire. *Presence: Teleoperators and Virtual Environments*, 7(3), 225–240.

Yalom, I. (1980). *Existential psychotherapy*. New York, NY: Basic.

(2005). *Theory and practice of group psychotherapy*. New York, NY: Basic.

Yan, Z. (2012). *Encyclopedia of cyber behavior*. Hershey, PA: IGI Global.

Yee, N., & Bailenson, J. (2007). The Proteus effect: The effect of transformed self-representation on behavior. *Human Communication Research*, 33 (3), 271–290.

Young, K. (1998). *Caught in the net*. Hoboken, NY: Wiley.

Young, K., & Nabuco de Abreu, C. (Eds.). (2010). *Internet addiction: Handbook and guide to evaluation and treatment*. Hoboken, NJ: Wiley.

Zaheer, H., & Griffiths, M. (2008). Gender swapping and socializing in cyberspace: An exploratory study. *CyberPsychology and Behavior*, 11 (1), 47–53.

Zittrain, J. (2009). *The future of the Internet – and how to stop it*. New Haven, CT: Yale University Press.

Zubek, J. (Ed.) (1969). *Sensory deprivation: Fifteen years of research*. New York, NY: Appleton Century Crofts.

Zuckerman, M. (2007). *Sensation seeking and risky behavior*. Washington, DC: American Psychological Association.

INDEX

Lightning Source UK Ltd.
Milton Keynes UK
UKOW01f2105150817
307364UK00014B/289/P